Matchbox® Toys

compiled by Nancy Schiffer

77 Lower Valley Road, Atglen, PA 19310

Certain material has been gathered from the following copyrighted publications with permission:
The Toy Car Catalog: "Matchbox" 1-75 series, a major variation catalog, by Scott Mace. Box 1534, San Jose, California, 1981.
The Toy Car Catalog: "Matchbox" Two Pack, a major variation catalog, by Scott Mace. Box 1534, San Jose, California, 1981.
The Toy Car Catalog: "Matchbox" Major Pack, a major variation catalog, by Scott Mace. Box 1534, San Jose, California, 1981.
The Toy Car Catalog: "Matchbox" King Size K1 through K20, by Scott Mace. Box 1534, San Jose, California, 1981.
A Concise Catalog of 1-75 series "Matchbox" toys, 2nd edition, by Geoffrey Leake, 38 Park Avenue, Worcester, England, 1981.
"Matchbox" U.S.A. K21 Onward Catalog, 2nd edition, by Charles Mack, RR3, Box 216, Durham, Connecticut, 1981.
Collectors' Catalogue of "Matchbox" "Models of Yesteryear", 3rd edition, by H.M. and T.J. Gunner, 2a Clarence Road, Wallington, England, 1981.
U.K. Matchbox Club Magazine, volumes 1 through 6, 1977 to1982, Ray Bush, editor, 1 Tor Road, Plymouth, England.
"Matchbox" U.S.A. Club Magazine, monthly April 1980 through 1982. Charles Mack, editor, RR3, Box 216, Durham, Connecticut.
The Box Catalog, 1953-1980 The Models and Their Boxes, 1st edition, and 1953-1978 variations 2nd edition, by Graham Ward. Model & Hobby Shop. 256 Uttoxeter Road, Longton, Stoke-on-Trent, ST3 5QL, England.

Published by Schiffer Publishing Ltd.
77 Lower Valley Road
Atglen, PA 19310
Please write for a free catalog.
This book may be purchased from the publisher.
Please include $2.95 postage.
Try your bookstore first.

Table of Contents

	Picture	Written Description
Introduction and Identification System		5
History		9
Early Lesney toys	13	131
Matchbox 1-75 Series		
Regular Wheels	19	132
Superfast Wheels	34	134
Australian Issue Superfast	71	
Limited Edition Superfast	72	
Japanese Issue Superfast	74	
Pre-production Superfast	75	
Models of Yesteryear Series	76	178
Plated Models of Yesteryear	81	184
Pre-production Models of Yesteryear	82	
Promotional Models of Yesteryear	83	
One of a Kind	84	
Accessories	85	184
Major Packs	87	185
King Size	89	186
Super Kings	94	190
Adventure 2000	112	195
Regional Super Kings	113	
Buses	114	
Gift Sets	115	195
Skybusters	116	196
Matchbox Military	119	198
Battle Kings	119	199
Two-Packs	121	199
Sea Kings	124	200
Walt Disney Characters and Popeye Series	126	200
Glo-Racers	127	201
Boxes	128	
Gifts, Souvenirs and Heritage Series		202
Code Red		203
Convoy Series		203
Pocket Catalogs		204
Matchbox Collectors' Clubs		206
Bibliography		208

Acknowledgments

We are indebted to many people whose assistance and encouragement has resulted in this book. One never knows it all, but by all contributing, the subject has been covered in as much detail as seemed practical. Our very special thanks goes to Pat Lamagna and Charles Mack whose collections were photographed late into the nights and who answered many of our early questions. Ray Bush spent hours telling us about early Lesney toys. We thank Muriel and Keith Chandler and Ed Marcantonio for their assistance throughout the research. Fannie Stokes took the photographs and organized the material cleverly. Scott Mace, Graham Ward, Terry Gunner and Geoffrey Leake, through correspondance, cleared up detailed questions in their specialties. We appreciate the efforts of Elizabeth Wardley, Leonard Sausen, Eric Edwards and Dolores Huntemann at Lesney Products Corporation. And especially we thank Ellen Taylor for the typesetting and final design.

Introduction

The toys pictured and listed in this book represent the major variations of the most popular series made by Lesney Products from 1947 to June of 1982. There exist games, plastic models, dolls, roadways, and short-run toys which were made by Lesney but are not made from the die-cast metal and are not covered in this book. Toys released after June of 1982 were too late to meet our deadline and too new to have been analyzed for variations.

The international scope of Matchbox toys is quite apparent as one encounters catalogs, boxes, and labels for the toys printed in a dozen languages. Certain toys have been made for sale in specific stores, or to promote specific companies. Test markets are tried in selected countries and toys are sold in one part of the world before others. The numbering of the toys has been known to vary between catalogs for different countries. The result of all of these variables is a fascinating and infinite variety of Matchbox toys.

The public's consistent enthusiasm, and the long-term interest of children grown to adults have provided the necessary ingredients for Matchbox toys to become ideal collectible items. The old toys have become scarce and variations of newer toys have given the collectors a challenge to own each one. The collectors seek both toys and related catalogs, collector buttons, and boxes. Gradually, collectors were drawn by their common goals into organized clubs, a current list of

Introduction

which is included at the end of this book. The collector club magazines provide details of the countless variations as they are found and cataloged, and keep the members up-to-date on new toys released around the world.

As we anticipate Matchbox toys to extend long into the future, if continuous with today's series or in a new guise, we leave the continuing story for another, future time. It will be most interesting to see how Matchbox toys develope.

Introduction

The Matchbox toys identification system

Each Matchbox toy is identified precisely by means of a system of letters and numbers.
For example:

Y-2-A2   1911 "B" type London Bus   2⅔"   1956

The **first letter** represents an abbreviation for the series of the toy. (**Y** in the example stands for the Yesteryear series) A list of these abbreviations follows this explanation.

The **first number** represents the number of the toy in that series (The example is the number two toy in the Yesteryear series.)

The **second letter** represents, in alphabetical sequence, the order of the toys issued for that number. (In the example, this toy is the first (or A), number two toy issued in the Yesteryear series.)

The **second number** represents the variation listed for that toy. (The example is the number two variation listed in this book for the toy.)

Following the numbers are the name of the toy, its length, and the year it was first issued.

Introduction

The **series letters** are as follows:

    Early Lesney toys—no series letter. These are known only by their toy name.

    1-75 and Superfast—no series letter. These are known only by their toy number.

    Limited Edition series—known by Roman numerals.

    Code Red—no series letter. Known by the words "Code Red."

    Gifts, Souvenirs and Heritage series—no series letter. Known by their number.

A   Accessories
BK Battle Kings
CS Comic Strip characters (after Walt Disney characters)
CY Convoy series
G   Gift Sets
GR Glo-Racers
J   Japanese Issue Superfast (after 1-75 series)
K   King Size/Super Kings/Speed Kings/Adventure 2000
M   Major Packs
MG Matchbox Garages (part of Accessories)
MM Matchbox Military
SB Skybusters
SK Sea Kings
TP Two Packs (900 range)
WD Walt Disney characters
Y   Models of Yesteryear

History

Leslie Smith and Rodney Smith were unrelated school friends when they were reunited by chance in 1940, both serving in The English Royal Navy. They each shared an ambition of one day having their own engineering factory, and discussed joining each other, once the Second World War was over. Finally, they formed a partnership and began "Lesney Products" on June 19, 1947. The name was a composit of the founders' first names, and the word "Products" seemed appropriate because they had not yet decided what they would make. Leslie Smith was also employed by the J. Raymond Wilson Company, which confirmed overseas orders, in a position he continued for several years. He worked in the evenings keeping the financial records of Lesney until Lesney Products grew sufficiently to support him fulltime. Rodney Smith found employment with the engineering firm of Diecast and Machine Tools in London.

With about 600 pounds of combined revenue, the pair bought the old tavern "Rifleman" at Edmonton, London, and some government surplus die casting machinery. They now were determined to make pressure die casting products for industrial use.

Another employee at Diecast and Machine Tools was John W. Odell, always called Jack, who contributed his particular casting skill and joined into the Lesney venture. The three began in a small way producing small die-cast components as sub-contractors for industry. They were among many such small firms in London contributing to the rebuilding of the city.

The English business custom of taking stock inventory for taxation purposes on the first of January led to reduced orders for component suppliers during the last two months of the year. Therefore, the few Lesney employees were not kept busy producing die-castings during those months, and the founders considered alternate products. Some of the other small die-cast firms had made a few toys, and the Lesney people experimented with this, too. In 1949 the first of these toys was produced and sold locally in London in small shops. By 1952, Lesney was supplying a few toys to some of the Woolworth stores in London for the Christmas season.

The London toy distributors considered these little toys "Christmas cracker trash" and were not enthusiastic about handling them. Children, however, just loved them and the shopkeepers wanted more. By Christmas 1953, the Lesney people recognized that there was a market for their toys, and knew how to make them, but were not interested at this time in developing a sales force, storage facilities, and marketing techniques to distribute toys for a few months a year. They turned, instead, to agents who specialized in marketing to handle their toys. In the east end of London there were several agents well established long before the war. The one they contacted was Moko.

Moses Kohnstam was a German agent from Nuremberg who came to England about 1900 to develope the toy industry. He specialized in packaging, storing, distributing, and financial backing for many small toy manufacturers, for which he received a percentage of the selling price. Moses Kohnstam's company was Moko, and the toys he distributed carried his company's name—Moko, no matter what various small firm made them.

In 1953, Moses Kohnstams' successor Richard Kohnstam was in charge of the Moko company. Lesney Products and Richard Kohnstam entered into an agreement whereby Moko would package and distribute the toys. Eventually, Moko became the sole distributor of the toys worldwide. This was the year that Lesney began the small 1-75 series of toys.

By 1954, Lesney produced eighteen models which were distributed by Moko. The trademark "Matchbox" had been registered in 1953 and belonged 50% to Moko who continued to provide its services and financial backing of the toys. Rodney Smith by now had moved to Australia and left Lesney, which was being managed by Leslie Smith and Jack Odell.

During 1958, Leslie Smith felt there was potential for the toys in Asia, particularly Japan, but Richard Kohnstam disagreed. In order to open up the market, Lesney realized it had to go off on its own marketing course, so it must buy out the Moko interest in the toys. In 1959, Lesney concluded an agreement to buy "Moko", and produced their first catalog of toys. Since then Richard Kohnstam has formed his own firm Riko. In 1959, a second catalog was also produced including the new Models of Yesteryear series. In 1954, distribution of Lesney toys to the United States was conducted by a salesman from New York named Fred Bronner. He became the sole U.S. importer during the late

History

1950's. In 1964, Lesney Products (U.S.A.) was formed as a division of the English Lesney Products. Lesney acquired all of Fred Bronner's stock and he became the first president of Lesney Products (U.S.A.).

In 1960, when Lesney sold 400,000 shares of stock to the public at one pound each, the offering was over subscribed fifteen times. The name of the company was changed to Lesney Products Corporation in 1970 to incorporate the divisions in Canada and Australia. New markets were developed worldwide in response to the enormous success of the toys. By 1979, Lesney Products Corporation employed 6,500 workers in fourteen factories and made up to 5½ million toys a week.

Gradually, however, the company began to experience financial difficulty related to stresses in world-wide economic shifts. Rising labor, shipping and interest costs in England could not be off-set by charging higher prices because the competetive companies used less expensive labor in Asia to keep their costs low. During the Spring of 1982, rumors were proven correct when Lesney Products Corporation went into receivership. Then, on June 11, 1982, Lesney Products Corporation ceased to exist, and was replaced by its financial receivers by new companies. The company "Matchbox Toys" was formed to handle only the toy division of the former firm. This company was in turn sold on September 24, 1982 to Universal International, a toy die-cast company based in Hong Kong with an office in Chicago for the United States' market and an office in London for the European market.

Early Lesney Toys

When Lesney Products began manufacturing metal die-cast toys in 1948, it started with the Aveling Barford diesel road roller. By 1953, seventeen other toys joined the Lesney line. The order in which these seventeen were released is not certain, and therefore the dates 1948—1953 can be used in most cases for the group unless a more precise date can be determined. The variety of toys in this group reflects the uncertain direction of this branch of the company at that time. Mechanical animals, vehicles with wheels, and even a fishing novelty item were all tried before the success of the wheeled vehicles eclipsed efforts in the other directions.

The three major versions of the Early Lesney Road Roller.
- No man, flywheel with cast boss.
- No cast boss for a flywheel.
- With a man, no boss for a flywheel.

This was scaled down for the first 1-75 series toy.

Early Lesney Toys

Between 1950 and 1952, the English government restricted the use of zinc for non-essential products during the Korean War, and therefore no die-cast toys could be made. Only the "Jumbo-the-Elephant" of tin was made by Lesney during this period. During 1953, Jack Odell began designing smaller scale toys. The first 6 were smaller versions of the original Lesney toys. These small toys were enormously successful, and were continued to become the 1-75 series. With the growing success of the small series, the larger toys were phased out by 1954.

Each of the early Lesney toys was packaged in a cardboard box which was printed with a picture of the toy, its name, and in some cases the name of the distributor of the toy Moko. (See the chapter on History for an explanation of Moko.)

From a collector's point of view, the toy is more interesting with its original box in good condition—and some collectors have made a science of the boxes themselves.

Soap Box Racer.

Caterpillar Tractor, Caterpillar Bulldozer.

Caterpillar Tractor.

Early Lesney Toys

Bread Bait Press.

Muffin the Mule

One of the few preliminary models for a Quarry Truck which was never produced. This truck was, however, scaled down to be released as the No. 6A Quarry Truck of the 1-75 series, shown resting on top.

Jumbo the Elephant.

Quarry Truck.

Early Lesney Toys

-Originally the King was included inside the coach.

-Eventually the King was cut off at the seat.

-The box label for the coronation coach.

-Entire Coronation Coach and horses.

Rag and Bone Cart.

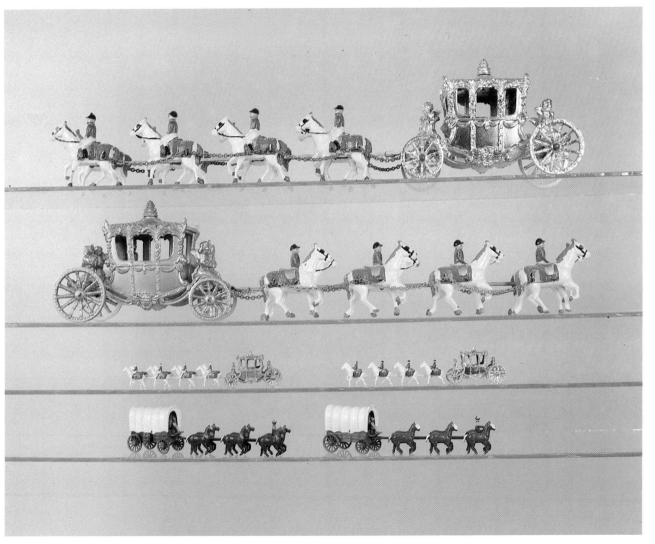

Row 1
Large silver Coronation Coach.

Row 2
Large gold Coronation Coach.

Row 3
Small gold Coronation Coach, small silver Coronation Coach.

Row 4
Covered Wagon, Covered Wagon.

Row 1
**Hand Cement Mixer,
Massey Harris Tractor,
Hand Cement Mixer.**

Row 2
**Aveling Barford Diesel
Road Roller, Horse-
drawn Milk Float.**

Row 3
**Prime Mover, Trailer and
Bulldozer.**

Row 1
1-A1 **Road Roller**, 1-B2 **Road Roller**, 1-C3 **Road Roller**, 1-D2 **Road Roller**.

Row 2
1-E1 **Mercedes Truck**, 2-A2 **Dumper**, 2-A1 **Dumper**, 2-B1 **Dumper**.

Row 3
2-C1 **Muir Hill Dumper**, 2-D2 **Mercedes Trailer**, 3-A2 **Cement Mixer**, 3-B1 **Bedford Tipper**.

Row 4
3-C1 **Mercedes Ambulance**, 4-A1 **Massey-Harris Tractor**, 4-B3 **Massey-Harris Tractor**, 4-C2 **Triumph Motorcycle & Sidecar**.

Row 5
4-D2 **Stake Truck**, 5-A2 **London Bus**, 5-B1 **London Bus**, 5-C2 **London Bus**, 5-D1 **London Bus**.

19

Row 1
6-A3 **Quarry Truck**, 6-B1 **Euclid Quarry Truck**, 6-C3 **Euclid Quarry Truck**, 6-D1 **Ford Pick-up.**

Row 2
7-A2 **Horse Drawn Milk Float**, 7-B1 **Ford Anglia**, 7-C3 **Ford Refuse Truck**, 8-A1 **Caterpillar Tractor**, 8-A2 **Caterpillar Tractor.**

Row 3
8-B3 **Caterpillar Tractor**, 8-C1 **Caterpillar Tractor**, 8-D3 **Caterpillar Tractor**, 8-E1 **Ford Mustang**, 8-F3 **Ford Mustang.**

Row 4
9-A1 **Dennis Fire Escape**, 9-A2 **Dennis Fire Escape**, 9-B4 **Merry-Weather Fire Engine**, 10-D3 **Boat & Trailer.**

Row 5
10-A1 **Mechanical Horse & Trailer**, 10-B1 **Mechanical Horse & Trailer**, 10-C2 **Sugar Container Truck**, 10-D1 **Pipe Truck.**

Row 1
11-A5 **Road Tanker**, 11-A4 **Road Tanker**, 11-A1 **Road Tanker**, 11-B1 **Road Tanker**, 11-C1 **Jumbo Crane.**

Row 2
11-D **Scaffolding Truck**, 12-A1 **Land Rover**, 12-B3 **Land Rover Series 2**, 12-C5 **Safari Land Rover**, 12-C1 **Safari Land Rover.**

Row 3
13-B1 **Wreck Truck**, 13-A1 **Wreck Truck**, 13-C1 **Thames Wreck Truck**, 13-C3 **Thames Wreck Truck**, 13-D7 **Dodge Wreck Truck.**

Row 4
13-D4 **Dodge Wreck Truck**, 14-A1 **Ambulance**, 14-B6 **Daimler Ambulance**, 14-C1 **Bedford Ambulance.**

Row 5
14-D1 **ISO Grifo**, 15-A2 **Truck Tractor**, 15-B3 **Atlantic Tractor**, 15-C4 **Tippax Refuse Truck.**

*Matchbox 1—75 Series
Regular Wheels*

Row 1
16-B2 **Volkswagen 1500,**
16-A1 **Atlantic Trailer,**
16-A2 **Atlantic Trailer,**
16-B4 **Atlantic Trailer.**

Row 2
16-C5 **Mountaineer Dump Truck,** 16-C1 **Mountaineer Dump Truck,** 16-D4 **Case Tractor,** 16-D3 **Case Tractor.**

Row 3
17-A5 **Removals Van,**
17-A3 **Removals Van,**
17-A1 **Removals Van,**
17-A2 **Removals Van,**
17-B3 **Austin Taxi.**

Row 4
17-C3 **Hoveringham Tipper,** 17-D2 **Horse Box,** 18-A1 **Caterpillar Bulldozer,** 18-B1 **Caterpillar Bulldozer.**

Row 5
18-C3 **Caterpillar Bulldozer,** 18-C1 **Caterpillar Bulldozer,** 18-D3 **Caterpillar Bulldozer,** 18-D4 **Caterpillar Bulldozer.**

Matchbox 1—75 Series
Regular Wheels

Row 1
18-E3 **Field Car**, 18-E1 **Field Car**, 19-A1 **MG Sports Car**, 19-B1 **MG Sports Car**, 19-B2 **MG Sports Car.**

Row 2
19-C3 **Aston Martin**, 19-C5 **Aston Martin**, 19-D1 **Lotus Racing Car** 19-D2 **Lotus Racing Car.**

Row 3
20-A5 **Stake Truck**, 20-A1 **Stake Truck**, 20-A2 **Stake Truck**, 20-B1 **ERF 686 Truck.**

Row 4
20-C7 **Chevrolet Impala Taxi**, 20-C1 **Chevrolet Impala Taxi**, 21-A **Long Distance Coach**, 21-B3 **Long Distance Coach.**

Row 5
21-C1 **Milk Delivery Truck**, 21-C7 **Milk Delivery Truck**, 21-D1 **Foden Concrete Truck**, 22-A2 **Vauxhall Sedan.**

Row 1
22-B9 **Vauxhall Cresta**,
22-B1 **Vauxhall Cresta**,
22-C3 **Pontiac Grand Prix**, 23-A **Berkeley Cavalier Trailer.**

Row 2
23-B2 **Bluebird Dauphine Trailer**, 23-C1 **House Trailer Caravan**, 24-A2 **Weatherhill Hydraulic Excavator**, 24-B6 **Weatherhill Hydraulic Excavator.**

Row 3
24-C1 **Rolls Royce Silver Shadow**, 25-A5 **Dunlop Truck**, 25-B4 **Volkswagon**, 25-C1 **BP Petrol Tanker.**

Row 4
25-C4 **"Aral" Petrol Tanker**, 25-D2 **Ford Cortina**, 26-A2 **Concrete Truck**, 26-B1 **Concrete Truck.**

Row 5
26-C **G.M.C. Tipper Truck**, 27-A1 **Bedford Low Loader**, 27-B2 **Bedford Low Loader**, 27-C9 **Cadillac Sixty Special.**

Row 1
27-D2 **Mercedes 230SL Convertible**, 28-A2 **Bedford Compressor Truck**, 28-B6 **Thames Compressor Truck**, 28-C2 **Jaguar MK 10**.

Row 2
28-D2 **Mack Dump Truck**, 28-D3 **Mack Dump Truck**, 29-A1 **Bedford Milk Truck**, 29-B5 **Austin A55 Cambridge**.

Row 3
29-C2 **Fire Pumper**, 30-A2 **Ford Perfect**, 30-B5 **6-Wheel Crane Truck**, 30-C3 **8-Wheel Crane Truck**.

Row 4
31-A1 **American Ford Station Wagon**, 31-B7 **American Ford Station Wagon**, 31-B1 **American Ford Station Wagon**, 31-C1 **Lincoln Continental**.

Row 5
32-A1 **Jaguar XK140 Coupe**, 32-B3 **Jaguar XKE**, 32-C1 **Leyland Tanker**, 32-C2 **Leyland Tanker**.

Row 1
33-A8 **Ford Zodiac Sedan**, 33-B1 **Ford Zephyr 6 MK III**, 33-C3 **Lamborghini Miura**, 34-A4 **Volkswagen Panel Truck.**

Row 2
34-B4 **Volkswagen Camper**, 34-C **Volkswagen Camper**, 34-D1 **Volkswagen Camper**, 35-A4 **Marshall Horse Box.**

Row 3
35-B4 **Snow-trac Tractor**, 35-B3 **Snow-trac Tractor**, 35-B2 **Snow-trac Tractor**, 35-B1 **Snow-trac Tractor.**

Row 4
36-A5 **Austin A50**, 36-B2 **Lambretta Motorscooter & Side Car**, 36-C1 **Opel Diplomat**, 37-A1 **Coca Cola Lorry**, 37-C4 **Coca Cola Lorry.**

Row 5
37-D2 **Cattle Truck**, 38-A6 **Karrier Refuse collector**, 38-B5 **Vauxhall Victor Estate Car.**

Row 1
39-B3 Honda Motor-cycle & Trailer, 38-C2 Honda Motorcycle & Trailer, 39-A1 Ford Zodiac Convertible, 38-B3 Pontiac Convertible.

Row 2
39-C1 Ford Tractor, 40-A2 Bedford Tipper Truck, 40-B3 Leyland Royal Tiger Coach, 40-C1 Hay Trailer.

Row 3
41-A1 D-type Jaguar, 41-B10 D-type Jaguar, 41-C3 Ford GT, 42-A1 Bedford Evening News Van.

Row 4
42-B2 Studebaker Station Wagon, 42-C1 Iron Fairy Crane, 43-A2 Hillman Minx, 43-B4 Aveling Barford Tractor Shovel.

Row 5
43-C1 Pony Trailer, 44-A8 Rolls Royce Silver Cloud, 44-B3 Rolls Royce Phantom V.

Row 1
44-C1 **Refrigerator Truck**, 44-A1 **Vauxhall Victor Sedan**, 45-B1 **Ford Corsair with boat**, 46-A3 **Morris Minor.**

Row 2
46-B2 **Pickford's Removal Van**, 46-B13 **Beals Bealson Removal Van**, 46-C1 **Mercedes 300SE**, 47-A1 **Brooke Bond Trojan Van.**

Row 3
47-B1 **Commer Ice Cream Truck**, 47-B4 **Commer Ice Cream Truck**, 47-B13 **Commer Ice Cream Truck**, 47-C1 **DAF Tipper.**

Row 4
48-A4 **Meteor Boat & Trailer**, 48-B1 **Boat & Trailer**, 48-C1 **Dump Truck**, 49-A2 **Army Personnel Carrier.**

Row 5
49-B4 **Unimog**, 50-A11 **Commer Pick-up Truck**, 50-B1 **John Deere Tractor**, 50-C1 **Kennel Truck.**

Row 1
51-A6 **Albion Chieftan,** 51-A10 **Albion Chieftan,** 51-B1 **John Deere Trailer,** 51-C9 **8-Wheel Tipper.**

Row 2
51-C2 **8-Wheel Tipper,** 52-A2 **Maserati 4CLT,** 52-A8 **Maserati 4CLT,** 52-B3 **BRM Racer.**

Row 3
53-A1 **Aston Martin,** 53-B1 **Mercedes Benz 220 SE,** 53-C2 **Ford Zodiac MK IV,** 54-A1 **Saracen Personnel Carrier.**

Row 4
54-B1 **S & S Cadillac Ambulance,** 55-A1 **D.U.K.W.,** 55-B4 **Ford Fairlane Police Car,** 55-C2 **Ford Galaxie Police Car.**

Row 5
55-D3 **Mercury Police Car,** 56-A1 **London Trolly Bus,** 56-A7 **London Trolley Bus,** 56-B2 **Fiat 1500.**

Row 1
57-A5 **Wolseley 1500,**
57-B4 **Chevrolet Impala,**
57-C2 **Land Rover Fire
Truck,** 58-A2 **BEA
Coach.**

Row 2
58-A3 **BEA Coach,** 58-
B3 **Drott Excavator,** 58-
C1 **DAF Girder Truck,**
59-A7 **Ford Thames Van.**

Row 3
59-B1 **Ford Fairlane Fire
Chief's Car,** 59-C2 **Ford
Galaxie Fire Chief's
Car,** 60-A5 **Morris J2
Pick-up,** 60-A8 **Morris J2
Pick-up.**

Row 4
60-B1 **Site Hut Truck,**
61-A1 **Ferret Scout Car,**
61-A1 **Ferret Scout Car,**
61-B1 **Alvis Stalwart.**

Row 5
61-B5 **Alvis Stalwart,** 62-
A1 **Army General Lorry,**
62-B2 **T.V. Service Van,**
62-B8 **T.V. Service Van.**

Row 1
62-C **Mercury Cougar**, 63-A2 **Army Service Ambulance**, 63-B1 **Fire-fighting Crash Tender**, 63-C1 **Dodge Crane Truck**.

Row 2
64-A4 **Scammel Breakdown Truck**, 64-B **MG 1100**, 65-A2 **3.4 litre Jaguar**, 65-B4 **3.8 Litre Jaguar**.

Row 3
65-C1 **Claas Combine Harvester**, 66-A3 **Citroen D.S. 19**, 66-B1 **Harley Davidson Motorcycle & Side Car**.

Row 4
66-C1 **Greyhound Coach** 66-C2 **Greyhound Coach** 67-A1 **Saladin Armoured Car**, 67-B2 **Volkswagon 1600 TL**.

Row 5
68-A1 **Austin MK2 Radio Truck**, 68-B2 **Mercedes Coach**, 68-B1 **Mercedes Coach**, 69-A4 **Nestle Delivery Truck**.

Row 1
69-B7 **Hatra Tractor Shovel**, 69-B6 **Hatra Tractor Shovel**, 69-B8 **Hatra Tractor Shovel**, 69-B1 **Hatra Tractor Shovel**.

Row 2
69-B3 **Hatra Tractor Shovel**, 69-B2 **Hatra Tractor Shovel**, 70-A1 **Thames Estate Car**, 70-A6 **Thames Estate Car**.

Row 3
70-B3 **Atkinson Grit Spreader**, 71-A2 **Austin 200 Gallon Water Truck**, 71-B1 **Jeep Gladiator Pick-up Truck**, 71-B7 **Jeep Gladiator Pick-up Truck**.

Row 4
71-C2 **Ford Heavy Wreck Truck**, 72-A5 **Fordson Tractor**, 72-A1 **Fordson Tractor**, 72-A8 **Fordson Tractor**.

Row 5
72-A9 **Fordson Tractor**, 72-A2 **Fordson Tractor**, 72-A6 **Fordson Tractor**.

Row 1
72-B1 **Standard Jeep**, 73-A3 **R.A.F. 10 Ton Pressure Refueller Tanker**, 73-B2 **Ferrari F1 Racer**, 73-B1 **Ferrari F1 Racer**.

Row 2
73-C1 **Mercury Commuter**, 74-A2 **Mobile Refreshment Canteen**, 74-A4 **Mobile Refreshment Canteen**, 74-A1 **Mobile Refreshment Canteen**.

Row 3
74-B4 **Daimler Bus**, 74-B2 **Daimler Bus**, 74-B3 **Daimler Bus**.

Row 4
75-A1 **Ford Thunderbird**, 75-A6 **Ford Thunderbird**, 75-B1 **Ferrari Berlinetta**.

Row 5
75-B4 **Ferrari Berlinetta**, 75-B3 **Ferrari Berlinetta**, 75-B2 **Ferrari Berlinetta**.

Matchbox 1—75 Series
Superfast Wheels

Row 1
1-F4 **Mercedes Truck,**
1-F6 **Mercedes Truck,**
1-F5 **Mercedes Truck.**

Row 2
1-F15 **Mercedes Truck,**
1-G1 **Mod Rod,** 1-G3
Mod Rod.

Row 3
1-G18 **Mod Rod,** 1-H1
Dodge Challenger, 1-H8
Dodge Challenger.

Row 4
1-I **Revin' Rebel,** 2-E3
Mercedes Trailer, 2-E6
Mercedes Trailer.

Row 5
2-E8 **Mercedes Trailer,**
2-E14 **Mercedes Trailer,**
2-F1 **Jeep Hot Rod.**

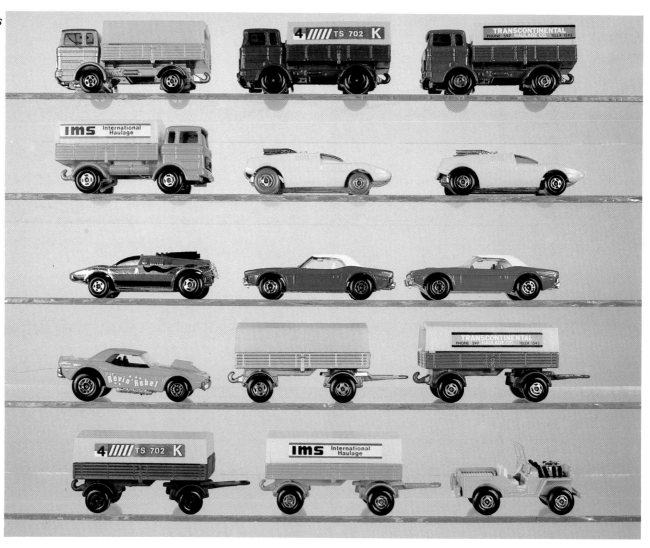

Row 1
2-F14 **Jeep Hot Rod**,
2-F17 **Jeep Hot Rod**,
2-G1 **Hovercraft**.

Row 2
2-G3 **Hovercraft**, 2-G13
Hovercraft, 2-H2 **S-2Jet**.

Row 3
2-H3 **S-2 Jet**, 3-D1 **Mercedes Ambulance**, 3-D8
Mercedes Ambulance.

Row 4
3-E1 **Monteverdi Hai**, 3-F1 **Porshe Turbo**, 3-F3
Porshe Turbo.

Row 5
3-F11 **Porshe Turbo**, 3-F15 **Porshe Turbo**, 4-E1
Dodge Cattle Truck.

Matchbox 1—75 Series
Superfast Wheels

Row 1
4-F1 **Gruesome Two-some**, 4-F14 **Gruesome Twosome**, 4-G5 **Pontiac Firebird.**

Row 2
4-H3 **57 Chevy**, 4-H5 **57 Chevy**, 5-E1 **Lotus Europa.**

Row 3
5-E5 **Lotus Europa**, 5-E14 **Lotus Europa**, 5-F3 **Seafire Boat.**

Row 4
5-F9 **Seafire Boat**, 5-F10 **Seafire Boat**, 5-F12 **Seafire Boat.**

Row 5
5-G2 **U.S. Mail Jeep**, 5-H **4x4 Golden Eagle Jeep**, 6-E1 **Ford Pickup.**

Row 1
6-F1 **Mercedes 350SL,**
6-F7 **Mercedes 350SL,**
6-F13 **Mercedes 350SL.**

Row 2
6-F10 **Mercedes 350SL,**
6-F20 **Mercedes 350SL,**
6-F22 **Mercedes 350 Convertible.**

Row 3
7-D1 **Ford Refuse Truck,**
7-E30 **Hairy Hustler,** 7-E28 **Hairy Hustler.**

Row 4
7-E3 **Hairy Hustler,** 7-F1 **V.W. Golf,** 7-F5 **V.W. Golf.**

Row 5
7-F12 **V.W. Golf,** 7-F21 **V.W. Golf,** 7-G1 **Rompin Rabbit.**

Row 1
8-F1 **Ford Mustang**, 8-F2 **Ford Mustang**, 8-G1 **Wildcat Dragster**.

Row 2
8-H1 **DeTomaso Pantera**, 8-H7 **DeTomaso Pantera**, 8-I1 **Rover**.

Row 3
9-D1 **Boat and Trailer**, 9-E8 **Javelin**, 9-E17 **Javelin**.

Row 4
9-E25 **Javelin**, 9-E29 **Javelin**, 9-E36 **Javelin**.

Row 5
9-F3 **Ford Escort RS 2000**, 9-F5 **Ford Escort RS 2000**, 9-F12 **Ford Escort RS 2000**.

Matchbox 1—75 Series
Superfast Wheels

Row 1
9-G1 **Fiat Abarth**, 10-E2 **Pipe Truck**, 10-F1 **Piston Popper.**

Row 2
10-F11 **Piston Popper**, 10-G5 **Plymouth Gran Fury**, 11-E1 **Scaffolding Truck.**

Row 3
11-F1 **Flying Bug**, 11-G2 **Car Transporter**, 11-G18 **Car Transporter.**

Row 4
11-H1 **Cobra Mustang**, 12-D3 **Safari Land Rover**, 12-E3 **Setra Coach.**

Row 5
12-E5 **Setra Coach**, 12-E8 **Setra Coach**, 12-F3 **Big Bull.**

Matchbox 1—75 Series
Superfast Wheels

Row 1
12-G2 **Citroen CX**, 12-G9 **Citroen CX**, 12-H **1982 Pontiac Firebird**.

Row 2
13-E2 **Dodge Wreck Truck**, 13-F1 **Baja Dune Buggy**, 13-G2 **Snorkel Fire Engine**.

Row 3
13-H **4x4 Mini Pickup**, 14-E1 **Iso Grifo**, 14-E6 **Iso Grifo**.

Row 4
14-E5 **Iso Grifo**, 14-F1 **Mini-Haha**, 14-G1 **Rallye Royale**.

Row 5
14-G2 **Rallye Royale**, 14-H2 **Leyland Tanker**, 15-E1 **Volkswagen 1500**.

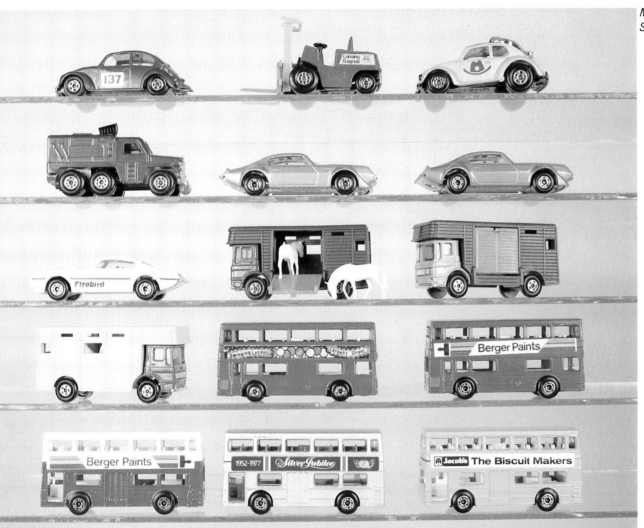

Row 1
15-E5 **Volkswagen 1500,**
15-F1 **Fork Lift Truck,**
15-G1 **Hi Ho Silver.**

Row 2
16-E1 **Badger Explora-
tion Truck,** 16-F1 **Pontiac,** 16-F5 **Pontiac.**

Row 3
16-G **Pontiac Trans-Am,**
17-E1 **Horse Box,** 17-E2
Horse Box.

Row 4
17-E4 **Horse Box,** 17-F1
Londoner Bus, 17-F3
Londoner Bus.

Row 5
17-F2 **Londoner Bus,** 17-
F17 **Londoner Bus,** 17-
F14 **Londoner Bus.**

Matchbox 1–75 Series
Superfast Wheels

Row 1
17-F22 **Londoner Bus,**
17-F25 **Londoner Bus,**
17-F32 **Londoner Bus.**

Row 2
17-G3 **Londoner Bus,**
17-G1 **Londoner Bus,**
18-F1 **Field Car.**

Row 3
18-F8 **Field Car,** 18-F16 **Field Car,** 18-F15 **Field Car.**

Row 4
18-F34 **Field Car,** 18-F32 **Field Car,** 18-G3 **Hondarora.**

Row 5
18-G4 **Hondarora,** 18-G12 **Hondarora,** 18-G14 **Hondarora.**

Row 1
19-E1 **Lotus Racer**, 19-F1 **Road Dragster**, 19-F12 **Road Dragster**.

Row 2
19-G1 **Cement Mixer**, 19-G17 **Cement Mixer**, 19-H **Peterbilt Cement Truck**.

Row 3
20-D1 **Lamborghini Marzal**, 20-D3 **Lamborghini Marzal**, 20-D5 **Lamborghini Marzal**.

Row 4
20-E7 **Police Patrol**, 20-E25 **Police Patrol**, 20-E6 **Police Patrol**.

Row 5
20-E24 **Police Patrol**, 20-E45 **Police Patrol**, 20-F **4x4 Jeep [Desert Dawg]**.

*Matchbox 1–75 Series
Superfast Wheels*

Row 1
21-E1 **Foden Cement Truck**, 21-F2 **Road Roller**, 21-F4 **Road Roller**.

Row 2
21-G1 **Renault 5TL**, 21-G5 **Renault 5TL**, 21-G8 **Renault 5TL**.

Row 3
21-G29 **Renault 5TL**, 22-D1 **Pontiac GP Sports Coupe**, 22-E6 **Freeman Inter-city Commuter**.

Row 4
22-E3 **Freeman Inter-city Commuter**, 22-F10 **Blaze Buster**, 22-G **Ford Mini Pickup/Camper**.

Row 5
23-D3 **Volkswagen Camper**, 23-D5 **Volkswagen Camper**, 23-D10 **Volkswagen Camper**.

Row 1
23-E8 **Atlas Truck**, 23-E7
Atlas Truck, 23-E9 **Atlas
Truck**.

Row 2
23-F **G.T. 350**, 23-G
Audi Quattro, 24-D1
**Rolls Royce Silver
Shadow**.

Row 3
24-F1 **Shunter**, 24-F4
Shunter, 24-E1 **Team
Matchbox**.

Row 4
24-E6 **Team Matchbox**,
24-E10 **Team Matchbox**,
24-E3 **Team Matchbox**.

Row 5
24-G1 **Datsun 280 ZX**,
24-H **Datsun 280** [Pre-
production], 25-E1 **Ford
Cortina**.

*Matchbox 1—75 Series
Superfast Wheels*

Row 1
25-E2 **Ford Cortina**, 25-F4 **Mod Tractor**, 25-F10 **Mod Tractor**.

Row 2
25-G2 **Flat Car**, 25-G5 **Flat Car**, 25-H6 **Celica GT**.

Row 3
25-J **Celica GT**, 25-1 **Ambulance**, 26-C **GMC Tipper Truck**.

Row 4
26-E1 **Big Banger**, 26-F1 **Site Dumper**, 26-F9 **Site Dumper**.

Row 5
26-F12 **Site Dumper**, 26-G1 **Cosmic Blues**, 27-D2 **Mercedes 230 SL**.

Row 1
27-E4 **Mercedes 230 SL**, 27-F1 **Lamborghini**, 27-F14 **Lamborghini**.

Row 2
27-G1 **Swing Wing Jet**, 28-E1 **Mack Dumper**, 28-E-5 **Mack Dumper**.

Row 3
28-F1 **Armoured Vehicle**, 28-F3 **Armoured Vehicle**, 28-G2 **Lincoln Continental MK V**.

Row 4
28-H **Formula Racing Car**, 29-D1 **Fire Pumper**, 29-D2 **Fire Pumper**.

Row 5
29-E1 **Racing Mini**, 29-E12 **Racing Mini**, 29-F7 **Tractor Shovel**.

47

Row 1
29-F3 **Tractor Shovel,**
29-F28 **Tractor Shovel,**
30-D2 **Wheel Crane
Truck.**

Row 2
30-E2 **Beach Buggy,** 30-
F1 **Swamp Rat,** 30-G1
Articulated Truck.

Row 3
30-H **Peterbilt Quarry
Truck,** 31-D2 **Lincoln
Continental,** 31-E17
Volksdragon.

Row 4
31-F11 **Caravan,** 31-G1
Mazda RX-7, 31-G5 **Mazda RX-7.**

Row 5
31-H **Mazda RX-7,** 32-E1
Maserati Bora, 32-E11
Maserati Bora.

Row 1
32-D1 **Leyland Tanker,**
32-D2 **Leyland Tanker,**
32-D5 **Leyland Tanker.**

Row 2
32-F1 **Field Gun,** 32-G1
Atlas Excavator, 32-G3
Atlas Excavator.

Row 3
33-D2 **Lamborghini
Miura,** 33-D3 **Lamborghini Miura,** 33-E9 **Datsun 128X.**

Row 4
33-F7 **Police Motor
Cyclist,** 33-F5 **Police
Motor Cyclist,** 33-F6
Police Motor Cyclist.

Row 5
34-E1 **Formula,** 34-E3
Formula, 34-E4 **Formula.**

Row 1
34-E7 **Formula**, 34-F1
Vantastic, 34-F6 **Vantastic**.

Row 2
34-G3 **Chevy Pro Stock-
er**, 35-C2 **Merryweather
Fire Engine**, 35-D1 **Fandango**.

Row 3
35-D22 **Fandango**, 35-E
Zoo Truck, 35-F **Trans
Am "T" Roof**.

Row 4
36-D1 **Opel Diplomat**,
36-E1 **Hot Rod Draguar**,
36-E6 **Hot Rod Draguar**.

Row 5
36-F1 **Formula 5000**, 36-
F5 **Formula 5000**, 36-G1
Refuse Truck.

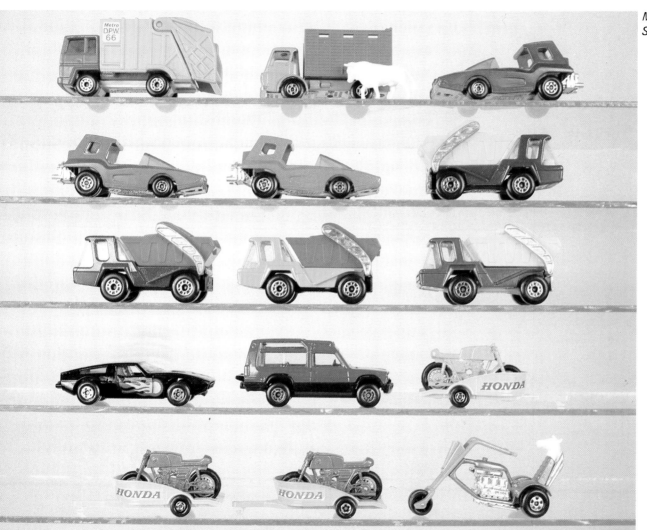

Matchbox 1–75 Series
Superfast Wheels

Row 1
36-G4 **Refuse Truck**, 37-E1 **Cattle Truck**, 37-F3 **Soopa Coopa**.

Row 2
37-F8 **Soopa Coopa**, 37-F10 **Soopa Coopa**, 37-G3 **Skip Truck**.

Row 3
37-G8 **Skip Truck**, 37-G6 **Skip Truck**, 37-G13 **Skip Truck**.

Row 4
37-H1 **Sunburner**, 37-I **Matra Rancho**, 38-D2 **Honda & Trailer**.

Row 5
38-D3 **Honda & Trailer**, 38-D4 **Honda & Trailer**, 38-E3 **Stingaroo Cycle**.

51

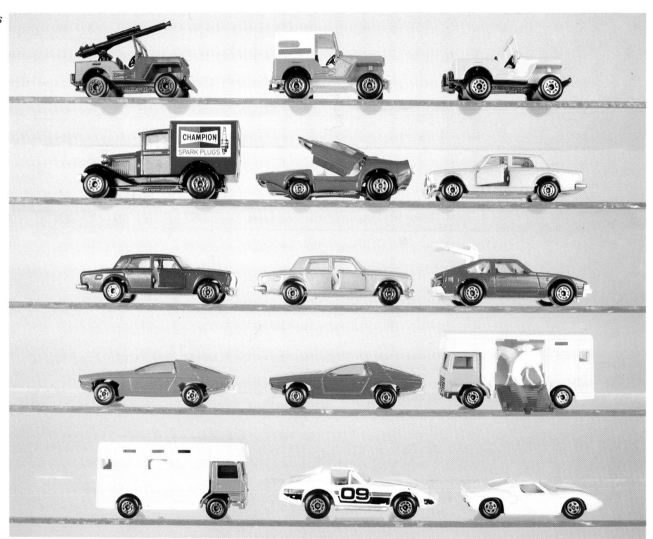

Matchbox 1—75 Series Superfast Wheels

Row 1
38-F1 **Jeep**, 38-F10 **Jeep** 38-F9 **Jeep**.

Row 2
38-H **Model "A" Truck**, 39-D3 **Clipper**, 39-E1 **Rolls Royce Silver Shadow II**.

Row 3
39-E2 **Rolls Royce Silver Shadow II**, 39-E1 **Rolls Royce Silver Shadow II**, 39-F **Toyota Celica Supra**.

Row 4
40-D1 **Guildsman**, 40-D9 **Guildsman**, 40-E4 **Horse Box**.

Row 5
40-E6 **Horse Box**, 40-F **Corvette "T" Roof**, 41-D1 **Ford GT**.

Row 1
41-D4 **Ford GT**, 41-E1
Siva Spider, 41-E11 **Siva
Spider**.

Row 2
41-F1 **Ambulance**, 41-
F2 **Ambulance**, 41-F13
Ambulance.

Row 3
41-F7 **Ambulance**, 41-G
Kenworth ® **Conventional Aerodyne**, 42-D4 **Iron
Fairy Crane**.

Row 4
42-E5 **Tyre Fryer**, 42-E7
Tyre Fryer, 42-F1 **Mercedes Container Truck**.

Row 5
42-F3 **Mercedes con-
tainer Truck**, 42-F11
**Mercedes Container
Truck**, 42-F14 **Mercedes
Container Truck**.

53

*Matchbox 1—75 Series
Superfast Wheels*

Row 1
42-F12 **Mercedes Con-
tainer Truck**, 42-F13
**Mercedes Container
Truck**, 42-G **'57 Ford
T-Bird.**

Row 2
43-D1 **Pony Trailer**, 43-
D3 **Pony Trailer**, 43-D5
Pony Trailer.

Row 3
43-E2 **Dragon Wheels**,
43-F1 **0-4-0 Steam Loco**,
43-F2 **0-4-0 Steam Loco.**

Row 4
43-G **Peterbilt®** Con-
ventional, 44-D1 **Refrigerator Truck**, 44-D2 Re-
frigerator Truck.

Row 5
44-E3 **Boss Mustang**,
44-F1 **Passenger Coach**,
44-F12 **Passenger
Coach.**

Row 1
44-G **Chevy Van**, 45-C1
Ford Group 6, 45-C9
Ford Group 6.

Row 2
45-C20 **Ford Group 6**,
45-D1 **BMW 3.0 CSL**, 45-
D3 **BMW 3.0 CSL.**

Row 3
45-D6 **BMW 3.0 CSL**,
45-D12 **BMW 3.0 CSL**,
45-E **Kenworth**® **Cab-
over Aerodyne.**

Row 4
46-D1 **Mercedes 300 SE**,
46-D4 **Mercedes 300 SE**,
46-D5 **Mercedes 300 SE.**

Row 5
46-D7 **Mercedes 300 SE**,
46-E1 **Stretcha Fetcha**,
46-E13 **Stretcha Fetcha.**

Row 1
46-E11 **Stretcha Fetcha**, 46-F8 **Ford Tractor**, 46-F4 **Ford Tractor**.

Row 2
46-G **Hot Chocolate**, 47-D1 **DAF Tipper Truck**, 47-E1 **Beach Hopper**.

Row 3
47-F2 **Pannier Tank Loco**, 47-G **Jaguar SS100**, 48-D4 **Dump Truck**.

Row 4
48-E3 **Pie-eyed Piper**, 48-E5 **Pie-eyed Piper**, 48-F8 **Sambron Jacklift**.

Row 5
48-G1 **Red Rider**, 49-C3 **Unimog**, 49-C8 **Unimog**.

Row 1
49-D2 **Chop Suey**, 49-E5 **Crane Truck**, 49-E1 **Crane Truck**.

Row 2
49-E10 **Crane Truck**, 50-D1 **Kennel Truck**, 50-D7 **Kennel Truck**.

Row 3
50-E1 **Articulated Truck**, 50-E18 **Articulated Truck**, 50-E20 **Articulated Truck**.

Row 4
50-G1 **Harley Davidson Cycle**, 51-D1 **Wheel Tipper Truck**, 51-E3 **Citroen SM**.

Row 5
51-E11 **Citroen SM**, 51-F1 **Combine Harvester**, 51-G1 **Midnight Magic**.

Matchbox 1–75 Series
Superfast Wheels

Row 1
52-C5 **Dodge Charger,**
52-C9 **Dodge Charger,**
52-D4 **Police Launch.**

Row 2
52-D6 **Police Launch,**
52-E1 **BMW-M1,** 53-D3
Ford Zodiac.

Row 3
53-D6 **Ford Zodiac,** 53-E1 **Tanzara,** 53-E4 **Tanzara.**

Row 4
53-F7 **CJ6 Jeep,** 53-F9 **CJ6 Jeep,** 53-F10 **CJ6 Jeep.**

Row 5
53-G **Flareside Pick-up,** 54-C1 **Cadillac Ambulance,** 54-D3 **Ford Capri.**

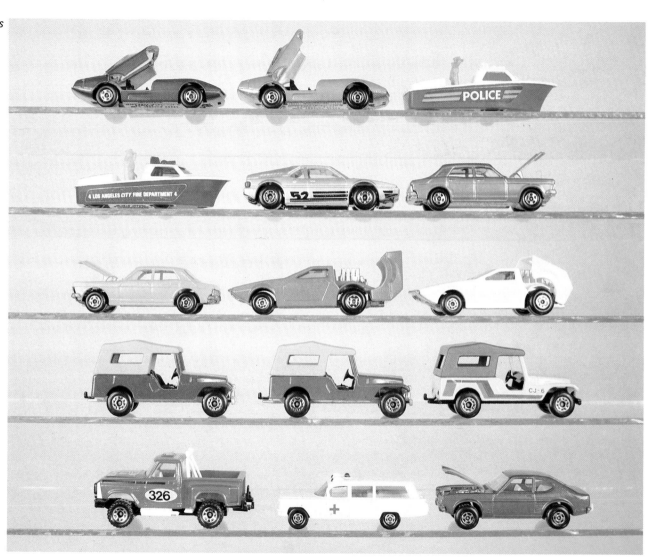

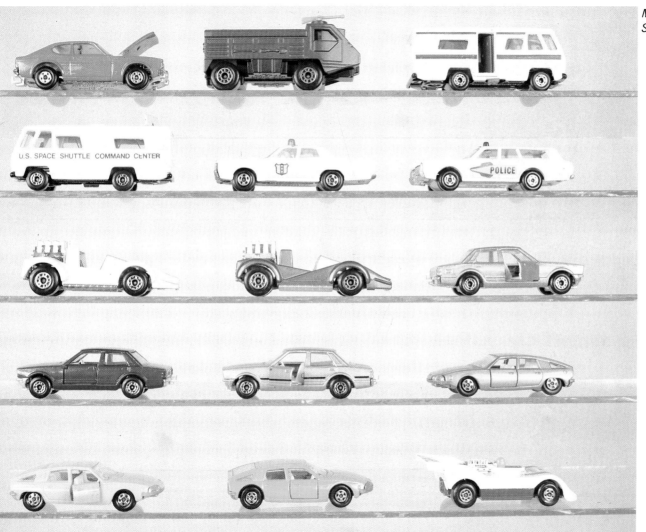

Row 1
54-D8 **Ford Capri**, 54-E1
Personnel Carrier, 54-F8
Moblie Home.

Row 2
54-G **NASA Tracking Vehicle**, 55-E1 **Mercury Police Car**, 55-F4 **Mercury Police Stationwagen.**

Row 3
55-G1 **Hellraiser**, 55-G3
Hellraiser, 55-H4 **Ford Cortina.**

Row 4
55-H5 **Ford Cortina**, 55-I
Cortina 1600GL, 56-C1
Pininfarina.

Row 5
56-C6 **Pininfarina**, 56-C2
Pininfarina, 56-D5 **Hi-Tailer.**

Row 1
56-E2 **Mercedes 450SL**,
56-F2 **Mercedes Taxi**,
56-G **Peterbilt ® Tanker.**

Row 2
57-D1 **Land Rover Fire Truck**, 57-E1 **Eccles Caravan**, 57-E8 **Eccles Caravan.**

Row 3
57-E11 **Eccles Caravan**, 57-E12 **Eccles Caravan**, 57-F1 **Wildlife Truck.**

Row 4
57-F10 **Wildlife Truck**, 57-G **Charmichael Commando**, 57-H **4x4 Mini Pick-up.**

Row 5
58-D1 **Girder Truck**, 58-D2 **Girder Truck**, 58-E3 **Woosh-n-Push.**

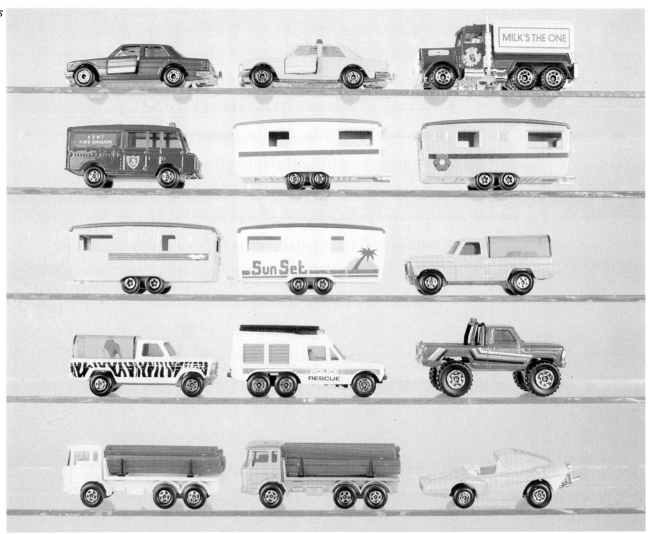

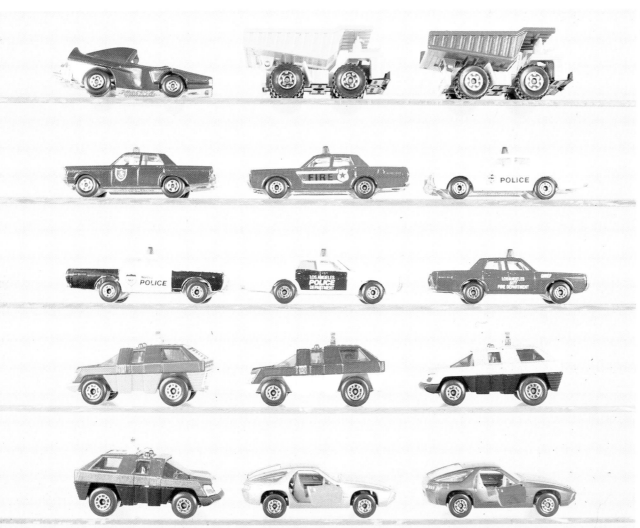

Row 1
58-E6 **Woosh-n-Push,**
58-F1 **Faun Dump
Truck,** 58-F4 **Faun
Dump Truck.**

Row 2
59-D3 **Ford Galaxie Fire
Chief,** 59-E13 **Mercury
Fire Chief Car,** 59-E14
Mercury Fire Chief Car.

Row 3
59-E18 **Mercury Fire
Chief Car,** 59-E16 **Mercury Fire Chief Car,**
59-E17 **Mercury Fire
Chief Car.**

Row 4
59-F1 **Planet Scout,** 59-
F6 **Planet Scout,** 59-F7
Planet Scout.

Row 5
59-F13 **Planet Scout,** 59-
G6 **Porsche 928,** 59-G20
Porsche 928.

Matchbox 1–75 Series
Superfast Wheels

Row 1
59-G28 **Porsche 928**, 60-
C1 **Site Hut Truck**, 60-D1
Lotus Super Seven.

Row 2
60-D3 **Lotus Super
Seven**, 60-E2 **Holden
Pick-up**, 60-E4 **Holden
Pick-up.**

Row 3
60-E8 **Holden Pick-up**,
60-E11 **Holden Pick-up**,
60-E9 **Holden Pick-up.**

Row 4
60-F **Piston Popper**, 61-
C4 **Blue Shark**, 61-D4
Wreck Truck.

Row 5
61-D21 **Wreck Truck**, 61-
D13 **Wreck Truck**, 61-D8
Wreck Truck.

Row 1
61-E **Peterbilt®️ Wreck Truck**, 62-G1 **Chevrolet Corvette**, 62-G8 **Chevrolet Corvette**.

Row 2
62-D2 **Mercury Cougar**, 62-E2 **Mercury Cougar "Rat Rod"**, 62-E5 **Mercury Cougar "Rat Rod"**.

Row 3
62-F3 **Renault 17TL**, 62-F1 **Renault 17TL**, 63-D1 **Dodge Crane Truck**.

Row 4
63-E2 **Freeway Gas Truck**, 63-E1 **Freeway Gas Truck**, 63-E4 **Freeway Gas Truck**.

Row 5
63-E15 **Freeway Gas Truck**, 63-E9 **Freeway Gas Truck**, 63-E21 **Freeway Gas Truck**.

Row 1
63-E27 **Freeway Gas Truck**, 63-E26 **Freeway Gas Truck**, 63-E28 **Freeway Gas Truck.**

Row 2
63-F1 **Freeway Gas Tanker Trailer**, 63-F2 **Freeway Gas Tanker Trailer**, 63-F4 **Freeway Gas Tanker Trailer.**

Row 3
63-G1 **Dodge Challenger**, 63-G3 **Dodge Challenger**, 63-H **Snorkel Fire Engine.**

Row 4
64-C1 **MG 1100**, 64-C2 **MG 1100**, 64-D1 **Slingshot Dragster.**

Row 5
64-D4 **Slingshot Dragster**, 64-D2 **Slingshot Dragster**, 64-E2 **Fire Chief.**

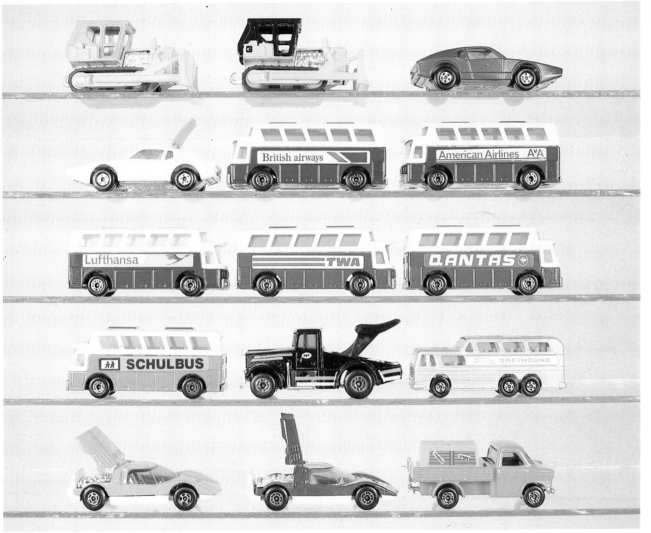

Row 1
64-F2 **Caterpillar® Bulldozer**, 64-F9 **Caterpillar® Bulldozer**, 65-D2 **Saab Sonnet**.

Row 2
65-D5 **Saab Sonnet**, 65-E5 **Airport Coach**, 65-E4 **Airport Coach**.

Row 3
65-E8 **Airport Coach**, 65-E16 **Airport Coach**, 65-E17 **Airport Coach**.

Row 4
65-E18 **Airport Coach**, 65-F **Tyrone Malone Bandag Bandit**, 66-D1 **Greyhound Bus**.

Row 5
66-E3 **Mazda RX500**, 66-E15 **Mazda RX500**, 66-F1 **Ford Transit**.

Row 1
66-F12 **Ford Transit**, 66-E9 **Mazda RX500**, 66-G **Tyrone Malone Super Boss.**

Row 2
67-C1 **Volkswagen 1600-TL**, 67-C2 **Volkswagen 1600TL**, 67-C5 **Volkswagen 1600TL.**

Row 3
67-D1 **Hot Rocker**, 67-D5 **Hot Rocker**, 67-E1 **Datsun 260Z 2 + 2.**

Row 4
67-E2 **Datsun 260Z 2 + 2**, 67-E10 **Datsun 260Z 2 + 2**, 67-E13 **Datsun 260Z 2 + 2.**

Row 5
68-C1 **Porsche 910**, 68-C3 **Porsche 910**, 68-D5 **Cosmobile.**

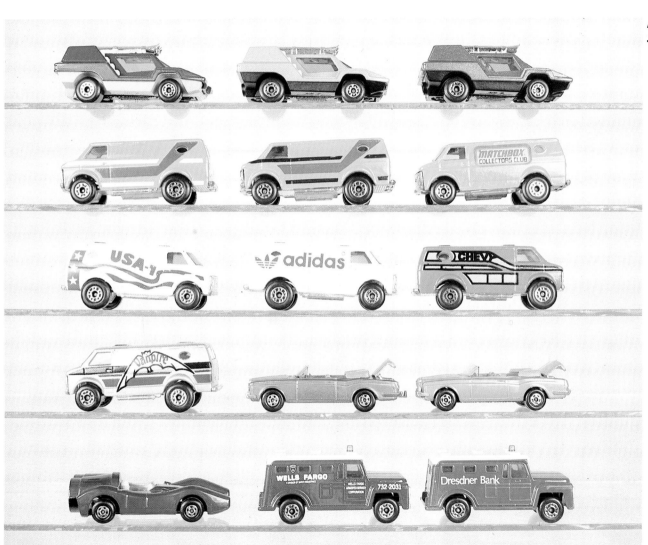

Row 1
68-D8 **Cosmobile**, 68-D10 **Cosmobile**, 68-D17 **Cosmobile**.

Row 2
68-E3 **Chevy Van**, 68-E9 **Chevy Van**, 68-E15 **Chevy Van**.

Row 3
68-E14 **Chevy Van**, 68-E16 **Chevy Van**, 68-E17 **Chevy Van**.

Row 4
68-E20 **Chevy Van**, 69-C1 **Rolls Royce Silver Shadow Coupe**, 69-C4 **Rolls Royce Silver Shadow Coupe**.

Row 5
69-D2 **Turbo Fury**, 69-E1 **Armored Truck**, 69-E6 **Armored Truck**.

Matchbox 1—75 Series
Superfast Wheels

Row 1
69-F **1933 Willy's Street Rod**, 70-C2 **Grit Spreader**, 70-D11 **Dodge Dragster.**

Row 2
70-D12 **Dodge Dragster**, 70-E1 **Self-Propelled Gun**, 70-F1 **Ferrari 308 GTB.**

Row 3
71-D1 **Wreck Truck**, 71-D4 **Wreck Truck**, 71-D5 **Wreck Truck.**

Row 4
71-E1 **Jumbo Jet Motorcycle**, 71-F3 **Cattle Truck**, 71-F6 **Cattle Truck.**

Row 5
71-F25 **Cattle Truck**, 71-F19 **Cattle Truck**, 71-G **1962 Corvette.**

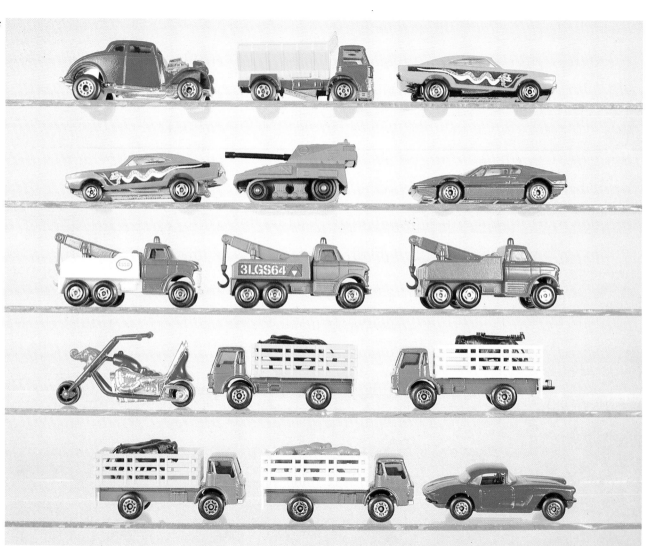

Row 1
72-C1 **Jeep**, 72-D2 **Hovercraft**, 72-E1 **Bomag Road Roller.**

Row 2
72-F1 **Maxi Taxi**, 72-G **Dodge Delivery Truck**, 73-D1 **Mercury Stationwagon.**

Row 3
73-E3 **Mercury Stationwagon**, 73-F1 **Weasel**, 73-F2 **Weasel.**

Row 4
73-G2 **Model "A" Ford**, 73-G6 **Model "A" Ford**, 73-G9 **Model "A" Ford.**

Row 5
74-C2 **Daimler Bus**, 74-C6 **Daimler Bus**, 74-D9 **Toe Joe.**

Matchbox 1–75 Series
Superfast Wheels

Row 1
74-D3 **Toe Joe**, 74-D22 **Toe Joe**, 74-D16 **Toe Joe**.

Row 2
74-E1 **Cougar Villager**, 74-E4 **Cougar Villager**, 74-F1 **Orange Peel**.

Row 3
75-C1 **Ferrari Berinetta**, 75-C4 **Ferrari Berinetta**, 75-D3 **Alfa Carabo**.

Row 4
75-E1 **Alfa Carabo**, 75-E3 **Alfa Carabo**.

Row 5
75-F4 **Seasprite Helicopter**, 75-G1 **Helicopter**.

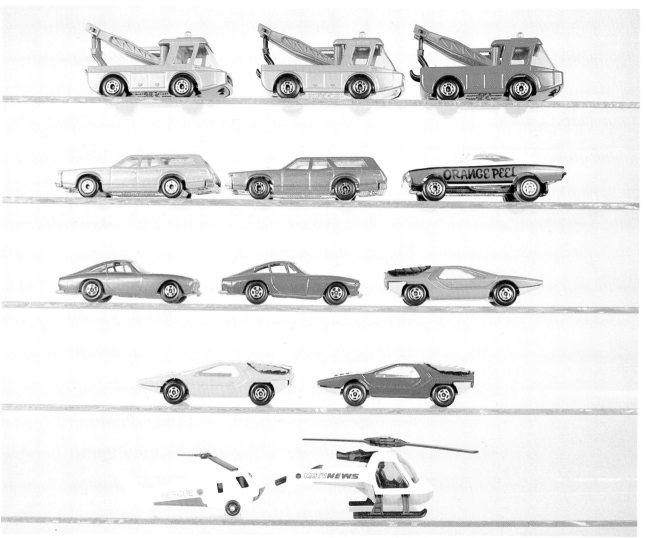

Row 1
76-A **Mazda RX7** [Australian] and box.

Row 2
77-A **Toyota Celica** [Australian] and box.

Row 3
78-A **Datsun 280Z** [Australian] and box.

Row 4
79-A **Galant Eterna** [Australian] and box.

Matchbox 1—75 Series
Limited Edition
Superfast

Row 1
I **Silver Streak**, II **Sleet-n-snow**, III **White Lightning**.

Row 2
IV **Flying Beetle**, V **Hot Smoker**.

Row 3
VI **Lady Bug**, VII **Brown Sugar**, VIII **Black Widow**.

Row 4
IX **Flamin' Manta**, X **Golden X**.

Limited Edition Superfast I to X.

72

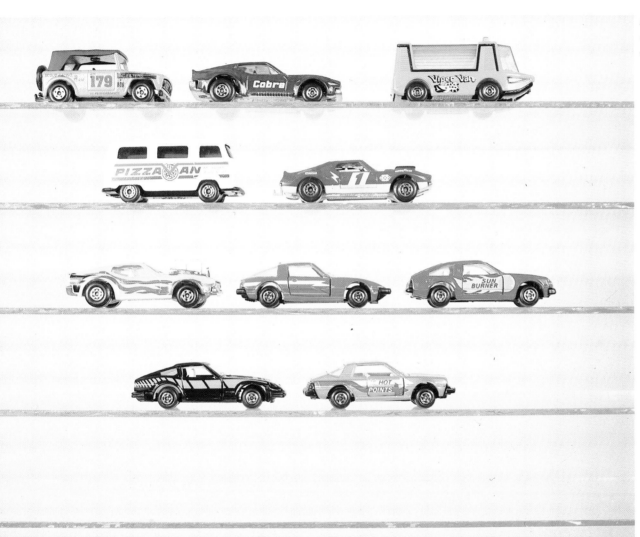

Row 1
Bush Wacker, Cobra Mustang, Viper Van.

Row 2
Pizza Van, Can Cracker.

Row 3
Hot Popper, Boulevard Blaster, Sun Burner.

Row 4
Phantom Z, Hot Points Challenger.

**Limited Edition Superfast.
Second series, unnumbered.**

73

Matchbox 1—75 Series
Japanese Issue
Superfast

Row 1
5 Datsun 280Z, 2 Mazda RX7

Row 2
J-21 **Toyota Celica,** J-22 **Galant Eterna,** J-22 **Galant Eterna.**

Row 3
J-4 **Black Box,** 24-D **Rolls Royce.**

Row 4
33-D **Lamborghini,** 38 **Colored Box.**

Row 5
31 **White Box,** 27-E **Mercedes.**

Row 1
33-D **Lamborghini**, 8-H **Panterra**, 10-G **Police Car**.

Row 2
28-G **Lincoln**, 28-F **Stoat**, 54-F **Mobil Home**.

Row 3
16-E **Badger**, 26-E **Big Banger**, 29-F **Tractor Shovel**.

Row 4
32-G **Excavator**, 21-G **Renault**, 7-G **V.W. Rabbit**.

Experimental models, not sold in these colors.

75

Models of Yesteryear Series

Row 1

Y-1-A1 **1925 Allchin 7-NHP Traction Engine**, Y-1-B4 **1911 Model "T" Ford**, Y-1-C2 **1936 Jaguar SS100**.

Row 2

Y-2-A2 **1911 "B" type London bus**, Y-2-B3 **1911 Renault Two-seater**, Y-2-C2 **1914 Prince Henry Vauxhall**, Y-2-C8 **1914 Prince Henry Vauxhall**.

Row 3

Y-3-A1 **1907 London "E" class Tramcar**, Y-3-B8 **1910 Benz Limousine**, Y-3-B10 **1910 Benz Limousine**, Y-3-C2 **1934 Riely MPH**, Y-3-D **1912 Model "T" Ford Petrol Tanker**.

Row 4

Y-4-A8 **Sentinel Steam Wagon**, Y-4-B2 **Shand Mason Horse-drawn Fire Engine**, Y-4-C12 **1909 Opel Coupe**, Y-4-C6 **1909 Opel Coupe**.

Row 5

Y-4-D2 **1930 Duesenberg Model "J" Town Car**, Y-4-D3 **1930 Duesenberg Model "J" Town Car**.

Row 1
Y-5-A4 **1929 Le Mans Bentley**, Y-5-B1 **1929 4-1/2 litre [S] Bentley**, Y-5-C1 **1907 Peugeot** Y-5-C5 **1907 Peugeot.**

Row 2
Y-5-D2 **Talbot Van**, Y-5-D3 **Talbot Van**, Y-5-D11 **Talbot Van**, Y-5-D17 **Talbot Van.**

Row 3
Y-6-A2 **1916 A.E.C. "Y" type Lorry**, Y-6-B2 **1923 type 35 Bugatti**, Y-6-B10 **1923 type 35 Bugatti.**

Row 4
Y-6-C1 **1913 Cadillac**, Y-6-C10 **1913 Cadillac**, Y-6-C **1920 Rolls Royce Fire Engine.**

Row 5
Y-7-A5 **4 Ton Leyland Lorry**, Y-7-B3 **1913 Mercer Raceabout**, Y-7-B11 **1913 Mercer Raceabout**, Y-7-C1 **1912 Rolls Royce**, Y-7-C8 **1912 Rolls Royce.**

Models of Yesteryear Series

Row 1
Y-8-A3 **Morris Cowley 1926 "Bullnose"**, Y-8-B2 **1914 Sunbeam Motorcycle with Milford sidecar**, Y-8-C2 **1914 Stutz**, Y-8-D1 **1945 MG TC**, Y-8-D6 **1945 MG TC.**

Row 2
Y-9-A2 **1924 Fowler "Big Lion" Showmans Engine**, Y-9-B1 **1912 Simplex**, Y-9-B8 **1912 Simplex.**

Row 3
Y-10-A8 **1908 'Grand Prix" Mercedes**, Y-10-B1 **1928 Mercedes Benz 36/220.**

Row 4
Y-10-C2 **1906 Rolls Royce Silver Ghost**, Y-10-C3 **1906 Rolls Royce Silver Ghost**, Y-10-C6 **1906 Rolls Royce Silver Ghost.**

Row 5
Y-11-A6 **1920 Aveling & Porter Steam Roller**, Y-11-B5 **1912 Packard Landaulet**, Y-11-C6 **1938 Lagonda Drop-head Coupe**, Y-11-C1 **1938 Lagonda Drop-head Coupe.**

Row 1
Y-12-A1 **1899 London Horse-drawn Bus,** Y-12-B6 **Thomas Flyabout,** Y-12-B2 **1909 Thomas Flyabout.**

Row 2
Y-12-C1 **1912 Model "T" Ford-Coleman's Mustard,** Y-12-C5 **1912 Model "T" Ford-Coca Cola,** Y-12-C12 **1912 Model "T" Ford-Blue Bird Custard Powder.**

Row 3
Y-13-A1 **1862 American "General" Loco "Santa Fe",** Y-13-B1 **1911 Daimler,** Y-13-C2 **1918 Crossley R.A.F. Tender,** Y-13-C6 **1918 Crossley Coal & Coke Tender.**

Row 4
Y-14-A1 **1903 "Duke of Connaught" Loco,** Y-14-B5 **1911 Maxwell Roadster,** Y-14-C6 **1931 Stutz Bearcat,** Y-14-C7 **1931 Stutz Bearcat.**

Row 5
Y-15-A2 **1907 Rolls Royce Silver Ghost,** Y-15-B3 **1930 Packard Victoria,** Y-15-B13 **1930 Packard Victoria.**

Models of Yesteryear Series

Row 1
Y-16-A2 **1904 Spyker,** Y-16-A8 **1904 Spyker,** Y-16-B6 **1928 Mercedes SS.**

Row 2
Y-16-B5 **1928 Mercedes SS,** Y-16-B1 **1928 Mercedes SS,** Y-16-B7 **1928 Mercedes SS.**

Row 3
Y-17-A6 **1938 Hispano Suiza,** Y-17-A1 **1938 Hispano Suiza.**

Row 4
Y-18-A1 **1937 Cord 812,** Y-19-A1 **1935 Auburn Speedstar.**

Row 5
Y-20-A **1938 Mercedes 540-K,** Y-21-A **1929 Woody Wagon.**

Row 1
Y1-B **1911 Model T Ford,**
Y2-B **1911 Renault,** Y2-C
1914 Prince Henry Vaux-
hall.

Row 2
Y3-C **1934 Riley,** Y4-C
1909 Opel Coupe, Y14-B
1911 Maxwell Roadster.

Row 3
Y5-B **1929 Bentley,** Y7-C
1912 Rolls Royce, Y10-B
1928 Mercedes Benz.

Row 4
Y10-C **1906 Rolls Royce**
Silver Ghost, Y13-B
1911 Daimler, Y13-C
1918 Coal and Coke
Truck.

Models of Yesteryear
Pre-preduction
Models of Yesteryear

Row 1
Y-8 **Stutz,** Y-8 **Stutz,**
Y-13 **Daimler.**

Row 2
Y-9 **Simplex,** Y-1 **Ford,**
Y-5 **Peugeot.**

Row 3
Y-20 **Mercedes,** Y-4
Duesenburg, Y-13 **Coal
& Coke Truck.**

Row 4
Y-10 **Rolls Royce,** Y-7
Rolls Royce, Y-15 **Pack-
ard.**

Row 5
Y-11 **Packard Landaulet,**
Y-2 **Prince Henry Vaux-
hall,** Y-2 **Prince Henry
Vauxhall.**

**Experimental models,
not sold in these colors.**

Row 1
Y-5 **Nestle's Milk,** Y-12
Suze.

Row 2
Y-12 **25** th **Anniversary,**
Y-12 **Smith's Potatoe
Chips.**

Row 3
Y-5 **Landendorf Bakery,**
Y-5 **Merita Bakery,** Y-5
Taystee Bakery.

**Some Lesney-made pro-
motional Yesteryears.**

These were tool-makers'
ideas, prototypes that
almost made it, but
never went into produc-
tion.

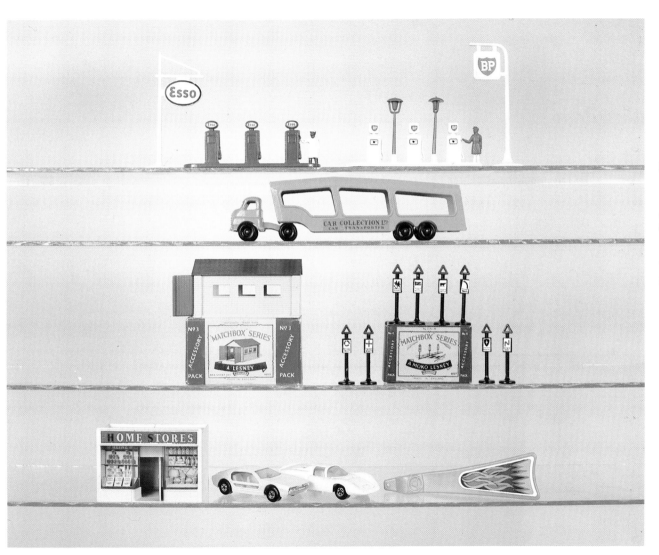

Row 1
A1-A **Petrol Pumps and Sign—Esso**, A1-B **Petrol Pumps and Sign— BP.**

Row 2
A2-A **Bedford Articulated Four Car Transporter Truck.**

Row 3
A3-A **Metal Lock-up Garage**, A4-A **Road Signs** [set of eight].

Row 4
A5-A **Home Store**, A3-B **Brroomstick** [or **Zingomatic**].

Row 1
MG1-C **Matchbox Garage.**

Row 2
MG3-A **Texaco Garage & Restaurant**

Row 1
M1-A **Caterpillar Earth Scraper**, M1-B **BP Auto Tanker.**

Row 2
M2-A2 **Bedford Ice Cream Truck**, M2-B1 **Bedford Tractor & York Trailer.**

Row 3
M2-B3 **Bedford Tractor & York Trailer**, M3-A4 **Thorneycraft Antar with Sanky 50-ton tank transporter and Centurion MK III tank.**

Row 4
M4-A2 **Ruston Bucyrus Power Shovel**, M5-A1 **Massey Ferguson Combine Harvester.**

Row 1
M6-A **Pickfords 200 Ton Transporter**, M6-B **Racing Car Transporter.**

Row 2
M7-A3 **Jennings Cattle Truck**, M8-A1 **Mobilgas Petrol Tanker.**

Row 3
M8-B2 **Guy Warrior Car Transporter**, M10-A1 **Dinkum Dumper.**

Row 4
M9-A6 **Interstate Double Freighter.**

Row 5
M9-A4 **Interstate Double Freighter.**

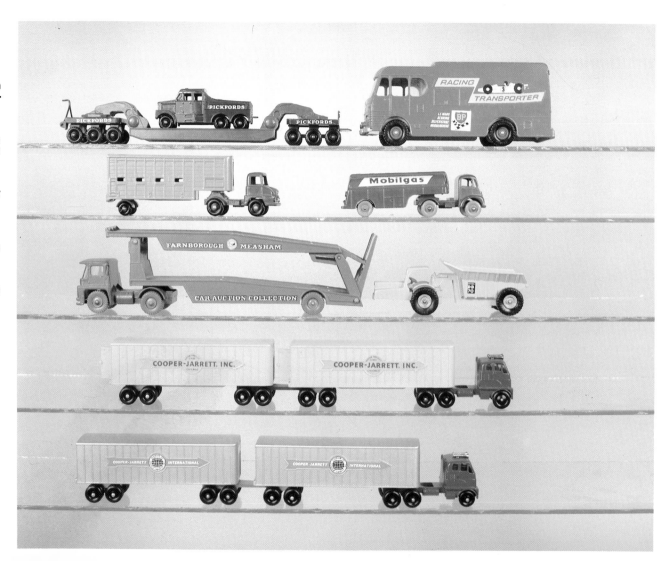

Row 1
K1-A **Weatherhill Hy-draulic Shovel**, K1-B **8-Wheel Tipper Truck**, K2-A2 **Muir Hill Dumper**, K2-A1 **Muir Hill Dumper**.

Row 2
K2-B **K.W. Dump Truck**, K2-C2 **Scammell Heavy Wreck Truck**, K2-C3 **Scammell Heavy Wreck Truck**.

Row 3
K3-C **Massey Ferguson Tractor & Trailer**, K3-A5 **Caterpillar Bulldozer**, K3-A6 **Caterpillar Bull-dozer**.

Row 4
K3-B1 **Hatra Tractor Shovel**, K4-A1 **Inter-national Tractor**, K4-A4 **International Tractor**.

Row 5
K4-B1 **GMC Tractor with Fruehauf Hopper Train**.

Row 1
K4-C1 **Leyland Tipper,**
K4-C4 **Leyland Tipper,**
K4-C3 **Leyland Tipper.**

Row 2
K5-A1 **Foden Tipper Truck,** K6-A1 **Allis-Chalmers Earth Scraper,** K6-B2 **Mercedes Benz Ambulance.**

Row 3
K7-A **Curtiss—Wright Rear Dumper,** K7-B Refuse Truck.

Row 4
K8-A7 **Prime Mover & Transporter with Caterpillar Crawler Tractor.**

Row 5
K8-B4 **Guy Warrior Car Transporter.**

Row 1
K8-C2 **Caterpillar Trax-cavator**, K9-A2 **Diesel Road Roller**, K9-B5 **Claas Combine Harvester**.

Row 2
K9-B1 **Claas Combine Harvester**, K10-A2 **Aveling Barford Tractor Shovel**.

Row 3
K10-B1 **Pipe Truck**, K11-A4 **Fordson Tractor & Farm Trailer**.

Row 4
K11-B1 **DAF Car Transporter**.

Row 5
K11-B2 **DAF Car Transporter**.

91

Row 1
K12-A1 **Heavy Break-
down Wreck Truck**, K13-
A1 **Ready-Mix Concrete
Truck.**

Row 2
K15-A1 **Merryweather
Fire Engine**, K14-A2
Taylor Jumbo Crane.

Row 3
K16-A1 **Dodge Tractor**
with twin tippers.

Row 4
K17-A1 **Low Loader and
Bulldozer.**

Row 1
K18-A1 **Articulated Horse Box**, K19-A1 **Scammell Tipper Truck.**

Row 2
K20-A2 **Tractor Transporter & Tractors.**

Row 3
K21-A1 **Mercury Cougar**, K23-A1 **Mercury Police Car**, K24-A1 **Lamborghini Miura.**

Row 1
K1-C3 **O & K Excavator,**
K2-D3 **Car Recovery Ve-**
hicle.

Row 2
K3-D1 **Mod Tractor &**
Trailer, K4-D4 **Big Tip-**
per.

Row 3
K3-E1 **Grain Trans-**
porter.

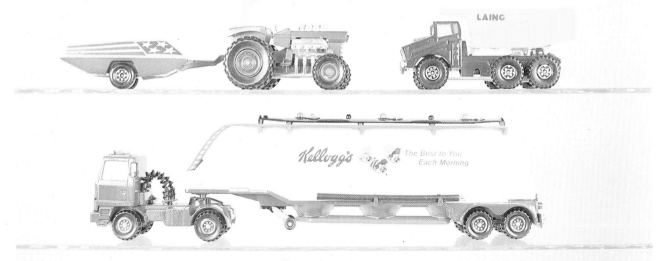

Row 1
K5-C2 **Muir Hill Tractor & Trailer.**

Row 2
K6-C2 **Cement Mixer,** K6-D2 **Motorcycle Transporter.**

Row 3
K7-B4 **Refuse Truck,** K7-C8 **Racing Car Transporter.**

Row 4
K8-D2 **Animal Transporter.**

95

King Size
Super Kings

Row 1
K9-C1 **Fire Tender**, K11-D1 **Dodge Delivery Van.**

Row 2
K10-C2 **Car Transporter.**

Row 3
K10-D **Bedford Car Transporter.**

Row 4
K11-C1 **Tow Truck**, K11-C4 **Tow Truck.**

Row 1
K12-C1 **Hercules mobile Crane**, K13-B5 **Building Transporter.**

Row 2
K13-C6 **Aircraft Transporter**, K14-B2 **Freight Truck.**

Row 3
K13-C2 **Aircraft Transporter**, K14-C2 **Heavy Breakdown Truck.**

Row 1
K15-B1 **The Londoner Swinging London Carnaby Street**, K15-B6 **The Londoner-Hamleys.**

Row 2
K15-B5 **The Londoner-Harrods**, K15-B7 **The Londoner-Tourist London by Bus.**

Row 3
K15-B11 **The Londoner-Visit The London Dungon**, K15-B4 **The Londoner-Silver Jubilee.**

Row 4
K15-B12 **The Londoner-The Royal Wedding**, K15-B13 **The Londoner-1979 Royal Visit [Trial Run].**

Row 1
K16-B1 **Petrol Tanker-Texaco.**

Row 2
K16-B2 **Petrol Tanker-Quaker State.**

Row 3
K16-B5 **Petrol Tanker-Aral.**

Row 4
K16-B9 **Petrol Tanker-Chemco.**

99

Row 1
K17-B6 **Articulated Container Truck-Gentransco**

Row 2
K-17B **Articulated Container Truck-Ginny Vogue Dolls.**

Row 3
K17-B17 **Articulated Container Truck-Penguin.**

Row 4
K17-B18 **Articulated Container Truck-7-UP.**

King Size
Super Kings

Row 1
K18-B4 **Articulated Tipper Truck**, K19-B2 **Security Truck.**

Row 2
K20-B5 **Cargo Hauler & Pallet Loader**, K20-C4 **Peterbilt Wrecker.**

Row 3
K21-B3 **Cougar Dragster**, K21-C **Tractor Transporter.**

Row 4
K21-D3 **Ford Transcontinental.**

101

King Size
Super Kings

Row 1
K22-A **Dodge Charger,**
K22-B2 **Dodge Dragster,**
K22-C1 **SRN6 Hover-**
craft.

Row 2
K23-B1 **Lowloader &**
Bulldozer, K24-B1
Scammell Container
Truck.

Row 3
K24-B3 **Scammell Con-**
tainer Truck, K25-A1
Powerboat & Trailer.

Row 4
K25-B2 **Digger & Plough**
K26-A2 **Mercedes Am-**
bulance, K26-B1 **Ce-**
ment Truck.

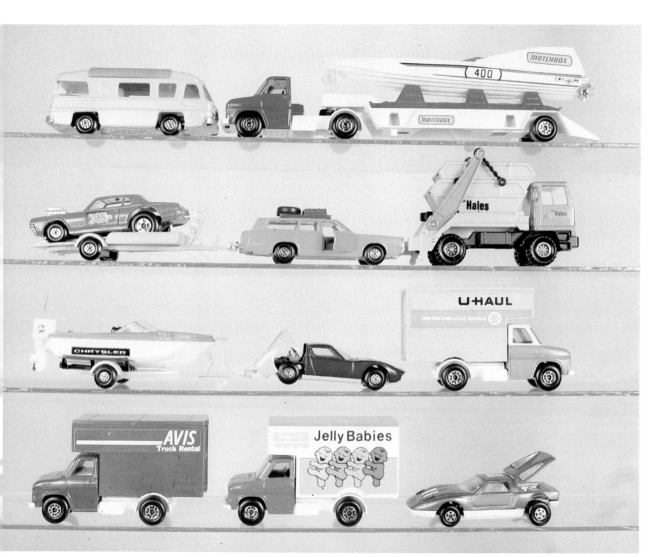

Row 1
K27-A1 **Camping Cruiser**, K27-B2 **Boat Transporter**.

Row 2
K28-A2 **Drag Pack**, K28-B1 **Skip Truck**.

Row 3
K29-A3 **Muira Seaburst Set**, K29-B1 **Ford Delivery U-haul Van**.

Row 4
K29-B2 **Ford Delivery Van-Avis**, K29-B7 **Ford Delivery Van-Jelly Babies**, K30-A4 **Mercedes C,111**.

103

King Size
Super Kings

Row 1
K30-B3 **Unimog & Com-
pressor,** K31-A1 **Bertone
Runabout.**

Row 2
K31-B3 **Peterbilt Refrigerator Truck-Coca-Cola.**

Row 3
K31-B6 **Peterbilt Refrig-
erator Truck-Burger
King.**

Row 4
K31-B5 **Peterbilt Refrigerator Truck-Pepsi.**

Row 1
K32-A1 **Shovel Nose**, K32-B1 **Farm Unimog & Trailer.**

Row 2
K33-A1 **Citroen SM**, K33-B1 **Cargo Hauler.**

Row 3
K34-A2 **Thunderclap**, K34-B1 **Pallet Truck & Forklift.**

Row 4
K35-A1 **Lightning**, K35-B **Massey Ferguson Tractor & Trailer.**

Row 5
K36-A6 **Bandalero**, K36-B2 **Construction Transporter**, K37-A1 **Sandcat.**

King Size
Super Kings

Row 1
K37-B **Leyland Tipper,**
K38-A1 **Gus's Helper,**
K38-B **Dodge Ambu-lance.**

Row 2
K39-A1 **Milligan's Mill,**
K39-B **Simon Snorkel
Fire Engine.**

Row 3
K40-A4 **Blaze Trailer,**
K40-B1 **Pepsi Delivery
Truck,** K41-A5 **Fuzz
Buggy.**

Row 4
K41-B1 **Brabham BT,**
K41-C **JCB Excavator,**
K42-A1 **Nissan 270X.**

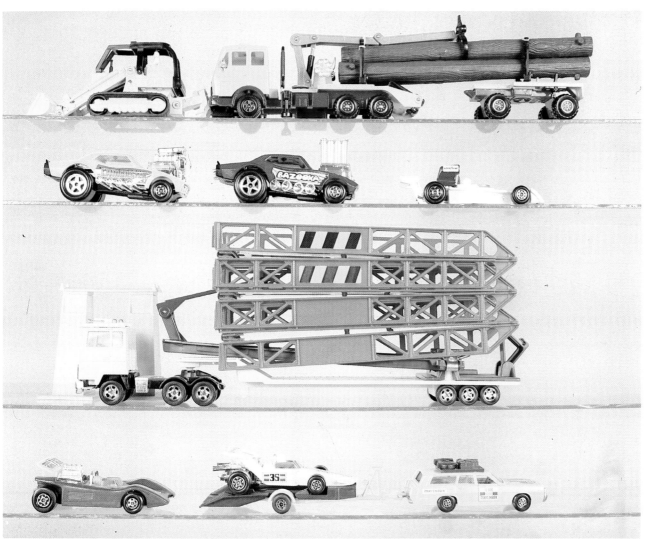

Row 1
K42-B **Traxcavator Road Ripper**, K43-B **Log Transporter.**

Row 2
K43-A3 **Cambuster**, K44-A5 **Bazooka**, K44-B **Surtees Formula 1.**

Row 3
K44-C **Bridge Layer.**

Row 4
K45-A5 **Marauder**, K46-A1 **Racing Car Pack.**

King Size
Super Kings

Row 1
K47-A1 **Easy Rider,** K48-A2 **Mercedes 350 SLC,** K49-A1 **Ambulance.**

Row 2
K50-A4 **Street Rod,** K51-A8 **Barracuda,** K52-A1 **Datsun Rally Car.**

Row 3
K53-A2 **Hot Fire Engine,** K54-A5 **AMX Javelin,** K55-A1 **Corvette Caper Car.**

Row 4
K56-A6 **Maserati Bora,** K57-A2 **Javelin Drag Racing Set.**

Row 5
K58-A2 **Corvette Power Boat Set,** K59-A1 **Ford Capri MK II.**

Row 1
K60-A **Ford Mustang II,**
K60-B2 **Cobra Mustang,**
K61-A1 **Mercedes Police
Car.**

Row 2
K62-A2 **Doctor's Emergency Car,** K63-A1 **Mercedes Benz Ambulance,**
K64-A5 **Range Rover
Fire Engine.**

Row 3
K65-A1 **Plymouth Trail
Duster,** K66-A8 **Jaguar
xj12 Police Patrol,** K67-A2 **Dodge Monaco Fire
Chief Car.**

Row 4
K68-A1 **Dodge Monaco
& Trailer,** K70-A1
Porsche Turbo.

Row 5
K69-A2 **Jaguar Sedan
and Europa Caravan**
K71-A **Porsche Polizei
Patrol.**

Row 1
K72-A2 **Brabham BT 44B**, K73-A2 **Surtees Formula 1**, K74-A1 **Volvo Estate.**

Row 2
K75-A1 **Airport Fire Tender**, K76-A2 **Volvo Rally Set.**

Row 3
K77-A1 **Highway Rescue Vehicle**, K78-A1 **Gran Fury Police Car**, K79-A **Gran Fury U.S. Taxi.**

Row 4
K80-A3 **Dodge Custom Van**, K81-A **Suzuki Motorcycle**, K82-A2 **BMW Motorcycle.**

Row 1
K83-A **Harley Davidson Police Motorcycle**, K84-A **Peugeat 305**, K86-A **V.W. Golf.**

Row 2
K87-A **Massey Ferguson Tractor & Rotary Rake**, K88-A **Money Box.**

Row 3
K90-A **Matra Rancho**, K91-A **Motorcycle Racing Set.**

Row 4
K98-A **Forestry Unimog**, K99-A **Range Rover Polizei Set.**

Super Kings
Adventure 2000

Row 1
K2001 **Raider Command
[in two parts]**.

Row 2
K2002 **Flight Hunter,**
K2003 **Crusader.**

Row 3
K2004 **Rocket Striker.**

Row 4
K2006 **Shuttle Launcher.**

Row 1
K77 **Highway Rescue—Germany**, K65 **Plymouth Trail Duster—Germany**, K75 **Airport Rescue—Germany**.

Row 2
K29 **Ford Delivery Van—Germany**, K28 **Skip Truck—Germany**, K26 **Cement Truck—Germany**.

Row 3
K38 **Dodge Ambulance—Germany**, K29 **Ford Delivery Van—Germany**, K64 **Range Rover—Sweden**.

Row 4
K21 **Tandem Truck—Germany**.

These Super Kings were made for regional markets only.

Row 1
Buy "Matchbox" Series, Buy "Matchbox" Series, Players Please, BP Visco-static.

Row 2
Pegram, The Baron of Beef, BP Visco-static.

Row 3
Drink Peardrox, Players Please, BP Visco-static, BP Longlife.

Row 4
Drink Peardrox, Drink Peardrox.

Regular series double-decker beauties.

G2-D **Railway Set.**

Skybusters

Row 1
SB1-A **Learjet**, SB2-A3 **Corsair A7D**, SB3-A **A300B Airbus**.

Row 2
SB3-B **NASA Space Shuttle**, SB4-A2 **Mirage F1**, SB5-A **Starfighter**.

Row 3
SB6-A3 **MIG 21**, SB7-A1 **Junkers A7B**, SB8-A5 **Spitfire**.

Row 4
SB9-A **Cessna 402**, SB10-A5 **Boeing 747**, SB10-B **Air Force-1**.

Row 5
SB11-A2 **Alpha Jet**, SB12-A1 **Douglas Skyhawk A-4E**, SB12-B **Pitts Special**.

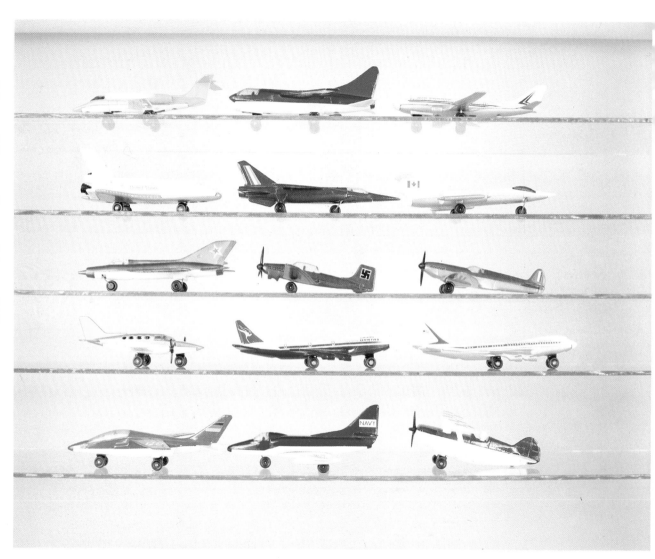

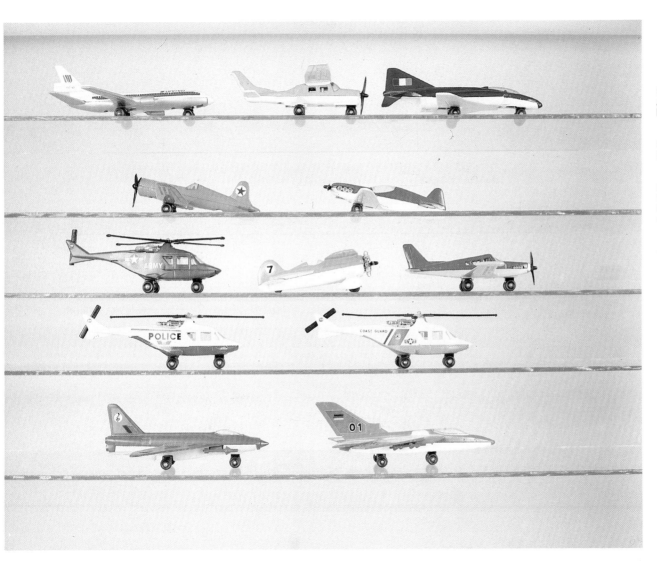

Row 1
SB13-A5 **DC10**, SB14-A2 **Cessna 210**, SB15-A1 **Phantom F4E.**

Row 2
SB16-A3 **Corsair F4U-5N**, SB17-A **RamRod.**

Row 3
SB20-A1 **Helicopter**, SB18-A **Wild Wind**, SB19-A **Piper Commanche.**

Row 4
SB20-A3 **Helicopter**, SB20-A2 Helicopter.

Row 5
SB21-A **Lightning**, SB22 A1 **Tornado [M.R.C.A.].**

Row 1
SB23-A1 **Super Sonic Transport**, SB24-A **F-16.**

Row 2
SB25-A2 **Rescue Helicopter, Code Red,** SB25 A1 **Rescue Helicopter.**

Row 3
SB26-A **Cessna 210 Float Plane,** SB27-A **Harrier Jet.**

Row 4
SB10-A **Boeing 747 (plated)**

Row 5
Gold plated Super Sonic transport mounted on pen stand.

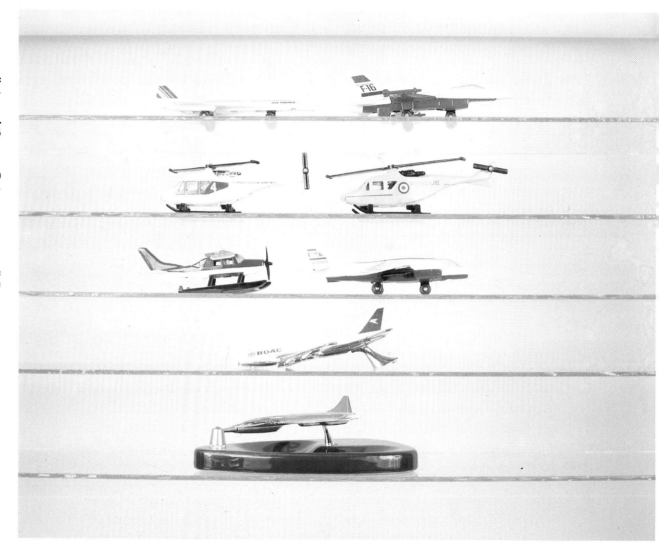

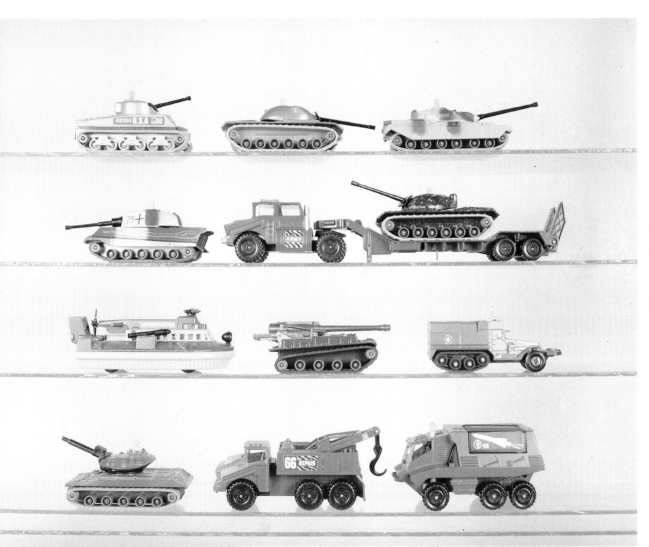

Row 1
BK101 **Sherman Tank,**
BK102 **M48 AZ Tank,**
BK103 **Chelftan Tank.**

Row 2
BK104 **King Tiger Tank,**
BK106 **Tank Transporter
with** (BK102) **M48 AZ
Tank.**

Row 3
BK105 **Hover Raider,**
BK107 **155 mm Self-
propelled Howitzer Gun,**
BK108 **M3A1 Half Track
A.P.C.**

Row 4
BK109 **Sheridan Tank,**
BK110 **Recovery Vehi-
cle,** BK111 **Missile
Launcher.**

Row 1
BK112 **DAF Ambulance,**
BK114 **Army Aircraft
Transporter.**

Row 2
BK113 **Military Crane
Truck,** BK115 **Military
Petrol Tanker.**

Row 3
BK116 **Troop Carrier and
Howitzer,** BK117 **Self-
propelled "Hawk" Rock-
et Launcher.**

Row 4
BK118 **Kaman Seasprite
Army Helicopter,** MM2-
A **Army Tank Transport-
er.** [Matchbox Military
series].

Row 1
TP7-B **Jeep and Glider set.**

Row 2
TP16-C **Articulated Truck and Trailer.**

Row 3
TP19-A **Cattle Truck and Trailer.**

Row 4
TP20-A **Shunter and Side Tipper.**

Row 5
TP21-A **Motorcycle Transporter Set.**

Row 1
TP22-A **Double Container Truck.**

Row 2
TP23-A **Covered Container Truck.**

Row 3
TP24 **Preproduction Kodak Box Container Truck.**

Row 4
TP24-A **Box Container Truck.**

Row 5
TP24-A **Box Container Truck.**

TP24-A **Box Container Truck.**

Row 2
TP25-A **Pipe Truck.**

Row 3
TP26-A **Boat Transporter.**

Row 4
TP2-C **Articulated Petrol Tanker.**

Row 5
PS1 **Double Container Truck [from the Play Set].**

Sea Kings

Row 1
SK301 **Frigate.**

Row 2
SK302 **Corvette.**

Row 3
SK303 **Battleship.**

Row 4
SK304 **Aircraft Carrier.**

Row 5
SK305 **Submarine
Chaser.**

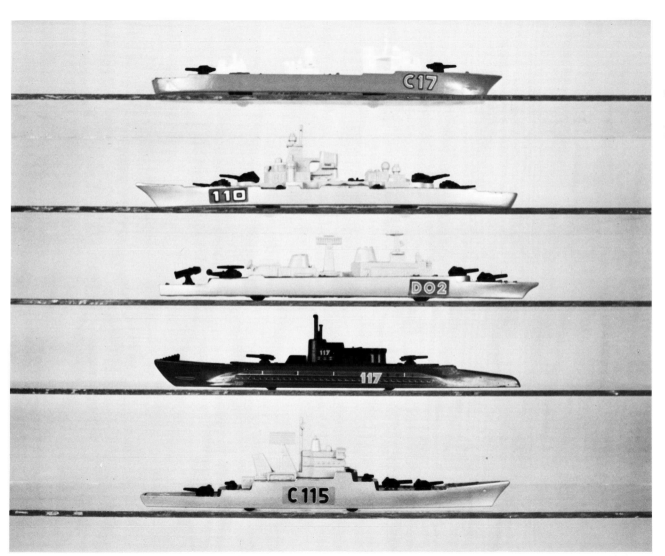

Row 1
SK306 **Convoy Escort.**

Row 2
SK307 **Helicopter Carrier.**

Row 3
SK308 **Guided Missile Destroyer.**

Row 4
SK309 **Submarine.**

Row 5
SK310 **Anti-aircraft Cruiser.**

*Walt Disney
Characters and
Popeye Series*

Row 1
WD1-A **Mickey Mouse
Fire Engine**, WD2-A
**Donald Duck Beach
Buggy**, WD3-A1 **Goofy
Beetle**, WD3-A2 **Goofy
Beetle**.

Row 2
WD4-A **Minnie Mouse
Lincoln**, WD5-A1 **Mickey Mouse Jeep**, WD6-A
Donald Duck Jeep,
WD7-A **Pinnochio's
Travelling Theatre**.

Row 3
WD8-A **Jiminy Cricket's
Old Timer**, WD9-A
Goofy's Sports Car,
WD10-A **Goofy's Train**,
WD11-A **Donald Duck's
Ice Cream Van**.

Row 4
WD12-A **Mickey Mouse
Corvette**, CS13-A **Popeye's Spinach Wagon**,
CS14-A **Bluto's Road
Roller**, CS15-A **Olive
Oyl's Sports Car**.

Row 1
GR1 **Light Beamer**, GR2 **Speed Blazer**, GR3 **Flamin' Vette.**

Row 2
GR4 **Streak Ray**, GR5 **Twilight TR.**

Row 3
GR6 **Quicksilver**, GR9 **Turbo Flash**, GR10 **Dark Rider.**

Row 4
GR11 **Flash Fire**, GR12 **Night Bird.**

A variety of Matchbox boxes, for early Yester-year, and King Size, and a progression of 1-75 series toys.

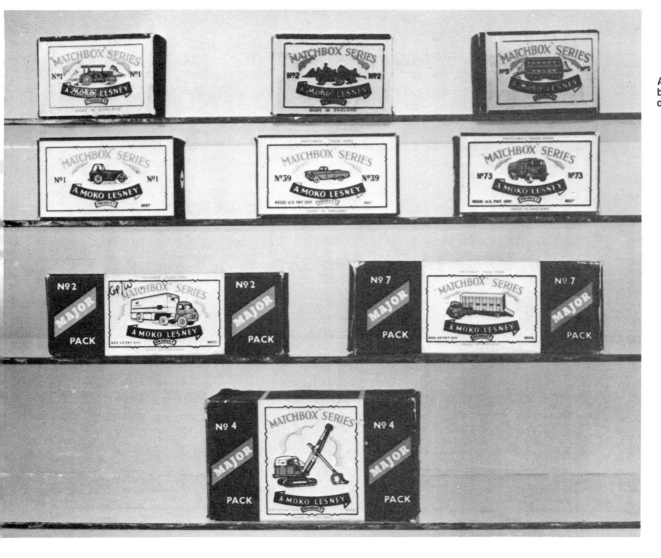

A progression of Match-
box boxes from the first
design to the latest.

Row 1
The K-15 bus for the 1979 Royal Visit and 1981 Royal
Wedding.

Row 2
Two models of Yesteryear boxes and a European
issued ambulance in clear packs.

Boxes for specialized toys.

Early Lesney Toys

Aveling Barford Diesel Road Roller 4-3/8" 1948
This toy was made also by several other companies in 1948-9, but the following details identify the Lesney-made toy.Green body and roof with unpainted gray metal wheels with crimped axles, no baseplate, tow hook at the rear. The first toys had no lettering; later toys have "Lesney-England" embossed under the roof.

1. No drivers' body is cast in the seat and a cast boss with yellow 7/8" diameter flywheel is on the left side.
2. No driver, and flywheel and cast boss are removed.
3. Driver cast on the seat.

Soap Box Racer 3-1/8" est. 1948-49
Bronze colored body with a movable front axle and notches where a rubber band joins the axle with the driver's hands. The removable driver was painted dark brown with a pink face. The baseplate is lettered "A Lesney product, Made in England".

Caterpillar Bulldozer 4½" est. 1948-50
The body has been found in these color variations: Pale green body and blade, orange body and blade, or yellow body with red blade. The treads are black or green rubber on red rollers which can be found solid or with 4 holes on the inner side. The blade was cast plain, unlike a very similar bulldozer of the Prime Mover set which had cast lettering on the back side of the blade reading "Lesney-Moko Made in England". A handle can appear on the blade, or have been cast with no handle.

Caterpillar Tractor 3-1/8" est. 1948-50
The green body is similar to the Caterpillar Bulldozer without a blade. This model, however, has a tan driver and black treads. This is the large model from which the no. 8 Matchbox 1-75 series was copied.

Ruston Bucyrus 10RB Excavator 4" est. 1948-50
Maroon body with side black lettering "10RB", and three maroon stripes, below a cream colored roof. The lower chassis is painted army green with four wheels at the corners in matching green paint. The chassis is marked "Moko, Made in England" on its under side. The wheels are joined by rubber tracks. A black handle on the right side of the excavator body operates the height of the green painted shovel by an attached black string. This toy was the prototype for the Major Pack 4-A shovel which has some modifications and is of smaller size.

Rag and Bone Cart 5¼" est. 1948
British television had produced a popular show entitled "Steptoe & Son" in the years after World War Two, about a rag and bone merchant with horse and cart which had been common on the streets of London in the early years of this century. Lesney produced a toy version of the horse-drawn cart with 8 pieces of 'junk'. The cart was painted yellow on top with red wheels with the axle rivetted at one end & crimped at the other. An oval panel above each side was lettered "Rag and Bone Merchants". The horse had a hollow body with solid tail, neck & head all finished gunmetal color. The horse was attached to the cart by two studs from the cart shafts which fit into a hole in each of the animal's shoulders. The driver was cast separately without hands and painted brown. The eight pieces of junk included the frame of a man's bicycle, a toilet cistern, a tin bath tub, a wheel, a slatted box, the handle section of a wooden roller mangle, an iron bedstead headboard, and a bucket. The junk was left unpainted except for the sides of the box which were painted dull gray.

Horse Drawn Milk Float 5-3/8" est. 1949
The cart was painted blue or orange with white lettering "Pasteurised Milk" with metal wheels painted black, gray or charcoal, axles with one or both ends crimped or rivetted. Variations in the castings do exist at the junction of the roof and drivers' seat. The driver is painted white with black shoes and pink hands and face, with black eyes and mouth. Six separate milk bottle crates were painted white, some with red or silver tops. Replacement crates were made and can be identified in 2 versions. The horse was painted dark brown with a white tail, mane and hooves.

Hand Cement Mixer 3-9/16" est. 1949
The body was painted dark green, pale green or red with a rotating barrel painted dark green, pale green or red. The arm joining the barrel and body has raised lettering "Made in England". The 2 wheels can be found colored dark green, yellow, red, or black. A small version of this toy appeared as the number 3 Matchbox toy in the 1.75 series.

The Prime Mover, Trailer, & Bulldozer Set 18" est. 1949
The Prime Mover is 5" long, painted orange with 2 removable, dark green engine covers. The orange driver is cast separately but rivetted to the cab on his right foot. Six metal wheels are painted gray. The engine trim, tow hook, and side fuel tanks are painted gold. The door has cast lettering painted white. The lettering "Made in England" is cast under the cab roof. The trailer, 8½" long, is painted orange or blue with 6 wheels painted gray. The towing brace matches the trailer in color or is silver. The removable triangular chocks (wedges) are blue. The under side of the trailer has cast lettering "A Lesney-Moko Toy Made in England". The bulldozer, 4½" long, is very similar to the Caterpillar Bulldozer issued separately but the one issued with the Prime Mover set has the lettering "Lesney-Moko Made in England" on the inside, back edge of the blade. The body of the bulldozer of the Prime Mover set can be found green with a green blade, orange with an orange blade, and yellow with a red blade. The red wheels have green rubber tracks and are rivetted at one end and crimped at the opposite end with a small brass washer.

Bread Bait Press 2" est. 1949
This novel idea satisfied the fishermen at Lesney Products who lost soggy bread from their hooks before the fish found it. This device is a 3-part metal die-cast tool to compress bread into a dense pellet with a small hole for attaching to the hook. The top wing nut is unpainted and attached to a second part by a metal pin. The second part is flat at one end and housed within the third section-a red painted open rectangle. To operate, a section of bread is placed within the open rectangle, and compressed by the second flat edge as the wing nut screws down. The original version of this press was made to be sold by a shop named Milbourne's on Camden Road, Holloway, London N.W.II. Therefore, the side of each press was cast with lettering, reading "Milbo Lesney Bread Bait Press Made in England Pat. Pen". After a year the press no longer sold well at Milbourne's, so to expand marketing the Lesney workers removed the word Milbo from the lettering. Most presses which remain are without Milbo.

Jumbo the Elephant 4" 1950-51
When the Korean War broke out in 1949, the English (United Kingdom) government restricted the use of zinc to essential, primarily military, products. Therefore, the use of zinc for die-cast toys was impossible until the government lifted the restriction in 1952. During these two years, only 1 toy was made by Lesney, a tin Jumbo the Elephant. The original version of Jumbo was made in American occupied Germany about 1947-48. Somehow one made its way to England where Lesney employees copied it exactly-but replaced the wording on the back left side "Made in the United States occupied zone of Germany" with the wording "Made in England". The tin body is painted gray with yellow & red details and the name "Jumbo". A clockwork motor is concealed inside and is activated by a winding key. The motor activates the four legs to "walk". A black wool tail is attached appropriately.

Muffin the Mule 5½" 1952
The British television network featured a puppet character Muffin the Mule in 1951 which was quite popular. Seeing potential in producing a replica die-cast toy of Muffin, Mr. Alf Gilson, a neighbor of Lesney Products in London, secured the licensing rights to manufacture a Muffin toy. Mr. Gilson used the firm Moko, to act as factor to provide advance capital and distribute the toy under the Moko name. (See more on Moko in the chapter on the history of the company). During this period of the Korean War, a restriction on the use of zinc to make toys depressed many small toy manufacturers, including Alf Gilson. Mr. Gilson decided to close his business and emigrate to Canada. Lesney Products then acquired the Gilson premesis as an expansion of their own successful die-cast business. Soon, they agreed to also acquire the rights to produce Muffin with Moko's help, and when the ban on zinc used for toys was lifted in 1952, they went into production. Muffin the Mule was a zinc alloy marionet toy weighing over ½ pound and is painted white with red and black details. The front legs have 2 movable joints while the back has only 1 movable joint. Strings attached to the body at the head, shoulders and hips maneuver the figure. The lettering "Made in England" is embossed on the inside of the right back leg.

Large Coronation Coach 15¾" 1953
The silver wedding celebrations of King George VI and Queen Elizabeth (now known as the Queen Mother) in 1949 rekindled popular interest in the British royalty. Also, England was planning a huge "Festival of Britain" for 1951 in London. The staff at Lesney decided to produce for the 1951 festival a toy replica of the golden Coronation Coach and eight horses as a souvenir for visitors. When the molds were made and ready for production, the British government restricted the use of zinc for toy-making as one part in their Korean War effort. For two years the molds for the coach lay unused. In 1952, King George VI died and the throne passed on to his oldest daughter Elizabeth. Shortly after the King's death, the restrictions on zinc were lifted, and Lesney went into production on the large coach. About 200 coaches were produced from the original molds with figures of both the King and Queen inside. Then, it was learned that the new Queen, Elizabeth, would ride alone to her coronation on June 2, not with her husband Philip. The staff at Lesney then removed the King from the mold, and at the same time conformed to a new government regulation of including the country of origin on all products, and added "Made in England" under the right side of the coach. The production of about 32,800 coaches were then made with these modifications. The coach was originally produced painted gold, and most toys were released this way. However, a small number of coaches with the Queen alone were released with a gold plated exterior or an intermediary silver plated finish. The eight horses are joined by a 10" long square connecting bar with four hollow, cylindrical cross pieces which secured the horses. The cross pieces can be found in bare metal or painted gold or white. An additional pin passes through the back of each horse. The horses are painted white with gray manes, tails & hooves, red, white & gold blankets & gold saddles. The horses on the left side have mounted riders dressed in black hats and boots, white breeches, and red and gold tunics. Gold chains on each side extend from the lead horses to small hooks on each back horse and joining the front coach axle.

1. King and Queen riding in gold painted coach.
2. Queen riding in gold painted coach with "Made in England" underneath.
3. Queen riding in gold plated coach with "Made in England" underneath.
4. Queen riding in silver plated coach with "Made in England" underneath.

Small Coronation Coach 4½" 1953
This is a scaled-down version of the large Coronation Coach by Lesney with a few variations. The basic description follows that of the large coach. The coach was chrome plated or painted gold with plain doors and the back panel either plain or with lettering "England" followed by a dash. The horses and central bar were cast in one piece and painted white with red blacket, gold saddle, and on the left side the riders were painted with red tunic, black breeches, and black hat. The top of the center bar is embossed "A Moko toy by Lesney, British Made". Very similar coaches were made by Lesney's neighbor Bembros, but these

Early Lesney Toys

have lettering "Made in England" on the upper face of the central bar, and initials E II R on the coach doors.

Massey Harris Tractor   7-13/16"   1953-54
(Proposed large series No. 1)

The red body has white rasied letters "Massey Harris" and letters "745 D" on each side. The red or beige steering wheel turns and steers the front wheels. The beige wheels have black rubber tires, small ones in front and large rear ones lettered "Made in England by Lesney". The left inner mud guard is lettered "A Lesney Product", while the right inner mud guard is lettered "Made in England". A smaller version of this toy appeared as the number 4 in Matchbox 1.75 series.

Quarry Truck   1953
(Proposed large series No. 2.) Never produced.

This was the second large scale toy attempted by Lesney, but only a few preliminary models ever were made; none were released for sale. The toy was 10¾" long and painted yellow. This was the original from which the smaller No. 6A Quarry Truck in the 1.75 series was made.

Diesel Road Roller   1953
(Proposed large series No. 3.) Never produced.

A larger version of the first Lesney toy, but only 1 preliminary toy was made. None were ever sold.

Covered Wagon   4-7/8"   1954

Following the success of the small Coronation Coach, Lesney produced this second miniature horse drawn vehicle. This toy was inspired by American Conestoga type covered wagons which were a popular vehicle used by pioneers to penetrate the western regions of the country. The wagon body & wheels are painted green with a separate white painted canopy & a pair of water barrels. A separate horsebar has the embossed inscription "Made in England by Lesney" on the upper side, and to it are attached six horses. The horses and bar are painted dark brown with white applied to the horses tails and foreheads. A single rider on the left lead horse is painted with a tan shirt and hat and a red neck bandana.

The first Covered Wagon toys had each horse with a gold painted collar, but later horses lack this collar. The driver of the wagon is cast separately and painted tan with a red neck kerchief. The original casting of the wagon included two water barrels while on the later casting these are omitted.

The Matchbox® Series 1-75

The extraordinary success of the small coronation coach in 1953 encouraged Lesney personnel to proceed with plans to make small sized toys for the 1953 selling year. They began by making scaled-down versions of seven of their earlier toys in this order: (1-A) Diesel Road Roller, (2-A) Dumper, (3-A) Cement Mixer, (4-A) Massey Harris Tractor, (6-A) Quarry Truck, (7-A) Horse-drawn Milk Float, and (8-A) Caterpillar Tractor. The (5-A) London Bus was designed especially for this small series. These toys were immediately successful with the children, and more new toys were made each successive year.

When the personnel gathered to design a box for the new small toys, they struck on the idea of using a style resembling a match box. This was not a new thought, for earlier in the 1900's toys from Germany were made with this style box. The Lesney people did, however, register the name Matchbox for this series and that name has identified their toys since. Lesney Products was then using the distribution and packaging facilities of Moko for its toys, and Moko had a significant financial interest in the new series.

The actual design of the printing on the box is now known to have derived from a Scandinavian match box cover for Norvic Safety Matches (Shown here):

From this design, the Lesney and Moko people substituted their own wording and created the first Matchbox box. The front and back are yellow with red letters "Matchbox® Series" in an arch above a black and red drawing of each toy inside. On both sides of the drawing, the number of the toy in this series is placed. Below the drawing, a scroll with lettering "A Moko Lesney" appears. The word "Product" is in a small arch below the scroll. For this design, the word Moko is written in script lettering. This box design was used only for the first seven toys in the Matchbox series which were made in 1953 and 1954.

A second box design was created in 1955; the script lettering of Moko changed to block lettering, and the number of the toy usually was added to the end flaps. Another change was made in 1960 to reflect the independent distribution of its toys by Lesney. Then the word Moko was omitted from the box.

A fourth change in the box design was made in 1961 when the scroll below the drawing of the model was eliminated. This precident ushered in the more modern designs which have followed. In all, 12 different designs have been made for the Matchbox 1-75 series boxes to the present.

The Matchbox® Series 1-75 /Superfast

Throughout the production of each of these toys, variations have been made in colors, wheel styles, casting changes, and minor parts to create an endless variety of finished toys. The variations noted in the lists of toys for each series represent the most important changes, but we are sure that countless more variations will be found and reported.

By 1960, a total of seventy-five different toys—regardless of variations—had been made, and some of the dies from the early toys were beginning to wear out. A decision was made to limit the series to seventy-five toys and issue different toys to replace some of the earlier numbered toys. This practice was carried out gradually and without regard to numerical progression, and that is what makes collecting these toys such a challenge today. Since 1960, there have been up to 9 different issues for each number, with some numbers remaining relatively stable with only a few changes.

In 1969, the winds of change blew hard at Lesney. That year, the Mattel Company introduced their "Hot Wheels" series of toy cars with frictionless wheels which moved more quickly than the conventional wheels Lesney had been using. "Hot Wheels" were enormously successful and posed a threat to all the other die-cast toys on the market. The staff at Lesney responded by designing their own styles of frictionless wheels for the 1-75 series and the King-size series which by now had been introduced. These new wheels ushered in the new line of modern, fast running toys which Lesney registered as "Superfast". Collectors today designate toys prior to 1969 as "Regular Wheels", and those made from 1969 on as "Superfast". This designation was continued in the Matchbox catalogs until 1982 when the term "Matchbox" was used for all the 1-75 series once more.

This is an opportune place to describe the eleven types of Superfast wheels which have been used on Matchbox toys since 1969. That year, the current toys were simply assembled with the new wheels. The names of these new wheels were made gradually by collectors as new styles were identified. Therefore, there exists today a variety of terms for the same style. The descriptions of the Superfast wheels in this book may reflect this variety of terms. The most current and widely acknowledged names are as follows:

Superfast Wheels

Style A—**Four spoke wheel.**   Style B—**Five spoke wheel.**   Style C—**Five spoke wheel with center cut-out.**

Style D—**Five crowns wheel**-some-
times called reverse ac-
cent wheel.

Style E—**Five arches wheel**-some-
times called five-spoke
accent wheel.

Style F—**Maltese Cross wheel**-
sometimes called clover-
leaf wheel.

Style G—**Dot-Dash or Morse-
code wheel**-some-
times called multi-
spoke wheel.

Style H—**New eight-spoke wheel
with tread.**

Style I—**Spiro wheel.**

Style J—**Eight bolt head wheel.**

Style K—**New five-spoke wheel
with tread.**

Other types of wheels do exist for specific toys, but are not
generally found throughout the 1-75 series or the King size series.
Examples are those wheels made for railroad cars, motorcycles,
tractors, harvesters, airplanes, and boats.

1-A   Diesel Road Roller   1-7/8"   1953
Green body, flat canopy, red metal rollers, crimped axles, tow hook, gold trim, no number cast on body, tan driver.
1. Dark green body.
2. Light green body.

1-B   Road Roller   2¼"   1955
Pale green body, high peaked canopy, with & without gold trim, tow hook, no number cast on body, light or dark tan driver.
1. Dark tan driver.
2. Light tan driver.

1-C   Road Roller   2-3/8"   1958
Green body, high peaked canopy, red metal rollers, crimped or round axles, tow bar, no trim color, with number cast inside body, & green driver.
1. Light green body, metal rollers, crimped axels.
2. Dark green body, metal rollers, crimped axles.
3. Dark green body, metal rollers, rounded axles.
4. Dark green body, metal rollers ¼" wide, rounded axles.

1-D   Aveling Barford Road Roller 2-5/8"   1962
Green body, high peaked canopy, red plastic rollers, no trim color, with tow hook, one hole in baseplate, & green driver.
1. "Made in England" cast on baseplate.
2. "Made in England" cast under canopy roof.

1-E   Mercedes Benz Lorry   3"   1967
Pale green body, removable orange plastic canopy, silver plastic grille & front base, tow hook.
1. Plain base & front bumper.
2. License plate under front bumper.
3. License plate & tow marks on baseplate.

1-F   Mercedes Benz Lorry   3"   1970
Metallic gold, removable canopy, red or black axle covers.
1. Orange canopy, large four spoke wheels.
2. Orange canopy, small five spoke wheels.
3. Yellow canopy, large four spoke wheels.
4. Yellow canopy, small five spoke wheels.
5. Red body, dark blue windows, black grille and baseplate, bright yellow canopy with white. green and black "Transcontinental Haulage Co." labels on each side, four spoke wide wheels, no number on base. (TP-1).
6. Military olive green body, dark blue windows, black grille and baseplate, tan canopy with U.S. flag and USA 48350 or 4TS 702K on olive green side labels, large five spoke wide wheels, no hub cap, no number on base. (TP-15-G-11).
7. Same as 6, tan canopy with olive green, red and white '4TS 702 K' or 'USA 48350' side labels, small five spoke wide wheels, no hub caps.
8. Same as 7, large four spoke wide wheels, no hub caps.
9. Same as 7, large five spoke wide wheels, no hub caps. (G-11)
10. Military olive drab, dark blue windows, black grille and baseplate, tan canopy with U.S. flag and USA 48350 or 4TS 702 K on olive green side labels, large five spoke wide wheels, no hub caps, no number on base. (TP-15)
11. Same as 10, large four spoke wheels, no hub caps.
12. Same as 5, "1978" added to baseplate inscription. (TP-1)
13. Same as 8, "1978" added to baseplate inscription. (TP-15)
14. Same as 12, "1978" on base, orange/yellow plastic canopy. (TP-1)
15. Light blue body, dark blue plastic windows, black plastic grille and baseplate, orange/yellow plastic canopy, black "IMS" and "International Haulage" on long yellow side labels iwth red borders, added casting reinforcement above gas tanks on right side, four spoke wide wheels, no number on base. (TP-1)
16. Same as 14, "1978" on base, orange/yellow plastic canopy, added casting reinforcement above gas tank on right side. (TP-1)

1-G   Mod Rod   2-7/8"   1971

Yellow body, amber tinted windows, orange interior, silver rear motor, sticker label brown faced cat, metal baseplate.
1. Red wheels, light & dark interiors.
2. Black wheels, light & dark interiors.
3. Black wheels, flower sticker (same as No. 13).
4. Black wheels, spotted cat sticker.
5. Black wheels, spotted cat sticker, red interior.
6. Black wheels, spotted cat sticker, dark orange interior, silver/gray painted baseplate.
7. Black wheels, spotted cat label, red interior, silver/gray baseplate.
8. Black wheels, spotted cat label, light orange interior, unpainted metal baseplate.
9. Black wheels, black and red on white round Scorpion label on hood, light orange interior, unpainted metal baseplate.
10. Black wheels, black and red on white round Scorpion label on hood, light orange interior, silver/gray baseplate.
11. Black wheels, black & red on white round Scorpion label on hood, dark orange interior, unpainted metal baseplate.
12. Black large five spoke rear wheels, small five spoke front wheels, spotted cat label on hood, unpainted metal baseplate, orange interior.
13. Black large four spoke front & rear wheels, spotted cat label on hood, unpainted metal baseplate, orange interior.
14. Black large five spoke rear wheels, small five spoke front wheels, spotted cat label on hood, unpainted metal baseplate, large 'Mod Rod' lettering at rear.
15. Black large five spoke rear wheels, small five spoke front wheels, spotted cat label on hood, silver/gray painted baseplate, large 'Mod Rod' lettering at rear.
16. Black large five spoke rear wheels, small five spoke front wheels, red on white round Scorpion label on hood, silver/gray painted baseplate, large 'Mod Rod' lettering at rear.
17. Same as 12, small five spoke wheels front and rear.
18. Chrome plated body, unpainted metal baseplate, black plastic window, rear engine and exhaust pipes, red and black tempa imprint each side, small five spoke front wheels, large four spoke rear wheels. This model is SF Special Issue No. 1 with original SF 1-2 baseplate.
19. Same as 18, baseplate now reads "No: 1 SILVER STREAK".
20. Same as 14, baseplate now reads "No. 1 Silver Streak".
21. Same as 16, red and white round scorpion label on hood, unpainted metal baseplate, large "MOD ROD" lettering at rear.

1-H   Dodge Challenger   2-15/16"   1976
Red body, white plastic top, silver plated interior and air scoops on hood, wide five spoke accent wheels, unpainted metal baseplate & grille.
1. Clear windshield.
2. Same as 1, small multi-spoke wheels.
3. Same as 1, wide five spoke accent wheels, white plastic interior and air scoops on hood.
4. Same as 3, wide five spoke accent wheels, white plastic interior and air scoop on hood, smoky gray tinted windows.
5. Blue body, white plastic top, clear windshield, red plastic interior and air scoops on hood, unpainted metal baseplate, wide five spoke accent wheels.
6. Same as 1, wide five spoke accent wheels, red plastic interior and air scoop on hood.
7. Same as 5, wide five spoke accent wheels, red plastic interior and air scoop on hood, smoky gray tinted windows.
8. Dark blue body, white plastic top, red plastic interior and air scoop on hood, unpainted metal baseplate, wide five spoke accent wheels.

1-I   Revin' Rebel   1982
Orange body, blue roof, black interior, large 5 spoke back wheels, small 5 spoke front wheels, clear front window.

2-A   Dumper   1-5/8"   1953
Green body, red dumper, gold trim, metal wheels, crimped axles, no number cast on body, & slim tan driver.
1. Green painted wheels, nail holds dumper to body.
2. Unpainted wheels, nail holds dumper to body.

2-B   Dumper   1-7/8"   1957
Green body, red dumper, no trim color, number cast inside under front fender, & hefty tan driver.
1. Metal wheels, crimped axles, dumper snaps into pins in rear of body.
2. Dark gray plastic wheels, crimped axles, dumper connected by rivet to body.
3. Dark gray plastic wheels, round axles.
4. Light gray plastic wheels.
5. Light gray plastic wheels, drivers hands cast in 'V' shape.
6. Smaller front wheels.
7. No hat on driver.

2-C   Muirhill Dumper   2-1/6"   1961
Red cab and chassis, green dumper, "Laing" decal on right door, black plastic wheels, round axles.
1. Red cab & chassis, green dumper, thin brace holds front wheels, no hole in base.
2. With hole in base under front axle.
3. Thick brace holds front wheels.
4. Green cab & chassis, red dumper, thin brace holds front wheels, no hole in base and this could be a pre-production model. The front left bumper comes connected or seperated from body, front grilles come with/without silver paint.

2-D   Mercedes Trailer   3½"   1968
Pale green body, removable orange canopy, tow hook, rotating tow bar, black plastic wheels.
1. Thin brace in rear inside corner of body.
2. Thick brace in rear inside corner of body.

2-E   Mercedes Trailer   3¼"   1970
Metallic gold, removable canopy, rotating tow bar, colors vary on the body and canopy.
1. Orange canopy, large four spoke wheels, two raised lines on front of trailer body above tow bar. (Same as regular wheel trailer).
2. Orange canopy, four spoke wheels, two raised lines on front of trailer body over tow bar, reinforcement panel directly behind raised lines inside front panel.
3. Yellow canopy, four spoke wheels, two raised lines on front of trailer body, reinforcement panel.
4. Orange canopy, four spoke wheels, recess center panel on front of trailer body, reinforcement panel.
5. Yellow canopy, four spoke wheels, recess center panel on front of trailer body, reinforcement panel.
6. Red trailer bed, black axle covers, bright yellow canopy with white, green & black "Transcontinental Haulage Co." labels on each side, four spoke wide wheels, no number on base. (TP-1).
7. Military olive green body, black axle covers, tan canopy with U.S. flag and white "USA 48350" or "4TS 702 K" on olive green side labels, large four spoke wide wheels, no hub caps, no number on base. (TP 15-G-1)
8. Same as 7, tan canopy with olive green, red & white '4TS 702 K' or 'USA 48350' labels. Can be found with identical labels on both sides or different labels so that the 'K' may be to the front on both sides.
9. Same as 8, large five spoke wide wheels, no hub caps.
10. Same as 8, small five spoke wide wheels, no hub caps. (G-11)
11. Military olive drab body (very dark almost brown), black axle covers, tan canopy with olive green, red & white '4TS 702 K' or 'USA 48350' labels, small five spoke wide wheels, no hub caps. (G-11)

Matchbox 1-75 Series/Superfast

12. Same as 11, large four spoke wide wheels, no hub caps.
13. Same as 6, orange/yellow plastic canopy.
14. Light blue trailer bed, black axle covers, orange/yellow canopy, black "IMS" and "International Haulage" on long yellow side labels with red borders, four spoke wide wheels, no number on baseplate. (TP-1)

2-F   Jeep Hot Rod   2-5/16"   1971
Cream seats and tow hook, silver motor, black plastic wxhaust pipes, large wide four spoke wheels.
1. Pink body, light green base.
2. Pink body, dark green base.
3. Orchid body, light green base.
4. Orchid body, dark green base.
5. Pink body, dark green base, wide baseplate bracket (tool chest holder) on right side of tow hook.
6. Pink body, dark green base, wide baseplate bracket, white interior.
7. Pink body, dark green base, wide baseplate bracket, yellow interior.
8. Pink body, dark green base, wide baseplate bracket, cream interior, wide five spoke wheels.
9. Pink body, short rear panel on body, dark green base, wide baseplate, bracket, cream interior, large wide four spoke wheels.
10. Pink body, short rear panel on body, dark green base, wide squared off baseplate bracket, cream interior, large four spoke wheels.
11. Pink body, short rear panel on body, white painted baseplate, squared off brackets on baseplate, cream interior, large four spoke wheels.
12. Dark red body, short panel, green baseplate baseplate squared off brackets, cream interior, large four spoke wheels.
13. Dark red body, short panel, green baseplate baseplate, squared off brackets, ivory interior, large four spoke wheels.
14. Dark red body, short panel, white painted baseplate squared off brackets, cream interior, large four spoke wheels.
15. Dark red body, short panel, white painted baseplate, squared off brackets, cream interior, five spoke wheels.
16. Dark red body, short panel, white painted baseplate, squared off brackets, cream interior, small wide clover leaf wheels.
17. Military olive green body, black painted baseplate, black plastic steering wheel interior and tow hook, green and white circle label with white star in center on hood, large four spoke wheels, no hub caps. (TP-11)
18. Same as 17, reinforcements above wheels under front fender. (TP-11).
19. Same as 17, no reinforcement, 'Jeep' only on base, number and "Hot Rod" has been removed. (TP-11).
20. Same as 19, reinforcements above wheels under front fender. This model is now found in G1 gift sets with new base showing no. 38 and 1972 date. (TP-11).
21. Same as 19, Military olive drab body.

2-G   Hovercraft   3-1/8"   1976
Metallic lime green upper structures, tan plastic lower half and baseplate, (baseplate shows no. 72 and 2 and 1972 date), silver plastic engines & front air scoop, amber windows, thin wheels.
1. Black "RESCUE" letters on orange & dark olive green label on rear fin, also found without label on rear fin.
2. Same as 1, metallic green body.
3. Metallic green body, black plastic lower half & baseplate, black "RESCUE" on orange and dark olive green label on rear fin.
4. Light avocado green, black plastic lower half & baseplate, purple plastic windows, black "RESCUE" on orange & dark olive green label on rear fin. (K-2005)
5. Same as 1, beige plastic lower half and baseplate.
6. Same as 4, amber plastic windows. (K-2005)
7. Same as 2, red plastic windows.
8. Same as 2, purple plastic windows.
9. Same as 4, black "2000" on avocado green rear fin.
10. Same as 4, black "2000" on avocado green rear fin, red

plastic engines and front air scoop.
11. Same as 4, red plastic engine and front air scoop.
12. Same as 4, no plastic window insert.
13. Tan body, black base, red plastic engine & front air scoop.

2-H   S-2 Jet   3"   1981
Yellow under fuselage, black upper fuselage, tail fin & horizontal stabilizers, yellow/orange plastic folding wings, four black plastic wheels.
1. Amber plastic canopy.
2. Red plastic canopy.
3. Silver upper fuselage, white under fuselage & wings with red stripe and white words "viper".

3-A   Cement Mixer   1-5/8"   1953
Blue body & rotating barrel, orange metal wheels, crimped axles, no number cast on body.
1. Small handle on rear compartment, 4 paddles inside barrel, grooved nail used for axles.
2. Small handle on rear compartment, 4 paddles inside barrel, plain wire used for axles.
3. No handle on rear compartment.
4. No handle on rear compartment, no paddles inside barrel.
5. Four ribs inside motor compartment.
6. Four ribs inside motor compartment, dark gray plastic wheels.
7. Four ribs inside motor compartment, dark gray plastic wheels, round axles.
8. Light gray plastic wheels.

3-B   Bedford Ton Tipper   2½"   1961
Gray cab & chassis, number '3' cast on black front base, 2 round axles, two front wheels, double rear wheels, with or without silver painted grilles, headlights, bumpers.
1. Maroon dumper, knobby gray plastic wheels, without support on dumper over rear wheels.
2. Maroon dumper, knobby black plastic wheels, without support on dumper over rear wheels.
3. Maroon dumper, fine tread black plastic wheels, without support on dumper over rear wheels.
4. Maroon dumper, fine tread black plastic wheels, with support on dumper over rear wheels.
5. Maroon dumper, fine treads, with support, small no. 3 cast on front baseplate.
6. Red dumper, fine tread gray plastic wheels.
7. Red dumper, fine tread black plastic wheels.
8. Red dumper, fine tread black plastic wheels, with reinforced rear floor on rear of dumper.

3-C   Mercedes Benz Ambulance   2-7/8"   1968
White interior & stretcher, blue tinted windows & dome light, metal grille & baseplate with tow slot, black plastic wheels. Body colors vary in shades. Two dies were used to produce the baseplates on this model. The lettering will read either front to back or back to front on all variations listed. Model changed to Superfast wheels.
1. Off white body, red cross decals on door.
2. Cream body, red cross decals on door.
3. Cream body, red cross labels on door.

3-D   Mercedes Ambulance   2-7/8"   1970
Ivory interior, red cross label on side doors in various sizes, blue tinted windows & dome light, baseplate lettering reads from front to back & back to front.
1. Cream body, five spoke thin wheels, small wheel wells. (Same as regular wheel versions).
2. Off white body, five spoke thin wheels, medium wheel wells.
3. Off white body, five spoke thin wheels, wide wheel wells.
4. Off white body, five spoke wide wheels, wide wheel wells.
5. Off white body, five spoke wide wheels, wide wheel wells, dark blue windows & dome light.
6. Off white body, slick wheels, wide wheel wells, dark blue windows and dome light.
7. Off white body, rear door does not open, unpainted metal baseplate, bumper & grille, head lights now part of body casting, blue

tinted windows & dome light, multi-spoke wide wheels, no number on baseplate, square red cross side labels. (TP-10)
8. Same as 7, military olive green body, multi-spoke wide wheels, no hub caps. (TP-14)
9. Same as 8, military olive green body, multi-spoke wide wheels, with chrome hub caps. (TP-14)

3-E   Monteverdi Hai   2-7/8"   1973
Dark orange body, blue tinted windows, ivory interior, five spoke wide wheels, yellow/orange/black label on hood.
1. Metal baseplate, blue tinted windows.
2. Silver/gray painted baseplate, blue tinted windows.
3. Metal baseplate, light blue tinted windows.
4. Metal baseplate, light & dark blue tinted windows, light yellow interior.
5. Silver/gray baseplate, light blue tinted windows, ivory interior.
6. Metal baseplate, dark blue windows, ivory interior, no label on hood.
7. Metal baseplate, dark blue windows, light yellow interior, no labels.
8. Metal baseplate, light blue windows, light yellow interior, no labels.
9. Metal baseplate, dark blue windows, ivory interior, no. 16 on white & yellow stripe label on hood.
10. Metal baseplate, dark blue windows, ivory interior, no. 16 on white & yellow stripe label on hood.
11. Unpainted metal baseplate, very dark blue windows, ivory interior, no. 3 yellow/orange/black label on hood.
12. Flat black painted baseplate, blue tinted windows, ivory interior, no. 3 yellow/orange/black label on hood.
13. Flat black painted baseplate, blue tinted windows, ivory interior, green no. 6 in black bordered white circle on yellow, green & red stripes on label on hood. (62-C label)

3-F   Porshe Turbo   3"   1978
Metallic brown painted body, glossy black painted metal baseplate, light yellow plastic interior and tow hook, wide five spoke accent wheels.
1. Clear plastic windows.
2. Same as 1, clear plastic windows, unpainted metal baseplate.
3. Same as 1, metallic silver gray body, red plastic interior and tow hook, clear plastic windows.
4. Same as 1, metallic silver gray body, light yellow plastic interior and tow hook, clear plastic windows.
5. Same as 3, metallic silver gray body, red plastic interior & tow hook, clear plastic windows, metallic brown painted baseplate.
6. Metallic silver gray body, tan plastic interior & tow hook, clear plastic windows, black painted metal baseplate.
7. Metallic silver gray body, tan plastic interior & tow hook, clear plastic windows, charcoal gray painted baseplate.
8. Metallic silver gray body, tan plastic interior & tow hook, clear plastic windows, metallic brown painted metal baseplate.
9. Metallic gray body, red plastic interior & tow hook, clear plastic windows, charcoal gray painted baseplate.
10. Metallic brown body, light yellow plastic interior and tow hook, clear plastic windows, charcoal gray painted baseplate.
11. Metallic brown body, orange/yellow plastic interior and tow hook, clear plastic windows, charcoal gray painted baseplate.
12. Metallic silver gray body, light yellow plastic interior and tow hook, clear plastic windows, charcoal gray painted baseplate.
13. Metallic green body, red plastic interior and tow hook, clear plastic windows, charcoal gray painted baseplate.
14. Metallic green body, orange/yellow plastic interior and tow hook, clear plastic windows, glossy black painted metal baseplate.
15. Red body, light yellow plastic interior and tow hook, white lettering 90 on door, porshe and emblem on hood, turbo in black on roof.

4-A   Massey Harris Tractor   1954
Red body with rear fenders, tan driver, gold hubs and motor, subject to color variances, 4 spoke metal front wheels, solid metal rear wheels, no number cast on body, "Lesney-England" cast on inside of fenders near driver, open or closed above motor area.

1. Left fender-Lesney, right fender-England, area above motor open.
2. Same as 1, area above motor closed.
3. Left fender-England, right fender-Lesney, area above motor open.
4. Same as 3, area above motor closed.
5. Left fender-Lesney, right fender-Lesney, area above motor open.
6. Same as 5, area above motor closed.
7. Left fender-England, right fender-England, area above motor open.

4-B   Massey Harris Tractor   1-5/8''   1957
Red body, no fenders, tan driver of varying shades connected to rear axle from below, solid metal front wheels, hollow inside rear wheels, open above motor area, ''Lesney/England & No. 4 cast inside body'', gold hubs of various shades.
1. Metal wheels, crimped axles.
2. Gray plastic wheels, crimped axles.
3. Gray plastic wheels, round axles.

4-C   Triumph Motorcycle & Sidecar   2-1/8''   1960
Silver blue body, wire wheels, black plastic tires.
1. Fender connected part way, knobby treads, small thin raised line between cycle & car on base.
2. Fender connected part way, fine treads.
3. Fender connected full, fine treads.
4. Fender connected full, fine treads, blocks connect sidecar to cycle on base.

4-D   Stake Truck   2-7/8''   1967
Yellow cab & chassis, green tinted windows, unpainted metal baseplate & grille, 6 black plastic wheels on 3 axles. Model changed to Superfast wheels.
1. Blue stake body.
2. Green stake body.
3. Green stake body, tow slot on front baseplate.

4-E   Stake Truck   2-7/8''   1970
1. Yellow/orange cab & chassis, four spoke wide wheels.
2. Yellow/orange cab & chassis, eight spoke wide wheels.
3. Bright yellow cab & chassis, four spoke wide wheels.
4. Yellow/orange cab and chassis, cloverleaf (eight spoke) wide front wheels, four spoke wide rear wheels.

4-F   Gruesome Twosome   2-7/8''   1971
Metallic gold body, silver motors front & rear, wide five spoke wheels, metal baseplate, body colors vary from light to very dark shades of gold.
1. Yellow interior, purple tinted windows, front & rear motor mounts.
2. Yellow interior, purple tinted windows, rear motor mounts only.
3. Cream interior, purple windows, front & rear motor mounts.
4. Cream interior, purple windows, rear motor mounts only.
5. Yellow interior, amber windows, front & rear motor mounts.
6. Yellow interior, amber windows, rear motor mounts only.
7. Yellow interior, purple windows, motor mounts reinforced, floor under motor filled in.
8. Yellow interior, light purple windows, motor mounts reinforced, floor under motor filled in.
9. Yellow interior, purple windows, motor mounts reinforced, floor under motor filled in, silver/gray baseplate.
10. Cream interior, purple windows, motor mounts reinforced, floor under motor filled in.
11. White interior, purple windows, motor mounts reinforced, floor under motor filled in.
12. Cream interior, light purple windows, motor mount reinforced, floor under motor filled in.
13. Cream interior, purple windows, motor mount reinforced, floor under motor filled in, silver/gray baseplate.
14. Orange red body, cream interior, purple windows, motor mount reinforced, floor under motor filled in, unpainted metal baseplate.
15. Metallic gold body, white interior, white windows, motor mount reinforced, floor under motor filled in, silver gray painted baseplate.
16. Orange red body, yellow interior, motor mount reinforced, floor under motor filled in, silver gray painted baseplate.
17. Orange red body, bright yellow interior, motor mounts reinforced,

floor under motor filled in, unpainted metal baseplate.

4-G   Pontiac Firebird   2-7/8''   1975
Metallic blue body, unpainted metal baseplate & grille, silver plated plastic interior & air scoop on hood, small multi spoke slicks front and rear.
1. Amber windows.
2. Amber windows, cloverleaf wheels (same as 50-2).
3. Light amber windows, small multi-spoke slicks front and rear.
4. Amber windows, five spoke accent wheels.
5. Dark metallic blue body, amber windows, small multi-spoke front and rear wheels.

4-H   '57 Chevy   2-15/16''   1979
Light metallic mauve body, unpainted metal baseplate, chrome plated plastic interior, motor, grille, bumpers and side exhaust pipes, five spoke accent front wheels, larger five spoke reverse accent rear wheels. Most '57 Chevies may now be found in a much darker shade of mauve, or in combination of dark hood and light body or light hood and dark body.
1. Clear windows, front hood opens.
2. Same as 1, five spoke accent wheels front and rear.
3. Same as 2, mulit-spoke front wheels, large five spoke reverse accent rear wheels.
4. Same as 3, large five spoke reverse accent wheels front and rear.
5. Red body, white interior, side lettered ''Cherry'' bomb. (1982)

5-A   London Bus   2''   1954
Red body, gold grille, No. 5 cast on upper front & rear of body, ''Buy ''MATCHBOX'' SERIES'' sticker label glued to sides, metal wheels, crimped axles.
1. Small recessed square on lower rear of body.
2. Without recessed square.

5-B   London Bus   2¼''   1957
Red body, No. 5 cast on upper front & rear of body.
1. 'Buy ''MATCHBOX'' Series' bright yellow decal metal wheels, crimped axles, gold grille.
2. 'Buy ''MATCHBOX'' Series' dull yellow decal, metal wheels, crimped axles, gold grille.
3. 'Buy ''MATCHBOX'' Series' dull yellow decal, small gray plastic wheels, crimped axles, gold grille.
4. 'Buy ''MATCHBOX'' Series' dull yellow decal, small gray plastic wheels, crimped axles, silver grille.
5. 'PLAYERS PLEASE' decals, small gray plastic wheels, crimped axles, silver grille.
6. 'PLAYERS PLEASE' decals, large gray plastic wheels, crimped axles, silver grille.
7. 'PLAYERS PLEASE' decals, small gray plastic wheels, round axles, silver grille.
8. 'VISCO-STATIC' decals, small gray plastic wheels, round axles, silver grille.

5-C   London Bus   2-9/16''   1961
Red body, silver grille & headlights, No. 5 cast on baseplate.
1. 'PLAYERS PLEASE' decals, small gray plastic wheels.
2. 'VISCO-STATIC' decals, small gray plastic wheels.
3. 'DRINK PEARDRAX' decals, small gray plastic wheels. The 'DRINK PEARDRAX' decals were sold to collectors after the model was released, so it is now impossible to authenticate the originals.
4. 'DRINK PEARDRAX' decals, small black plastic wheels, criss cross marks inside upper roof.
5. 'VISCO-STATIC' decals, small gray plastic wheels, criss cross marks inside upper roof.
6. 'VISCO-STATIC' decals, small black plastic wheels, criss cross marks inside upper roof.

5-D   London Bus   2¼''   1965
Red body, white plastic seats, black plastic wheels.
1. 'LONG LIFE' decals, 5 lettered line base.
2. 'VISCO-STATIC' decals, 5 lettered line base.
3. 'VISCO-STATIC' decals, 4 lettered line base, shallow cutout under front axle on baseplate.

4. 'VIXCO-STATIC' labels, 4 lettered line base, shallow cutout under front axle on baseplate.
5. 'VISCO-STATIC' labels, full cutout under front axle.
6. 'VISCO-STATIC' labels, full cutout under front axle, wing support in front of front axle.
7. 'VISCO-STATIC' decals, full cutout under front axle, wing support in front of front axle.
8. 'VISCO-STATIC' labels, cream color seats.
9. 'VISCO-STATIC' labels, cream top seats, white bottom seats.
10. 'VISCO-STATIC' labels, white top seats, cream bottom seats.

5-E   Lotus Europa   2-7/8''   1969
Clear windows, ivory interior & tow hook, metal baseplate, colors vary from light to dark shades. All blue models have a short pin under the roof holding the plastic windshield. Early pink models also have this pin. Later pink models are without pin. Some of the pink models, thin wheels and small wheel wells are found without the pin but with the hole in the plastic where the pin should be inserted.
1. Metallic blue body, five spoke thin wheels, without the word ''Superfast'' cast on the front of the baseplate.
2. Metallic blue with ''Superfast'' cast on the front of the baseplate.
3. Metallic blue, No. 20 labels on doors & hood. (from G-3 Gift sets).
4. Pink body, no labels.
5. Pink body, with No. 20 labels.
6. Pink body, wide wheels, wide wheel wells.
7. Pink body, wide wheels, wide wheel wells, tow box.
8. Pink body, wide wheels, wide wheel wells, tow box, silver/gray baseplate.
9. Pink body, wide wheels, wide wheel wells, tow hole, No. 20 label on hood and sides.
10. Pink body, wide wheels, wide wheel wells, silver/gray base, narrow tow box.
11. Pink body, wide wheels, wide wheel wells, unpainted metal baseplate, narrow tow box.
12. Pink body, five spoke wide wheels (same as 3-B) wide wheel wells, unpainted metal baseplate, narrow tow box.
13. Pink body, five spoke wide wheels (same as 75-B) wide wheel wells, unpainted metal baseplate, narrow tow box.
14. Black body, ivory interior and tow hook, clear windows, unpainted metal baseplate, narrow tow box, gold tempa imprint monogram ''JPS'' on hood, gold trim line around roof, hood and grille, five spoke wide wheels. (Sold in Japan in special black box numbered J-2) may be found with the wide or narrow tow box.
15. Same as 14, no tempa printing on hood or sides. (MP-1)
16. Same as 15, no tempa imprint on hood or sides, mulit-spoke wheels. (MP-1).

5-F   Seafire Boat   2-15/16''   1975
White deck, blue plastic hull (baseplate), four small thin wheels inserted in holes in baseplate, silver plastic engine, red plastic exhaust pipes, Sea-fire label may be found in light or dark blue.
1. Blue driver, blue 'Sea Fire' and yellow and red flame on white label front of driver.
2. Blue 'Sea Fire' and yellow and red flame on white label front of driver, black plastic exhaust pipes.
3. Blue ''Sea Fire'' and yellow and red flame on white label front of driver, yellow/orange driver, red plastic exhaust pipes.
4. Same as 3, modified casting of engine block (block is new filled half way up the silver plated plastic cylinder heads.)
5. Red deck, white plastic hull, four small thin plastic wheels fitted in holes in baseplate, silver plated plastic engine, red plastic exhaust pipes, ''SEA FIRE'' label on hood, yellow/orange plastic driver, modified engine block. (TP-18)
6. Same as 4, black plastic exhaust pipes.
7. Same as 4, light yellow plastic driver.
8. Same as 5, light yellow plastic driver. (TP-18).
9. Red deck, blue plastic hull, four thin black plastic wheels, silver plated plastic engine, red plastic exhaust pipes, blue ''SEAFIRE'' with yellow and red flames label front of driver, light yellow

plastic driver.

10. White deck, brown plastic hull, four thin black plastic wheels, silver plated plastic engine, red plastic exhaust pipes, blue "SEA-FIRE" with red and yellow flames on label in front of driver, yellow/orange plastic driver (found in 3-pack sold in the U.K.)
11. Same as 10, light yellow plastic driver. (Found in 3-pack sold in U.K.)
12. Same as 5, with white plastic driver.

5-G   U.S. Mail Jeep   2-3/8''   1978
Blue body, white painted baseplate, bumpers and gas can, black plastic front seat, steering wheel and tow hook, white plastic canopy with textured finish, white five spoke reverse accent wheels. This model previously listed under 38-C has now appeared with a new baseplate with 'No. 5 U S Mail Truck'.
1. Large white "US MAIL" tempa imprint on hood, red stripe label each side of canopy.
2. Same as 1, wide five spoke reverse accent wheels, no hub caps.
3. Yellow body, charcoal gray painted baseplate, bumpers and gas can, black plastic front seat, steering wheel and tow hook, blue, white and orange wings on hood, "GLIDING CLUB" label on hood, cast metal rear seats with canopy mounting holes, wide five spoke reverse accent wheels. (TP-7).
4. Same as 3, white painted metal baseplate and gas can. (TP-7).
5. Same as 3, flat black painted metal baseplate and gas cans. (TP-7)
6. Same as 1, cream painted metal baseplate and gas can.

5-H   4x4 Golden Eagle Jeep (off-road)   1982
Comes in shades of light to dark brown, 4 spoke wide wheels, yellow eagle decal on hood.

6-A   Quarry Truck   2-1/8''   1954
Orange cab & chassis, gray dumper with 6 vertical ribs, gold radiator & side trim, no number cast on body, 2 front, 4 rear metal wheels, crimped axles.
1. 1/8 inch space between front axle and body.
2. 1/32 inch space between front axle and body.
3. Gray plastic wheels, crimped axles.

6-B   Euclid Quarry Truck   2½''   1957
Yellow body, 4 vertical ribs on dumper sides, small round decal on front doors, 2 front, 4 rear plastic wheels.
1. Gray plastic wheels, crimped axles, flat rivet holds dumper to body.
2. Black plastic wheels, crimped axles, flat rivet holds dumper to body.
3. Black plastic wheels, rounded axles, flat rivet holds dumper to body, added brace behind gas tank.
4. Black plastic wheels, rounded axles, rounded rivet holds dumper to body, added brace behind gas tank.

6-C   Euclid Quarry Truck   2-5/8''   1964
Yellow body, 3 round axles, 2 front black plastic wheels, 2 solid rear duel wheels each side, with & without silver grille, letter 'A' or 'B' cast on dumper base.
1. Front hubs peaked, rear wheels solid, letter 'A'.
2. Same as 1, letter 'B'.
3. Front hubs flat, rear wheels solid, letter 'A'.
4. Same as 3, letter 'B'.
5. Front hubs flat, rear wheels double, letter 'A'.

6-D   Ford Pick-up   2¾''   1968
Red body, white removable plastic canopy, clear plastic wheels, front wheels pivet, ivory interior, model changed to superfast wheels.
1. White plastic grille.
2. White plastic grille, letter 'A' on baseplate.
3. Silver plastic grille, letter 'A' on baseplate.

6-E   Ford Pick-up   2¾''   1970
Red body, ivory interior, white removable canopy, five spoke wheels.
1. Silver grille, thin wheels, black baseplate.
2. Silver grille, thin wheels, green baseplate.
3. Silver grille, thin wheels, metallic green baseplate.

4. White plastic grille, thin wheels, green baseplate.
5. White plastic grille, wide wheels, green baseplate.
6. White plastic grille, wide wheels, charcoal baseplate.
7. White plastic grille, wide wheels, gray baseplate.
8. White plastic grille, wide wheels, black baseplate.
9. Silver plastic grille, wide wheels, black baseplate.
10. Silver plastic grille, wide wheels, green baseplate.
11. Silver plastic grille, wide wheels, metallic green baseplate.
12. Silver plastic grille, wide wheels, charcoal baseplate.
13. White plastic grille, wide wheels, unpainted metal base.
14. Silver plastic grille, wide wheels, gray baseplate.
15. White plastic grille, thin wheels, unpainted metal baseplate.

6-F   Mercedes 350 SL   3''   1973
Orange body, black plastic convertible top with textured finish, light yellow interior, wide five spoke wheels.
1. Metal base and grille, amber tinted windshield.
2. Metal base & grille, clear windshield.
3. Metal base & grille, amber tinted windows, light yellow interior, small five spoke wheels (not slicks).
4. Metal base & grille, amber tinted windshield, ivory interior.
5. Unpainted metal baseplate, no patent no. on baseplate, wide five spoke accent wheels, amber tinted windshield, light yellow interior.
6. Yellow body, unpainted metal baseplate, no patent no. on base-plate, wide five spoke accent wheels, amber windshield, light yellow interior.
7. Orange body, unpainted metal baseplate, no patent number, wide five spoke accent wheels, clear windshield, light yellow interior.
8. Same as 7, small five spoke wheels, not slicks.
9. Metallic silver/gray body, unpainted metal baseplate, amber windows, black plastic roof, light yellow interior, black 'RENN-SERVICE' (Racing Service) on white side labels on doors, silver label with black and white checkered flag on hood, white oval label with red border and red letter 'AVD' on trunk, fine black letters on red border, wide five spoke accent wheels. (sold in Germany).
10. Metallic silver gray body, unpainted metal baseplate, amber windows, black plastic roof, light yellow interior, No label, wide five spoke accent wheels.
11. Same as 6, wide five spoke accent wheels, clear windshield, light yellow interior.
12. Same as 10, metallic brownish bronze body, no labels, black plastic convertible top with textured finish.
13. Same as 12, metallic brownish bronze body, no labels, white plastic convertible top with textured finish.
14. Same as 13, metallic brownish bronze body, no label, white plastic convertible top with textured finish, clear windshield.
15. Same as 14, frosted clear windshield.
16. Same as 14, metallic mahogany red body, clear windshield.
17. Same as 13, large five spoke reverse accent wheels.
18. Same as 13, smoky gray tinted plastic windshield.
19. Same as 13, smoky gray tinted plastic windshield, ivory plastic interior.
20. Red body, unpainted metal baseplate, white plastic textured convertible top, light yellow plastic interior, clear plastic windshield, wide five spoke accent wheels.
21. Same as 20, amber plastic windshield.
22. Top open-convertible, clear plastic windshield, wide five spoke accent wheels. 1982

7-A   Horse Drawn Milk Float   2¼''   1954
Orange body, white driver & bottle load, brown horse with white mane & hoofs, gold coller & harness, spoked metal wheels, crimped axles, no number cast on body. The horse hoofs are white or brown, the harness is gold trimmed or painted brown as same as horse. The model containing silver bottles can not be authenticated as having been produced by Lesney.
1. First casting, rear left bottle rack cast 1/16'' from edge.
2. Second casting, rear left bottle rack cast 1/8'' from edge.

3. Gray plastic wheels, crimped axles, orange driver with white cap.
4. Gray plastic wheels, round axles, orange driver with white cap, bottom hitch casting solid to sides of axles.
5. Gray plastic wheels, round axles, all orange driver.

7-B   Ford Anglia   2-5/8''   1961
Blue body, green tinted windows, silver radiator & front bumper, with or without silver rear bumper, with or without red painted tail lights, black baseplate with tow hook, No. 7 cast on flat baseplate or on raised platform.
1. Gray plastic wheels with knobby treads, No. 7 raised.
2. Same as 1, but No. 7 flat.
3. Same as 1, but fine treads.
4. Same as 1, No. 7 flat.
5. Silver plastic wheels, fine treads, flat No. 7.
6. Same as 5, flat No. 7.
7. Same as 5, fine treads.
8. Same as 7, No. 7 flat.
9. Black plastic wheels, knobby treads, No. 7 raised.
10. Same as 9, flat No. 7.
11. Same as 9, fine treads.
12. Same as 11, flat No. 7.

7-C   Ford Refuse Truck   3''   1966
Orange cab & chassis, gray plastic dumper, silver metal loader, green tinted windows, unpainted metal baseplate & grille, 4 black plastic wheels, rounded axles, model changed to Superfast wheels.
1. Straight arm on loader above rear wheels covering axle pin holding loader to dumper.
2. Curved cutout on loader above rear wheels.
3. Curved cutout on loader above rear wheels, tow slot on front baseplate.

7-D   Ford Refuse Truck   3''   1970
Gray plastic body, silver metal dumper, green tinted windows, metal baseplate and grille.
1. Orange cab & chassis, thin wheels, four spoke wheels, square long opening on inside of base.
2. Red/orange cab & chassis, thin four spoke wheels, square long opening on inside of base.
3. Orange cab & chassis, thin four spoke wheels, long "T" shaped opening on inside of base.
4. Orange cab & chassis, wide wheels, long square opening on inside of base.
5. Orange cab & chassis, wide wheels, long "T" shaped opening on inside of base.

7-E   Hairy Hustler   2-7/8''   1971
Metallic bronze, silver air scoop at rear, silver interior, No. 5 label on hood, No. 5 label on sides on yellow background, five spoke front wheels, clover leaf rear wheels.
1. Purple windows, black baseplate.
2. Purple windows, light gray baseplate.
3. Yellow windows, black baseplate.
4. Yellow windows, light gray baseplate.
5. Yellow windows, black baseplate, small tab like license plate attached to front back.
6. Yellow windows, gray baseplate, small tab like license plate attached to front back.
7. Yellow windows, black baseplate, blue labels on sides with 'lightning' background.
8. Unpainted metal baseplate.
9. Yellow windows, black baseplate, black & red on white Scorpion label on hood, small black on white No. 5 label on sides.
10. Light yellow windows, black base, black and red on white Scorpion label on hood, small black on white No. 5 label on sides.
11. Light yellow windows, black base, large black on white No. 5 on hood, yellow No. 5 and white lightning on blue background on sides.
12. Light yellow windows, green base, large black on white No. 5 on hood, yellow No. 5 and white lightning on blue background on

Matchbox 1-75 Series /Superfast

sides.
13. Dark yellow windows, green base, large black on white No. 5 on hood, yellow No. 5 and white lightning on blue background on sides.
14. Light yellow windows, green base, large black and white No. 5 on hood, no labels on sides.
15. Light yellow windows, black base, black and red on white scorpion label on hood, small black on white No. 3 label on sides.
16. Yellow windows, black base, black and red on white scorpion label on hood, small black on white No. 3 label on sides.
17. Yellow windows, green base, black and red on white scorpion label on hood, small black on white No. 3 label on sides.
18. Light yellow windows, black base, black and red on white scorpion label on hood, small black on white No. 137 label on sides.
19. Yellow windows, black base, large black on white No. 5 label on hood, no label on sides.
20. Yellow windows, black baseplate, large black on white No. 5 label on hood, small black on white No. 3 label on sides.
21. Yellow windows, green baseplate, large black on white No. 5 label on hood, no label on sides.
22. Light yellow windows, black baseplate, large black on white No. 5 label on hood, no label on sides.
23. Yellow windows, black baseplate, black and red on white round Scorpion label on hood, small black on white No. 137 labels on sides.
24. Yellow windows, green baseplate, black and red on white round Scorpion label on hood, small black on white No. 5 on sides.
25. Yellow windows, green baseplate, black and red on white round Scorpion label on hood, small black on white No. 137 labels on sides.
26. Same as 11, small five spoke wide wheels front and rear.
27. White body, (no streaker imprint) amber window, charcoal painted baseplate, silver plated plastic air scoop and interior, five spoke front wheels, large wide clover leaf rear wheels.
28. Yellow painted body, black painted baseplate, chrome plastic interior, rear air and rear panel, amber windshield, various "flame design" tempa imprint on front fenders, hood, roof and rear or air scoop, black design tempa imprints on each side of windshield, and on each rear fender, five spoke front wheels, large clover leaf rear wheels.
29. Same as 28, baseplate now reads, "No: IX Flaming Manta".
30. Streakers white body, red racing stripe top of fenders, black checkerboard stripe center front to rear. Five spoke wide front wheels, large wide clover leaf rear wheels, amber windows, & black painted baseplate.
31. Same as 30, but orange racing stripe.
32. Same as 30, but light amber window (pinkish), & red racing stripes.
33. Same as 30, small five spoke wide wheels front and rear.
34. Same as 30, charcoal painted baseplate.

7-F   V.W. Golf   2-7/8"   1976
Metallic green body, black painted metal baseplate and grille, small wide multi-spoke wheels.
1. Orange/yellow interior and tow hook, amber windows, black plastic roof rack and surfboards. May be found in two distinct shades of metallic green, light and dark.
2. Yellow body, yellow/orange interior and tow hook, amber windows, black painted baseplate and grille, four holes on roof, two covered by a white label with '201', front left hole holds an amber dome light, rear right hole holds a long black antenna, black 'ADAC' and black outline of an eagle on white label on hood, black border and black 'ADAC' (Automobile Club of Germany) on wide side labels on front doors, small multi-spoke wheels. (sold in Germany).
3. Same as 1, dark metallic green painted body.
4. Same as 1, dark metallic green painted body, center board bracket on roof rack is 5/32" wide.

5. Same as 4, red body. (TP-18)
6. Same as 4, dark amber windows.
7. Same as 4, glossy black painted baseplate.
8. Same as 4, light amber windows, yellow plastic interior.
9. Same as 4, amber windows, yellow/orange plastic interior, charcoal gray painted baseplate and grille.
10. Same as 4, light amber windows, yellow/orange plastic interior and tow hook, charcoal gray painted baseplate.
11. Same as 4, amber windows, red plastic interior and tow hook, charcoal gray painted baseplate and grille.
12. Yellow body, red plastic interior and tow hook, clear plastic windows, charcoal gray painted baseplate and grille, black plastic rack and surfboard on roof, small wide multi-spoke wheels.
13. Same as 4, amber plastic windows, bright lemon yellow plastic interior, charcoal gray painted metal baseplate.
14. Metallic green body, charcoal gray painted baseplate and grille, yellow/orange plastic interior and tow hook, cloudy amber plastic windows, black plastic rack and surf boards on roof, small wide multi-spoke wheels.
15. Yellow body, red plastic interior and tow hook, clear plastic windows, glossy black painted baseplate and grille, black plastic rack and surf boards on roof, small wide multi-spoke wheels.
16. Metallic green body, charcoal gray painted baseplate, red plastic interior and tow hook, cloudy amber plastic windows, black plastic roof rack and surf boards, small multi-spoke wheels.
17. Yellow body, red plastic interior and tow hook, clear plastic windows, blue/gray painted metal baseplate and grille, black plastic roof rack and surfboards, small multi-spoke wheels.
18. Red body, charcoal gray painted baseplate and grille, amber plastic windows, bright lemon yellow plastic interior and tow hook, black plastic roof and surfboards, small wide multi-spoke wheels. (TP-18)
19. Red body, glossy black painted metal baseplate and grille, clear plastic windows, orange/yellow plastic interior and tow hook, black plastic roof rack and surfboards, small wide multi-spoke wheels. (TP-18)
20. Same as 19, clear plastic windows, bright lemon yellow plastic interior and tow hook. (TP-18)
21. Same as 19, silver body.

7-G   Rompin' Rabbit   1982
1. White body, red plastic windows, side lettering on yellow stripe reads "Rompin' Rabbit". Black silhouette of rabbit on top, hood with 4x4 rabbit w. Clover leaf wheels.

8-A   Caterpillar Tractor   1½"   1955
No number on baseplate, drivers hat same color as body or painted black, metal rollers, crimped axles, rubber treads.
1. Orange body & driver, gold grille.
2. Yellow body & driver, silver grille.
3. All yellow body & driver, no trim.

8-B   Caterpillar Tractor   1-5/8"   1959
Yellow body & driver, No. 8 cast in base, large smoke stack, metal rollers, crimped axles, rubber treads.
1. Metal rollers, crimped axles.
2. Orange driver.

8-C   Caterpillar Tractor   1-7/8"   1961
Yellow body & driver, large smoke stack, rubber treads, rounded axles.
1. Metal rollers, no number showing.
2. Metal rollers, No. 18 in base.
3. Silver plastic rollers, no number showing.
4. Black plastic rollers, no number showing.

8-D   Caterpillar Tractor   2"   1964
Yellow body, no driver, large black plastic rollers, rubber treads, rounded axles, No. 8 cast on rear baseplate.
1. Large smoke stack.
2. Large smoke stack, with hole in front baseplate.
3. Small smoke stack, with hole in front baseplate.

8-E   Ford Mustang Fastback   2-7/8"   1966
White body, red interior, clear windows, recessed hole in base for steer-

ing, with or without silver painted grille. Model changed to Superfast wheels.
1. Silver hub caps, black plastic wheels, "patent pending" on flat base, steering slot not recessed.
2. Silver hub caps, black plastic wheels, "patent pending" on flat base, steering slot recessed.
3. Silver wheels, black plastic tires, "patent pending" on flat base, steering slot recessed.
4. Silver wheels, black plastic tires, "patent pending" on flat base, steering slot recessed. Low slot.
5. Silver wheels, black plastic tires, "Pat No. 1097556" on raised base, steering slot recessed, tow slot, this model comes with a shiny black or matt black baseplate.
6. Orange body, silver wheels, black plastic tires, Pat. No. on raised base, steering slot recessed, tow slot.

8-F   Ford Mustang   2-7/8"   1970
Wide five spoke wheels, with tow hook same color as interior.
1. White body, red interior.
2. Red body, red interior.
3. Red/orange body, red interior.
4. Red body, ivory interior.
5. Red/orange body, ivory interior.

8-G   Wildcat Dragster   2-7/8"   1970
Pinkish/orange body, yellow interior & tow hook, green windows, silver motor in hood, black & orange wildcat label on doors, small five spoke front wheels, large four spoke rear wheels.
1. Metal baseplate.
2. Black baseplate.
3. Yellow baseplate.
4. Light yellow baseplate.
5. Orange baseplate.
6. Charcoal baseplate.
7. Black baseplate, yellow & tan wildcat label.
8. Charcoal baseplate.
9. Gray baseplate.
10. Light gray baseplate.
11. Unpainted metal baseplate.
12. Black baseplate, sail boat label (same as No. 23-A3) on sides.
13. Green painted baseplate, yellow & tan Wild Cat labels on sides.
14. Black painted baseplate, 'RAT RQD' side labels (same as 62-E).

8-H   De Tomaso Pantera   3"   1975
White body, blue painted metal baseplate, cinnamon plastic interior and rear lid, cloverleaf front slicks, five spoke rear slicks. May be found with light or dark blue painted baseplate.

1. Clear windows, black No. 8 in cinnamon circle and white 'Pantera' on blue label on hood, black No. 8 in cinnamon lozenge and white 'Pantera' on white stripe label on each side.
2. Clear windows, black No. 8 in cinnamon circle and white "PANTERA" on blue label on hood, black No. 8 on cinnamon lozenge on white "PANTERA" on white stripe label on each side, unpainted metal baseplate.
3. Clear windows, black No. 8 in cinnamon circle and white 'PAN-TERA' on blue label on hood, black No. 8 on cinnamon lozenge and white 'PANTERA' on white stripe label on each side, Un-painted metal baseplate, small five spoke front wheels, large five spoke rear wheels.
4. Same as 4, light bright cinnamon plastic interior and rear lid, also frequently found without the side labels on doors.
5. Same as 4, no side labels, dark red plastic interior and rear lid.
6. Same as 1, cream body, no side label, cinnamon plastic interior and rear lid.
7. Blue body, glossy black painted metal baseplate, black plastic interior and rear lid, light gray and black tempa stripes on hood and rear, light gray tempa circles with blue "17" on roof and sides, cloverleaf front wheels, five spoke rear wheels, "Made in Hong Kong" on base.
8. Same as 1, light bright cinnamon plastic interior and rear lid,

yellow blue sunburst label on hood. (label from SF 47-2)
9. Same as 1, green "9" on black bordered white circle and yellow, green and red stripes on white label on hood. (label from SF62-3)

8-I   Rover   1982
Released in all countries but U.S.A.
1. Tan interior.
2. White interior.

9-A   Dennis Fire Escape Engine   2¼''   1955
Red body, no number cast in body, with & without gold trim on grille, drivers hat, booster under ladder, top of ladder railings, top of dash, metal wheels, crimped axles, no front bumper.
1. Three-eighths inch metal wheel at rear of ladder.
2. One half inch metal wheel at rear of ladder.

9-B   Merryweather Marquis Fire Engine   2½''   1959
Red body, silver grille & front bumper, with & without silver rear hose connections, with & without 4 upper rear hose connections, tan, gold or unplated (silver) top ladder, 17 rumgs in top ladder.
1. Dark gray wheels, knobby treads, crimped axles, tan top ladder, silver hose rim.
2. Same as 1, rounded axles.
3. Same as 2, rear hose trim same as body.
4. Same as 3, gold top ladder.
5. Light gray wheels, same as 4.
6. Black wheels, same as 5.
7. Same as 6, silver top ladder.
8. Same as 7, no rear hose trim.
9. Same as 8, gold top ladder.
10. Same as 9, fine treads.
11. Same as 10, silver top ladder, 18 rungs.
12. Same as 10, 18 rungs.

9-C   Boat and Trailer   3¼''   1966
White plastic hull, blue plastic deck on boat in various shades, clear windows, blue trailer in various shades with black plastic wheels, round axles. Model changed to Superfast wheels.
1. No side support on boat for trailer.
2. With side supports on boat for trailer.

9-D   Boat and Trailer   3¼''   1970
Blue deck, white hull, clear windows, five spoke wheels on trailer.
1. Light blue trailer.
2. Dark blue trailer.
3. Light blue, reinforced rounded tow hitch.
4. Dark blue, reinforced rounded tow hitch.
5. Light blue trailer, reinforced rounded tow hitch, small hubless accent wheels, riveted black axle cover, no number on base. (TP-5)
6. Light blue trailer, reinforced rounded tow hitch, smooth surface on platform between wheels, small hubless wheels, riveted black axle cover, smooth surface, no number "9" on base, boat with blue plastic deck, white plastic hull and clear plastic windows. (TP-5)

9-E   Javelin   3''   1972
Metallic lime green, yellow interior & tow hook, amber windows, metal baseplate, five spoke wide wheels.
1. Silver air scoop on hood & silver dashboard.
2. Black air scoop and dashboard.
3. Black air scoop & dashboard, silver/gray baseplate.
4. Black air scoop and dashboard, unpainted metal base, light amber windows.
5. Black air scoop and dashboard, silver/gray baseplate, light amber windows.
6. Black air scoop and dashboard, unpainted metal baseplate, amber windows, light yellow interior.
7. Black air scoop & dashboard, unpainted metal baseplate, amber windows, orange interior.
8. Black air scoop & dashboard, unpainted metal baseplate, amber windows, light orange interior.
9. Black air scoop & dashboard, silver/gray baseplate, amber windows, orange interior.
10. Black air scoop & dashboard, unpainted metal baseplate, amber

windows, yellow interior, small wide cloverleaf wheels.
11. Black air scoop & dashboard, unpainted metal baseplate, amber windows, orange interior, clover leaf wheels.
12. Black air scoop & dashboard, unpainted metal baseplate, light amber windows, yellow interior, clover leaf wheels.
13. Black air scoop & dashboard, unpainted metal baseplate, light amber windows, orange interior, five spoke wide wheels.
14. Black air scoop and dashboard, silver/gray painted baseplate, amber windows, light yellow interior, five spoke wide wheels.
15. Black air scoop and dashboard, unpainted metal baseplate, amber windows, light yellow interior, small wide cloverleaf wheels.
16. Black air scoop and dashboard, unpainted metal baseplate, amber windows, white interior, five spoke wide wheels.
17. Metallic blue body, yellow interior & tow hook, amber windows, unpainted metal baseplate, black air scoop & dashboard, five spoke slicks. (TP-3)
18. Metallic green body, black air scoop and dashboard, unpainted metal baseplate, amber windows, yellow/orange interior, five spoke accent wheels.
19. Metallic blue body, black air acoop and dashboard, unpainted metal baseplate, amber windows, yellow/orange interior, five spoke accent wheels. (TP-3)
20. Same as 18, light pinkish amber windows.
21. Same as 18, silver/gray painted metal baseplate.
22. Same as 19, silver/gray painted baseplate. (TP-3)
23. Same as 19, dark metallic blue body, silver/gray painted metal baseplate.
24. Metallic green body, unpainted metal baseplate, amber windows, blue plastic interior, five spoke accent wheels.
25. Blue body, silver gray painted baseplate, amber plastic windows, doors now cast as part of body, black plastic air scoop on hood and dashboard, yellow/orange plastic interior and tow hook, all following design in grayish/white tempa print: wide stripe front to rear on top, stripe each side at base of body, parallelogram on each door with large blue "1", 'GOOD YEAR' logo above each front wheel well, 'UNION' logo above each rear wheel well, lightning bolt rear of each foor, five spoke accent wheels. (LEM)
26. Same as 19, metallic blue body, unpainted metal baseplate, doors are now cast as a part of the body.
27. Same as 25, unpainted metal baseplate. (LEM)
28. Same as 19, metallic blue body, silver gray painted baseplate, doors as part of body.
29. Dark metallic green body, doors solid with body, unpainted metal baseplate, yellow/orange plastic interior, grille and tow hook, black plastic scoop on hood, black plastic dashboard, five spoke accent wheels. (TP-3)
30. Same as 29, unpainted metal baseplate, no number on baseplate. (TP-3)
31. Same as 25, silver gray painted metal baseplate, no number on baseplate. (LEM)
32. Same as 25, unpainted metal baseplate, no number on baseplate. (LEM)
33. Same as 19, metallic blue body, doors solid with body, unpainted metal baseplate, no number on baseplate. (TP-3)
34. Same as 29, dark metallic green body, doors solid with body, silver gray painted baseplate. (TP-3)
35. Same as 29, dark metallic green body, doors solid with body, silver gray painted baseplate, no number on baseplate. (TP-3 and 4)
36. Same as 29, red body.

9-F   Ford Escort RS2000   3''   1978
White body, black glossy painted metal baseplate and grille, tan plastic interior and tow hook, clear windows, mulit-spoke wide wheels.
1. Blue and yellow stripes, red '9' in yellow circle and white 'DUN-LOP CIBIE' side labels, light and dark blue and yellow stripes with red 'shell' logo label on roof, light and dark blue and yellow stripes with white on blue 'FORD' logo and red 'RS2000' label on hood.

2. Same as 1, flat black painted metal baseplate and grille.
3. Same as 1, amber plastic windows.
4. Same as 1, clear plastic windows, charcoal gray painted baseplate.
5. Light blue body, tan plastic interior and tow hook, clear plastic windows, glossy black painted baseplate, white "PHANTOM", white and dark blue stripes on light blue label on hood and on each side on door, light blue "9" and dark blue "V" on white background on light blue label on roof, multi-spoke wide wheels.
6. Same as 5, charcoal gray painted metal baseplate.
7. Same as 6, charcoal gray painted metal baseplate, very light amber tinted plastic windows.
8. Same as 4, clear plastic windows, charcoal gray painted metal baseplate, light tan plastic interior and tow hook.
9. Same as 1, charcoal gray painted metal baseplate, light tan plastic interior and tow hook.
10. Same as 1, clear plastic windows, charcoal gray painted metal baseplate, tan plastic interior and tow hook.
11. White body, tan plastic interior and tow hook, clear plastic windows, glossy black painted metal baseplate and grille, white "PHANTOM", white and dark blue stripes on light blue label on hood and each side on doors, light blue "9" and dark blue "V" on white background on light blue label on roof, multi-spoke wide wheels. (TP-5)
12. Tan interior, green body with black & white labels.

9-G   Fiat Abarth   1982
White body, red interior. (listed as no. 74 everywhere but U.S.A.)
1. Stripes red and orange.
2. Stripes red and brown.

10-A   Mechanical Horse and Trailer   2-3/8''   1955
Red cab with 3 metal wheels, gold trim, gray trailer with 2 metal wheels, crimped axles, smooth bed in trailer, no number.
1. Without support under rear wheels on trailer.
2. With support under rear wheels on trailer.

10-B   Mechanical Horse and Trailer   2-15/16'' 1958
Red cab, gold trim, ribbed bed in trailer, no number. The front wheels of the cabs are metal. May or may not have gas tanks.
1. Metal wheels, crimped axles, gold trim, light tan trailer.
2. Gray plastic wheels, crimped axles, gold trim, dark tan trailer.
3. Same as 2, silver trim.
4. Same as 3, rounded axles.
5. Same as 4, no trim.

10-C   Sugar Container Truck   2-5/8''   1961
Blue body, "Tate & Lyle" decals on sides & rear, with and without 'crown' on top of rear decal, 4 axles, 8 plastic wheels, with and without small hole in base, thin or thick brace between 2nd & 3rd axle.
1. With crown decal, gray wheels, knobby treads, no hole in base, thin base support.
2. No crown decal, same as 1.
3. Same as 2, silver wheels.
4. Same as 3, thick base support.
5. Same as 4, gray wheels.
6. Same as 5, hole in base.
7. Same as 6, black wheels.
8. No crown decal, silver wheels, fine treads, hole in base, thick base support.
9. Same as 8, gray wheels.
10. Same as 8, black wheels and with florescent or bright red lettering on decals.

10-D   Pipe Truck   2-7/8''   1966
Red body, gray pipes, with 'Leyland' or 'Ergomatic' on front base, white or silver plastic grille & base, blue tinted windows, 8 black plastic wheels on 4 round axles, with or without supports over axles.
1. Base marked 'Leyland', silver grille, no supports over axles, no tow slot.
2. Base marked 'Ergomatic', same as 1.
3. Base marked 'Ergomatic', white grille, no supports over axles, tow slot.

4. Same as 3, but with support over axles.
5. Same as 4, silver grille.

10-E Pipe Truck   **2-7/8''**   **1970**
Blue tinted windows, black pipe racks, eight-5 spoke thin wheels.
1. Red cab and chassis, silver plastic grille and baseplate, gray plastic pipe.
2. Orange cab & chassis, silver grille & baseplate, gray plastic pipes.
3. Orange cab & chassis, gray plastic grille & baseplate, gray plastic pipes.
4. Orange cab & chassis, silver grille & baseplate, yellow plastic pipes.
5. Orange cab & chassis, gray plastic grille & baseplate, yellow plastic pipes.
6. Orange cab & chassis, gray plastic grille & baseplate, yellow plastic pipes, small lettered ''Pat App'' on baseplate.

10-F Piston Popper   **2-7/8''**   **1973**
Metallic blue body, white interior, silver motor in hood with clear 'pistons' that move up and down operated by front wheel pins, (Rolamatic) small wide five spoke front wheels, larger clover leaf rear wheels, metal baseplate.
1. Amber windows.
2. Amber windows, silver/gray baseplate.
3. Light amber windows, metal baseplate.
4. Light amber windows, silver/gray baseplate.
5. Amber windows, unpainted metal baseplate, thick long braces each side of axle housing.
6. Amber windows, unpainted metal baseplate with braces, small clover leaf front wheels, large clover leaf rear wheels.
7. Amber windows, unpainted metal baseplate, thick long braces each side of axle housing, small 5 spoke wide wheels front & rear.
8. Light amber windows (pinkish), unpainted metal baseplate with braces, small five spoke front wheels, large cloverleaf rear wheels.
9. Amber windows, unpainted metal baseplate with braces, small five spoke front wheels, large cloverleaf rear wheels, Pat. App. 12174/72 replaced by Pat. No. 1424808.
10. Same as 1, ''SUPERFAST'' on baseplate instead of ''ROLOMATIC'' (would appear to be first issue)
11. Same as 9, white painted body. This model previously listed and later thought of doubtful source has now been reported found in five packs (MP-1) in Germany.
12. Same as 9, light amber windows.
13. Yellow body, white plastic interior, amber plastic windows, silver plated plastic motor on hood, with clear plastic cylinders and red plastic pistons, unpainted metal baseplate, grille and bumpers, red flames tempa print designs on hood and sides, black flames tempa print designs around rear deck, small five spoke front wheels, large clover leaf rear wheels, no. 10 on baseplate (LEM)
14. Same as 13, dark amber plastic windows. (LEM)

10-G Plymouth Gran Fury   **3''**   **1979**
Police car, white body, black tempa print covering front and back fenders, unpainted metal baseplate, grille and bumpers, black tempa print ''POLICE'' and shield over side doors, white plastic interior, multi-spoke wheels.
1. Amber windows, square blue opaque plastic rectangular lights on roof.
2. Amber windows, square light blue transparent plastic rectangular lights on roof.
3. Same as 1, dark amber windows.
4. Same as 2, dark amber windows.
5. Same as 1, blue plastic windows and lights on roof.
6. Same as 2, light amber plastic windows.
7. Same as 2, dark blue plastic windows, blue plastic lights on roof.
8. Same as 2, light blue plastic windows, blue plastic lights on roof.

11-A Road Tanker   **2''**   **1955**
Trim on front grille, headlights, gas tanks, tank covers on top, no number cast, metal wheels, crimped axles.
1. Green body, flat base between cab & body, gold trim.
2. Butterscotch body, flat base between cab & body, silver trim.

---

3. Light yellow body, flat base, silver trim.
4. Light yellow body, half round base between cab & body, silver trim.
5. Red body, half round base between cab & body, silver trim.
6. Red body, half round base between cab & body, gold trim, small 'Esso' decal at rear.
7. Red body, half round base between cab & body, gold trim, large 'Esso' decal at rear.

11-B Road Tanker   **2½''**   **1958**
Red body, No. 11 on baseplate, large 'Esso' decals at rear, comes with or without silver trim on grille, headlights, gas tanks, tank covers on top, with and without square hole under rear axle, with and without small round hole in front base, with flat or half rounded brace on small base, with and without thin brace between cab and tank body.
1. Metal wheels, crimped axles, no brace between cab, half-round brace on base, rear axle hole, no hole in base.
2. Same as 1, gray plastic wheels.
3. Same as 1, but metal wheels and thin brace between cab.
4. Same as 2, thin brace between cab.
5. Same as 4, rounded axles.
6. Same as 5, flat brace on base and hole in base.
7. Same as 5, with hole in base.
8. Same as 7, no rear axle hole.
9. Same as 8, black wheels.
10. Same as 8, black wheels.

11-C Jumbo Crane   **3''**   **1965**
Yellow body, red plastic hydraulic lifter sleeve, black plastic wheels, comes with and without red weight box, with and without braces in crane top and bottom, with and without small brace at inside top of crane, red double, red single or yellow single crane hook.
1. Small rear wheels, yellow weight box, open crane braces, no top crane brace, double red hook.
2. Same as 1, large rear wheels.
3. Same as 2, red weight box.
4. Same as 3, closed crane brace, single yellow crane hook.
5. Same as 4, double red crane hook.
6. Same as 5, with top crane brace.
7. Same as 6, single red crane hook.

11-D Scaffolding Truck   **2½''**   **1969**
Silver body, red plastic base and grille, green tinted windows, yellow plastic scaffolding, stick labels ''Builders Supply Company'' black plastic wheels, model changed to Superfast wheels.

11-E Scaffolding Truck   **2½''**   **1969**
Silver/gray body, red plastic grille and baseplate, green tinted windows, yellow pipes.
1. Long black axle cover on front.
2. Short black axle cover on front.
3. Short black axle cover on front wheels, light yellow scaffolding.

11-F Flying Bug   **2-7/8''**   **1972**
Metallic red, gray windows, silver helmit on driver, flesh colored face, yellow jets, five spoke small front wheels, large five spoke rear wheels, metal baseplate.
1. Square cut label on hood.
2. Heart shaped label on hood.
3. Heart shaped label on hood, wing supports on front baseplate, in front of front wheels.
4. Heart shaped label on hood, silver/gray painted base.
5. Heart shaped label on hood, unpainted metal baseplate, large four spoke front wheels.
6. Heart shaped label on hood, unpainted metal baseplate, five spoke small front wheels, blue non-transparent plastic windows.
7. Orange painted body, black painted baseplate, black plastic windows and air scoops, flesh colored plastic driver's face with chrome plated helmet, black and white ''bee design'' tempa imprint on hood, baseplate now reads ''No: IV Flying Beetle'': small wide five spoke front wheels, large wide five spoke rear wheels.

11-G Car Transporter   **3''**   **1976**
Orange body, black painted baseplate and grille, ivory plastic car rack,

---

one each red, blue and orange plastic cars, small multi-spoke wheels. May be found with either dark or light blue plastic car on carrier. May be found with yellow car in front or red car, red car in front of yellow car or two yellow cars on top of carrier.
1. Dark blue windows.
2. Dark blue windows, five spoke accent wheels.
3. Dark blue windows, dark blue plastic car on carrier, small multi-spoke wheels.
4. Same as 1, small multi-spoke wheels, no hub caps.
5. Same as 1, bone white plastic car rack, small multi-spoke wheels.
6. Same as 1, bone white plastic car rack, blue car behind red car on top. Blue car on bottom, small multi-spoke wheels.
7. Same as 1, ivory plastic car rack, blue car behind red car on top, blue car on bottom, small multi-spoke wheels. The yellow plastic car found on top rear may be found in various shades of yellow, dark to light, and orange/yellow.
8. Same as 1, ivory plastic car rack, small multi-spoke wheels, dark green plastic windows.
9. Same as 1, ivory plastic car rack, small multi-spoke wheels, blueish green plastic windows.
10. Same as 1, charcoal gray painted baseplate.
11. Same as 1, ivory plastic car rack, small multi-spoke wheels, purple plastic windows.
12. Same as 1, light yellow plastic car rack, small multi-spoke wheels, dark green plastic windows.
13. Bright red cab, unpainted metal baseplate and grille, bone white plastic car rack, purple plastic windows.
14. Same as 1, ivory plastic car rack, small multi-spoke wheels, dark blue plastic windows, unpainted metal baseplate.
15. Bright red cab, unpainted metal baseplate, bone white plastic car rack, dark blue plastic windows, small multi-spoke wheels.
16. Same as 8, ivory plastic car rack, small multi-spoke wheels, dark green plastic windows, charcoal gray painted baseplate.
17. Same as 1, ivory plastic car rack, small multi-spoke wheels, purple plastic windows.
18. Red cab, silver gray painted baseplate and grille, ivory plastic car rack, dark blue plastic windows, small multi-spoke wheels.
19. Same as 18, silver gray painted baseplate, purple plastic windows.

11-H Cobra Mustang   **1982**
Orange body with lettering on doors, ''The Boss''.
1. White lettering.
2. Black lettering.
3. White lettering outlined in black.

12-A Land Rover   **1¾''**   **1955**
Olive green body, tan driver, with and without silver headlights and bumper, no number cast, metal wheels, crimped axles.
1. Small brace platform inside between front axles.
2. No platform between front axles.

12-B Land Rover   **2¼''**   **1959**
Olive green, no driver, black baseplate and tow hook, with and without silver headlights and bumper, thick or thin steering post, with and without brace inside hood.
1. Black wheels with knobby treads, crimped axles, thick steering post, no hood brace.
2. Same as 1, rounded axles.
3. Gray wheels, fine treads, rounded axles, thin steering post, with hood brace.
4. Same as 5, black wheels.

12-C Safari Land Rover   **2-1/3''**   **1965**
Clear windows, white plastic interior and tow hook, black plastic wheels, rounded axles, black baseplate with and without small 'tab' behind tow hook, brown or tan luggage on roof.
1. Green body, brown luggage, no rear base tab, no tow slot.
2. Same as 1, with rear base tab.
3. Blue of varying shades, brown luggage, no rear base tab, no tow slot.
4. Same as 3, with rear base tab.

5. Same as 3, tan luggage.
6. Same as 5, with rear base tab.
7. Same as 5, with tow slot.
8. Same as 7, with rear base tab.

12-D Safari Land Rover   2-13/16" 1970
Metallic gold, tan roof luggage, clear windows, black baseplate, five spoke thin wheels.
1. With small support behind tow hook on baseplate.
2. Without small support.
3. Red roof rack.

12-E Setra Coach   3" 1970
Clear windows, ivory interior, five spoke thin wheels, rear plastic lights same color as upper body.
1. Tannish/gray upper roof, metallic gold body, thin reinforced rear baseplate.
2. Tannish/gray upper roof, metallic gold body, thick reinforcement at rear of baseplate.
3. White upper roof, metallic gold body, thin reinforced rear baseplate.
4. White upper roof, metallic gold body, thick reinforcement at rear baseplate.
5. White upper roof, yellow body, thin reinforced rear baseplate.
6. White upper roof, yellow body, thick reinforcement at rear baseplate.
7. White upper roof, metallic dark red body, thin reinforcement at rear of baseplate, clear windows.
8. White upper roof, metallic dark red body, thin reinforcement at rear of baseplate, green windows.
9. White upper roof, metallic dark red body, thick reinforcement at rear of baseplate, green windows.
10. White upper roof, magenta (purple) body, thin reinforcement at rear of baseplate, green windows.
11. White upper roof, magenta (purple) body, thick reinforcement at rear of baseplate, green windows.

12-F Big Bull   2½" 1975
Light orange body, green blade, baseplate and side panels, chrome seat, hood exhaust, motor and rear side plates, orange rollers.
1. Black rubber treads, casting No. 1 (left dial on right side of dozer set at 12 o'clock).
2. Black rubber treads, casting No. 2 (left dial on right side of dozer set at 11 o'clock).
3. Same as 1 or 2, triangular reinforcements have been added back of blade where mounts connect to blade.
4. Same as 3, triangular reinforcement on blade, light yellow plastic rollers.

12-G Citroen CX   3" 1979
Metallic light blue body of various shades, silver/gray painted metal baseplate, bumpers and head lights, blue plastic rear hatch door, multi-spoke wheels.
1. Clear plastic windows, yellow plastic interior and tow hook.
2. Clear plastic windows, light yellow plastic interior and tow hook.
3. Blue plastic windows, light yellow plastic interior and tow hook.
4. Same as 2, dark blue metallic body, clear plastic windows, light yellow plastic interior and tow hook.
5. Same as 2, unpainted metal baseplate, clear plastic windows, light yellow plastic interior and tow hook.
6. Metallic blue body, glossy black painted baseplate, bumpers and headlights, clear plastic windows, light yellow plastic interior and tow hook, multi-spoke wheels.
7. Metallic blue body, unpainted metal baseplate, bumpers and headlights, clear plastic windows, light yellow plastic interior and tow hook, multi-spoke wheels.
8. Same as 7, charcoal gray painted metal baseplate.
9. Same as 6, but yellow body.

12-H Pontiac Firebird   1982
Preproduction used for picture purposes. Red. (listed as 51 for every-

where but U.S.A.)

13-A Bedford Wreck Truck   2" 1955
Tan body, red metal crane and hook, crane attached to body just above rear axle, curved sides of truck, silver grille.
1. Metal wheels, crimped axles.

13-B Bedford Wreck Truck   2-1/8" 1958
Tan body, red metal crane and hook, crane attached to rear axle, sides of truck longer, silver grille, No. 13 cast inside cab roof, brace between cab and body extends to top.
1. Metal wheels, crimped axles.
2. Gray plastic wheels, crimped axles.
3. Gray plastic wheels, rounded axles.

13-C Thames Wreck Truck   2½" 1961
Red body, with and without silver grille, ornament, bumper and parking lights, with and without black out lined decal: "MATCHBOX GAR-AGES" black front base, with and without open lined lattice crane, with and without parking lamps, red, silver or gray hook, rounded axles.
1. Gray wheels, knobby treads, open crane lattice, decal outlines, no parking lamps, red metal hook.
2. Same as 1, silver metal hook.
3. Same as 2, black wheels.
4. Same as 3, closed crane lattice.
5. Gray wheels, fine treads, open crane lattice, no decal outlines, no parking lamps, gray plastic hook.
6. Same as 5, closed crane lattice, parking lamps which may have only one side cast.
7. Black wheels, fine treads, closed crane lattice, decal outlines, no parking lamps, silver metal hook.
8. Gray wheels, fine treads, closed crane lattice, no decal outlines, no parking lamps, gray plastic hook.
9. Same as 8, black wheels.
10. Same as 9, with parking lamps which may have only one side cast.
11. Same as 10, small black wheels.

13-D Dodge Wreck Truck   3" 1965
Yellow cab & crane, green body & baseplate, green windows, red dome light, "BP" decals on body sides, black plastic wheels, round axles.
1. Yellow cab & crane, green body, gray plastic hook.
2. Red plastic double cable hook.
3. Red plastic single cable hook.
4. Red plastic single cable hook, "BP" labels.
5. Red plastic single cable hook, "BP" labels, bright yellow (dark) cab.
6. Green cab & crane, yellow body, gray plastic hook of thin casting, may be a pre-production model.
7. In 1970, models with green cab, yellow body, red plastic hook, BP labels, & black plastic wheels with crimped axles were hand produced in the Lesney factory and sold to collectors as 'authen-tic' products.

13-E Dodge Wreck Truck   3" 1970
Green rear body, red plastic hook, green windows, red dome light: green baseplate, five spoke thin wheels, "BP" labels on side of body.
1. Yellow cab and boom.
2. Bright yellow cab and boom.
3. Bright yellow cab and boom, small five spoke wheels.

13-F Baja Dune Buggy   2-5/8" 1971
Metallic green, orange interior, silver motor, black exhaust pipes, flower label on hood, metal baseplate, clover leaf balloon wheels. Most models can be found with flower stick color from light orange to red and with light to heavy black outline around flower. Body may be found in metallic tones from dark lime green to lime green to light yellow green.
1. Red flower label, 12 vents on side.
2. Red flower label, 13 vents on side.
3. Orange flower label, 12 vents on side.
4. Orange flower label, 13 vents on side.
5. Orange flower label, 13 vents on sides, light orange interior.
6. Orange flower label, 13 vents on sides, orange interior, brace on

each side of motor.
7. Orange flower label, 13 vents on sides, motor braces, red exhaust pipes.
8. Orange interior, red exhaust pipes, blue and red on white shield label.
9. Red interior, red exhaust pipes, blue and red on white shield label.
10. Red interior, red exhaust pipes, light & dark orange flower label.
11. Orange two seater interior (same as 47-B), red exhaust pipes, orange flower label.
12. Dark metallic lime green, four seater orange interior, red exhaust pipes, orange flower label on hood.
13. Same as 12, yellow sunburst label on hood. (from SF 47-B), found in G-17 Car Ferry.
14. Same as 9, pale orange interior.

13-G Snorkel Fire Engine   3" 1977
Red body, unpainted metal baseplate, and pump on front bumper, yellow/orange plastic snorkel and fire fighter, wide five spoke accent wheels.
1. Blue plastic windows and dome light.
2. Blue plastic windows and dome light, silver gray painted metal baseplate.
3. Amber plastic windows and dome lights, unpainted metal baseplate. (G-7)
4. Dark red body, light blue plastic windows and dome lights, unpainted metal baseplate.
5. Same as 4, dark red body, silver gray painted metal baseplate.

13-H 4x4 Mini Pick-up   1982
Orange body. (Same as 63 everywhere but U.S.A.)

14-A Daimler Ambulance   1-7/8" 1956
Cream body, silver trim, no number cast on body, "AMBULANCE" cast on sides, metal wheels, crimped axles.
1. Without red cross painted on roof.
2. With red cross painted on roof.

14-B Daimler Ambulance   2-5/8" 1958
Silver trim, black baseplate with number 14 cast, "AMBULANCE" cast on sides, red cross on roof.
1. Cream body, metal wheels, crimped axles.
2. Cream body, gray plastic wheels, crimped axles.
3. Off white body, gray plastic wheels, crimped axles.
4. Cream body, gray plastic wheels, rounded axles.
5. Off white body, gray plastic wheels, rounded axles.
6. Off white body, silver plastic wheels, rounded axles.

14-C Bedford Ambulance   2-5/8" 1962
White body (varying from off white to pure white), silver trim, red cross and LCC AMBULANCE on side decals, two rear doors open, black baseplate with number 14 cast.
1. Dark gray wheels, knobby treads, crimped axles, white interior, no cross outline on roof.
2. Same as 1, rounded axles.
3. Silver wheels, knobby treads, rounded axles, white interior, with cross outline on roof.
4. Same as 3, but cream interior.
5. Same as 4, but black wheels and no cross outline on roof.
6. Same as 5, white interior.
7. Same as 6, but thick or thin black wheels, fine treads, and various shades of blue-black lettering.

14-D Iso Grifo   3" 1968
Blue body, in various shades of dark, medium & light blue. Light blue interior, metal grille and baseplate, silver plastic hubs, light blue tow hook, clear windows. Model changed to Superfast wheels.
1. Black plastic tires.

14-E Iso Grifo   3" 1969
Tow hook same color as interior, clear windows, metal baseplate, five spoke wheels.
1. Metallic dark blue, light blue interior, thin wheels.
2. Metallic dark blue, bright blue interior, thin wheels.

3. Light blue, white interior, thin wheels.
4. Light blue, white interior, wide wheels.
5. Light blue, white interior, wide wheels, dot inside square on front hood.
6. Medium blue, white interior, wide wheels, dot inside square on front hood.
7. Medium blue, white interior, wide wheels, dot inside square on front hood, silver/gray baseplate.
8. Medium blue, white interior, wide wheels, no dot inside square on front of hood, silver/gray painted base.
9. Dark blue, white interior, wide wheels, dot inside square on front of hood, metal baseplate.
10. Metallic dark blue, white interior, thin wheels, metal baseplate.
11. Dark blue, white interior, thin wheels, metal baseplate, no dot inside square on front hood.
12. Powder blue body, white interior, unpainted metal baseplate, five spoke wide wheels. (Sold in Japan in special black box numbered J-3)
13. Same as 12, small multi-spoke wheels. (MP-1)

14-F   Mini-Haha   2-3/8"   1975
Red body, pink driver with brown helmet, peeking out through roof, unpainted metal baseplate, small cloverleaf front slicks, large spoke rear slicks, silver plated engine front of driver.
1. Blue non-transparent plastic windows, red, white, blue and yellow bull's eyes on sides.
2. Blue non-transparent windows, red center, blue outer ring circular side labels. (label same as SB-22)
3. Same as 1, face and shoulder of driver in very light pink (almost white) plastic.
4. Same as 2, face and shoulder of driver in very light pink (almost white) plastic, may show a purple or lavender shade.
5. Same as 1, multi-spoke front wheels.
6. Same as 2, multi-spoke front wheels.
7. Same as 1, face and shoulders of driver in light purple plastic.
8. Same as 1, pink plastic driver, dark chocolate brown plastic helmet.
9. Red body, dark blue non-transparent plastic windows, pink plastic driver, dark chocolate brown helmet, unpainted metal baseplate, red, white and blue bull's eye side labels, silver plated plastic rotary engine front of driver, small cloverleaf front wheels, large five spoke rear wheels.
10. Same as 9, pink plastic driver, brown plastic helmet.
11. Same as 9, light purple plastic driver, dark chocolate brown helmet.
12. Same as 9, light purple plastic driver, brown plastic helmet.

14-G   Rallye Royale   2-7/8"   1973
Metallic pearl gray body, flat black painted metal baseplate, black plastic interior, black tempa "14" on wide blue tempa stripe bordered by thin black stripes on hood, wide blue tempa stripe bordered by thin black tempa stripes on roof, five spoke wide wheels, "Made In Hong Kong" on baseplate. (formerly SF3)
1. Clear plastic windows.
2. White body, blue number 8 on wide blue stripe bordered by thin red stripes on hood, blue "8" on doors, red stripe under door.

14-H   Leyland Tanker   1982
Released in all countries but, U.S.A.
1. Label "F".
2. Decal "F".

15-A   Prime Mover   2-1/8"   1956
Silver trim on grille & tank behind cab, tow hook same color as body.
1. Yellow body, 6 metal wheels, crimped axles.
2. Dark orange body, 6 metal wheels, crimped axles.
3. Dark orange body, 10 gray plastic wheels, crimped axles.

15-B   Atlantic Tractor Super   2-5/8"   1959
Orange body, silver trim on grille, with tow hook, spare wheel behind cab on body.
1. Large gray plastic wheels, crimped axles.
2. Large gray plastic wheels, rounded axles.
3. Large black plastic wheels, rounded axles.

15-C   Refuse Truck   2½"   1963
Blue body & chassis, gray dumper with opening door, 6 black plastic wheels, with & without silver trim, with & without brace between gas tanks, thick or thin rear door hinges, square cut or rounded off decal, with & without small hole in front of dumper body.
1. Large wheels, knobby treads, no dumper hole, no brace between gas tanks, thin rear hinge, full decal.
2. Same as 1, with dumper hole.
3. Same as 1, but fine treads and with dumper hole.
4. Small wheels, fine treads, no dumper hole, with brace between gas tanks, thin rear hinge, full decal.
5. Same as 4, thick rear hinge.
6. Same as 5, square decal.
7. Same as 5, square label.

15-D   Volkswagon 1500 Saloon   2-7/8"   1968
Off white body in various shades, ivory interior, clear windows, with tow hook, black number '137' (small or large) on doors, silver hubs, black plastic tires. Model changed to Superfast wheels.
1. Decals on doors.
2. Labels on doors.

15-E   Volkswagon 1500 Saloon   3"   1970
Clear windows, ivory interior & tow hook, metal baseplate & headlights, red decal on front bumper, black thick or thin numbered labels on sides '137', five spoke thin wheels.
1. Off white body, decals on side doors.
2. Off white body, labels on side doors.
3. Cream body, labels on side doors.
4. Metallic red body.
5. Metallic red body, split rear bumper.
6. Metallic red body, split rear bumper, 'sun burst' front bumper.
7. Same as 3, cream body, decals on side doors.
8. Off white body, split rear bumper, 'sun burst' front bumper, black "137" on white labels on side doors. (Sold in Japan in special black box numbered J-6 also) (TP-6)

15-F   Fork Lift Truck   2½"   1972
Red body, yellow hoist, gray plastic forks in various shades, a black steering wheel & baseplate, five spoke wide rear wheels, clover leaf spoked front wheels, yellow/red/ & black labels on sides. Fork of fork lift may be found in light or dark gray plastic.
1. Horse on label faces front.
2. Horse on label faces rear.
3. Unpainted metal baseplate.
4. Green painted baseplate.
5. Charcoal painted baseplate.
6. Black painted baseplate, no Pat. No., small multi-spoke rear wheels, large wide clover leaf front wheels.
7. Black painted baseplate, no Pat.No., small multi-spoke rear wheels, large wide multi-spoke front wheels.
8. Unpainted metal baseplate no Pat. No., small multi-spoke rear wheels, large wide multi-spoke front wheels.
9. Unpainted metal baseplate, no patent number, unpainted metal lift uprights, yellow plastic lift forks, small multi-spoke rear wheels, large wide multi-spoke front wheels.
10. Same as 7, charcoal painted baseplate.
11. Same as 9, black painted baseplate.
12. Black painted baseplate, no patent number, unpainted metal lift uprights, yellow plastic lift forks, steering wheel a part of the body casting, small multi-spoke rear wheels, large multi-spoke front wheels.
13. Same as 12, gray plastic lift forks.
14. Same as 12, long red plastic lift forks & rubber band spring motion. (K-34)
15. Same as 14, long red plastic lift and forks, unpainted metal baseplate, casting modified, vertical steering box front of driver seat has been removed. (K-40)
16. Same as 12, casting modified, vertical steering box front of driver seat has been removed.

17. Same as 16, casting modified, vertical steering box front of driver seat has been removed, unpainted metal baseplate.

15-G   Hi Ho Silver   2½"   1971
Metallic pearl gray body, flat black painted metal baseplate, bumpers and headlights, chrome plated plastic rear engine and air scoop, red tempa "HI HO SILVER" on trunk lid front of car, red tempa sheriff's hat on side doors, black tempa over entire roof with pearl gray "31", small five spoke front wheels, large five spoke rear wheels, "Made In Hong Kong" on baseplate. (formerly SF31-2)
1. Clear plastic windows, red plastic interior.

16-A   Atlantic Trailer   3-1/8"   1956
Tan body, movable rear ramp, 6 metal wheels, crimped axles, tan tow bar.
1. No supports inside rear ramp.
2. With supports inside ramp.

16-B   Atlantic Trailer   3¼"   1957
Ridged ramp, front tow bar, 8 plastic wheels with knobby treads on 4 axles.
1. Tan body, tan tow bar, gray wheels.
2. Orange body, orange tow bar, gray wheels.
3. Same as 2, black tow bar.
4. Same as 3, black wheels.
5. Same as 3, black wheels.
6. Same as 5, unpainted tow bar.

16-C   Scammel Mountaineer Dump Truck   3"   1964
with snow plough
Gray cab & chassis, gray dumper body, with & without open side steps, with red/white or orange/white decal on blade, with No. 16 cast beside front rivet on baseplate, or cast under cab, with & without hole in base, 6 plastic wheels with fine treads, 2 axles.
1. Gray wheels, hole in base, closed steps, red/white decal.
2. Same as 1, black wheels.
3. Same as 2, orange/white decal.
4. Same as 2, open steps.
5. Same as 3, open steps.
6. Same as 4, no hole in base.
7. Same as 6, orange/white decal.

16-D   Case Tractor Bulldozer   2½"   1969
Red body, yellow base, motor & blade, yellow removable canopy, black plastic rollers.
1. No brace support at cab, green rubber treads.
2. With brace support at cab, green rubber treads.
3. With brace support at cab, green rubber treads, bright red body.
4. Dark red body, black rubber treads.

16-E   Badger Exploration Truck   2¾"   1974
Metallic red body, silver grille, bumpers, front winch & radar scoop on roof, six wide clover leaf wheels, rolamatic action.
1. Gray plastic baseplate, dark green windows.
2. Gray plastic baseplate, dark green windows, small tail lights.
3. Gray plastic baseplate, two braces in front forming tow box (back of winch) dark green windows, small tail lights.
4. Gray plastic baseplate, two braces in front forming tow box, dark green windows, large tail lights.
5. Gray plastic baseplate, dark green windows, cream radar antenna, (unplated radar antenna) the baseplate on this model is made of a glossier and light gray plastic than the original model, a small portion of the baseplate around the rivet back of the front axle and extending to the front axle is slightly raised.
6. Military olive drab, (almost dark brown) unpainted metal baseplate and grille, gray plastic insert on baseplate, light yellow radar antenna, six wide clover leaf wheels, no hub caps. (Military carry case)
7. Military olive green, unpainted metal baseplate and grille, gray plastic insert on baseplate, light yellow radar antenna, six wide clover leaf wheels, no hub caps. (TP-14)
8. Military olive green, unpainted metal baseplate and grille, dark gray insert plastic on baseplate, light yellow radar antenna, six

wide clover leaf wheels, no hub caps. Pat. App. 12174/72 replaced by Pat. No. 1424808. (TP-14)

9. Metallic red body, unpainted metal baseplate grille, dark gray plastic insert on baseplate, light yellow radar antenna, six wide cloverleaf wheels, Pat. No. on base.
10. Same as 9, black plastic insert on baseplate.
11. Same as 9, dark gray plastic insert, light blueish green plastic windows.
12. Same as 10, black plastic insert, light blueish green plastic windows.
13. Same as 9, redesigned black plastic insert on baseplate, (the word "Rolomatic" on front axle cover, "Lesney" on first rear axle cover and "England" on last one).
14. Same as 9, redesigned dark gray plastic insert on baseplate.
15. Same as 14, redesigned dark gray plastic insert on baseplate, black plastic radar antenna.
16. Same as 13, redisgned black plastic insert on baseplate, ivory radar plastic radar antenna.
17. Same as 14, redesigned dark gray plastic insert on baseplate, ivory plastic radar antenna.
18. Same as 15, redesigned dark gray plastic insert on baseplate, black plastic radar antenna, light blueish green tinted plastic windows.
19. Same as 13, redesigned black plastic insert on baseplate, black plastic radar antenna, dark green plastic windows.
20. Same as 15, redesigned light gray plastic insert on baseplate, black plastic radar antenna, dark green plastic windows.
21. Same as 19, redesigned black plastic insert on baseplate, black plastic antenna, light blueish green plastic windows.
22. Same as 15, redesigned dark gray plastic insert on baseplate, black plastic radar antenna, light blueish/green plastic windowc.
23. Same as 10, black plastic insert on baseplate (old insert), ivory plastic antenna.
24. Metallic red body, unpainted metal baseplate, bumpers and grille, black plastic inserts on baseplate, black plastic radar antenna, purple tinted plastic windows, wide clover leaf wheels.

16-F Pontiac   3''   1979
Metallic light gold body, unpainted metal baseplate, headlights and rear bumper, red plastic interior and rear panel, multi-spoke wide wheels.
1. Clear plastic windows, brown, tan and yellow firebird on tan background label on hood.
2. Same as 1, clear plastic windows, light chocolate brown, tan and yellow firebird on goldish green background label on hood.
3. Metallic greenish gold body, unpainted metal baseplate, headlights and rear bumper, red plastic interior and rear panel, clear plastic windows, light chocolate brown, tan and yellow firebird on goldish green background label on hood, multi-spoke wheels.
4. Same as 3, five spoke accent wheels.
5. Dark gold body, unpainted metal baseplate, headlights and rear bumper, red plastic interior and rear panel, clear plastic windows, light chocolate brown, tan and yellow firebird on goldish green background label on hood, multi-spoke wheels.

16-G Pontiac Trans Am   1982
White body, red interior, clear windows, blue decal of eagle with open wings on hood.

17-A Bedford Removals Van   2-1/8''   1956
No number cast, radiator cast to front bumper, peaked roof, gold or silver grille, "MATCHBOX REMOVALS SERVICE" decal in white or outlined in black, rear window cast in cab through rear body, crimped axles.
1. Maroon body, gold grille, metal wheels, white decal.
2. Blue body, silver grille, metal wheels, white decal.
3. Same as 2, but green body.
4. Same as 3, but decal outlined.
5. Same as 4, but gray wheels.

17-B Austin Taxi Cab   2¼''   1960
Maroon body, comes in various shades which appear to be maroon, dark maroon, or dark red, silver grille & bumpers, tan driver, No. 17 cast one baseplate, rounded axles.

1. Dark gray wheels, light gray interior and baseplate.
2. Light gray wheels, light gray interior and baseplate.
3. Silver wheels, light gray interior and baseplate.
4. Silver wheels, pale light gray interior and baseplate.

17-C Hoveringham Tipper   2-7/8''   1963
Red body & chassis, orange dumper, with & without silver grille, with & without plastic springs under front & 3rd axle, with & without front axle support, with & without hole under 3rd axle on baseplate, 8 black plastic wheels, "HOVERINGHAM" decals on sides of tipper.
1. Black baseplate, two tinted green springs, no front axle support, no third axle support.
2. Same as 1, but two white plastic springs.
3. Same as 2, but red baseplate.
4. Red baseplate, one white plastic spring, no front axle support, with third axle support.
5. Red baseplate, no springs, pin point front axle support, with third axle support.
6. Same as 5, but peaked front axle support.

17-D Horse Box, Ergomatic Cab   1969
Red cab & chassis, green plastic box, gray side door, silver plastic grille & half base, with tow slot, 2 axles, 4 black plastic wheels, blue tinted windows.
1. No reinforcement under side door on baseplate.
2. Reinforcement under side door on baseplate.

17-E Horse Box   2¾''   1970
Blue tinted windows, five spoke thin wheels, white plastic horses inside box, silver grille and front baseplate.
1. Red cab & chassis, green box with gray side door.
2. Mustard cab & chassis, green box with gray door.
3. Red/orange cab & chassis, green box with gray door.
4. Red/orange cab & chassis, light tannish/gray box with light brown side door.
5. Light orange cab & chassis, light tannish/gray box with light brown side door.

17-F Londoner Bus   3''   1972
Red body, white interior, five spoke wide wheels, black baseplate, labels on sides.
1. "Swinging London-Carnaby Street" labels, die cast doors No. 1 & 2.
2. "Berger Paints" label, paint brush faces left, die cast doors No. 1 & 2.
3. "Berger Paints" label, paint brush faces right, die cast doors No. 1 & 2.
4. Unpainted metal baseplate, die cast doors No. 1 & 2.
5. Londoner Bus, red, black baseplate, "Ty-Phoo Puts the T in Britain" labels. "Ty-Phoo" in white lettering on black background. The remainder of the lettering in white is on a blue background with the British flag at the end.
6. "Berger Paints" label, die cast doors No. 1 & 2, black baseplate, long axle braces over axle channels on baseplate.
7. No label, die cast doors No. 1 & 2, black baseplate, long axle braces.
8. New "Swinging London-Carnaby Street" labels, die cast doors No. 1 & 2, black baseplate, long axle braces.
9. New "Swinging London Carnaby Street" labels, die cast doors No. 1 & 2, black baseplate, no braces.
10. New "Swinging London Carnaby Street" label, die cast doors No. 1 & 2, charcoal gray painted baseplate, long axle braces.
11. "ESSO EXTRA PETROL" labels, die cast doors, 1 & 2, black painted baseplate, long axle braces.
12. 'Berger Paints' labels, die cast doors 1 & 2, black painted baseplate long axle braces, wide axle covers, multi-spoke wide wheels.
13. 'Berger Paints' labels with rounded corners, black painted baseplate, long axle braces, wide axle covers, multi-spoke wide wheels.
14. Orange body, black on white 'JACOB's The Biscuit Makers' round side labels, black painted baseplate with long axle braces and wide axle covers, multi-spoke wide wheels, die cast doors 1 & 2.

15. "Berger Paints" side labels with round corners, charcoal gray painted baseplate, long axle braces, wide axle covers, multi-spoke wide wheels.
16. "Berger Paints" side labels with round corners, unpainted metal baseplate, long axle braces, wide axle covers, multi-spoke wide wheels.
17. Silver gray body, red interior, blue, white, red and yellow "Silver Jubilee" labels, unpainted metal baseplate, multi-spoke wide wheels.
18. Silver gray body, red interior, blue, white, red and yellow "Silver Jubilee" labels, charcoal gray painted baseplate, multi-spoke wide wheels.
19. Silver gray body, red plastic interior, "Berger Paints" rounded corners side labels, charcoal gray painted baseplate, multi-spoke wide wheels.
20. Same as 8, unpainted metal baseplate, long axle braces over axle channels on baseplate, two screw-in mounts on baseplate. (from fancy goods ashtray).
21. Same as 15, "BERGER PAINTS" side labels with square corners.
22. Light blue body, charcoal painted baseplate, blue on white "Deutschlands Autopartner No. 1" and "ARAL" logo round corner side labels, white interior, multi-spoke wide wheels. (Sold in Germany).
23. Same as 22, flat black painted metal baseplate, 17-B (22) and (23), may be found with logo on label either at front or rear of bus.
24. Same as 15, flat black painted metal baseplate.
25. Same as 22, glossy black painted metal baseplate, yellow and red "MATCHBOX" logo, yellow, orange and red stripes, black "1953-1978" on white side labels with round corners: This is the "MATCHBOX" Silver Anniversary.
26. Same as 25, light blue body, glossy black painted baseplate. "MATCHBOX" Silver Anniversary label each side.
27. Same as 25, light blue body, charcoal painted baseplate "MATCH-BOX" Silver Anniversary label each side.
28. Same as 15, glossy black painted metal baseplate, "BERGER PAINTS" labels, colored stripes on label cover full width.
29. Same as 15, metallic brown painted metal baseplate.
30. Same as 14, red body, glossy black painted baseplate, black and white "JACOB's the Biscuit Maker" side labels, multi-spoke wide wheels.
31. Same as 25, light blue body, metallic brown painted baseplate, "MATCHBOX" Silver Anniversary' labels each side.
32. Same as 15, glossy black painted baseplate, multi-color on yellow side labels, on right side "BISTO — THE BISTO BUS" and two young faces, on the other side "YOU CAN'T KID A BISTO KID" and two young faces. (Found in a small toy shop in the U.K. as a regular merchandise).
33. Same as 21, "BERGER PAINTS" side labels with square corners, black plastic baseplate.
34. Same as 33, "BERGER PAINTS" side labels with rounded corners, black plastic baseplate.
35. Red body, white plastic interior, black plastic baseplate, multi-color on yellow side labels, on right side "BISTO — THE BISTO BUS" and two faces on left side "YOU CAN'T KID A BISTO KID" and two young faces, multi-spoke wide wheels.

17-G Londoner Bus   1982
1. (Chesterfield label), green body, 1882.
2. **Blue body and white top, greek writing.**
3. Laker Skytrain label, 1982

18-A Caterpillar D8 Bulldozer   1-7/8''   1956
Yellow body and driver, red blade & side supports, no number cast, with and without black hat on driver, metal rollers, crimped axles, green rubber treads.

18-B Caterpillar Bulldozer   2''   1958
Yellow body & driver, yellow blade, no number cast on body, No. 18 cast on back of blade, metal rollers, crimped axles, green rubber treads.

1. No. 8 cast inside body.
2. No. 18 cast inside body.

18-C Caterpillar Bulldozer   2¼"   1961
Yellow body with driver, rounded axles, green rubber treads.
1. Metal rollers, no number showing.
2. Metal rollers, No. 18 inside base.
3. Silver plastic rollers, no number showing.
4. Black plastic rollers, no number showing.

18-D Caterpillar Crawler Bulldozer   2-3/8"   1964
Yellow body, no driver, rounded axles, green rubber treads, number 18
cast on rear of baseplate.
1. Silver plastic rollers, large smoke stack.
2. Black plastic rollers, large smoke stack.
3. Black plastic rollers, small smoke stack, hole in front baseplate.

18-E Field Car   2-5/8"   1969
Yellow body, tan plastic roof, ivory interior & tow hook, spare tire
mounted on rear of body, black plastic tires.
1. Black base & grille, red wheels.
2. Metal unpainted base & grille, red wheels.
3. Metal unpainted base & grille, green wheels. Model changed to
   Superfast wheels.

18-F Field Car   2-5/8"   1970
Yellow body, ivory interior & tow hook, tan roof, black spare tire
mounted at rear, metal baseplate. Most models come with & without
an imprint on the rear shelf interior.
1. No 'Pat App' on baseplate at bottom of lettering, five spoke wide
   wheels.
2. No 'Pat App' on baseplate at bottom of lettering, four spoke thin
   wheels.
3. 'Pat. App.' on baseplate, five spoke wide wheels.
4. 'Pat. App.' on baseplate, four spoke thin wheels.
5. 'Pat. App.' on baseplate, four spoke wide wheels.
6. 'Pat. App.' on baseplate, four spoke wide wheels, inside roof
   brace filled in.
7. 'Pat. App.' on baseplate, four spoke wide wheels, inside roof
   brace filled in, silver/gray baseplate.
8. Military olive green body, black painted baseplate, black plastic
   interior and tow hook, white "A" on red and blue square side
   labels, four spoke wide wheels no hub caps, filled roof brace with
   raised triangles, no number 18 on base. (TP-12)
9. Same as 8, smooth filled roof brace. (TP-12)
10. Same as 9, smooth filled roof braces, small five spoke wide wheels,
    no hub caps. (TP-12)
11. Military olive drab body (very dark, almost brown), black painted
    baseplate, black plastic interior and tow hook, white "A" on red
    and blue square side labels, small five spoke wide wheels, no hub
    caps, smooth filled roof braces, no number 18 on base. (Found in
    military carry case).
12. Military olive green body, black painted baseplate, black plastic
    interior and tow hook, No. 3 on red/yellow/red stripe and white
    "RA391" letters on olive green background label on hood, smooth
    filled roof braces, small five spoke wide wheels, no number
    18 on base. (TP-12)
13. Same as 12, four spoke wide wheels, no hub caps. (TP-12)
14. Military olive drab, black painted baseplate, black plastic interior
    and tow hook, white "A" on red and blue square side labels, large
    four spoke wide wheels, no hub caps, filled roof braces with
    raised triangles, no number 18 on base. (TP-12)
15. Orange body, black painted baseplate, black plastic roof interior
    and tow hook, smooth filled roof braces, black and white check-
    ered label on hood, large four spoke wide wheels. (TP-8)
16. White body, black painted baseplate, black plastic roof, interior
    and tow hook, smooth filled roof braces, black and white check-
    ered label on hood, large four spoke wide wheels. (TP-8)
17. Same as 8, filled roof braces, raised triangles, small five spoke wide
    wheels, no hub caps.
18. Same as 15, five spoke wide slicks. (TP-8)

19. Same as 15, large four spoke, wide wheels, no hub caps. (TP-8)
20. Same as 12, textured tan plastic roof. (TP-12)
21. Same as 15, textured black plastic roof.
22. Metallic red body, black painted metal baseplate: textured tan
    plastic roof, black plastic interior and tow hook, black and red
    "CHAMPION" logo, black "GOOD YEAR" logo and large black
    '44' on white and yellow label on hood, large four spoke wide
    wheels. (TP-9)
23. Same as 15, textured black plastic roof, large four spoke wide
    wheels, no hub caps.
24. Same as 22, textured tan plastic roof, large four spoke wide
    wheels, no hub caps. (TP-9)
25. Metallic red body, silver gray painted metal baseplate, no number
    18 on baseplate, textured tan plastic roof, black plastic interior
    and tow hook, black and white checkered label on hood, large
    four spoke wide wheels. (TP-9)
26. Dark orange body, dull black painted metal baseplate, no number
    18 on baseplate, textured black plastic roof, black plastic interior
    and tow hook, all tempa print designs, large black '179' on doors,
    orange 'AC FILTERS' on black stripe above front wheel wells,
    black 'SCOUT RACING TEAM' above rear wheel wells, black
    "HIGH PERFORMANCE" below side doors, large four spoke wide
    wheels. (LEM)
27. Same as 15, textured black plastic roof, silver gray painted base-
    plate, large four spoke wide wheels. (TP-8).
28. Same as 26, silver gray painted metal baseplate, textured black
    plastic roof. (LEM)
29. Same as 28, silver gray painted metal baseplate, textured tan
    plastic roof. (LEM)
30. Same as 28, silver gray painted metal baseplate, textured black
    plastic roof, five spoke wide wheels. (LEM)
31. Dark orange body, flat black painted metal baseplate and grille, no
    number 18 on baseplate, textured black plastic roof, black plastic
    interior and tow hook, large four spoke wide wheels. (TP-8)
32. Metallic red body, silver gray painted metal baseplate, textured
    dark tan plastic roof, black plastic interior and tow hook, black
    and red "CHAMPION" logo, black "GOOD YEAR" logo and large
    '44' on white and yellow label on hood, large four spoke wide
    wheels, no hub caps. (TP-9)
33. Same as 32, textured light tan plastic roof, white and black check-
    ered flag label on hood, large four spoke wide wheels, no hub
    caps. (TP-9)

18-G Hondarora Motorcycle   2-3/8"   1975
Red frame and rear fenders, silver plastic handlebars, front fender and
suspension, silver plastic engine and exhaust pipes, black plastic seat,
wire wheels and black tires.
1. Purple label with orange border and white "honda" lettering on
   each side of gas tank.
2. Purple label, orange border and white "Honda" each side of gas
   tank, long frame connector (to front wheel assembly), filled in
   triangle (frame near foot rest right side), no block and hollow
   space top of front fender, silver handlebar and front wheel
   assembly.
3. Black handlebar and front wheel assembly. May be found without
   labels.
4. Orange frame, black handlebar and front assembly. This variation
   is found in the new K-6 Transporter.
5. Military olive green frame, black engine and exhaust pipes, black
   handlebar and front assembly. (TP-11)
6. Military olive drab frame, black engine and exhaust pipes, black
   plastic handlebar and front assembly. (TP-11)
7. Same as 3, black handlebar and front wheel assembly, thin black
   plastic seat (only half as thick over rear mud guard).
8. Same as 5, thin black plastic seat. (TP-11)
9. Same as 7, black plastic handlebars and front wheel assembly, thin
   seat, black plastic engine and exhaust pipes.
10. Same as 7, black plastic handlebars and front wheel assembly, thin

seat, no label on gas tank, chrome plated engine and exhaust pipes,
black plastic one piece tire and mag wheels with five spokes.
11. Same as 7, black plastic handlebars and front wheel assembly, thin
    seat, no label on gas tank, black plastic engine and exhaust pipes,
    black plastic one piece tire and mag wheel with five spokes.
12. Metallic green frame and rear fender, black plastic handlebars,
    front wheel assembly and front fender, black plastic seat, wide
    spoke mag wheels and tires, chrome plated plastic engine and
    exhaust pipes.
13. Metallic green frame and rear fenders, black plastic handlebars,
    front wheel assembly, front fender, seat, wide spoke mag wheels
    and tires, black plastic engine and exhaust pipes.
14. Yellow frame and rear fender, black plastic handlebars, mag wheels
    and tires, with brown rider.

19-A MG Sports Car (midget)   2"   1956
Silver grille & headlights, tan driver, red painted seats, spare tire mounted on rear, no number cast on body.
1. Cream body, metal wheels, crimped axles.
2. White body, metal wheels, crimped axles.

19-B MGA Sports Car   2¼"   1958
Color of body varies from white/off white to light creamish colors, silver
or gold grilles, tan driver, with or without steering post of steering
wheel, with/without red taillights.
1. Metal wheels, crimped axles, short steering post, silver grille.
2. Same as 1, gray wheels.
3. Same as 2, gold grille.
4. Same as 2, no steering post, silver grille.
5. Same as 3, rounded axles.
6. Same as 5, silver wheels.

19-C Aston Martin Racing Car   2½"   1961
Metallic green (various shades), metal steering wheel & wire wheels,
black plastic tires, white circle decal with black numbers.
1. Gray driver, decal 52.
2. Gray driver, decal 41.
3. Gray driver, decal 5.
4. Gray driver, decal 19.
5. White driver, decal 19.
6. White driver, decal 3.

19-D Lotus Racing Car   2¾"   1966
White driver & steering post, unpainted metal rear motor & exhaust
pipes, white circle number '3' decal or label on sides, white circle number
'3' on front of hood with yellow stripe, yellow plastic hubs, small front
tire, large rear tire. The common issued model was the orange body
model. The green model was issued with the orange one in gift sets
G-4 Racetrack and others.
1. Orange body, decal.
2. Green body, decal.
3. Orange body, label.
4. Green body, label.

19-E Lotus Racing Car   2¾"   1970
Metallic purple, white driver, metal rear motor & exhaust pipes &
baseplate, five spoke wide wheels with clover leaf design.
1. No. 3 label on sides, No. 3 label on hood on yellow stripe.

19-F Road Dragster   2-7/8"   1970
Ivory interior, silver plastic motor, metal baseplate & grille, clear windows, five spoke front wheels, large clover leaf rear wheels, black No. 8
label on hood & trunk inside yellow/orange circle.
1. Label run horizontally, red body, thick rim wide rear wheels.
2. Label run vertically, red body, thick rim wide rear wheels.
3. Labels run vertical, red/orange body.
4. Red/orange body, silver/gray baseplate.
5. Red/orange body, unpainted base, No. 8 label on trunk only.
6. Red/orange body, unpainted metal baseplate, black and red on white
   round Scorpion labels front & back.
7. Red/orange body, silver/gray painted baseplate, black and red on
   white round scorpion labels front and rear.
8. Red/orange body, unpainted metal baseplate, no labels.

9. Metallic purple body, unpainted metal baseplate, black No. 8 inside yellow and orange circles on hood and trunk.
10. Red orange body, unpainted metal baseplate, black No. 8 inside yellow and orange circles on hood and trunk, small five spoke front wheels (same as 5-A), large clover leaf rear wheels.
11. Same as 10, white interior.
12. Metallic purple body, unpainted metal baseplate, black No. 8 inside yellow and orange circles on hood and trunk, five spoke front wheels, large clover leaf rear wheels, white interior.
13. Now found in Multi-pack (MP-1) without label.
14. Same as 12, small five spoke front wheels (same as 5-A).
15. Metallic red body, unpainted metal baseplate, black No. 8 inside yellow and orange circles on label on hood & trunk, five spoke front wheels, large clover leaf rear wheels, ivory interior.
16. Metallic purple body, unpainted metal baseplate, black & red on white Scorpion label on hood and trunk, five spoke front wheels, large clover leaf rear wheels, ivory interior.

19-G Cement Truck   3''   1976
Red body, mustard yellow with red stripes plastic barrel, black plastic barrel support arms, large wide five spoke reverse accent wheels. Black or red design on barrel of model (2) or (3) may be found slanted in two directions.
1. Green tinted windows, unpainted metal baseplate and grille, mustard yellow plastic barrel with red stripes, steps on side doors extend to lower edge of door.
2. Same as 1, 3 steps on door end 3/32'' from lower edge of door.
3. Same as 3, mustard yellow plastic barrel with black stripes.
4. Same as 3, no stripe on plastic barrel.
5. Same as 2, light blueish green plastic windows.
6. Same as 2, green tinted windows, red stripes on light gray plastic barrel.
7. Same as 6, blueish/green plastic windows.
8. Same as 2, mustard yellow plastic barrel with red stripes, no windows, with a redesigned rear wheel well, where the rear cut-out has been rounded.
9. Same as 6, gray plastic barrel with red stripes, no window, with a redesigned rear wheel well, where the rear cut-out has been rounded.
10. Same as 2, mustard yellow plastic barrel with red stripes, light purple plastic windows, with a redesigned rear wheel well, where the rear cut-out has been rounded.
11. Red body, mustard yellow plastic barrel with red stripes, black plastic barrel support arms, unpainted metal baseplate, green tinted plastic windows, redesigned wheel wells, large five spoke reverse accent wheels.
12. Same as 11, green tinted plastic windows, bright yellow plastic barrel with red stripes.
13. Same as 11, light purple plastic windows, bright yellow plastic barrel with red stripes.
14. Same as 11, green tinted plastic windows, gray plastic barrel with red stripes.
15. Red body, gray plastic barrel with red stripes, black plastic barrel support arms, unpainted metal baseplate, front bumper and grille, purple tinted plastic windows, redesigned wheel wells, large five spoke reverse accent wheels.
16. Same as 15, bright yellow plastic barrel with red stripes, purple tinted plastic windows.

19-H Peterbilt Cement Truck   1982
Green body with orange barrel, decal ''Big Pete'' on front hood, silver plastic grille and dual high exhaust pipes.

20-A Stake Truck   2-3/8''   1956
Silver or gold trim on front grille and side gas tanks, ribbed bed, no number cast on body, crimped axles.
1. Maroon body, metal wheels, gold grille, gold side tanks.
2. Same as 1, but silver grille and silver side tanks.
3. Same as 2, but dark red body.

4. Same as 2, but maroon color and gray wheels.
5. Same as 2, but gray wheels and dark red side tanks.

20-B ERF 686 Truck   2-5/8''   1959
Dark blue body, silver radiator, headlights & bumper, No. 20 cast on black base, 8 plastic wheels on 4 axles, ''Ever Ready For Life'' decal on sides of body, rounded axles except 1, plastic wheels.
1. Crimped axles, small dark gray wheels.
2. Rounded axles, small dark gray wheels.
3. Small light gray wheels.
4. Large dark gray wheels.
5. Large light gray wheels.
6. Small silver wheels.
7. Small black wheels.

20-C Chevrolet Impala Taxi Cab   3''   1965
Orange/yellow or bright yellow body, ivory or red interior & driver, red 'TAXI' decal or label on hood, clear windows, with tow slot on front baseplate, with tow hook. The background of the decals come in orange, orange/yellow, all yellow, etc., and make up a number of variations although only majors are being listed.
1. Orange/yellow body, large gray wheels, ivory interior, unpainted metal baseplate, red decal.
2. Same as 1, but small black wheels.
3. Same as 2, but baseplate painted light gray.
4. Same as 2, but red interior and yellow label.
5. Bright yellow body, small black wheels, ivory interior, unpainted metal baseplate, orange label.
6. Same as 5, but red interior.
7. Same as 6, but yellow label.

20-D Lamborghini Marzel   2¾''   1969
Amber windows, ivory interior, metal baseplate & grille. All models come with curved or square hood design.
1. Metallic dark red, five spoke thin wheels.
2. Metallic dark red, five spoke thin wheels, No. 2 label on hood, Avon labels on sides, rear of car.
3. Pinkish/salmon body, five spoke thin wheels.
4. Pinkish/salmon body, five spoke thin wheels, No. 2 label on hood, Avon labels on sides, rear of car.
5. Yellowish/green body, five spoke wide wheels, wide wheel wells, (produced for the European market as ''Broomstick'' models).
6. Pinkish/salmon body, five spoke wide wheels, wide wheel wells.
7. Pinkish/salmon body, five spoke wide wheels, wide wheel wells, No. 2 label on hood, Avon labels on sides, rear of car.
8. Pinkish/salmon body, five spoke wide wheels, wide wheel wells, silver/gray painted baseplate.
9. Pinkish/salmon body, five spoke wide wheels, wide wheel wells, silver/gray painted baseplate, light amber windows.
10. Pinkish/salmon body, five spoke wide wheels, wide wheel wells, unpainted metal baseplate, light amber windows.
11. Pinkish/salmon body, five spoke wide wheels, wide wheel wells, unpainted metal baseplate, wide raised axle cover on baseplate, amber windows.
12. Silver/gray painted baseplate, wide raised axle cover on baseplate, amber windows.

20-E Police Patrol   2-7/8''   1975
White body, unpainted metal baseplate, clover leaf slicks, black 'Police' on long orange stripe label on sides, orange interior and light, 'Rolamatic'.
1. Clear domelight, frosted windows, black 'POLICE' 15/16'' long on orange stripe label each side.
2. Light blue tinted domelight, light blue tinted frosted windows, black 'POLICE' 15/16'' long on orange strip label each side.
3. Clear domelight, frosted windows, black 'POLICE' 11/16'' long on thin orange strip label each side.
4. Military olive green body, unpainted metal baseplate and grille, black 'Police' on red and yellow arrow shaped side labels, clear dome light, frosted windows, orange interior, clover leaf wheels, no hub caps. (TP-12)
5. Same as 4, clover leaf wheels with hub caps. (TP-12)

6. Orange body, unpainted metal baseplate, clover leaf slicks, 'Site Engineer' white and red chevrons side labels, orange interior and light, clear domelight, frosted windows.
7. Military olive green body, unpainted metal baseplate and grille, ''AMBULANCE'' and Red Cross on white rectangular side labels, clear domelight, frosted windows, orange interior, small five spoke slick wheels, no hub caps, (found in military carry case).
8. White body, unpainted metal baseplate and grille, 'POLICE' side labels, clear domelight, frosted windows, orange interior, small five spoke slicks.
9. Military olive green body, unpainted metal baseplate and grille, 'POLICE' side labels, clear domelight, frosted windows, orange interior, small five spoke slicks, no hub caps. (TP-12)
10. Military olive drab, (very dark, almost brown), unpainted metal baseplate and grille, ''AMBULANCE'' and Red Cross on white rectangular labels, clear domelight, frosted windows, orange interior, small five spoke slicks, no hub caps, (Found in Sears military set)
11. White body, unpainted metal baseplate, and grille 'POLICE' side labels, clear domelight, frosted windows, orange interior, clover leaf slicks, Pat. Appr. 12174/70 replaced by No. 1424808.
12. Same as 6, Pat. No. 1424808 on base.
13. Military olive green body, Pat. No. 1424808 on unpainted metal baseplate and grille, 'AMBULANCE' and red cross on white rectangular side labels, clear domelight, frosted windows, orange interior clover leaf wheels, no hub caps.
14. Orange body, Pat. No. 1424808 on unpainted baseplate, five spoke wide wheels, no hub caps, 'Site engineer' and white and red chevrons side labels, orange interior and light, clear domelight, frosted windows. (G-2)
15. Same as 5, Pat. No. 1424808 on unpainted baseplate.
16. Same as 5, Pat. No. 1424808 on unpainted metal baseplate.
17. Same as 9, clover leaf wheels, no hub caps.
18. Same as 9, black 'POLICE' on red and yellow arrow shaped side labels, clover leaf wheels, no hub caps.
19. Same as 12, light blue tinted frosted plastic windows and dome light.
20. Same as 12, orange body, black ''POLICE'' on orange stripe side labels.
21. Same as 14, ''Site Engineer'' with white and red chevrons side labels.
22. Same as 14, small five spoke wheels.
23. Same as 11, clover leaf slicks, no hub caps.
24. Same as 11, light blue tinted frosted plastic windows and dome light.
25. Same as 11, amber/orange frosted plastic windows and dome light.
26. White body, unpainted metal baseplate and grille, black ''POLICE'' on orange stripe side labels, clear frosted plastic windows and dome on roof, blue plastic interior rear and dome light, clover leaf slicks.
27. Same as 26, blue plastic interior rear and dome light, gray tinted frosted plastic windows and dome on roof.
28. Same as 26, blue plastic interior rear and dome light, clear frosted plastic windows and dome on roof, flat black painted metal baseplate and grille.
29. White body, unpainted metal baseplate and grille, black ''POLICE'' on orange stripe side labels, clear frosted plastic windows and dome on roof, orange plastic interior rear and blue plastic dome light, clover leaf slicks.
30. Same as 29, orange plastic interior rear and blue plastic dome light, gray tinted frosted plastic windows and dome on roof.
31. Same as 29, orange plastic interior rear and blue plastic dome light, clear frosted plastic windows and dome on roof, black ''POLICE'' on white stripe side labels.
32. Same as 29, orange plastic interior rear and blue plastic dome light, gray tinted frosted plastic windows and dome on roof, black ''POLICE'' on white stripe side labels.
33. White body, unpainted metal baseplate and grille, black ''POLICE''

on orange stripe side labels, clear frosted plastic windows and dome on roof, cream plastic interior rear and lemon yellow plastic dome light, clover leaf slicks.

34. Same as 33, orange plastic interior rear and lemon yellow plastic dome light, clear frosted plastic windows and dome on roof, black "POLICE" on white stripe side labels.

35. Same as 33, orange plastic interior rear and lemon yellow plastic dome light, gray tinted frosted plastic windows and dome on roof, black "POLICE" on white stripe side labels.

36. White body, unpainted metal baseplate and grille, black "POLICE" on orange stripe side labels, clear frosted plastic windows and dome on rear, blue plastic interior rear and lemon yellow plastic dome light, clover leaf slicks.

37. Same as 36, blue plastic interior rear and lemon yellow plastic dome light, gray tinted frosted plastic windows and dome on roof.

38. Same as 36, blue plastic interior rear and lemon yellow plastic dome light, clear frosted plastic windows and dome on roof, black "POLICE" on white stripe side labels.

39. White body, flat black painted baseplate and grille, black "POLICE" on orange side labels, clear frosted plastic windows and dome on roof, orange plastic interior rear and blue plastic dome light, clover leaf wheels.

40. White body, unpainted metal baseplate and grille, black "POLICE" on orange stripe side labels, gray tinted frosted plastic windows and dome light on roof, orange plastic interior rear and dome lights, clover leaf wheels.

41. White body, charcoal brown painted metal baseplate and grille, side labels with black "POLICE" and shield on yellow stripe bordered by red thin stripes, above three rows of black and white checkers, clear frosted windows and dome on roof, blue plastic interior rear and dome light, clover leaf wheels.

42. Same as 41, glossy black painted metal baseplate and grille, clear frosted plastic windows and dome on roof, blue plastic interior rear and dome light.

43. Same as 26, blue plastic interior rear and dome light, clear frosted plastic windows and dome on roof, glossy black painted metal baseplate and grille.

44. Blue body, orange plastic interior rear and dome on roof, unpainted metal baseplate and grille, dark blue "SECURITY—RALLYE PARIS—DAKAR 81" on yellow side labels, gray tinted frosted windows and dome on roof, clover leaf wheels.

45. White body, blue plastic interior rear and dome light, unpainted metal baseplate and grille, blue "COUNTY SHERIFF" and white star on blue on white side labels, blue roof tempa imprint with white "017", blue stripes and circle containing a white star and blue "SHERIFF" tempa imprint on hood, clear frosted windows and dome on roof, cloverleaf wheels.

46. White body, unpainted metal baseplate and grille, black "POLICE" on white stripe side labels, clear frosted plastic windows and dome on roof, blue plastic rear interior and dome light, clover leaf slicks.

47. Same as 41, flat black painted metal baseplate and grille, clear frosted plastic windows and dome on roof, blue plastic interior rear and dome light.

48. Same as 41, unpainted metal baseplate and grille, clear frosted plastic windows and dome on roof, blue plastic interior rear and dome light.

49. Same as 44, clear frosted plastic windows and dome on roof, orange plastic interior rear and dome light.

20-F Desert Dawg 4x4 Jeep 1982
White body, red top, red side stripe with white letters JEEP, clover leaf wheels, Desert Dawg decal in yellow, red and green on hood.

21-A Long Distance Coach 2¼" 1956
Light green body, black base, no number cast on body, silver grille, orange lettered decal, "London to Glasgow" on sides, metal wheels, crimped axles.

21-B Long Distance Coach 2-5/8" 1958
Green body, black base, number 21 cast on black baseplate, silver

grille, orange lettered "London to Glasgow" decal on sides.
1. Light green body, metal wheels, crimped axles.
2. Same as 1, but dark gray plastic wheels.
3. Dark green body, same as 2.
4. Same as 3, rounded axles.

21-C Commer Milk Truck 2¼" 1961
Pale green body, with clear or green tinted windows, with ivory or cream bottle load, with bottle or cow decal on doors, with clear or white decal on roof panel, with snap-in front & rear base or 2 front rivets holding base to body, with or without silver front bumpers.
1. Clear top decal, bottle decal on side, silver wheels, knobby treads, cream bottle load, snap-in baseplate. No. 1 also comes with clear or tinted windows.
2. Same as 1, but white bottle load.
3. Same as 1, but cow side decal.
4. Same as 3, but white bottle load.
5. Same as 4, but white top decal.
6. Same as 5, but white bottle load.
7. Same as 6, but with small gray wheels.
8. Same as 6, but with large gray wheels.
9. Same as 6, but with black wheels and fine treads.
10. Same as 9, but with 2 rivets in baseplate. Comes with thin or thick front bumper.

21-D Foden Concrete Truck 3" 1968
Orange/yellow body & rotating barrel & gear under body, green tinted windows, 8 black plastic wheels on 4 rounded axles, with & without reinforced braces under 3rd & 4th axles, with metal or plastic pin holding rear barrel, & with & without hole in base under 3rd axle. Model changed to Superfast wheels.
1. Metal barrel pin, no reinforcement under 3rd & 4th axles, no hole in baseplate.
2. Same as 1, but reinforced under 3rd and 4th axles.
3. Same as 1, but with plastic barrel pin.
4. Same as 3, but reinforced under 3rd and 4th axles.
5. Same as 4, but with a hole in baseplate.

21-E Foden Concrete Truck 2-7/8" 1970
Green tinted windows, green plastic baseplate, five spoke thin wheels, red chassis, pale orange revolving barrel.
1. Yellow cab, cab connects into front bumper.
2. Yellow cab, cab does not connect to bumper.
3. Bright yellow cab.
4. Bright yellow cab, dark red chassis, darker green baseplate.

21-F Road Roller 2-5/8" 1973
Yellow body, red seat, black steering wheel, black plastic rollers, blue 'flame' label on hood.
1. Red metallic rear hubs, green plastic baseplate.
2. Red plastic rear hubs. (Light & dark shades). Green plastic baseplate.
3. Black plastic rear hubs, green plastic baseplate.
4. Black plastic rear hubs, black plastic baseplate.
5. Orange-yellow body, black plastic rear hub, black plastic baseplate.
6. Orange-yellow body, black plastic rear hubs, green plastic baseplate.
7. Yellow body, black plastic rear hubs, green plastic base, rounded handles on steering bar, open slot for steering mechanism on roller frame. Now found without flame label.
8. Same as 3, black plastic rear hubs, green plastic base, closed slot for steering mechanism on roller frame, rounded handles on steering bar.

21-G Renault 5TL 2-11/16" 1978
Yellow Renault body, silver/gray painted metal baseplate, grille and bumpers, yellow plastic movable rear hatch, tan plastic interior and tow hook, small multi-spoke wheels.
1. Clear plastic windows, black tempa imprints stripes and "LE CAR" on sides.
2. Metallic dark blue body, clear windows, no tempa imprint.
3. Same as 1, flat black painted body, grille and bumpers.

4. Same as 2, flat black painted metal baseplate and bumper.
5. Metallic silver gray body, flat black painted metal baseplate, grille and bumpers, silver gray plastic moveable rear hatch, red plastic interior and tow hook, clear plastic windows.
6. Same as 5, two thin tempa print red stripes, closed at each end running from front to rear, red "A5" between stripes at rear.
7. Same as 2, silver gray painted metal baseplate, small multi-spoke wheels, no hub caps. (G-1)
8. Same as 2, silver gray painted metal baseplate, grille and bumpers, red plastic interior and tow hook.
9. Same as 3, black painted metal baseplate, grille and bumpers, red plastic interior and tow hook.
10. Same as 4, flat black painted metal baseplate and bumpers, red plastic interior and tow hook. (G-1)
11. Same as 1, yellow body, silver/gray painted metal baseplate, tan plastic interior and tow hook, amber plastic windows.
12. Same as 2, metallic blue body, silver/gray painted metal baseplate, tan plastic interior and tow hook, amber plastic windows.
13. Same as 3, yellow body, black painted metal baseplate, tan plastic interior and tow hook, amber plastic windows.
14. Same as 3, silver-black painted metal baseplate, tan plastic interior and tow hook, clear plastic windows, pale yellow plastic rear hatch.
15. Same as 1, silver gray painted baseplate, red plastic interior and tow hook.
16. Same as 2, flat black painted baseplate grille and bumpers, tan plastic interior and tow hook, amber plastic windows.
17. Same as 1, charcoal gray painted baseplate grille and bumpers, tan plastic interior and tow hook, amber plastic windows.
18. Metallic silver gray body, silver gray painted metal baseplate, grille and bumpers, silver gray moveable plastic rear hatch, tan plastic interior and tow hook, clear plastic windows.
19. Same as 1, yellow body, charcoal gray painted baseplate, grille and bumpers, tan plastic interior and tow hook, clear plastic windows.
20. Same as 2, metallic blue body, charcoal gray painted baseplate, grille and bumper, grayish/yellow plastic interior and tow hook, clear plastic windows.
21. Metallic silver gray body, silver gray painted metal baseplate, grille, and bumpers, silver gray plastic rear hatch, red plastic interior and tow hook, clear plastic windows, small multi-spoke wheels.
22. Same as 21, silver gray painted metal baseplate, two thin red tempa print stripes closed at each end and running from front to rear on each side and red "A5" between stripes at rear.
23. Metallic silver gray body, charcoal gray painted metal baseplate, grille, and bumpers, silver gray plastic rear hatch, red plastic interior and tow hook, clear plastic windows, red tempa print stripes and red tempa print "LE CAR" on each side, small multi-spoke wheels.
24. Yellow body, charcoal gray painted metal baseplate, grille and bumpers, yellow plastic rear hatch, grayish/yellow plastic interior and tow hook, clear plastic windows, black tempa print stripes and black tempa print "LE CAR" on each side, small multi-spoke wheels.
25. Same as 23, black painted metal baseplate, grille and bumpers.
26. Same as 23, charcoal gray painted metal baseplate, grille and bumpers, amber plastic windows.
27. Same as 23, glossy black painted metal baseplate, grille and bumpers, amber plastic windows.
28. Metallic silver gray body, glossy black painted metal baseplate, grille and bumpers, silver gray plastic rear hatch, red plastic interior and tow hook, clear plastic windows, small multi-spoke wheels.
29. White boyd, green decals with black "4 Renault" on hood and doors and green Renault on top. 1982.

22-A Vauxhall Sedan 2½" 1956
Dark red body, cream or off white roof, silver grille & headlights, black baseplate with tow hook, no windows, no number cast on body, metal

wheels, crimped axles, a small brace appears over the middle of the front axle with later models breaking the brace.
1. Cream roof.
2. Off white roof.

22-B Vauxhall Cresta   2-5/8''   1958
With & without silver grilles, bumpers, tail lights painted, with & without light green tinted windows, black baseplate & tow hook, knobby treads (except 12 & 13), plastic wheels, rounded axles (except 1 and 3).
1. Pinkish cream body, gray wheels, crimped axles, no windows.
2. Cream body.
3. Pinkish cream body, green windows.
4. Same as 3, but turquoise/bronze body and crimped axles.
5. Same as 3, rounded axles.
6. Same as 3, lilac/gray body.
7. Same as 6, silver wheels.
8. Same as 7, deep dark gold body.
9. Same as 7, light gold body.
10. Same as 3, bronze body.
11. Same as 10, black wheels.
12. Same as 11, fine treads.
13. Same as 12, no windows.

22-C Pontiac Gran Prix Sports Coupe   3''   1964
Body color ranges dark red to orange red, light gray interior & tow hook, clear windows, silver grille & headlights, with & without patent number on rear of baseplate, with & without license plate under front bumper, with & without tow slot behind license plate, with plastic or metal door springs, black base, 2 axles, 4 black plastic wheels. Model changed to Superfast wheels.
1. Plastic door springs, without patent number, without license plate - without tow slot.
2. Same as 1, but with patent number.
3. Metal door springs, with patent number, without license plate, without tow slot.
4. Same as 3, but with license plate.
5. Same as 4, but with tow slot.

22-D Pontiac Gran Prix Sports Coupe   3''   1970
Light gray interior, clear windows, black baseplate, five spoke thin wheels.
1. Metallic dark purple body.
2. Light purple.
3. Light purple, pink axles.

22-E Freeman Inter-city Commuter   3''   1970
Clear windows, invory interior, metal baseplate & grille, five spoke wide wheels.
1. Metallic purple.
2. Metallic purple, with yellow & black labels on sides.
3. Metallic gold, with labels.
4. Metallic dark red, with labels.
5. Metallic dark red, with labels, silver/gray painted baseplate.
6. Metallic dark red, no label on sides, silver/gray baseplate.
7. Metallic dark red, no label on sides, metal baseplate.
8. Metallic dark red, label on sides, unpainted baseplate, white interior.

22-F Blaze Buster   3''   1975
Red body, unpainted metal baseplate, silver plastic interior and accessories, red 'Fire' and black crossed axes on shield on yellow label on sides, small five spoke slicks.
1. White plastic ladder, amber windows and dome lights.
2. Yellow plastic ladder, amber windows and dome lights.
3. Black plastic ladder, amber windows and dome light.
4. Yellow plastic ladder, amber windows and dome light, black painted baseplate and grille.
5. Yellow plastic ladder, light amber windows and dome light, black painted baseplate and grille.
6. Yellow plastic ladder, amber windows and dome light, black painted baseplate and grille, large four spoke wide wheels, front and rear.
7. Same as 4, white plastic interior and accessories.

8. Same as 4, white plastic interior and accessories, light amber windows and dome lights.
9. Same as 4, pale yellow plastic ladder.
10. Dark red body, (same color as red dumper on 26-C Side Dumper) yellow plastic ladder, white plastic interior & accessories, amber plastic windows and dome lights, black painted metal baseplate.
11. Same as 10, charcoal gray painted metal baseplate.
12. Same as 7, white plastic interior and accessories, charcoal gray painted metal baseplate.
13. Same as 11, silver plated plastic interior and accessories, charcoal gray painted metal baseplate.
14. Same as 10, black painted metal baseplate, silver plated plastic interior and accessories.
15. Same as 6, large four spoke wide wheels, light amber plastic windows.
16. Same as 10, charcoal gray painted baseplate, light amber plastic windows.

22-G Ford Mini Pick-up/Camper   1982
Silver cab and white camper top, black "26" & "Big Foot" on yellow stripe with black borders on sides, clover leaf wheels.

23-A Berkeley Cavalier Trailer   2½''   1956
Decal on lower right rear of trailer, "On Tow MB23", with flat or reinforced circle on front tow hook, heavy door outline, 2 small pins in baseplate hold baseplate to body, open axles, numbered 23 on base.
1. Pale blue body, slight door outline, metal wheels, flat tow hook, closed crimped axles.
2. Same as 1, heavy door outline, open crimped axles.
3. Same as 2, reinforced tow hook.
4. Same as 2, but lime green body.
5. Same as 3, but lime green body.
6. Same as 4, but gray plastic wheels.
7. Same as 6, but reinforced tow hook.
8. Same as 6, but rounded axles.

23-B Bluebird Dauphine Trailer   2½''   1960
Decal on lower right rear of trailer, "On Tow MB23", door on left rear side opens, 2 small pins on baseplate hold base to body, open rounded axles, flat or reinforced front tow hook.
1. Metallic lime green body, large gray wheels, knobby treads, flat tow hook.
2. Metallic tan body, small gray wheels, knobby treads, flat tow hook.
3. Metallic tan body, large gray wheels, knobby treads, reinforced tow hook.
4. Same as 2, but fine treads.
5. Same as 3, but fine treads.
6. Same as 2, but small silver wheels.
7. Same as 6, but reinforced tow hook.

23-C Trailer Caravan   2-7/8''   1965
Yellow or pink body with white roof, blue removable interior, open or closed axles, left door top even with roof or ends below roof, open or closed axles, knobby or fine treads on black plastic wheels.
1. Yellow body, open axles, knobby treads, & door top even with roof.
2. Same as 1, fine treads.
3. Same as 1, closed axles, knobby treads.
4. Same as 1, closed axles and fine treads.
5. Same as 4, pink body.
6. Same as 5, door top ends below roof.

23-D Volkswagon Camper   2-1/8''   1970
Dark orange roof, clear windows, metal baseplate & bumpers, five spoke thin wheels. Variations: 1 to 9 display numbers "VMV 252H" on the registration plate at rear of vehicle; 10 to 15 display number "DGY 833H
1. Blue, with gas tank lid on left rear side, orange interior.
2. Blue, without gas tank lid.
3. Blue, with sail boat label on rear sides.
4. Dark orange, white interior.
5. Light orange, white interior.
6. Orange body, orange interior, sail boat label on sides.

7. Orange body, white interior, small wheels, sail boat label on sides.
8. Orange body, white interior, small wheels, no labels.
9. Yellow body, white interior, sail boat label on sides.
10. Military olive green body, black painted baseplate, baseplate has been revised: "No: 23 Volkswagon Camper" removed, tail pipe added, "Dormobile" moved, "Superfast" removed, date changed to 1976, no interior, roof now part of body, square Red Cross labels on roof and sides, deep blue windows, multi-spoke wheels with chrome hub caps. (TP-12)
11. Same as 10, multi-spoke wheels, no hub caps.
12. White body, glossy black painted metal baseplate, same base as 23-A (10), red and green tempa print designs each side, "PIZZA VAN", "WE DELIVER DAY AND NIGHT" dark green plastic windows, multi-spoke wheels, no hub caps. (LEM)
13. Same as 12, multi-spoke wheels, with hub caps. (LEM)
14. Same as 12, flat black painted metal baseplate, multi-spoke wheels, no hub caps. (LEM)
15. Same as 12, flat black painted metal baseplate, multi-spoke wheels, with chrome hub caps.
16. Same as 12, flat black painted metal baseplate, multi-spoke wheels, with chrome hub caps, lighter green plastic windows.

23-E Atlas Truck   3''   1975
Metallic blue cab and chassis, orange dumper, yellow and red chevron labels each side of dumper, large clover leaf wheels, silver interior, may be found without labels on sides.
1. Amber windows, unpainted metal baseplate, may be found with or without side labels.
2. Amber windows, unpainted metal baseplate modified axle covers, no patent number on front axle cover, wide large multi-spoke wheels, without labels.
3. Clear windows, dull gray interior, unpainted metal baseplate, modified axle covers, no patent number on front axle cover, wide multi-spoke wheels, without labels.
4. Amber windows, dull gray interior, unpainted metal baseplate, modified axle covers, no patent number on front axle cover, wide large multi-spoke wheels, without labels.
5. Same as 3, silver gray painted baseplate, without labels.
6. Same as 4, amber windows, dull gray interior, silver gray painted baseplate.
7. Metallic blue cab and chassis, silver gray painted dumper, clear plastic windows, dull gray plastic interior, silver gray painted baseplate, wide large multi-spoke wheels.
8. Metallic blue body, orange dumper, silver gray painted metal baseplate, clear plastic windows, yellow orange plastic interior, wide large multi-spoke wheels.
9. Red body and chassis, silver gray dumper, silver gray painted metal baseplate, clear plastic windows, dull gray plastic interior, wide large multi-spoke wheels.

23-F G.T. 350   2-7/8''   1970
White body, flat black painted metal baseplate, two wide blue tempa stripes on hood, roof and rear deck, blue tempa stripes and "G.T. 350" on sides, chrome plasted plastic engine protruding from hood, five spoke accent wheels, "Made In Hong Kong" on baseplate. (formerly SF8-2)
1. Clear plastic windows, blue plastic interior and tow hook.

23-G Audi Quattro   1982
White body, clear windows, black letters Audi Sport on doors, black and red rectangles on sides, hood and top. (listed as 25 everywhere but U.S.A.)

24-A Weatherhill Hydraulic Excavator   2-3/8''   1956
Metal front & rear wheels, crimped axles, 'Weatherhill Hydraulic' decal on rear of body, numbered '24' inside body, 'Lesney' cast inside scoop.
1. Orange body.
2. Yellow body.

24-B Weatherhill Hydraulic Excavator   2-5/8''   1959
Yellow body, small & medium front wheels, large rear wheels, crimped & rounded axles.
1. Small, dark gray front wheels, crimped axles, knobby treads.

2. Same as 1, rounded axles.
3. Same as 2, light gray wheels.
4. Same as 2, medium dark gray front wheels.
5. Same as 3, medium front wheels.
6. Medium black front wheels, rounded axles, fine treads.

24-C   Rolls Royce Silver Shadow   3"   1967
Metallic red body, ivory interior, clear windows, black 4 or 5 line baseplate depending with or without patent number, with & without tow slot on front baseplate, silver hub caps or solid silver wheels, metal grille. Model changed to Superfast wheels.

1. Black plastic wheels, silver hub caps, no patent number, no tow slot.
2. Black plastic wheels, silver hub caps, no patent number, no tow slot, with license plate under front bumper.
3. Silver wheels, black tires, no patent number, with license plate under front bumper.
4. Silver wheels, black tires, with patent number on baseplate, with license plate under front bumper, with tow slot behind license plate on baseplate.

24-D   Rolls Royce Silver Shadow   3"   1970
Ivory interior, clear windows, metal grille & bumpers, five spoke wheels. Most models come with narrow & / or wide wheel wells.

1. Metallic red, black baseplate, thin wheels.
2. Dark metallic red, black baseplate, thin wheels.
3. Metallic green baseplate, wide wheels.
4. Pink baseplate, wide wheels.
5. Silver/gray baseplate, wide wheels.
6. Charcoal baseplate, wide wheels.
7. Gray baseplate, wide wheels.
8. Black baseplate, wide wheels.
9. Black painted baseplate, small thin wheels (same as 25-A).
10. Metallic gold body, black painted metal baseplate, ivory interior, clear windows, metal grille and front bumper, five spoke wheels. (Sold in Japan in special black box numbered J-4)

24-E   Team Matchbox   2-7/8"   1973
White driver, silver motor, wide clover leaf wheels.

1. Yellow body, blue, yellow & red '8' label, thin roll bar behind driver.
2. Yellow body, blue, yellow & red '4' label, thick roll bar.
3. Metallic red body, blue, yellow & red '8' label, thick roll bar.
4. Metallic green body, red, yellow & black '5' label, thick roll bar.
5. Metallic blue body, yellow, and black '1' label, thick roll bar.
6. Metallic blue body, red, yellow & black '5' label, thick roll bar.
7. Metallic red body, red, yellow & black '5' label on hood, thick roll bar, large 5 spoke accent rear wheels.
8. Metallic red body, blue yellow and red '8' label, thick roll bar, large wide five spoke accent rear wheels.
9. Metallic red body, blue yellow and red '8' label, thick roll bar, large wide five spoke accent rear wheels.
10. Metallic green body, blue, yellow and red '8' label, thick roll bar, small clover leaf front wheels, large clover leaf rear wheels. (G-14)
11. Metallic red body, thick roll bar, black and red "CHAMPION" logo, black 'GOOD YEAR' logo and large black '44' on white and yellow label on hood, small clover leaf front wheels, large clover leaf rear wheels. (TP-9) and (G-14).
12. Same as 10, dark metallic green body. (G-14)
13. Orange body, thick roll bar, black and red "CHAMPION" logo, black "GOOD YEAR" logo and black "44" on white and yellow label on hood, butterscotch plastic driver, small clover leaf front wheels, large clover leaf rear wheels. (G-3)

24-F   Shunter   3"   1978
Metallic green body, red metal undercarriage bumpers, and front tow ring, red plastic baseplate, black plastic tan tow hook, tan plastic instrument panel, no window, black plastic wheels.

1. White on red "RAIL FREIGHT" side labels.
2. Same as 1, white on red "D1496-RF" side labels.
3. Same as 2, yellow body, white on red "D1496-RF" side labels.

May be found in various shades of yellow, from a light canary yellow to a darker mustard yellow, may be found without the plastic instrument panel inside cab.

4. Same as 3, yellow body, light brown plastic instrument panel or no instrument panel.
5. Yellow body, red metal undercarriage, bumpers and front tow ring, red plastic baseplate, black plastic rear tow hook, no instrument panel, no windows, white on red "D1496-RF" square corner side labels, black plastic wheels.
6. Same as 5, white on red "D1496-RF" rounded corners side labels.

24-G   Datsun 280ZX   2-7/8"   1979
Black body, black painted metal baseplate and bumpers, no number 24 on baseplate, (Made in Hong Kong), clear plastic windows, five spoke wide wheels.

1. Black with white outline "DATSUN" tempa stripe on sides, two black with white outline "280ZX" on wide red tempa on hood, red plastic interior.
2. Same as 1, white plastic interior.

24-H   Datsun 280   1982
Preproduction used for picture purposes.

25-A   Dunlop Truck (Bedford 12 cwt van)   2-1/8"   1956
Dark blue body, silver grille, black baseplate, numbered '25' 'Lesney England' on baseplate, "Dunlop" decal in orange or yellow on sides.

1. Metal wheels, crimped axle, orange decal.
2. Same as 1, but large gray plastic wheels.
3. Same as 2, but yellow decal.
4. Same as 3, but rounded axles.
5. Same as 4, but small gray plastic wheels.

25-B   Volkswagen 1200 Sedan   2½"   1960
Silver blue body, with & without silver grille, thin, clear or green tinted windows, black baseplate, rounded axles, with or without red painted tail lights.

1. Clear windows, dark gray plastic wheels with knobby treads.
2. Same as 1, but green windows.
3. Same as 2, but light gray plastic wheels.
4. Same as 2, but silver plastic wheels, with or without brace at rear of baseplate.
5. Same as 4, but light gray plastic wheels and fine treads.

25-C   BP Petrol Tanker   3"   1964
Yellow hinged cab, white tanker body, 6 wheels on 3 axles, with & without silver grille, "BP" or "Aral" decals on sides and rear of tank body.

1. Yellow cab, dark green chassis, BP decal, gray wheels, silver grille.
2. Same as 1, black wheels.
3. Same as 2, yellow grille.
4. Blue cab, grille and chassis, Aral decal. This model was produced only for the European market.

25-D   Ford Cortina G.T.   2-7/8"   1968
Light brown body in various shades, ivory interior & tow hook, clear windows, metal baseplate with tow slot, black baseplate. Model changed to Superfast wheels.

1. No roof rack.
2. Yellow plastic roof rack, found in gift sets G-4 (1969).

25-E   Ford Cortina   2¾"   1970
Clear windows, ivory interior & tow hook, metal baseplate & grille, thin five spoke wheels.

1. Light brown body.
2. Light metallic blue body.
3. Dark metallic blue body.

25-F   Mod Tractor   2-1/8"   1972
Metallic purple, orange/yellow seat & tow hook, silver motor & exhaust pipes, black steering wheel & baseplate, small wide wheels on front, large wheels on rear, clover leaf design.

1. With headlights cast to rear fenders.
2. With "V" cast to rear fenders.
3. Unpainted metal baseplate.
4. Black baseplate, red seats & tow hook.

5. "V" cast on rear fenders, black baseplate, yellow seat & tow hook, four spoke front wheels. (Same as SF 2-2).
6. Red body, orange/yellow seat & tow hook, silver motor & exhaust pipes, black steering wheel & baseplate, small wide clover leaf front wheels, large wide clover leaf rear wheels. (TP-2) Also found in blister-packs.
7. Metallic purple body, orange/yellow seat and tow hook silver motor and exhaust pipes, black steering wheel and baseplate, small wide reverse accent front wheels, large five clover leaf rear wheels.
8. Red body, orange/yellow seat and tow hook, silver motor and exhaust pipes, black steering wheel and baseplate, small wide reverse accent front wheels, large clover leaf rear wheels. (TP-2)
9. Metallic purple body, orange/yellow seat and tow hook, silver motor and exhaust pipes, black steering wheel and baseplate, small wide five spoke front wheels, large clover leaf rear wheels.
10. Red body, orange/yellow seat and tow hook, silver motor and exhaust pipes, black steering wheel and baseplate, small five spoke wide front wheels, large clover leaf rear wheels. (TP-2)

25-G   Flat Car & Container   3"   1978
Black metal flat bed on black plastic undercarriage, baseplate, tow ring and tow hook, deep tan container box with red movable plastic doors and red plastic roof, no number 25 on baseplate, black plastic wheels.

1. Red and white stripe flag and black on white "NYK WORLD WIDE SYSTEM" side labels.
2. Same as 1, red and blue "United States Lines" with red and blue eagle on white side labels.
3. Same as 1, red, white and black "SEALAND" side labels.
4. Same as 1, black on white "OCL OCLU 026909 4 GBx2000" side labels. Lettering on black plastic baseplate may be found reading from hook to ring or from ring to hook, may be found with darker red labels.
5. Same as 1, chocolate brown plastic container, "NYK Worldwide System" side labels. G-2
6. Same as 1, light tan plastic container box, "NYK WORLDWIDE SYSTEMS" side labels.
7. Same as 1, charcoal gray painted flat bed, dark tan plastic container box, "NYK WORLDWIDE SYSTEMS" side labels.

25-H   Celica GT   2-15/16"   1978
Pale blue body, black painted metal baseplate and bumpers, no number 25 on baseplate, (Made in Hong Kong), clear plastic windows, large blue with white outline "78" on white tempa rectangle on roof and on doors, wide white tempa racing stripe with thin black tempa stripe on hood and rear hatch door, black thin tempa stripe on sides from front to rear, black tempa design on sides between door and rear window.

1. Ivory plastic interior, old baseplate, with "MATCHBOX" SUPER-FAST and Toyota Celica, (1978) clover leaf wheels.
2. Ivory plastic interior, old baseplate with "MATCHBOX" SUPER-FAST and Toyota Celica, (1978) five spoke wheels.
3. Dark blue plastic interior, old baseplate with "MATCHBOX" SUPERFAST and Toyota Celica, (1978) five spoke wide wheels.
4. Dark blue plastic interior, new baseplate with "MATCHBOX" and "CELICA GT" (1979) five spoke wide wheels.
5. Dark blue plastic interior, new baseplate with "MATCHBOX" and "CELICA GT" (1979) no black tempa stripe on sides and no black tempa design on sides between door and rear window, five spoke wide wheels.
6. White plastic interior, old baseplate with "MATCHBOX" SUPER-FAST and Toyota Celica (1978) clover leaf wheels.

25-I   Ambulance
Says 41 on base but, was released as 25. (See 41-F)

25-J   Celica GT   1982
Yellow body and clear windows with dark blue interior, red lettering on hood "Yellow Fever", wide blue and narrow red stripes on sides, small front wheels, large wide back wheels.

26-A   Foden Ready Mix Concrete Truck   1¾"   1956
Orange body & rotating barrel, silver or gold grille, short or long barrel stem, 4 wheels on two axles, numbered 26.

1. Gold grille, metal wheels, crimped axles, short barrel stem.
2. Same as 1, but silver grille.
3. Same as 2, but long barrel stem.
4. Same as 3, but dark gray plastic wheels.
5. Same as 4, but rounded axles.
6. Same as 5, but light gray wheels.
7. Same as 5, but silver plastic wheels.

26-B Foden Ready Mix Concrete Truck   2½''   1961
Orange body & chassis, plastic rotating barrel, with & without silver grille, with & without reinforcement at rear of baseplate sides, 6 wheels on 3 rounded axles.
1. Gray barrel, dark gray wheels, knobby treads, no reinforcement.
2. Same as 1, but orange barrel.
3. Same as 2, but with reinforcement.
4. Same as 3, light gray wheels.
5. Orange barrel, black wheels, knobby treads, no reinforcement.
6. Same as 5, with reinforcement.
7. Same as 6, but fine treads.
8. Same as 3, but fine treads.
9. Same as 8, black wheels.
10. Same as 8, but large black wheels.

26-C G.M.C. Tipper Truck   2-5/8''   1968
Red tipping cab, green chassis, silver tipper body with swinging door, green windows, 4 wheels on 2 rounded axles, black plastic axles, number 26 cast inside gas tank. Model changed to Superfast wheels.

26-D G.M.C. Tipper Truck   2½''   1970
Red cab, green chassis, silver/gray tipper, green windows, wide wheels, four spokes, black baseplate, baseplate reads from front to back or reverse.
1. Superfast on front of baseplate.
2. Pat App on front of baseplate.
3. Superfast on front of baseplate, number 26 cast inside gas tank.
4. Pat. App. on front baseplate, number 26 cast inside gas tank.

26-E Big Banger   3''   1972
Red body, blue windows, silver motor in hood, metal baseplate and plastic exhaust pipes, small front wheels, large rear wheels, clover leaf design.
1. "Big Banger" labels on sides in black lettering on orange background on yellow label.
2. "Big Banger" labels on sides black lettering on orange background on yellow label, inside body casting supports under rear window.
3. "Big Banger" labels on sides, inside body casting supports, amber windows.
4. Brown painted body, white painted baseplate, chrome plated plastic motor, grille and exhaust pipes, deep blue plastic windows, black plastic air scoop on motor, brown, red and green on yellow "Brown Sugar" side labels, small wide clover leaf front wheels, large wide clover leaf rear wheels, baseplate now reads: "No. VII Brown Sugar".
5. Same as 4, amber plastic windows. The cherry cluster on the labels can either be seen as full impression or only a thin outline.
6. Same as 4, amber plastic windows, light tan, red and green on yellow 'BROWN SUGAR' side labels.
7. Same as 4, blue plastic windows, light tan, red and green on yellow 'BROWN SUGAR' side labels.
8. Same as 4, amber plastic windows, brown, red and green on yellow "BROWN SUGAR" side labels.

26-F Site Dumper   2-5/8''   1976
Yellow cab, body and front dumper, black painted metal baseplate with black plastic center insert, large five spoke front wheels, small reverse accent rear wheels.
1. Black plastic interior.
2. Black plastic interior, small multi-spoke rear wheels.
3. Black plastic interior, large five spoke front wheels, small five spoke accent rear wheels, red painted front dumper.
4. Same as 3, redesigned baseplate, heavy raised baseplate edges, number 26 new over the front axle.

5. Same as 4, large five spoke accent front wheels, small five spoke reverse accent rear wheels.
6. Same as 5, black plastic interior, red painted dumper, metallic brown painted base, black plastic insert on base, number 26 over front axle, large five spoke accent wheels, small reverse accent rear wheels.
7. Same as 4, large five spoke, small five spoke accent rear wheels, no hub caps on rear wheels.
8. Same as 5, black plastic interior, red painted dumper, metallic brown painted base, black plastic insert on base, number 26 over front axle, large five spoke front wheels, small five spoke reverse accent wheels.
9. Yellow cab, red front dumper, charcoal gray painted metal baseplate, with black plastic insert, number 26 over front axle, black plastic interior, large five spoke accent front wheels, small five spoke reverse accent rear wheels.
10. Red cab, silver gray front dumper, charcoal gray painted one piece metal baseplate (no plastic insert) white plastic interior, large five spoke accent front wheels, small five spoke reverse accent rear wheels.
11. Same as 10, glossy black painted metal baseplate.
12. Same as 10, large five spoke accent front wheels with yellow hot stamp design, small five spoke reverse accent rear wheels with yellow hot stamp design.

26-G Cosmic Blues   2-7/8''   1970
White body, flat black painted metal baseplate, blue tempa stars and streaks on roof and rear deck, blue tempa "COSMIC BLUES" and stars and streaks on sides, chrome plated plastic engine protruding from hood and exhaust pipes on sides, small clover leaf front wheels, large clover leaf rear wheels, "Made In Hong Kong" on baseplate. (Formerly SF26-2)
1. Blue plastic windows.

27-A Bedford Low Loader   3-1/8''   1956
Silver grille & side gas tanks, 4 metal wheels on cab, 2 metal wheels on trailer, crimped axles.
1. Light blue cab which is the same color as number 17 blue van, dark blue trailer which is the same as number 25 Dunlop Truck.
2. Light green cab and tan trailer.

27-B Bedford Low Loader   3¾''   1959
Silver grille, 4 wheels on cab, 2 on trailer.
1. Light green cab, dark tan trailer, metal wheels, crimped axles.
2. Same as 1, dark gray plastic wheels.
3. Dark green cab, light tan trailer, dark gray plastic wheels, crimped axles.
4. Same as 3, rounded axles.

27-C Cadillac Sedan   2¾''   1960
With & without silver grilles, bumpers, with & without red painted tail lights, red or black baseplate & tow hook, clear or green windows, white or pink roof, green, silver/gray or lilac colored bodies, silver, gray or black plastic wheels.
1. Green body, white roof, clear windows, silver wheels, knobby treads, red base.
2. Same as 1, but silver/gray body.
3. Same as 2, but pink roof.
4. Same as 2, but green windows.
5. Lilac body, pink roof, green windows, silver wheels, knobby treads, black base.
6. Same as 5, but gray wheels.
7. Same as 6, but thin treads.
8. Same as 6, but thick treads.
9. Same as 6, but black wheels and knobby treads.
10. Same as 9, but fine treads.

27-D Mercedes Benz 230 SL   3''   1966
Unpainted metal grille & baseplate, red plastic interior & tow hook, clear windshield, black plastic wheels. Model changed to Superfast wheels.
1. Cream body, plastic door springs.
2. White body, plastic door springs.

3. White body, metal door springs.

27-E Mercedes Benz 230 SL   2-7/8''   1970
Blue tinted windshield, metal baseplate & grille, five spoke wheels.
1. Cream body, red interior & tow hook.
2. Off white body, red interior & tow hook.
3. Yellow body, red interior & tow hook.
4. Yellow body, black interior & tow hook.
5. Yellow body, black interior & tow hook, wide wheels.
6. Light yellow body, black interior & tow hook, wide wheels.
7. Mustard yellow body, black plastic interior and tow hook, five spoke wide wheels. (Sold in Japan in special black box numbered J-9).

27-F Lamborghini Countach   2-7/8''   1973
Yellow body, silver interior & motor, five spoke wide wheels, number 3 sticker on hood, unpainted metal baseplate. All baseplate (metal, black, silver/gray) may be found with or without ® outside of right leg of X at end of Matchbox.
1. Purple tinted windows.
2. Red windows.
3. Red windows, black baseplate.
4. Purple windows, black baseplate.
5. Light yellow body, purple windows, black baseplate.
6. Light yellow body, red windows, black baseplate.
7. Yellow body, purple windows, silver/gray baseplate.
8. Light yellow body, amber windows, black baseplate.
9. Orange/red body, red windows, black baseplate.
10. Orange/red body, amber windows, black baseplate.
11. Streaker red/orange body, number 8 in black block on hood, black and green designs front to back, silver motor & interior, five spoke wide wheels, may be found with or without ® next to the X of MATCHBOX. Red windows, black painted baseplate.
12. Amber windows, black painted baseplate.
13. Light amber windows, black painted baseplate.
14. Blue tinted windows, unpainted metal baseplate, silver plastic interior.
15. Blue tinted windows, unpainted metal baseplate, dull gray plastic interior.
16. Blue tinted windows, black painted baseplate, silver plastic interior.
17. Blue tinted windows, black painted baseplate, dull gray plastic interior.
18. Amber windows, unpainted metal baseplate, silver plastic interior.
19. Blue tinted windows, unpainted metal baseplate, dull gray interior, forest green streaker design.
20. Green tinted windows, black painted baseplate, dull gray interior, light yellow green streaker design.
21. Green tinted windows, black painted baseplate, dull gray interior, forest green streaker design.
22. Same as 21, metallic brown painted baseplate, blue tinted windows, dull gray plastic interior.
23. Same as 22, metallic brown painted baseplate, blue tinted windows, dark gray plastic interior.
24. Same as 17, charcoal gray painted metal baseplate, dull gray plastic interior.
25. Same as 17, charcoal gray painted baseplate, dark gray plastic interior.
26. Same as 17, charcoal gray painted baseplate, yellow plastic interior.
27. Same as 17, charcoal gray painted baseplate, dull gray plastic interior, smoky gray plastic windows.
28. Same as 27, charcoal gray painted baseplate, white plastic interior, smoky gray plastic windows.
29. Same as 17, charcoal gray painted metal baseplate, white plastic interior, blue tinted plastic windows.
30. Same as 17, charcoal gray painted metal baseplate, tan plastic interior, blue tinted plastic windows.
31. Same as 17, charcoal gray painted metal baseplate, tan plastic interior, clear plastic windows.

32. Red/orange body, black and avocado green streaker designs, black painted metal baseplate, white plastic interior, clear plastic windows, five spoke wide wheels.

33. Red/orange body, black and avocado green streaker designs, black painted metal baseplate, tan plastic interior, clear plastic windows, five spoke wide wheels.

34. Same as 33, blue tinted plastic windows.

35. Red/orange body, black and avocado green streaker designs, black painted metal baseplate, dark gray plastic interior, purple plastic windows, five spoke wide wheels.

36. Same as 35, charcoal gray painted metal baseplate, tan plastic interior, purple plastic windows.

37. Same as 35, charcoal gray painted metal baseplate, dull gray plastic interior, purple plastic windows.

38. Same as 35, charcoal brown painted metal baseplate, tan plastic interior, purple plastic windows.

39. Same as 35, blue/gray metal baseplate, tan plastic interior, purple plastic windows.

27-G Swing Wing Jet   **3"**   **1981**
White under fusalage and horizontal stabilizers, red upper structure and tail fins, white plastic retractable wings, four small black plastic wheels.
1. Amber/red plastic canopy.
2. Red plastic canopy.

28-A Bedford Compressor Truck   **1¾"**   **1956**
Silver front & rear grilles, front bumper & tanks behind cab, metal wheels, crimped axles, numbered 28.
1. Orange body.
2. Yellow body.

28-B Thames Trader Compressor Truck   **2¾"**   **1959**
Yellow body, front & rear grilles &/or bumper are silver or plain, round rivet on front base, spread rivet rear base, single front black wheels, duel rear black wheels.
1. Large wheels, crimped axles, knobby treads, silver rear grille.
2. Same as 1, but rounded axles.
3. Same as 1, but yellow rear grille.
4. Same as 2, but rounded axles.
5. Same as 4, but yellow rear grille.
6. Same as 3, but fine treads.

28-C Mark 10 Jaguar   **2¾"**   **1964**
Light brown body, ivory interior & tow hook, front hood opens exposing motor, black baseplate, 4 plastic wheels, with & without silver bumpers.
1. Gray plastic wheels, tan motor.
2. Black plastic wheels, tan motor.
3. Black plastic wheels, unpainted metal motor.

28-D Mack Dump Truck   **2-5/8"** **1968**
Orange body, green windows, unpainted metal grille & baseplate, 3 open steps under each door, 4 large black plastic wheels, with & without metal brace under front fenders holding front base in position. Model changed to Superfast wheels.
1. Red plastic wheels, no brace under front fenders.
2. Red plastic wheels, brace under front fenders.
3. Yellow plastic wheels, brace under front fenders.

28-E Mack Dump Truck   **2-5/8"** **1970**
Pea green body, green windows, large balloon wheels with clover leaf design, metal baseplate & grille, black or red axle covers.
1. Open steps on ladder, open rear axle.
2. Open steps on ladder, open rear axle, large clover leaf flat wheels.
3. Closed steps on ladder, open rear axle, large clover leaf flat wheels.
4. Closed steps on ladder, closed rear axle, large clover leaf flat wheels.
5. Military olive green body, black painted metal baseplate and grille, closed steps on ladder, wide multi-spoke large wheels, no hub caps, no number 28 on base. (TP-16)
6. Military olive drab body, black painted metal baseplate and grille, closed steps on ladder, wide multi-spoke large wheels, no hub caps, no number 28 on base. (TP-16) In TP-16 with this model was R number 16-4 Case tractor also in olive drab.

28-F Stoat Armored Truck   **2-5/8"** **1974**
Metallic gold body, brown plastic observer coming out of turret, five spoke wheels, rolamatic action.
1. Unpainted metal baseplate and grille, black plastic center baseplate strip.
2. Black metal baseplate and grille, black plastic center baseplate strip.
3. Military olive green body, black metal baseplate and grille, black plastic center insert, five spoke slicks, no hub caps. (TP-13)
4. Same as 2, Pat. App. 12174/72 replaced by Pat. No. 1424808.
5. Same as 3, Pat. App. 12174/72 replaced by Pat. No. 1424808.
6. Same as 3, military olive drab body. Pat. App. 12174/72. (TP-13)
7. Same as 3, five spoke wide wheels, chrome hub caps.
8. Same as 4, no hub caps.
9. Same as 1, Patent number 1424808, five spoke wide wheels, chrome hub caps.

28-G Lincoln Continental MK V   **3"**   **1979**
Red painted body, unpainted metal baseplate grille and bumpers, tan plastic interior, multi-spoke wheels.
1. Clear windshield and rear window, textured white plastic convertible roof.
2. Same as 1, darker chocolate tan plastic interior.
3. Same as 1, light gray plastic interior.
4. Pinkish/red body, unpainted metal baseplate, grille and bumpers, tan plastic interior, clear plastic windows, textured white plastic convertible roof, multi-spoke wheels.
5. Same as 1, brown plastic interior.

28-H Formula Racing Car   **1982**
Gold body with white driver, silver engine and exhaust pipes behind white "Champion" & black "8" label on front, "8"on sides w/black rectangles and 2 white circles. 4 large clover leaf back wheels, 2 small reverse accent front wheels.

29-A Bedford Milk Delivery Van   **2¼"**   **1956**
Tan body, white bottle load & baseplate, numbered 29, with & without silver grille, bumpers, headlights.
1. Metal wheels, crimped axles.
2. Large dark gray plastic wheels, crimped axles.
3. Large dark gray plastic wheels, rounded axles.

29-B Austin A55 Cambridge Sedan   **2¾"**   **1961**
Two-tone green, light green roof & rear top half of body, dark metallic green hood and lower body, with & without silver bumpers, grille & headlights, with & without rear painted tail lights, green tinted windows, black baseplate & tow hook.
1. Gray plastic wheels, knobby treads.
2. Silver plastic wheels, knobby treads.
3. Silver plastic wheels, finer treads.
4. Black plastic wheels, finer treads.
5. Black plastic wheels, fine treads.

29-C Fire Pumper Truck   **3"**   **1966**
Red body, metal grille & baseplate, white plastic hose & ladders, blue windows & dome light, black plastic with & without "Denver" decals on side doors. Model changed to Superfast wheels.
1. Orange "Denver" decal on doors.
2. Yellow "Denver" decal on doors.
3. With tow slot.
4. With tow slot, no decals.
5. Raised door panels.

29-D Fire Pumper Truck   **3"**   **1970**
Red body, white plastic hose & ladder, blue windows & dome light, metal baseplate & grille.
1. Five spoke thin wheels.
2. Red body, unpainted metal baseplate with "PUMPER" and "1981", white plastic water gun, hoses, ladder and rear deck, blue plastic windows and dome light, large white tempa "LOS ANGELES CITY FIRE DEPARTMENT" on doors, multi-spoke wheels. (Code Red Issue)

29-E Racing Mini   **2¼"**   **1970**
Clear windows, metal baseplate & grille, black number 29 on yellow

label on sides, five spoke wide wheels.
1. Metallic bronze, ivory interior.
2. Dark orange, ivory interior.
3. Dark orange, cream interior.
4. Light orange, cream interior.
5. Dark orange, ivory interior, black number 29 on yellow label with green border.
6. Dark orange, cream interior, black number 29 on yellow label green border.
7. Dark orange, cream interior, black number 29 on yellow label green border, silver/gray baseplate.
8. Dark orange,cream interior, black number 29 on yellow label orange border, silver/gray baseplate.
9. Dark orange body, ivory interior, black number 29 on yellow label green border, silver/gray baseplate.
10. Dark orange body, cream interior, black large number 29 on yellow label green border, unpainted metal baseplate.
11. Dark orange body, ivory interior, black large number 29 yellow label green border, unpainted metal baseplate.
12. Red orange body, ivory interior, black large number 29 yellow green border label, unpainted metal baseplate.
13. Red body, ivory interior, large black number 29 on yellow with green border label each side, unpainted metal baseplate. (TP-6 also found in Blister)
14. Red body, ivory interior, large black number 29 on yellow with green border side labels, black painted baseplate and grille.
15. Same as 13, cream interior. (TP-6)
16. Same as 13, ivory interior, small hubless accent wheels. (TP-6)

29-F Shovel Nose Tractor   **2-7/8"** **1976**
Yellow body, yellow plastic baseplate, red plastic shovel, silver plastic motor, grille and air scoop.
1. Large clover leaf wheels, no windows.
2. No window, large clover leaf wheels, no hub caps.
3. Lime green body, yellow plastic shovel and baseplate, silver plastic motor, no window, large clover leaf wheels. (Sold in Germany only)
4. Mustard yellow body, yellow plastic baseplate, red plastic shovel, silver plated plastic motor, grille and air scoop, large clover leaf wheels.
5. Same as 4, black plastic motor, grille and air scoop.
6. Same as 5, black plastic motor, grille and air scoop, deep ivory plastic baseplate.
7. Same as 5, black plastic motor, grille and air scoop, yellow plastic baseplate, large clover leaf wheels, with yellow painted hub design.
8. Same as 5, black plastic motor, grille and air scoop, light ivory plastic baseplate.
9. Same as 5, black plastic motor, grille and air scoop, deep ivory plastic baseplate, large clover leaf wheels, with yellow painted hub design, dark red plastic shovel.
10. Same as 5, black plastic motor grille and air scoop, yellow plastic baseplate, large clover leaf wheels, with yellow painted hub designs, dark red plastic shovel.
11. Same as 5, black plastic motor, grille and air scoop, deep ivory plastic baseplate, large clover leaf wheels, with yellow painted hub designs, red plastic shovel.
12. Same as 5, black plastic motor, grille and air scoop, light ivory plastic baseplate, large clover leaf wheels with yellow painted hub designs, red plastic shovel.
13. Same as 12, black plastic motor, grille and air scoop, light ivory plastic baseplate, large clover leaf wheels with yellow painted hub designs, dark red plastic shovel.
14. Same as 5, black plastic motor, grille and air scoop, lemon yellow plastic baseplate, large clover leaf wheels, red plastic shovel.
15. Same as 5, black plastic motor, grille and air scoop, deep ivory plastic baseplate, large clover leaf wheels, black plastic shovel.

16. Same as 5, black plastic motor, grille and air scoop, black plastic baseplate, large clover leaf wheels, red plastic shovel.
17. Orange/red body, gray plastic motor, grille and air scoop, black plastic baseplate, large clover leaf wheels, red plastic shovel.
18. Orange/red body, gray plastic motor, grille and air scoop, black plastic baseplate, large clover leaf wheels, black plastic shovel.
19. Yellow body, black plastic motor, grille and air scoop, deep ivory plastic baseplate, large clover leaf wheels with yellow painted designs, black plastic shovel.
20. Same as 5, black plastic motor, grille and air scoop, deep ivory plastic baseplate, large clover leaf wheels, red plastic shovel.
21. Same as 18, yellow body.

30-A Ford Prefect 2¼'' 1956
Silver grille, headlights, bumpers, with & without red painted tail lights, black baseplate with tow hook. The colors come in various shades.
1. Tan body, metal wheels, crimped axles.
2. Same as 1, light blue body.
3. Same as 1, small gray plastic wheels.
4. Same as 3, rounded axles.
5. Same as 4, light blue body.

30-B 6-Wheel Crane Truck 2-5/8'' 1961
Silver body, orange crane, black front baseplate, open or closed lower section of crane, metal or plastic hook.
1. Gray wheels, knobby treads, open crane bottom, orange hook, flat hook rivet.
2. Silver wheels, knobby treads, open crane bottom, silver hook and flat hook rivet.
3. Same as 2, but rounded hook rivet.
4. Same as 3, but black wheels.
5. Same as 4, but closed crane bottom.
6. Same as 5, but gray hook.
7. Same as 6, but gray wheels and fine treads.
8. Same as 6, but fine treads.

30-C 8-Wheel Crane Truck 3'' 1965
Green body, orange crane, metal half base & grille, with & without tow slot, red or yellow plastic hook, with & without metal brace under body base, 8 black plastic wheels on 4 axles.
1. No brace under rear base, yellow hook.
2. With brace under rear base, red hook.
3. With brace under rear base, yellow hook.
4. Same as 3, with tow slot.

30-D 8-Wheel Crane Truck 3'' 1970
Yellow plastic hook, red body, five spoke thin wheels, metal baseplate and grille.
1. Orange crane.
2. Metallic gold crane.

30-E Beach Buggy 2½'' 1970
Pink, yellow paint splatters, clear windows, large clover leaf design wheels.
1. White interior and gas tanks, balloon tires.
2. Yellow interior & gas tanks, balloon tires.
3. White interior & gas tank, thin rim wide wheels.
4. Yellow interior & gas tank, thin rim wide wheels.
5. Yellow interior & gas tank, thick rim wide wheels.
6. Yellow interior & gas tank, thin rim wide wheels, same motor as 37-F.
7. Yellow interior & gas tank, thick rim wide wheels, same motor as 37-F.
8. Light yellow interior & gas tank, thin rim wide wheels, same motor as 37-F.
9. Yellow interior & gas tank, thick rim wide wheels, same motor as 37-F, no Pat. App. under rear motor.

30-F Swamp Rat 3'' 1976
Military olive green deck, yellow plastic hull and tan soldier, black plastic engine and propeller, small thin wheels, in hull.
1. Yellow and olive green side labels with 'Swamp Rats' in white.

2. Same as 1, dark brownish tan plastic hull.
3. Same as 1, dark pinkish tan plastic hull.

30-G Articulated Truck 3'' 1981
Metallic blue cab, silver gray dumper, white plastic grille on cab, black plastic baseplate on cab and dumper, five spoke accent wheels on cab and dumper.
1. Red plastic windows, no "LEYLAND" cast on front of cab.
2. Red plastic windows, "LEYLAND" cast on front of cab.

30-H Peterbilt Quarry Truck 3'' 1982
Yellow body with gray dumper and silver plastic gas tanks, exhaust pipes, door labels "Dirty Dumper" in black letters, 6 wheels.

31-A Ford Customline Station Wagon 2-5/8'' 1957
Yellow body, with and without silver grille, headlights, bumpers and hood ornament, single headlights, black baseplate, no windows, with and without red painted tail lights.
1. Metal wheels, crimped axles.
2. Dark gray plastic wheels, crimped axles.
3. Dark gray plastic wheels, round axles.

31-B Ford Fairlane Station Wagon 2¾'' 1960
With & without silver grilles, bumpers, headlights, with & without red painted tail lights, green or clear windows, double headlights, red or black baseplate & tow hook.
1. Yellow roof, yellow body, silver wheels, clear windows, red base.
2. Same as 1, pink roof, green body.
3. Same as 2, green windows.
4. Same as 3, but finer treads.
5. Same as 4, but black base.
6. Same as 5, but gray wheels.
7. Same as 5, but black base.

31-C Lincoln Continental 2-7/8'' 1964
Clear windows, ivory interior, metal baseplate with & without tow slot, black plastic wheels. Model changed to Superfast wheels.
1. Metallic blue body.
2. Metallic blue body, with tow slot.
3. Mint green body, with tow slot.

31-D Lincoln Continental 2¾'' 1970
Ivory interior, clear windows, metal baseplate & grille, five spoke wheels.
1. Mint green body.
2. Metallic lime green body, thin wheels.
3. Metallic lime green body, thin wheels, wide wheel wells.
4. Metallic lime green body, wide wheels, wide wheel wells.

31-E Volks Dragon 2½'' 1971
Red body, purple tinted windows, silver air scoop at rear, metal baseplate & grille, small front wheels, larger rear wheels, five spokes, black-yellow label on hood.
1. Cream interior.
2. Cream interior, 3 ribs on air scoop.
3. Bright yellow interior, 3 ribs on air scoop, clear windows.
4. Bright yellow interior, 3 ribs on air scoop, clear windows, silver-gray baseplate.
5. Bright yellow interior, 3 ribs on air scoop, clear windows, silver/gray baseplate.
6. Bright yellow interior, 3 ribs on air scoop, purple tinted windows, silver/gray baseplate.
7. Bright yellow interior, 3 ribs on air scoop, purple windows, unpainted metal baseplate, orange flower on hood.
8. Bright yellow interior, 3 ribs air scoop, purple tinted windows, silver/gray baseplate, orange flower label on hood.
9. Bright yellow interior, 3 ribs air scoop, purple tinted windows, unpainted metal baseplate, no label on hood.
10. Bright yellow interior, 3 ribs air scoop, purple tinted windows, silver/gray baseplate, no label on hood.
11. Bright yellow interior, purple windows, unpainted metal baseplate, silver/gray painted front bumper & lights, orange flower on hood.
12. Light yellow interior, 3 ribs air scoop, purple tinted windows, silver/gray baseplate, orange flower on hood.
13. White interior, 3 ribs air scoop, purple tinted windows, unpainted

metal baseplate, yellow orange and black eyes label on hood.
14. Light yellow interior, 3 ribs air scoop, purple tinted windows, unpainted metal baseplate, orange flower on hood.
15. Bright yellow interior, 3 ribs air scoop, purple tinted windows, unpainted metal baseplate, yellow orange and black eyes label on hood, small five spoke front wheels (same as 5-1).
16. Light yellow interior, 3 ribs air scoop, purple tinted windows, unpainted metal baseplate, yellow orange and black eyes label on hood.
17. Red body, yellow/orange and black "eyes" label on hood, bright yellow interior, 3 rib air scoop, purple tinted windows, unpainted metal baseplate with "no. VI LADY BUG" instead of "no. 31 VOLKS-DRAGON". (Special Issue 1978 baseplate)
18. Black painted body, red "beetle outline" tempa imprint on hood, yellow and two tone red "flame design" tempa imprint on roof, light yellow interior, 3 rib air scoop, purple tinted windows, baseplate now reads, "No. VI Lady Bug".

31-F Caravan 2-11/16'' 1977
White body, unpainted metal baseplate, yellow plastic interior and tow hitch, orange plastic side door and door closing trigger, small multi-spoke wheels.
1. Amber windows and skylights, white bird silhouette and orange and red stripes on an elongated side labels.
2. Amber windows and skylights, white bird silhouette and orange and red stripes on elongated side labels, yellow plastic door and door closing trigger.
3. Same as 1, ivory plastic interior and tow hitch.
4. Same as 2, yellow plastic door and door closing trigger, reinforced plastic tow hitch.
5. Same as 4, bright orange plastic door and door closing trigger, reinforced plastic tow hitch.
6. Same as 1, light amber plastic windows.
7. Same as 2, yellow plastic door and door closing trigger, ivory plastic interior and tow hook.
8. Same as 1, orange plastic door and door closing trigger, reinforced plastic tow hitch, tan plastic interior and tow hitch.
9. White body, unpainted metal baseplate, yellow plastic interior and tow hitch, light blue plastic door and closing trigger, amber plastic windows and skylights, white bird silhouette on orange and red stripes side labels, multi-spoke wheels.
10. Same as 9, tan plastic interior and tow hitch.
11. White body, unpainted metal baseplate, yellow plastic interior and tow hitch, light blue plastic door and closing trigger, amber plastic windows and skylights, white bird silhouette on dark blue and light blue stripes side labels, multi-spoke wheels.
12. White body, unpainted metal baseplate, light brown plastic interior and tow hitch, orange plastic door and closing trigger, amber plastic windows and skylights, white bird silhouette on orange and red stripes on side labels, multi-spoke wheels.
13. White body, unpainted metal baseplate, yellow plastic interior and tow hitch, royal blue plastic door and closing trigger, amber plastic windows and skylights, white bird silhouette on dark and light blue stripes on side labels, multi-spoke wheels.

31-G Mazda RX-7 3'' 1979
White body, black painted metal baseplate and bumpers, no number 31 on baseplate (Made in Hong Kong), wide burgundy tempa stripe on hood with black "RX-7", clear plastic windows.
1. Ivory plastic interior, wide burgundy tempa stripe on sides with large white "RX-7", old baseplate with "MATCHBOX" SUPER-FAST and SAVANNA RX 7" (1979), clover leaf wheels.
2. Tan plastic interior, wide burgundy tempa stripe on sides with large white "RX-7", new baseplate with "MATCHBOX" and Mazda RX-7" (1979), five spoke wide wheels.
3. Same as 2, two thin burgundy tempa stripes on sides with small white "RX-7".
4. Same as 1, small five spoke wheels.
5. Same as 2, black body with brown wide side stripes.

31-H Mazda RX-7   **1982**
Preproduction shown, newer casting used for pictures. Gray body with sun roof outlined on top, black interior and fenders, clover leaf wheels.

32-A Jaguar XK140 Coupe   **2-3/8"**   **1957**
With & without silver grille, headlights, bumpers, with & without red painted tail lights, black baseplate numbered 32, knobby treads, both colors have shades varying light to dark.
1. Cream body, metal wheels, crimped axles.
2. Same as 1, dark gray wheels.
3. Same as 2, rounded axles.
4. Same as 3, red body.
5. Same as 4, light gray wheels.

32-B Jaguar XKE   **2-5/8"**   **1962**
Metallic red body, with varying shades, ivory interior, clear or green tinted windows, black baseplate, thin or thick tires on wire metal wheels.
1. Green windows, thin gray plastic tires.
2. Green windows, thin black plastic tires.
3. Clear windows, thin gray plastic tires.
4. Clear windows, thin black plastic tires.
5. Clear windows, thick black plastic tires.

32-C Leyland Petrol Tanker   **3"**   **1968**
Green cab & chassis, white tank body, blue tinted windows, silver or white plastic grille & baseplate, 8 plastic wheels on 4 axles, "BP" decals or labels on tank body, with & without tow slot, with & without small block brace behind cab on left side connecting chassis. The Aral labels were made for the European market only. All models come with & without the wording 'Ergomatic' on a flat base or raised platform on the front baseplate. Model changed to Superfast wheels.
1. Green cab and chassis, silver grille and baseplate, "BP" labels, no tow slot.
2. Blue cab and chassis, Aral labels, then same as 1.
3. Same as 1, with tow slot.
4. Same as 3, white grille and baseplate.
5. Same as 2, with tow slot.

32-D Leyland Petrol Tanker   **3"**   **1970**
Green cab & chassis, white tank body, blue tinted windows, five spoke thin wheels, silver plastic grille & baseplate. Most models/variations come with a small brace between the cab & tank more noticable on the left side.
1. "BP" label on front sides of tank.
2. "ARAL" labels on side & rear, blue cab & chassis, white tank. (Produced for the German market only)
3. "BP" label in middle of tank.
4. Gray plastic grille & baseplate.
5. Metallic purple cab and chassis, gray tank with special decal reading "National Association of Matchbox Collectors" in black, (not a Lesney product).

32-E Maserati Bora   **3"**   **1972**
Metallic burgandy, clear windows, bright yellow interior, light green baseplate, grille & rear bumper, wide five spoke wheels.
1. No. 8 on green stripe label on hood.
2. Unpainted metal baseplate.
3. Medium green baseplate.
4. Dark green baseplate.
5. All green baseplate, no label on hood.
6. Large five spoke wheels. (same as 52-A).
7. Small five spoke wheels. (same as 40-A).
8. Green painted metal baseplate, no patent no. on divided axle covers, wide five spoke accent wheels.
9. Green painted metal baseplate, no Pat. No. on divided axle covers, wide five spoke accent wheels, yellow orange and black stripe no. 3 label on hood. (from SF 3-2)
10. Metallic green painted baseplate, no Pat. No. on divided axle covers wide five spoke accent wheels.
11. Metallic gold body, silver/gray painted metal baseplate, no number 32 on baseplate, clear windows, yellow/orange plastic interior and tow hook, five spoke accent wheels. (TP-4)

12. Same as 11, bright yellow plastic interior.

32-F Field Gun   **3"**   **1978**
Military olive green, black plastic gun barrel with spring action plunger, very large five spoke accent wheels, no hub caps.
1. Tan plastic soldiers, diorama and shells.

32-G Atlas Excavator   **3"**   **1981**
Red orange body, charcoal gray platform and turret, gray plastic undercarriage and fake treads, black plastic wheels.
1. Black plastic boom and shovel.
2. Black platform and turret, black plastic boom and shovel.
3. Same as 2, yellow body.

33-A Ford Zodiac MK II Sedan   **2-5/8"**   **1957**
With & without silver grille, bumper, headlights, with & without red painted tail lights, with & without light or dark green tinted windows, black baseplate & tow hook, the shades each color vary from light to dark.
1. Light blue body, no windows, metal wheels, crimped axles.
2. Same as 1, light green body.
3. Same as 1, dark green body.
4. Same as 3, gray plastic wheels.
5. Same as 4, rounded axles.
6. Two-tone tan/orange body, large gray wheels with knobby treads.
7. Same as 6, small gray wheels.
8. Same as 7, with windows.
9. Two-tone silver and tan/orange body, with small gray wheels, knobby treads.
10. Same as 9, large silver wheels.
11. Same as 10, tan/orange body.
12. Same as 11, small silver wheels with finer treads.

33-B Ford Zephyr 6MKIII   **2-5/8"**   **1963**
Blue/green body of shades varying from light to dark, clear windows, ivory interior, black baseplate & tow hook, with & without silver grilles.
1. Gray plastic wheels.
2. Silver plastic wheels.
3. Black plastic wheels.

33-C Lamborghini Miura   **2¾"**   **1969**
Metal grille & baseplate, silver plastic wheels, black plastic tires, red or white interior, with & without tow slot, clear windshield, clear or frosted back window over motor. Model changed to Superfast wheels.
1. Yellow body with various shades, ivory interior, clear back window, with tow slot.
2. Same as 1, no tow slot.
3. Same as 2, red interior.
4. Same as 3, with frosted back window.
5. Metallic gold body, ivory interior, frosted back window, no tow slot.

33-D Lamborghini Miura   **2¾"**   **1970**
Clear windows, frosted rear window, five spoke wheels, metal baseplate and grille.
1. Bright yellow body, red interior, tow box on front baseplate.
2. Bright yellow body, red interior, no tow box.
3. Metallic bronze body, red interior.
4. Light metallic bronze, red interior.
5. Metallic gold body, red interior.
6. Metallic gold body, ivory interior.
7. Light metallic gold body, ivory interior.
8. Light metallic gold body, ivory interior, wide wheels.
9. Light metallic gold body, ivory interior, wide wheels, dark red baseplate and grille.
10. Light metallic gold body, ivory interior, dark florescent red base and grille.
11. Light metallic gold body, ivory interior, wide wheels, bright florescent base and grille.
12. Light metallic gold body, ivory interior, five spoke wide wheels, wide wheel wells, unpainted metal baseplate. (sold in Japan in special black box numbered J-1, also MP-1)
13. Light metallic gold body, ivory interior, multi-spoke wide wheels,

wide wheel wells, flat black painted baseplate. (MP-1)

33-E Datsun or 126X   **3"**   **1973**
Yellow body, amber windows, silver motor and interior, orange baseplate.
1. Wide five spoke slicks, orange baseplate, braces on wheel wells on baseplate do not extend past wheel well opening.
2. Braces on wheel wells on baseplate extend beyond wheel well opening.
3. Unpainted baseplate, long braces.
4. Orange baseplate, long braces, 3 ribs over front & rear axles between braces.
5. Three ribs over front & rear axles between braces, light amber windows.
6. Gold plated body, black painted baseplate, black plastic windshield, green tempa imprint on roof and hood, small black tempa imprint in front of hood over green imprint, black lines tempa imprint highlighting louvers on rear motor lid, five spoke wide wheels, baseplate now reads "Golden X".
7. Same as 6, bright Kelly green tempa imprints on roof and hood.
8. Streaker yellow body, orange painted baseplate, silver motor and interior, five spoke wide wheels, orange on red flame design front to rear, & amber windows.
9. Black on red flame design front to rear, amber windows.
10. Black & red flame design front to rear, light amber windows.
11. Same as 2, black & red flame designs, glossy black painted metal baseplate, baseplate now reads "GOLDEN X". (MP-1)

33-F Police Motor Cyclist   **2½"**   **1977**
White frame, silver plastic motor and exhaust pipes, white plastic seat and side bags, wire wheels with black plastic tires.
1. Black "POLICE" on white labels on bags, dark blue police rider.
2. Same as 1, white painted helmet and gloves and flesh painted face on dark blue plastic rider. (K-66)
3. Same as 1, navy blue (almost black) plastic police rider.
4. Same as 1, light blue plastic police rider.
5. Cream cycle frame, silver plastic motor and exhaust pipes, green plastic seat and side bags, wire wheels with black plastic tires, white 'POLIZIE" on dark green labels on bags, green plastic police rider, white painted helmet and gloves, flesh color painted face. (German issue of K-55)
6. Same as 5, light gray plastic police rider.
7. Same as 3, navy blue (almost black) plastic police rider, black plastic engine and exhaust pipes.
8. Same as 5, green plastic police rider, black plastic engine and exhaust pipes.
9. White cycle frame, silver plated plastic motor and exhaust pipe, green plastic seat and side bags, white "POLIZIE" on green label on bags, green plastic police rider, wire wheels with black tires. In German Blisterpack.
10. Same as 9, black plastic motor and exhaust pipes. In German Blister pack.
11. Same as 9, white cycle frame, black plastic motor and exhaust pipes, green plastic seat and side bags, white "POLIZIE" on green labels on bags, green plastic police rider with white helmet and gloves, flesh colored face. (German K. 71)
12. Same as 3, navy blue (almost black) plastic police rider with white helmet and gloves, flesh colored face, black plastic engine and exhaust pipes.
13. Same as 12, black plastic one piece tire and mag wheels with five spokes.
14. White frame, black plastic motor and exhaust pipes, white plastic seats and side bags, black plastic mag wheels and tires, black "POLICE" on white labels on bags, white painted helmet and gloves, flesh painted face on light blue plastic police rider. (K-66)
15. Black frame, chrome plated motor and exhaust pipes, black plastic mag wheels and tires, white plastic seat and saddle bags, black "L.A.P.D." on white labels on bags, light gray plastic police rider, (Code Red Issue).
16. White frame, black plastic motor and exhaust pipes, black plastic

mag wheels and tires, green plastic seat and saddle bags, white "POLIZIE" on green labels on bags, green plastic rider, white painted helmet and gloves, flesh colored face.

34-A   Volkswagen Microvan   2¼"   1957
Silver grille, headlights, bumper, with & without silver rear bumper, "MATCHBOX INTERNATIONAL EXPRESS" decals on sides, black baseplate.
1. Metal wheels, crimped axles, orange decal.
2. Same as 1, yellow decal.
3. Same as 1, large gray wheels.
4. Same as 2, large gray wheels.
5. Same as 2, large black wheels.
6. Small gray wheels, rounded axles, yellow decal.
7. Same as 6, large gray wheels.
8. Same as 6, large silver wheels.
9. Same as 6, large black wheels.

34-B   Volkswagen Camper   2-3/5"   1962
Light green body, dark green interior & baseplate, flat roof window tinted green, with & without silver grille, headlights, bumper.
The right inside box on the door is solid, first seat casting (I) has a raised rear section of seats and solid seat casting is held by two rivets in the baseplate.
The second seat casting (II) has the seat section reversed, with the raised section in front, ipen space under the seats, and the seats held by two rivets in the baseplate.
The third seat casting (III) has an opening under the front section, no end sections, the seats and table cast to the base, no rivets, and a snap-in baseplate. The right inside box on the door is thin.
1. Dark gray wheels, knobby treads, seat casting I.
2. Black wheels, knobby treads, seat casting I.
3. Dark gray wheels, fine treads, seat casting I.
4. Black wheels, fine treads, seat casting I.
5. Same as 1, seat casting II.
6. Large gray wheels, thick fine treads, seat casting III.
7. Same as 6, large black wheels.
8. Same as 7, thin fine treads.

34-C   Volkswagen Camper Car   2-5/8"   1967
Silver body, orange tinted windows, orange interior, raised roof with six windows, black plastic wheels.

34-D   Volkswagen Camper Car   2-5/8"   1968
Silver body, orange tinted windows, orange interior, short raised sun roof, with license plate under front bumper, with & without tow slot, short or long door handles, black plastic wheels.
1. Short door handle, license plate only.
2. Long door handle, license plate only.
3. Long door handle, license plate & tow slot.

34-E   Formula I Racing Car   2-7/8"   1971
Metallic pink, white driver, clear glass, metal baseplate & front fins, number 16 on white/yellow stripe label on hood, wide four spoke wheels.
1. First casting, rear body extends to lower axle.
2. Second casting, rear body stops at top of axle.
3. Yellow body, number 16 on blue stripe label on hood.
4. Metallic blue body, number 15 yellow strip label.
5. Orange body, number 16 blue strip label.
6. Orange body, number 16 blue strip label, medium clover leaf front wheels, large five spoke rear wheels.
7. Yellow body, number 16 blue strip label, large five spoke rear wheels, five spoke rear wheels.
8. Metallic blue body, number 15 yellow strip label, medium clover leaf rear wheels, large five spoke rear wheels.
9. Orange body, number 16 blue strip label, medium clover leaf rear wheels, large five spoke rear wheels, amber windows.
10. Yellow body, number 16 blue strip label, medium clover leaf front wheels, large five spoke rear wheels.
11. Metallic pink, (second casting) number 16 on white and yellow stripe, clear windshield, 8 spoke clover leaf design wheels.
12. Yellow body, number 16 on white and yellow stripe label on hood,

medium clover leaf front wheels, large five spoke rear wheels, clear windshield.
13. Yellow body, number 16 dark blue stripe label, medium clover leaf front wheels, large five spoke rear wheels, clear windshield.
14. Yellow body, number 16 dark blue stripe label, medium clover leaf front wheels, large fine spoke rear wheels, amber windshield.
15. Orange body, number 16 on white and yellow stripe label on hood, wide four spoke wheels, clear windshield.
16. Orange body, number 16 on white and yellow stripe label on hood, medium clover leaf front wheels, large five spoke rear wheels, clear windshield.
17. Yellow body, streamline casting trim on each side of body above rear wheels, number 16 on white and yellow stripe label on hood, medium clover leaf front wheels, large five spoke rear wheels, clear windshield.
18. Yellow body, streamline casting trim, number 16 dark blue stripe label on hood, medium clover leaf front wheels, large five spoke rear wheels, clear windshield.
19. Yellow body, no streamline casting trim, number 16 dark blue & yellow stripe label on hood, amber windshield, front & rear medium clover leaf wheels.
20. Metallic blue body, no streamline casting trim, number 16 dark blue & yellow stripe label on hood, medium clover leaf front wheels, large five spoke rear wheels, amber windows.
21. Yellow body, streamline casting trim, number 16 dark blue & yellow stripe label on hood, medium clover leaf wheels, large five spoke rear wheels, clear windows.
22. Yellow body, no streamline casting, number 16 dark blue & yellow stripe label on hood, medium clover leaf front wheels, large five spoke rear wheels, amber windshield, silver/gray painted baseplate.
23. Yellow body, no streamline casting trim, number 16 dark blue & yellow stripe label on hood, four spoke large wheels, clear windshield, metal base.
24. Yellow body, streamline casting trim, number 16 dark blue and yellow stripe label on hood, large five spoke wheels, clear windows.
25. Metallic blue body, streamline casting, number 15 yellow stripe label, medium clover leaf front wheels, large five spoke rear wheels, clear windshield, unpainted metal baseplate.
26. Yellow body, streamline casting, number 16 on dark blue and yellow stripe label on hood, large four spoke front wheels (same as 2-B) large five spoke rear wheels, clear windshield, unpainted metal baseplate.
27. Orange/yellow body, streamline casting, number 16 on dark blue and yellow stripe label on hood, large four spoke front wheels, large five spoke rear wheels, clear windshield, unpainted metal baseplate.
28. Yellow body, streamline casting, number 16 dark blue and yellow stripe label on hood, large four spoke front wheels, medium clover leaf rear wheels, clear windshield, unpainted metal baseplate.
29. Orange body, stream line casting trim, number 16 blue and yellow stripe label on hood, large four spoke front wheels, large five spoke rear wheels, clear windshield.
30. Yellow body with streamline casting trim, number 15 yellow and blue stripe label on hood, medium clover leaf front wheels, large five spoke rear wheels, clear windshield . (found in five packs sold at Zayre or Korvette stores.)

34-F   Vantastic   2-7/8"   1975
Orange body, white painted baseplate, white interior, silver plated plastic front engine, small five spoke accent front slicks, large multi-spoke rear slicks.
1. Blue/green tinted windows, black, white & orange fist sticker each side.
2. Blue/green tinted windows, black, white, and orange fist stickers on each side, unpainted metal baseplate.
3. Blue/green tinted windows, black, white and orange fist stickers on each side, white painted baseplate with flat front axle cover.

4. Same as 3, black, white and red side stickers.
5. Same as 3, black,white and red stripes side labels.
6. Orange body, white painted metal baseplate, white interior, engine removed-replaced by full hood, orange and black stripes and black "34" on white label on hood, black, white and red stripes side labels, blue/green tinted windows, small five spoke accent front wheels, large multi-spoke rear wheels. Now found without the black, white and red stripe side labels.
7. Same as 6, light blueish green plastic windows, no side labels.
8. Same as 6, clear plastic windows, no side labels.
9. Same as 6, small five spoke accent wheels, front and rear.
10. Same as 6, small multi-spoke front wheels, large multi-spoke rear wheels.
11. Same as 6, light blueish/green plastic windows, no label on sides, yellow and blue sunburst label on hood. (label from SF47-2).

34-G   Chevy Pro Stocker   3"   1981
White body, unpainted metal baseplate and bumpers, red plastic interior, clear plastic windshield and side windows, frosted plastic rear window, five spoke accent front wheels, large five spoke reverse accent wheels.
1. All tempa prints, large white "34" in blue square on roof, blue stripes on trunk and hood, blue "LIGHTNING" and red lightning symbol on hood, wide blue stripe each side, blue "34" and blue "LIGHTNING RACING" in white rectangle on side doors.
2. Same as 1, tempa prints on side omitted.
3. Same as 1, five spoke accent wheels front and rear.

35-A   Marshall Horse Box   2"   1957
Red cab & baseplate, brown horse box, silver grille & headlights, drop down door on right side of box, 3 rear windows in box.
1. Dark brown box, metal wheels, crimped axles.
2. Same as 1, brown box.
3. Same as 2, small dark gray wheels.
4. Same as 3, rounded axles.
5. Same as 4, small light gray wheels.
6. Same as 4, small silver wheels.
7. Same as 4, small black wheels.

35-B   Snowtrac Tractor   2-3/8"   1964
Red body, silver painted grille & baseplate & tow hook, green windows, white rubber treads, 6 small black plastic rollers.
1. Large "Snow-Trac" decals on sides.
2. Small "Snow-Trac" decals on sides.
3. "Snow-Trac" lettering cast to sides.
4. Plain, no lettering on sides.

35-C   Merryweather Fire Engine   3"   1969
Metallic red body, blue windows & dome lights, white removable ladder on roof, gray plastic baseplate & grille, labels on sides, five spoke thin wheels.
1. First casting, flat side panels, no "Pat. App" or "A" on front baseplate.
2. Second casting, with raised isde panels, lettering "A" inside circle on front base.
3. Letter "A" inside circle on front base.
4. Letter "A" inside circle on base, "Pat. App" now behind rear axle.
5. Florescent red body.
6. Wide wheels, gray baseplate & grille.
7. Light tan baseplate & grille, four rivets holding axle covers.
8. Gray baseplate and grille, four rivets holding axle covers, recessed "A" on base.
9. Gray baseplate and grille, four rivets holding axle covers, raised "A" on base.
10. Black baseplate & grille, four rivets holding axle covers, recessed "A" on base.
11. Gray baseplate & grille, four rivets holding axle covers, recessed "A" on base, eagle on label white instead of yellow.
12. Gray baseplate and grille, four rivets holding axle covers, recessed "A" on base, no label on sides.
13. Gray baseplate and grille, four rivets holding axle covers, raised "A" on base, white eagle on label.

14. Gray baseplate and grille, four rivets holding axle covers, recessed "A" on base, white eagle on label.
15. Same as 11, no number on baseplate, white removable ladder with rounded bumpers on one end, five spoke wide accent wheels. (TP-2)
16. Same as 15, no number on baseplate, multi-spoke wheels . (TP-2)
17. Red body, cab roof removed, gray plastic baseplate and side panels, unpainted metal insert on base with "SNORKEL" and "1981", white plastic snorkel and fire fighter, white tempa "LOS ANGELES CITY FIRE DEPARTMENT" on sides, black plastic interior, blue plastic windows and dome light, five spoke accent wheels. (Code Red Issue)

35-D Fandango 3'' 1975
White body, red interior, chrome plated turbo prop on rear engine, wide large five spoke rear wheels, wide small five spoke front wheels.
1. Clear windshield, red painted baseplate.
2. Clear windshield, red painted baseplate, red plastic turbo prop on rear engine. (unplated turbo prop).
3. Clear windshield, red painted baseplate, silver painted turbo prop, number 60 on blue stripe label on hood.
4. Same as 1, Pat. App. 12174/72 replaced by Pat. number 1424808.
5. Same as 4, unpainted metal baseplate.
6. Red body, red interior, rear mounted red and chrome turbo prop, red painted baseplate, clear windshield.
7. Red body, white interior, rear mounted red and chrome turbo prop, red painted baseplate, clear windshield.
8. Red body, white interior, rear mounted red and chrome turbo prop, unpainted metal baseplate, clear windshield.
9. Same as 4, unpainted metal baseplate, red plastic turbo prop on rear engine.
10. Same as 8, red plastic turbo prop on rear engine, (unplated turbo prop).
11. Same as 8, white painted metal baseplate.
12. Same as 11, blue plastic turbo prop on rear engine.
13. Same as 11, red plastic turbo prop on rear engine.
14. Same as 12, unpainted metal baseplate, blue plastic turbo prop on rear engine.
15. Same as 12, unpainted metal baseplate, dark (royal) blue plastic turbo prop on rear engine.
16. Same as 15, unpainted metal baseplate, dark (royal) blue plastic turbo prop on rear engine, light yellow plastic interior.
17. Same as 16, light purple plastic windows.
18. Same as 14, unpainted metal baseplate, blue plastic turbo prop on rear engine, light yellow plastic interior.
19. Same as 15, unpainted metal baseplate, dark (royal) blue turbo prop on rear engine, white plastic interior, light purple plastic windows.
20. Red body, white plastic interior, blue turbo prop on rear engine, unpainted metal baseplate, light purple plastic windows.
21. Red body, light yellow plastic interior, blue turbo prop on rear engine, unpainted metal baseplate, light purple plastic windows.
22. Red body, white plastic interior, blue turbo prop on rear engine, unpainted metal baseplate, clear plastic window, yellow and blue sunburst label on hood.
23. Same as 22, dark (royal) blue plastic turbo prop on rear engine, yellow and blue sunburst label on hood.

35-E Zoo Truck 1981
35-F Trans Am "T" Roof 1982
Black body, red interior, yellow "turbo" on doors, yellow eagle with spread wings on hood, reverse accent wheels.

36-A Austin A50 2-3/8'' 1957
Silver grille, headlights & front bumper, with & without silver rear bumper, with & without red painted tail lights, crimped axles, black baseplate with tow hook, no windows, number 36 on base, with & without brace above windshield. The colors all have varying shades.
1. Light turquoise body, metal wheels, no brace above windshield.
2. Same as 1, blue/green body.

3. Same as 1, with brace above windshield.
4. Same as 2, with brace above windshield.
5. Same as 2, small gray wheels.
6. Same as 5, with brace above windshield.
7. Same as 4, small gray wheels.
8. Same as 6, light blue/green body.

36-B Lambretta TV175 Motor Scooter & Sidecar 2'' 1961
Metallic green, 3 wheels.
1. Dark metallic green, knobby black plastic wheels.
2. Light metallic green, knobby black plastic wheels.
3. Light metallic green, fine tread black plastic wheels, with small brace behind sidecar wheel.

36-C Opel Diplomat 2¾'' 1966
Metallic light gold body, white interior & tow hook, clear windows, open hood with silver or unplated gray plastic motor, black plastic wheels, with & without tow slot and license plate, black baseplate. Model changed to Superfast wheels.
1. Plain baseplate.
2. Plain baseplate, license plate under front bumper.
3. Tow slot on front baseplate, no license plate.
4. Tow slot and license plate.
5. Tow slot and license plate, gray plastic motor.

36-D Opel Diplomat 2-7/8'' 1970
Ivory interior & tow hook, clear windows, black baseplate, silver motor, five spoke thin wheels.
1. Dark metallic gold body, short steering wheel, no silver trim on grille.
2. Dark metallic gold body, short steering wheel, silver trim on grille.
3. Light metallic gold body, long steering wheel, silver trim on grille.
4. Dark metallic gold body, long steering wheel, no silver trim on grille.
5. Dark metallic gold body, long steering wheel, silver trim on grille.
6. Light metallic gold body, short steering wheel, silver trim on grille.

36-E Hot Rod Draguar 2-13/16'' 1970
Metallic red body, clear canopy, silver motor in hood, metal baseplate & side exhaust pipes, wide five spoke wheels. Comes with/without silver "Draguar" label on rear trunk.
1. Dark cream interior.
2. Ivory interior.
3. Light yellow interior.
4. Light yellow interior, two small braces in front of motor.
5. Dark 'hot pink' body, light yellow interior.
6. Dark 'hot pink', amber windows.
7. Dark 'hot pink' body, white interior, no label, clear windows.
8. Dark hot pink, light yellow interior, no labels, yellow tinted windows.
9. Metallic red body, light yellow interior, no label, amber windows.
10. Dark 'hot pink' body, bright yellow interior, no labels, amber windows.
11. Dark 'hot pink', bright yellow interior, no labels, yellow tinted windows.
12. Dark 'hot pink' body, white interior, no label, amber windows.
13. Dark 'hot pink' body, bright yellow interior, no label, amber windows, five spoke wide wheels. (same as 5-A).

36-F Formula 5000 3'' 1975
Orange body, unpainted metal baseplate, silver rear mounted motor, small five spoke front slicks, large clover leaf rear slicks.
1. Blue driver, black number '3' and white 'Formula 5000' on orange-white and blue label on front, white 'Formula' and black '5000' on orange-white and blue label on rear air foil (several shades of orange).
2. Same as 1, large 5 spoke wide accent wheels on rear.
3. Same as 1, yellow/orange driver.
4. Red body, unpainted metal baseplate, silver rear mounted motor, yellow/orange driver, labels and wheels same as 1.
5. Same as 4, black 'MARLBORO' on red and white label on rear air foil, large red '11' and black 'TEXACO' and 'GOOD YEAR' on red and white label on hood.

6. Same as 5, no label on air foil.
7. Same as 5, red, white and black "CHAMPION" logo label on air foil.

36-G Refuse Truck 3'' 1980
Metallic red body, silver/gray painted metal baseplate & grille, orange-yellow plastic refuse container, five spoke accent wheels.
1. Red plastic windows, red plastic slide inside container providing mechanical dumping.
2. Red plastic windows, red plastic slide inside container, the name "COLLECTOMATIC" molded in orange/yellow plastic upper front of refuse container above driver's cab.
3. Same as 2, dark amber/orange plastic windows.
4. Same as 2, blue body and side label "Metro DPW 66" in black letters on yellow background on sides of container.

37-A Coca Cola Lorry 2¼'' 1956
Uneven case load, silver grille, headlights & bumper, open base, metal rear fenders, "Coca Cola" decals at top of load and rear of truck, 4 metal wheels, crimped axles, numbered 37 inside roof.
1. Large lettered decal at top of load, orange/yellow body.
2. Small lettered decal at top of load, orange/yellow body.
3. Small lettered decal at top of load, yellow body.

37-B Coca Cola Lorry 2¼'' 1957
Orange/yellow body, even case load, open base, metal rear fenders, small "Coca Cola" decals at top of load and rear of truck, silver grille, bumper and headlights.
1. Metal wheels, crimped axles.
2. Gray plastic wheels, crimped axles.

37-C Coca Cola Lorry 2¼'' 1960
Yellow body of various shades, even case load, with & without silver grille, headlights and bumper, black rear fenders & baseplate, small "Coca Cola" decals at top of load and rear of truck (cut short or long), knobby treads.
1. Dark gray plastic wheels and crimped axles.
2. Dark gray plastic wheels and rounded axles.
3. Same as 2, light gray plastic wheels.
4. Same as 2, black plastic wheels.

37-D Cattle Truck 2½'' 1966
Yellow body & chassis, gray plastic box with fold down rear door, black plastic wheels, silver plastic or metal grille & baseplate, with or without wing supports at rear side of tail gate, reversible rear door with half-round or round middle rib at bottom, with & without tow slot, green tinted windows, two white plastic cattle. Model changed to Superfast wheels.
1. Silver plastic baseplate and grille, without wing supports, light gray box, plain baseplate.
2. Same as 1, with wing supports.
3. Same as 2, metal baseplate and grille.
4. Same as 3, dark gray box.
5. Same as 4, with tow slot in baseplate.

37-G Skip Truck 2-11/16'' 1976
Red body, yellow plastic load bucket, unpainted moving arm, light amber windows, silver plastic interior, multi-spoke wide wheels. Load bucket may be found in various shades of yellow or orange/yellow.
1. Glossy black painted baseplate and grille.
2. Flat black painted baseplate and grille.
3. Flat black painted baseplate, clear windows, dull gray interior.
4. Orange body, flat black painted baseplate, clear windows, dull gray interior.
5. Red body, unpainted metal baseplate, clear windows, dull gray interior.
6. Orange body, flat black painted baseplate, clear windows, dull gray interior, red plastic load bucket. (Sold in Germany only)
7. Red body, flat black painted baseplate, amber windows, dull gray interior.
8. Red body, flat black painted baseplate, clear windows, dull gray interior, blue plastic load bucket.
9. Red body, yellow plastic load bucket, flat black painted metal

baseplate, very light blue tinted plastic windows, dull gray plastic interior.
10. Red body, yellow plastic load bucket, metallic brown painted metal baseplate, clear plastic windows, dull gray plastic interior.
11. Same as 9, red body, yellow plastic load bucket, charcoal gray painted metal baseplate, very light blue tinted windows, dull gray interior.
12. Red body, yellow plastic load bucket, unpainted moving arms, clear plastic windows, yellow/orange plastic interior, charcoal gray painted metal baseplate, multi-spoke wide wheels.
13. Metallic blue body, yellow plastic load bucket, unpainted moving arms, clear plastic windows, dull gray plastic interior, charcoal gray painted metal baseplate, multi-spoke wide wheels.
14. Red body, yellow plastic bucket, metallic brown painted metal baseplate, smokey gray tinted plastic windows, dull gray plastic interior.
15. Same as 13, silver gray painted metal baseplate.

37-H Sun Burner   3"   1972
Black body, flat black painted metal baseplate, red and yellow tempa flames on hood and sides, yellow tempa "SUN BURNER" on baseplate, five spoke wheels. "Made In Hong Kong" on baseplate. (formerly SF32)
1. Clear plastic windows, red plastic interior and tow hook.

37-I Matra Rancho   1982
Released in all countries except U.S.A. Preproduction shown in picture.

37-E Cattle Truck   2½"   1970
Green tinted windows, metal baseplate & grille, gray plastic box, white plastic cattle inside, five spoke thin wheels. The rear door panel comes with either rounded or half round middle brace.
1. Yellow/orange cab & chassis.
2. Orange/mustard cab and chassis.
3. Light yellow cab and chassis.

37-F Soopa Coopa   2-7/8"   1972
Metallic blue, amber windows, yellow interior, silver plastic motor, metal baseplate & grille. The rear motor is the same as on number 30 Beach Buggy and number 58 Woosh-n-push.
1. Clover leaf wide wheels, metal base, light blue body.
2. Clover leaf wide wheels, metal base, medium blue body.
3. Clover leaf wide wheels, metal base, dark blue body.
4. Clover leaf wide wheels, silver/gray painted base, medium blue body.
5. Clover leaf wide wheels, metal baseplate, light amber windows, (comes in 3 shades of blue).
6. Five spoke wide wheels (same as 22-B) unpainted metal baseplate, amber windows.
7. Five spoke slicks front wheels, clover leaf rear wheels, unpainted metal baseplate.
8. Metallic pink body, clover leaf wide wheels, orange/red flower (same as 13-B) on roof, unpainted metal baseplate.
9. Metallic pink body, clover leaf wide wheels, orange/red flower on roof, red painted baseplate and grille.
10. Same as 8, with orange body.

38-A Karrier Refuse Collector   2-3/8"   1957
Silver grille headlights & bumper, "Cleansing Department" decals on sides, with & without brace between cab & body, with & without decal cast lines on body.
1. Dark gray body, no side casting, orange decal, no cab brace, metal wheels, crimped axles.
2. Same as 1, gray body.
3. Same as 2, with side casting.
4. Same as 3, with cab brace.
5. Same as 4, with light or dark gray plastic wheels.
6. Same as 5, yellow decal.
7. Same as 5, rounded axles.
8. Same as 6, rounded axles.

38-B Vauxhall Victor Estate   2-5/8"   1963
Yellow body, red or green interior, clear windows, black baseplate & tow

hook, with & without silver grille, headlights, bumper.
1. Light green interior, small gray wheels, knobby treads.
2. Light green interior, silver wheels, finer treads.
3. Light green interior, large gray wheels, fine treads.
4. Same as 3, thin black wheels.
5. Light red interior, silver wheels, fine treads.
6. Same as 5, thin black wheels.
7. Same as 5, thick black wheels.
8. Same as 7, dark red interior.

38-C Honda Motorcycle & Trailer   2-7/8"   1967
Metallic blue/green cycle with wire wheels, black plastic tires, trailer comes with or without red lettered decal or label, "Honda", two black plastic wheels.
1. Red/orange trailer, no decal or label "Honda", short axle channel, no channel brace.
2. Yellow trailer, "Honda" decal, short axle channel, no channel brace.
3. Same as 3, long axle channel.
4. Same as 3, "Honda" label.
5. Same as 3, with channel brace.
6. Same as 4, with channel brace.

38-D Honda Motorcycle & Trailer   2-7/8"   1970
Yellow trailer with five spoke thin wheels, red lettered label on sides.
1. Light blue metallic cycle, left & right casting circles.
2. Pink cycle, left & right casting circle.
3. Metallic purple cycle, right & left casting circle.
4. Orange trailer, red "Honda" on white and yellow side labels, small hubless wheels, number 838 on base, with metallic green Honda cycle. (TP-8)

38-E Stingeroo Cycle   3"   1973
Light metallic purple body, ivory horse head at rear of seat, silver motor and exhaust pipes, orange front plate at handle bars, black wide front wheels, five spoke wide rear wheels.
1. Silver handle bars.
2. Light purple handle bars.
3. Light grayish/blue plastic handle bars.

38-F Jeep   2-3/8"   1976
Military olive green body, glossy black painted baseplate, black plastic interior, wide five spoke reverse accent wheels, no hub caps.
1. Green and white circle label with white star on hood. (G-11)
2. Green and white circle label with white star on hood, half circle punch out upper center of windshield. (G-11)
3. Dark olive green and white circle label with star and "21-11" on hood, half circle punch out upper center of windshield. (G-11)
4. Dark olive green/white label with star and "21-11" on hood, half circle punch out upper center of windshield, black plastic revolving gun mounted on rear of jeep, wide five spoke reverse accent wheels, chrome plated hub caps.
5. Same as 3, wide five spoke reverse accent wheels, no hub caps.
6. Military olive drab, same as 2. (TP-11)
7. Military olive green body, green and white circle label with white star on hood, half circle punch out upper center of windshield, black plastic revolving gun mounted on rear of jeep, wide five spoke reverse accent wheels, no hub caps.
8. Same as 2, high gloss black painted baseplate and tow hook.
9. Yellow body, blue, white, orange wings and 'GLIDING CLUB' on hood, half circle punch-out upper center of windshield, flat black painted baseplate and tow hook, black plastic interior, wide five spoke reverse accent wheels with chrome hub caps. (TP-7)
10. Light blue & blue body, white painted baseplate, bumpers and gas can, black plastic interior, white plastic canopy, large white "U.S. MAIL" tempa imprint on hood, red stripe side labels (light or dark) on canopy, wide five spoke reverse accent wheels with chrome hub caps. (This model is SF Special Issue 1978 No. 11 with original SF 38-3 baseplate) Has two 1/8" high tabs.
11. Same as 10, label now reads, "No II Sleet-N-Snow". (Labels light or dark).

12. Same as 9, baseplate now reads "No II Sleet-N-Snow".
13. Same as 4, no hub caps.
14. Same as 13, black painted baseplate now reads "No II Sleet-N-Snow".
15. Same as 9, raised metal tabs back of seats. (TP-7)
16. Same as 9, raised metal tabs back of seats, baseplate now reads "No. II Sleet-N-Snow". (TP-7).
17. Same as 13, no hub caps, metal body brace above tow hook.
18. Same as 14, no hub caps, baseplate reads 'No. II Sleet-N-Snow', metal body brace above tow hook.
19. Same as 16, "No. II Sleet-N-Snow" on baseplate, no hub caps.
20. Same as 17, "No. 38" on baseplate, chrome hub caps.
21. Same as 18, "No. II Sleet-N-Snow" on baseplate, chrome hub caps.
22. Same as 10, powder blue painted body, "No. 38 Jeep" on baseplate. Found in SF-5 U.S. Mail Truck Boxes.
23. Same as 11, powder blue painted body, "No. II Sleet-N-Snow" on baseplate. Found in SF-5 U.S. Mail Truck Boxes".
24. Same as 18, no hub caps, baseplate reads "No. II Sleet-N-Snow", metal body brace above tow hook, canopy mounting hole in rear seat.
25. Same as 18, no hub caps, "No. 38 Jeep" on baseplate, metal body brace above tow hook, canopy mounting holes in rear seats.
26. Same as 9, raised metal tabs back of seats, "No. 38 Jeep" on baseplate, canopy mounting holes in rear seats. (TP-7)
27. Same as 15, raised metal tabs back of seats, "No. 38 Jeep" on baseplate, no hub caps. (TP-7)
28. Same as 10, rear black plastic seats replaced by blue painted seats part of the body casting, "No. 38 Jeep" on baseplate, with smooth or textured white plastic canopy.
29. Same as 11, rear black plastic seats replaced by blue painted seats part of the body casting, "Sleet-N-Snow" on baseplate, with or without smooth or textured white plastic canopy.
30. Same as 9, raised metal tabs back of seats, "Sleet-N-Snow" on baseplate, canopy mounting holes in rear black plastic seats.
31. Same as 9, raised metal tabs back of seats, "Sleet-N-Snow" on baseplate, canopy mounting holes in rear black plastic seats, five spoke reverse accent wheels, no hub caps.
32. Same as 9, raised metal tabs in back of seats, 'No. 38 Jeep' on baseplate, canopy mounting holes in rear black plastic seats, five spoke reverse accent wheels, no hub caps.
33. Same as 9, "No. 38 Jeep" on baseplate, rear seats now part of body casting. (TP-7)
34. Same as 9, "Sleet-N-Snow" on baseplate, rear seats no part of body casting. (TP-7)

38-G Camper   3"   1980
Red body, unpainted metal baseplate, grille and front bumper, bone white plastic camper on back of pick-up, multi-spoke wheels.
1. Green plastic windows on pick-up.
2. Same as 1, light blueish/green plastic windows on pick-up.

38-H Model "A" Truck (Not released yet)   1982
Blue body with white roof, "Champion Spark Plug" label on sides, black running boards and fenders, silver headlights, grille and front bumper.

39-A Ford Zodiac Convertible   2-5/8"   1957
Peach/pink body of various shades, tan driver (no hat), silver grille, bumper, headlights, with & without red painted tail lights, turquoise interior of various shades, & baseplate with tow hook.
1. Metal wheels, crimped axles.
2. Dark gray plastic wheels, crimped axles.
3. Dark gray plastic wheels, rounded axles.
4. Light gray plastic wheels, rounded axles.
5. Silver plastic wheels, rounded axles.

39-B Pontiac Convertible   2¾"   1962
With & without silver grille, headlights & bumpers, cream or ivory interior, red, cream or ivory steering wheel, red or black baseplate with tow hook, green tinted windshield. Wheels are found light, dark, thick, thin, and with various treads. If not part of the interior, red & ivory steering wheels can be changed.

1. Purple body, red steering wheel, cream interior, red base, silver wheels.
2. Same as 1, ivory interior.
3. Same as 1, gray wheels.
4. Same as 2, gray wheels.
5. Same as 1, yellow body of various shades.
6. Same as 2, yellow body of various shades.
7. Same as 6, ivory steering wheel.
8. Yellow body, cream steering wheel, cream interior, black base, gray wheels.
9. Same as 8, but ivory interior and steering wheel.
10. Same as 7, but black base.

39-C Ford Tractor   2-1/8''   1967
Blue body, black plastic steering wheel & tires, yellow plastic wheels, with & without yellow hood, with long or short stack. Casting circle at both sides of body.
1. Dark blue body, yellow hood, large rear wheels as on number 50-B tractor, short stack.
2. Same as 1, but small rear wheels.
3. Dark blue body, dark blue hood, small rear wheels, long stack. (This model found only with K-20-Atransporters)
4. Same as 3, yellow hood.
5. Same as 2, light blue body.
6. Same as 5, light blue hood.
7. Same as 5, but orange body and orange hood.

39-D Clipper   3''   1973
Metallic dark pink, amber windows, bright yellow interior, dark green front headlight panels & baseplate, silver rear pipes that move up & down by pin on rear wheels, small clover leaf front wheels, large five spoke rear wheels.
1. "Rolamatic", Pat no. 1238927 on front axle cover.
2. Unpainted metal baseplate & headlights, Pat no. 1238927 on front
3. Dark green headlights & baseplate, clear windows, Pat no. 1238927 on front axle cover.
4. Metallic hot pink body, dark green headlights & baseplate, amber windows, pat no. 1238927 on front axle cover.
5. Same as 1, Pat. App. 12174/72 replaced by Pat. No. 1424808, pat. no. 1238927 on front axle cover.
6. Pat. no. 1424808 on unpainted metal baseplate, unpainted headlights, pat. no. 1238927 on front axle cover.
7. Pat. no. 1424808 on unpainted headlights, white plastic exhaust pipes, pat. no. 1238927 on front axle cover.
8. Pat. no. 1424808, green painted baseplate, white plastic exhaust pipes.
9. Pat. no. 1424808, green painted baseplate, white plastic exhaust pipes, clear windows.

39-E Rolls Royce Silver Shadow II   3-1/16''   1979
Metallic silver gray body, clear plastic windshield, red plastic interior, small multi-spoke wheels.
1. Unpainted metal baseplate, silver plated plastic grille, front bumper and light assemblies.
2. Metallic red body, unpainted metal baseplate, silver plated plastic grille, front bumper and light assemblies, clear plastic windows, ivory plastic interior, small multi-spoke wheels.
3. Same as 2, tan plastic interior.
4. Same as 1, light tan plastic interior.

39-F Toyato Celica Super   1982
Preproduction shown

40-A Bedford Tipper Truck   2-1/8''   1957
Red cab & chassis, silver grille, with & without silver headlights & bumper, tan tipper body, 2 front wheels, 4 duel rear wheels, rear tipper door, there are various shades of the red cab.
1. Tipper body dark tan, metal baseplate, knobby treads, crimped axles.
2. Same as 1, light tan tipper body.
3. Tipper body dark tan, dark gray wheels, knobby treads, crimped axles.

4. Same as 3, light tan tipper.
5. Same as 4, round axles.
6. Same as 5, small gray wheels.

40-B Leyland Royal Tiger Coach   3''   1961
Silver/gray body, green tinted windows, black baseplate with & without rear rivet, with & without small side hole connecting baseplate to body, with & without rear extended bumper & baseplate, with & without silver grille, headlights, with & without red painted tail lights., 4 plastic wheels.
1. Gray wheels, knobby treads, two holes in body sides, no rear rivet baseplate.
2. Same as 1, silver wheels.
3. Same as 2, black wheels, fine treads.
4. Black wheels, fine treads, without holes in body sides, with rear rivet baseplate.

40-C Hay Trailer   3¼''   1967
Blue body with tow bar, yellow plastic racks, yellow plastic wheels with black plastic tires, with & without holes in rear base which hold racks, with & without reinforced circle or octagon between rear axle. Last issued plastic racks came with a small brace at the top of the rack and could be placed on any model.
1. Blue body, without top rack brace, two holes in bed, two holes in baseplate, octagon rear axle brace.
2. Same as 1, rounded rear axle brace.
3. Same as 2, without holes in baseplate.
4. Same as 3, without holes in bed.
5. Same as 4, with top rack brace.
6. Same as 5, light blue body.

40-D Vauxhall Guildsman   3''   1971
Pink body, light green windows, light cream interior & tow hook, wide five spoke wheels, metal baseplate & grille. SF 40-1 has been reported with three different positions of the door handles.
1. White star inside black circle label on hood.
2. White star inside blue circle label on hood.
3. White star inside blue circle label on hood, silver/gray baseplate.
4. White star inside circle label on hood, unpainted metal baseplate, large wide five spoke wheels (same as SF 19-2 front).
5. White star inside circle label on hood, unpainted metal baseplate, wide five spoke wheels, yellow/green windows, new body rear casting (edge of trunk retouched and larger insert holes).
6. Red body, green tinted windows, light yellow interior & tow hook, unpainted metal baseplate, white star in blue circle and flame label on hood.
7. Red body, amber windows, light yellow interior and tow hook, unpainted metal baseplate, white star in blue circle and flame on hood, (TP-4).
8. Red body, amber windows, light yellow interior and tow hook, unpainted metal baseplate and grille, one piece solid rounded axle covers, white star in blue circle and flame on hood, multi-spoke wide wheels. (TP-4)
9. Streaker red orange body, blue number 40 on tan on hood, tan stripe front to rear, five spoke wheels, unpainted metal baseplate and grille, green tinted windows, & light yellow interior.
10. Same as 9, large five spoke wheels (same as 19-B).
11. Same as 9, pink body, streaker design on hood.
12. Same as 9, red body, amber windows, streaker design on hood, light yellow interior and tow hook.
13. Same as 9, red body, amber windows, streaker design on hood, one piece solid rounded axle covers, light yellow interior and tow hook, multi-spoke wide wheels.
14. Same as 13, silver gray painted baseplate. (TP-4)

40-E Horse Box   2-13/16''   1977
Orange painted cab, ivory plastic horse van with tan plastic side door, small multi-spoke wheels.
1. Flat black painted metal baseplate and grille, green windows, 2 white plastic horses in van.

2. Same as 1, five spoke accent wheels front and rear.
3. Same as 1, bone white plastic horse van.
4. Same as 1, dark brown plastic side door.
5. Same as 4, dark brown plastic side door, charcoal gray painted baseplate.
6. Metallic green cab, unpainted metal baseplate and grille, ivory plastic horse van with dark brown plastic side door, small multi-spoke wheels.
7. Metallic green cag, charcoal gray painted metal baseplate and grille, ivory plastic horse van with dark brown plastic side door, small multi-spoke wheels.
8. Same as 7, light metallic green cag.
9. Same as 4, dark brown plastic side door, unpainted metal baseplate and grille.
10. Orange cab, black painted metal baseplate and grille, ivory plastic horse van with dark brown plastic side door, clear plastic windows, small multi-spoke wheels.
11. Light metallic green cab, unpainted metal baseplate and grille, ivory plastic horse van with dark brown plastic side door, green plastic windows, small multi-spoke wheels.
12. Metallic green cab, unpainted metal baseplate and grille, ivory plastic horse van with chocolate brown plastic side door, small multi-spoke wheels.
13. Same as 12, charcoal gray painted metal baseplate and grille, chocolate brown plastic side door, ivory plastic horse van

40-F Corvette "T"-Roof   1982
(Preproduction shown)
White body, white interior, black 09 on door with red & black stripes, 2 red stripes on hood and trunk lid, large wheels.

41-A D-Type Jaguar   2-3/16''   1957
Dark green body, black baseplate, open air scoop in front, tan driver, white round decal with black number 41 on front & rear.
1. Metal wheels, crimped axles.
2. Large dark gray plastic wheels, crimped axles.

41-B D-Type Jaguar   2-7/16''   1960
Dark green body, black baseplate, with open & closed air scoop in front, white round decal on front & rear, tan driver.
1. Large dark gray wheels, crimped axle, knobby treads, open air scoop, decal number 41.
2. Same as 1, rounded axle.
3. Same as 2, closed air scoop.
4. Same as 3, light gray wheels.
5. Same as 4, small wheels.
6. Same as 4, large wheels with fine treads.
7. Wire wheels, thin black tires, fine treads, closed air scoop, number 41 decal.
8. Same as 7, number 5 decal.
9. Same as 8, thick black tires.
10. Same as 9, red wheels, black tires, number 41 decal.

41-C Ford GT   2-5/8''   1965
White or yellow body, red interior, clear windows, blue stripe white number 6 decal or label on front hood, with & without tow slot, with & without license plate under front bumper, yellow or red plastic wheels, black tires and baseplate, unpainted metal rear motor & exhaust pipes. All decal labels come in various shades from dark blue to light blue. Model changed to Superfast below.
1. White body, red wheels with thin and thick tires, decal number 6 dark blue, plain base plate.
2. Dark yellow body, yellow wheels, decal number 6 dark blue, plain baseplate.
3. White body, yellow wheels, decal number 6 dark blue, plain baseplate.
4. Same as 3, license plate.
5. Same as 4, tow slot.

6. Same as 3, tow slot.
7. Same as 5, decal number 6 upside down blue.
8. Same as 7, decal number 6 blue.

41-D Ford GT   2-5/8''   1970
White body, red interior, clear windows, number 6 on blue stripe label on hood, five spoke wheels. Labels come in various shades of blue. The motor comes in metal, silver, or tinted blue and can be found on any variation.

1. Black baseplate, thin wheels.
2. Dark green baseplate, thin wheels.
3. Light green baseplate, thin wheels.
4. Metallic red body, black baseplate, thin wheels.
5. Metallic red body, light yellow baseplate, thin wheels.
6. Metallic red body, dark yellow baseplate, thin wheels.
7. Metallic red body, black baseplate, wide wheels, wide wheel wells.
8. Metallic red body, green baseplate, wide wheels, wide wheel wells.
9. Metallic red body, dark yellow baseplate, wide wheels, wide wheel wells.
10. Metallic red body, light yellow baseplate, wide wheels, wide wheel wells.
11. Metallic red body, charcoal baseplate, wide wheels, wide wheel wells.
12. Metallic red body, gray baseplate, wide wheels, wide wheel wells.
13. Metallic red body, light gray baseplate, wide wheels, wide wheel wells.
14. Metallic red body, dark yellow baseplate, thin wheels, wide wheel wells.
15. Metallic red body, green baseplate, thin wheels, wide wheel wells.
16. Metallic red body, green baseplate, thin wheels, narrow wheel wells.
17. White body, black painted metal baseplate, wide wheels, wide wheel wells, (sold in Japan in special black box numbered J-5).
18. White body, black painted metal baseplate, wide wheels, wide wheel wells, green number 6 in black bordered white circle on yellow, green and white stripes label on hood. (label same as SF 62-3 sold in Japan in special black box numbered J-5).
19. Yellow body, black painted metal baseplate, multi-spoke wide wheels, wide wheel wells, no label on hood. (found in Italy in small carrying cases).
20. Same as 18, multi-spoke wheels.
21. White body, black painted metal baseplate, five spoke wide wheels, wide wheel wells, brown cat face label on hood (label same as SF-1-2 Modrod).

41-E Siva Spider   3''   1972
Metallic red body, cream interior, clear windows, metal baseplate, wide five spoke wheels.

1. Silver strap over body.
2. Black strap over body.
3. Black strap over body, 14 raised lines on top of strap.
4. Black strap over body, 14 raised lines on top of strap, white interior.
5. Black strap over body, ivory interior.
6. Black strap over body, ivory interior, large four spoke wheels, (same as 2-B).
7. Light blue body, unpainted metal baseplate, black plastic roof strap with raised lines, ivory interior, clear windows, black and white "spider on web" tempa imprint on hood, black and white "GOOD YEAR" logo tempa imprint on roof, wide five spoke wheels. (This model is SF special issue No. VIII with original SF 41-2 baseplate).
8. Same as 7, black windshield. (This model is SF special issue No. VIII with original SF 41-2 baseplate).
9. Same as 7, baseplate now reads, "No. VIII Black Widow".
10. Same as 8, baseplate now reads, "No. VIII Black Widow".
11. Streaker metallic blue body, white stars on hood, red & white stripe front to rear, white bordered blue number 8 on roof, clear windows, black strap over body, five spoke slicks, unpainted metal baseplate & grille, & ivory interior.

12. Unpainted metal baseplate & grille, ivory interior, five spoke wide wheels. (Same as 75-B)
13. Unpainted metal baseplate & grille, white interior, five spoke slicks.
14. Same as 11, unpainted metal baseplate & grille, baseplate now reads "No. VII BLACK WIDOW", ivory interior, five spoke slicks.

41-F Chrevrolet Ambulance   2-15/16''   1978
White body, unpainted metal baseplate, bumpers and grille, blue frosted windshield, blue tinted windows and dome light, light gray interior, multi-spoke wide wheels.

1. Red Cross, black "AMBULANCE" and yellow and red stripes on white side labels.
2. Blue registered emergency medical techicians logo on white and blue "EMERGENCY MEDICAL SERVICE" on pale greenish/yellow side labels.
3. Same as 1, dark blue windows and dome lights.
4. Same as 2, dark blue windows and dome lights.
5. Same as 2, light yellow plastic interior.
6. Same as 2, bright orange plastic interior.
7. Metallic silver gray body, light gray plastic interior, unpainted metal baseplate, bumpers and grille, blue plastic windows and dome light, black "RALLYE-81" and "PARIS-DAKAR" on yellow shield and blue and red stripes broken by gray "SFP" and dark blue "SFP" and red, blue and green squares in white oval with blue border all on silver gray background side labels, multi-spoke wide wheels, (sold in France).
8. Same as 1, "AMBULANCE" labels, light yellow plastic interior.
9. Same as 1, "AMBULANCE" labels, bright orange plastic interior.
10. Same as 2, pale blue plastic windows and dome lights.
11. Same as 2, dark blue plastic windows and dome lights, dark tan plastic interior.
12. White body, unpainted metal baseplate, bumpers and grille, blue frosted windshield, blue windows and dome lights, light gray plastic interior, black "AMBULANCE" on yellow background bordered by thin line and white on blue E.M.S. logo side labels, multi-spoke wide wheels. BP
13. Bright red body, unpainted metal baseplate, bumpers and grille, blue frosted windshield, blue plastic windows and dome lights, light gray plastic interior, white plastic rear doors, red "TEL-112" on white tempa rectangle on cab doors, red cross on white tempa door outline and red tempa "NOTARZT" on sides, multi-spoke wheels. (sold in Germany).
14. Same as 12, black "AMBULANCE" on narrow stripe white side labels.
15. White body, unpainted metal baseplate, bumpers and grille, blue frosted windshield, blue plastic windows and dome lights, yellowish/gray interior, white plastic rear doors, red tempa cross on roof and on side doors, red tempa stripe with white "PACIFIC AMBULANCE" on sides, red tempa stripe with white "PACIFIC" each side on hood, red tempa "101" and "EMERGENCY" on roof, multi-spoke wheels. (Code Red Issue).

41-G Kenworth Conventional Aerodyne   1982
Red cab and chassis, silver plastic gas tanks and side vertical exhaust pipes, white & black diagonal stripes behind side of cab and horizontal black & white stripes on door and side of hood.

42-A Bedford Evening News Van   2¼''   1957
Yellow/yellow orange body, silver grille, with & without silver headlights & bumpers, black baseplate, with red lettered decal "EVENING NEWS" on sides, "FIRST WITH THE NEWS" white letters on red background decal at top of hood, with 3 different braces inside holding rivet for sign, colors of models vary from yellow/orange to yellow.

1. Metal wheels, crimped axles, knobby treads, letter "A" inside cab roof.
2. Same as 1, dark gray wheels.
3. Same as 2, rounded axles.
4. Same as 3, light gray wheels.
5. Same as 4, black wheels.

6. Same as 5, dark gray wheels letter "B".
7. Same as 6, light gray wheels.
8. Same as 7, black wheels.
9. Light gray wheels, rounded axles, fine treads, letter "C".
10. Same as 9, black wheels.

42-B Studebaker Lark Wagonaire   3''   1965
Blue body, sliding rear roof panel, white plastic interior & tow hook, clear windows, metal baseplate & grille, black plastic wheels, white plastic hunter & dogs, with & without tow slot. Body colors vary from dark, medium and light shades.

1. Blue metal roof panel.
2. Blue metal roof panel, tow slot.
3. Light blue roof panel, tow slot.

42-C Iron Fairy Crane   3''   1969
Red body, yellow/orange crane, yellow plastic single cable hook, black plastic hydraulic sleeve holding unpainted metal piston, yellow/orange plastic baseplate & seat, black plastic wheels. The variations can be located by viewing the square hole in the baseplate. The thin seat casting hole is wider. Model changed to Superfast wheels.

1. Thin plastic seat.
2. Thick plastic seat.

42-D Iron Fairy Crane   3''   1970
Yellow plastic body, four spoke wheels, orange/yellow baseplate. May be found in most variations with either a bright yellow or darker yellow plastic hook.

1. Red body, yellow boom, wide wheels.
2. Red body, lime green boom, wide wheels.
3. Red/orange body, yellow boom, wide wheels.
4. Red/orange body, lime green boom, wide wheels.
5. Light red/orange body, lime green boom, wide wheels.
6. Light red/orange body, lime green boom, thin wheels.
7. Red/orange body, lime green boom, thin wheels.

42-E Tyre Fryer   3''   1972
Metallic blue, yellow interior, silver plastic motor with black cover, black baseplate.

1. Five spoke wide wheels, very light blue body.
2. Five spoke wide wheels, very dark blue body.
3. Five spoke wide wheels, blue body, unpainted baseplate.
4. Five spoke wide wheels, blue body, light yellow interior, black base.
5. Small clover leaf front wheels, large five spoke rear wheels, blue body, black painted baseplate, yellow interior.
6. Five spoke wide wheels front and rear, orange/yellow interior, black painted baseplate.
7. Orange body with label on front, yellow interior.

42-F Mercedes Container Truck   3''   1977
Red body, black painted baseplate and grille, removable ivory plastic container with red roof and rear door six small multi-spoke wheels.

1. Dark blue windows, red, white and black 'SEALAND' side labels on container, vertical ribs each side inside rear of container, no connecting rib on roof.
2. Same as 1, vertical ribs each side inside rear of container, with connecting rib on roof.
3. Yellow painted cab and chassis, black painted baseplate, removable yellow plastic container, vertical ribs each side inside rear of container with connecting rib on roof, dark blue windows, black 'DEUTSCHIE BUNDESPOST' on white side labels. ('DEUTSCHE BUNDESPOST' means German Post Office).
4. Same as 2, unpainted metal baseplate.
5. Same as 2, red and white stripe flag and black on white "NYK Worldwide Service" side labels.
6. Same as 4, red and white stripe flag and black on white "NYK Worldwide Service" side labels.
7. Same as 4, "SEALAND" labels, unpainted metal baseplate, six small multi-spoke wheels, no hub caps.
8. Same as 4, bone white plastic container, "SEALAND" labels.
9. Same as 4, bone white plastic container, "O.C.L." labels.
10. Same as 4, unpainted metal baseplate and grille, "SEALAND"

labels, ivory plastic container, multi-spoke wheels under cab, five spoke reverse accent wheels under container.

11. Red body and chassis, unpainted metal baseplate and grille, removable white plastic container with red plastic roof and rear doors, yellow and red "MATCHBOX" logo and yellow and red stripes on wide glossy white side labels, blue plastic windows, small multi-spoke wheels. The smooth raised platform on side of container where the label is applied has been extended all the way from the roof line to above the lift holes.

12. Blue body and chassis, unpainted metal baseplate and grille, blue plastic container with non-opening rear doors, black plastic snap-in section of container, white "KARSTADT" on blue background side labels, blue plastic windows, small multi-spoke wheels.

13. Metallic dark green body and chassis, unpainted metal baseplate and grille, dark green plastic container with orange/yellow roof and movable doors, red "MAYFLOWER" on yellow background and white sail ship on green background and white borders on side labels, blue plastic windows, small multi-spoke wheels.

14. Red body and chassis, unpainted metal baseplate and grille, removable white plastic container with red plastic roof and rear doors, black arrows and "CONFERN" and "MOBELTRANSPORTBETRIEBE" on wide red and orange side labels, blue plastic windows, small multi-spoke wheels. (sold in Germany).

15. Same as 13, purple plastic windows.

16. Same as 13, yellow plastic roof and movable rear doors, purple plastic windows.

42-G '57' Ford T. Bird   1982
Red body open convertible, white interior, silver spare tire cover mounted on trunk, clear windshield, silver grille.

43-A Hillman Minx   2-5/8''   1958
With & without silver grille, headlights and bumpers, with & without red painted tail lights, no windows, black baseplate & tow hook.

1. Body green, roof green, wheels metal, axles crimped.
2. Bluish/gray body, light gray roof, metal wheels, crimped axles.
3. Same as 2, dark gray wheels.
4. Light turquoise body, cream roof, dark gray wheels, crimped axles.
5. Same as 4, rounded axles.
6. Same as 5, light gray wheels.

43-B Aveling Barford Tractor Shovel 2-5/8'' 1962
Yellow body, with yellow or red driver, shovel and baseplate, 4 large black plastic wheels.

1. Yellow body, yellow driver and baseplate, yellow shovel.
2. Same as 1, red shovel.
3. Same as 2, red baseplate and driver, yellow shovel.
4. Same as 3, red shovel.

43-C Pony Trailer   2-5/8''   1968
Yellow body, clear windows, gray plastic rear fold-down door, tan or green baseplate & tow bar, two white plastic horses inside, 4 black plastic wheels on 2 open axles.

1. Tan baseplate, tow bar brace "A" rear door dark gray, rear door brace letter "A".
2. Same as 1, rear door brace letter "B".
3. Same as 2, green baseplate.
4. Same as 3, light gray rear door.
5. Green baseplate, "B" tow bar brace, dark gray rear door, rear door brace letter "C".
6. Same as 5, light gray rear door.

43-D Pony Trailer   2-5/8''   1970
Yellow body, clear windows, gray rear door, two white horses, five spoke thin wheels.

1. Dark green baseplate & tow hitch.
2. Light green baseplate & tow hitch.
3. Cinnamon body, clear windows, brown rear ramp door, two white horses, small hubless accent wheels, black painted baseplate & tow hitch, round red and white horse head label each side, no number 43 on base. (TP-3)

4. May be found with thin or thick rear bumpers, on the thin bumper, the license plate is more noticable.
5. Same as 3, thick fenders over wheels.
6. Tan body, clear windows, brown plastic rear ramp door, two white plastic horses, small hubless accent wheels, thick fenders over wheels, black painted baseplate and tow hitch, round red and white horse head labels on sides, no number 43 on base. (TP-3) Now without the horse head label on sides.
7. Same as 5, pale avocado green body.
8. Tan body, smoke tinted plastic windows, dark chocolate brown plastic rear ramp door, two white plastic horses, small hubless accent wheels, thick fenders over wheels, black painted metal baseplate and tow hitch, round red and white horse head side labels, no number 43 on baseplate. (TP-3).
9. Cinnamon body, clear plastic windows, brown rear ramp door, two white plastic horses, small hubless accent wheels, thick fender over wheels, charcoal gray painted metal baseplate and tow hitch, round red and white horse head side labels, no number 43 on baseplate. (TP-3)

43-E Dragon Wheels   2-13/16''   1972
(Volkswagen), light green body, amber windows, silver interior, red plastic lifter, small five spoke wide front wheels, larger clover leaf rear wheels, side door labels have black lettering "Dragon Wheels" on orange background.

1. Black baseplate.
2. Unpainted metal baseplate, darker green body.
3. Black painted baseplate, dark green body.
4. Black painted baseplate, dark green body, light amber windows.
5. Black painted baseplate, dark green body, light amber windows, five spoke wide front wheels, (same as SF 40-1).
6. Black painted baseplate, dark green body, light amber windows, five spoke wide front wheels (same as SF 40-1).
7. Charcoal (blueish) painted baseplate, dark green body, dark amber windows, five spoke front wheels (same as 40-1).
8. Gray painted baseplate, dark green body, dark amber windows, five spoke front wheels (same as 40-1)
9. Black painted baseplate, dark green body, dark amber windows, small multi-spoke front wheels, large multi-spoke rear wheels.
10. Same as 3, multi-spoke front wheels.
11. Black painted baseplate, dark green body, dark amber windows, small multi-spoke front wheels, large clover leaf rear wheels.

43-F 0-4-0 Steam Loco   3''   1978
Red painted metal cab, coal bin and water tanks, black plastic boiler, coal, baseplate, tow hook and tow ring, four black plastic wheels.

1. White "4345" and border on red background side labels.
2. Green metal cab, coal bin and water tanks, black plastic boiler, coal, baseplate, tow hook and tow ring, four black plastic wheels, red "N—P", black wreath on tan oval on green rectangular side labels. (TP-27).

43-G Peterbilt ® Conventional   1982
Black cab and chassis, silver plastic grille, fender, gas tanks and vertical exhaust pipes behind cab, red and white striped Z and lines on sides, 6 wheels.

44-A Rolls Royce Silver Cloud   2-5/8''   1958
Metallic blue body, no windows, with & without silver grille, headlights, bumpers, with & without red painted tail lights, black base. Colors will vary on most models listed.

1. Body metallic dark blue, metal wheels, knobby treads, crimped axles.
2. Same as 1, metallic blue.
3. Same as 2, dark gray wheels.
4. Same as 3, metallic light blue.
5. Metallic dark blue body, dark gray wheels, knobby treads, rounded axles.
6. Same as 5, silver wheels, thin or thick wheels.
7. Same as 6, finer treads.
8. Same as 7, metallic light blue.

44-B Rolls Royce Phantom V   2-7/8''   1964
Clear windows, ivory interior, black baseplate, black plastic wheels, with & without silver grille, headlights, bumpers, trunk opens.

1. Metallic gray body, black wheels, without rear body reinforcement.
2. Same as 1, metallic silver gray body.
3. Metallic pinkish tan, gray wheels, without rear body reinforcement.
4. Same as 3, black wheels.
5. Same as 4, with rear body reinforcement.
6. Same as 5, metallic light tan.

44-C GMC Refrigerator Truck   1967
Red ribbed roof cab & chassis, turquoise box with gray plastic rear door that opens, gray plastic quarter baseplate & grille, green windows, with & without tow slot, with & without small brace at rear of box. Model changed to Superfast wheels.

1. Plain baseplate, rear door light gray, without rear box reinforcement.
2. Same as 1, with rear box reinforcement.
3. Same as 2, tow slot baseplate.
4. Same as 3, rear box reinforcement.

44-D GMC Refrigerator Truck   2-13/16''   1970
Green windows, gray plastic grille & front baseplate, four spoke wheels, gray plastic rear door.

1. Red cab & chassis, turquoise box, thin wheels.
2. Yellow cab & chassis, red box, thin wheels.
3. Yellow cab & chassis, red box, wide wheels.

44-E Boss Mustang   2-7/8''   1972
Yellow body, amber windows, mat black hood, silver motor & interior, clover leaf wide wheels.

1. Metal baseplate.
2. Front motor under hood now grooved.
3. Grooved motor, silver/gray baseplate.
4. Grooved motor, metal baseplate, light amber windows.
5. Grooved motor, metal baseplate, light amber windows, glossy black hood.
6. Grooved motor, unpainted metal baseplate, amber windows, five spoke wide wheels (same as 3-B).
7. Dark green body, three white tempa stripes front to rear on top, white "COBRA" tempa print on doors, unpainted metal baseplate, number 44 on baseplate, amber plastic windows, chrome plated plastic interior and motor showing through hood, small clover leaf front wheels, large clover leaf rear wheels. (LEM).

44-F Railway Passenger Coach 3-1/16''   1978
Red painted metal lower half of coach, cream plastic upper half and roof, black plastic baseplate, railings and couplings, black plastic wheels.

1. Green tinted windows, cream "431'432" and cream frame line on red background side labels.
2. Green tinted windows, cream thin numbers "431-432" and cream line on red background side labels.
3. Same as 1, bone white plastic upper half of roof. May be found with the cream plastic upper half and roof mounted with narrow window toward the coupling ring or the wide window toward the coupling ring.
4. Same as 1, front and rear edge of baseplate reinforced.
5. Same as 4, dark green plastic windows.
6. Same as 4, blue plastic windows.
7. Same as 4, no windows, three metal dividers on floor inside coach.
8. Same as 4, no windows, one metal divider on floor inside coach.
9. Red painted metal lower half of coach, cream plastic upper half and roof, black plastic baseplate, railings and couplings, black plastic wheels, no windows, one metal divider, two black plastic dividers one on each side of the metal divider on floor inside coach, cream "431-432" and cream frame line on red background side labels.
10. Same as 4, clear plastic windows.
11. Same as 9, red accentuated "G.W.R." on green background side labels. (label from SF47-1).
12. Green metal lower half, cream upper plastic half with caboose roof,

black plastic baseplate, railings and couplings, black plastic wheels, red "5810-6102", black wreath on elongated tan and green side labels. (TP-27)

44-G Chevy 4x4 Van   **1982**
Green body, green tinted windows, white letters "Ridin' High" and black horse & fence on sides, large clover leaf wheels.

45-A Vauxhall Victor Saloon   **2-3/8"**   **1958**
Yellow body, with & without green tinted windows, with & without silver grille, headlights, bumper, with & without red painted tail lights, black baseplate with tow hook. Green windows come in various shades and may appear clear.
1. Without windows, metal wheels, knobby treads, crimped axles.
2. Same as 1, small gray wheels.
3. Same as 2, rounded axles.
4. Same as 3, green windows.
5. Same as 4, large gray wheels.
6. Same as 5, large silver wheels.
7. Same as 6, small silver wheels, finer treads.
8. Same as 7, small black wheels.
9. Same as 8, large black wheels.

45-B Ford Corsair w/Boat   **2-3/8"**   **1965**
Pale yellow body, clear windows, red interior & tow hook, metal baseplate & grille, green roof rack with green plastic boat.
1. Silver/gray painted baseplate, black plastic wheels.
2. Unpainted metal baseplate, gray plastic wheels.
3. Unpainted metal baseplate, black plastic wheels.

45-C Ford Group 6   **3"**   **1970**
Metallic green body, clear windows, ivory interior, silver motor, five spoke wide wheels. For most variations, others can be found in G-3 Gift Sets with a "Burmah" label on the rear side of the body.
1. Metal baseplate, round number 7 label.
2. Black baseplate, round number 7 label.
3. Black baseplate, square number 7 label.
4. Black baseplate, square number 45 label.
5. Yellow baseplate, square number 45 label.
6. Pink baseplate, square number 45 label.
7. Gray baseplate, square number 45 label.
8. Pink baseplate, square number 45 label, amber windows.
9. Lime green body, amber windows, yellow baseplate, square number 45 labels.
10. Lime green body, amber windows, pink baseplate, square number 45 labels.
11. Lime green body, amber windows, charcoal baseplate, square number 45 labels.
12. Lime green body, amber windows, gray baseplate, square number 45 label.
13. Lime green body, amber windows, black baseplate, square number 45 on label.
14. Lime green body, amber windows, light gray baseplate, square number 45 labels.
15. Charcoal baseplate, gray plastic motor & tail pipes.
16. Gray plastic motor & tail pipes, body at rear of baseplate is partly rounded.
17. Dark metallic red, silver motor, light & dark amber windows.
18. Dark metallic red, gray plastic motor, light & dark amber windows.
19. Dark metallic red, silver motor, light or dark amber windows, gray baseplate.
20. Dark metallic red, silver motor, amber windows, black baseplate, yellow/orange & black 'eyes' label on hood. (same as SF 31-2).
21. Kelly green body, metal baseplate, round number 7 label on hood, clear windows, silver motor.
22. Metallic green body, black baseplate, round number 7 label on hood, clear windows, silver motor, Burmah labels on sides.
23. Metallic green body, black baseplate, square number 7 label on hood, clear windows, silver motor, Burmah labels on sides.
24. Metallic green body, pink baseplate, square number 45 label on hood, clear windows, silver motor, Burmah labels on sides.

25. Lime green body, black baseplate, square number 45 label on hood, amber windows, gray motor.
26. Lime green body, gray baseplate, square number 45 label on hood, amber windows, silver motor, Burmah label on sides.
27. Dark metallic red, green baseplate, yellow/orange & black 'eyes' label on hood, amber windows, silver motor.
28. Dark metallic red, green painted baseplate, square number 45 label on hood, amber windows, silver motor.
29. Metallic magenta body, black baseplate, square number 45 label on hood, amber windows, gray motor.
30. Lime green body, black baseplate, square number 45 label on hood, light amber windows, silver motor.
31. Lime green body, black baseplate, square number 45 label on hood, light amber windows, gray motor.
32. Metallic green body, metal baseplate, square number 7 label on hood, clear windows, silver motor, Burmah labels on sides.
33. Metallic green body, yellow baseplate, square number 45 label on hood, clear windows, silver motor, Burmah labels on sides.
34. Metallic green body, charcoal gray painted baseplate, square number 45 label on hood, amber windows, silver motor.
35. Dark metallic red, green painted baseplate, square number 45 label on hood, amber windows, silver motor, white interior.
36. Dark metallic red, black baseplate, square number 45 label on hood, amber windows, silver motor, white interior.

45-D BMW 3.0 CSL   **2-7/8"**   **1976**
Orange body, light yellow interior, unpainted metal baseplate, wide five spoke accent wheels.
1. Green tinted windows, black, white & blue BMW logo on yellow and red stripe label on hood. May now be found without label on hood. Now found with the same plastic window insert found in 2 or 3. Molded with a depressed circle to allow the dome light of 2 or 3 to be fitted.
2. White body, light yellow interior, unpainted metal baseplate, amber dome light on roof over driver's seat, green tinted windows, green painted hood and trunk lids, black '123' on white label on hood, white 'POLIZEI' on green side labels on doors, wide five spoke accent wheels. (sold in Germany) Green tempa imprint is usually darker green than the same imprint on 45-B (3).
3. Same as 2, blue dome light on roof over the driver's seat.
4. Same as 1, reinforced hinges inside doors. May be found with or without label on hood.
5. White body, light yellow plastic interior, unpainted metal baseplate, green tinted plastic windows, green painted hood and trunk lid, wide five spoke accent wheels. (MP-1)
6. White body, light yellow plastic interior, unpainted metal baseplate, green tinted plastic windows, black, white and blue "BMW" logo on yellow and red stripe label on hood, black "J. Manhalter" signature on white label on trunk, wide five spoke accent wheels. (Promotional)
7. Same as 4, ivory plastic interior.
8. Same as 4, reinforced hinges inside doors, clear plastic windows.
9. Same as 4, reinforced hinges inside doors, dark green plastic windows.
10. Same as 4, reinforced hinges on doors, clear plastic windows, ivory plastic interior.
11. Same as 4, reinforced hinges on doors, dark green plastic windows, ivory plastic interior.
12. Same as 1, red body.

45-E Kenworth ® Caboner Aerodyne   **1982**
White body, silver plastic grille, gas tank and vertical exhaust pipes, 6 wheels, blue & brown broken stripes on sides.

46-A Morris Minor 1000   **2"**   **1958**
Dark green body, no windows, with & without silver grille, headlights & bumpers, with & without red painted tail lights, black baseplate. The green models come in various shades.
1. Dark green body, metal wheels, knobby treaks, crimped axles.
2. Same as 1, small gray wheels.

3. Same as 2, blue body.

46-B Pickford Removal Van   **2-5/8"**   **1960**
With & without silver grilles, bumpers, black baseplate, 3 die-cast models were produced with 3 different decals.
No. 1: single line seam in upper roof;
No. 2: double line seam in upper roof; with gas cap & tool box cast on left side of Van.
No. 3: extended rear bumper.
1. Dark blue body, die-cast number 1, 3 line decal, large dark gray wheels, knobby treads.
2. Same as 1, small dark gray wheels.
3. Same as 2, small light gray wheels.
4. Same as 3, die-cast number 2, 2 line decal.
5. Same as 4, light gray wheels.
6. Same as 5, 3 line decal, large silver wheels.
7. Green body, die-cast number 2, 3 line decal, small silver wheels, knobby treads.
8. Same as 7, large light gray wheels.
9. Same as 8, small dark gray wheels.
10. Same as 9, black wheels.
11. Same as 10, fine treads.
12. Same as 11, die-cast number 3.
13. Same as 12, die-cast number 2, decal "Beals Bealson", fine treads.

46-C Mercedes Benz 300 SE   **2-7/8"**   **1968**
Clear windows, ivory interior, metal grille & baseplate with tow slot, rear trunk & front doors open, black plastic wheels.
1. Green body.
2. Dark metallic blue body.
3. Light metallic blue body.

46-D Mercedes Benz 300 SE   **2-7/8"**   **1970**
Ivory interior, clear windows, metal baseplate & grille, five spoke thin wheels.
1. Metallic blue, front doors open.
2. Metallic dark gold, front doors open.
3. Metallic light gold, front doors open.
4. Metallic light gold, front doors cast shut.
5. Military olive green body, front doors and truck lid cast shut, number 46 on baseplate removed, white letter "STAFF" and red and yellow shield on olive green labels on side doors, five spoke accent wheels, no hub caps. (TP-14).
6. Same as 5, multi-spoke wheels, no hub caps.
7. Metallic silver gray body, unpainted metal baseplate, number 46 on baseplate removed, ivory plastic interior, clear windows, multi-spoke wheels.

46-E Stretcha Fetcha   **2¾"**   **1972**
White body, blue windows & dome lights, pale yellow interior, small wide clover leaf wheels, red baseplate, red cross label on sides.
1. Small mirror, red baseplate.
2. Larger mirror, red baseplate.
3. Unpainted metal baseplate, small & large mirror.
4. Red base, pale yellow interior, light blue tinted windows.
5. Red base, light cream interior, light blue tinted windows.
6. Red base, pale yellow interior, light blue tinted windows, plain red cross label on sides (without word AMBULANCE).
7. Red base, pale yellow interior, light blue tinted windows, plain red cross label on sides (without word Ambulance).
8. Red painted baseplate, pale yellow interior, blue tinted windows, red cross ambulance label on sides, small five spoke wide wheels.
9. Red painted metal baseplate, pale yellow interior, blue tinted windows and dome light, red cross ambulance labels on sides, four spoke wide wheels.
10. Red painted baseplate, pale yellow interior, very dark blue tinted windows and dome lights, red cross ambulance labels on sides, small wide clover leaf wheels.
11. Red body, red painted baseplate, pale yellow interior, blue tinted windows and dome lights, small wide clover leaf wheels,

black "UNFALL RETTUNG" on white side labels, black "NOTRUF 112" on white narrow label on roof between top of windows, this label reads from back to front. (sold in Germany)

12. White body, red painted baseplate, pale yellow interior, amber windows and dome lights, red cross and "AMBULANCE" labels on sides, small clover leaf wheels. (MP-1)

13. White body, red painted baseplate, pale yellow interior, amber windows and dome light, plain red cross label on sides, (without word AMBULANCE), small clover leaf wheels.

14. Bright green body, glossy black painted baseplate, number 46 on baseplate, all tempa print designs, black and white "VIPER VAN" and black and white triangle forward on each side, black thin stripe around side windows, white plastic rear door, pale yellow plastic interior, amber plastic windows and dome light, small clover leaf wheels. (LEM)

15. Same as 14, white painted metal baseplate. (LEM).

16. Same as 14, white painted metal baseplate, cream plastic interior.

46-F Ford Tractor   2-3/16"   1978
Blue body, unpainted metal baseplate, tow hook and motor, small black deep tread plastic front wheels, large black plastic rear wheels.

1. light yellow interior, yellow plastic harrow as a detached accessory.
2. Same as 1, dark mustard yellow plastic harrow.
3. Same as 1, light yellow interior, no harrow attached, yellow painted hub design. (TP-11).
4. Same as 1, light yellow interior, yellow painted hub design on large rear wheels, yellow tire rings on small front wheels. (farm set).
5. Same as 1, bright yellow interior.
6. Same as 4, white plastic interior, yellow painted hub design on rear wheels, yellow tire ring on small front wheels. The variation of light yellow or orange/yellow plastic harrow can be found with any of the other variations.
7. Same as 4, white plastic interior, yellow painted hub design on rear wheels, black plastic small front wheels.
8. Metallic lime green body, unpainted metal baseplate, tow hook and motor, yellow plastic interior, yellow detached plastic harrow, small seep thread plastic front wheels with yellow ring imprint, large deep thread black plastic rear wheels with yellow hub designs.
9. Same as 8, metallic green body.
10. Same as 8, metallic lime green body, the "FORD" name is now left off the baseplate and the front of the tractor.
11. Same as 8, metallic green body, the "FORD" is now left off the baseplate and the front of the tractor.
12. Same as 8, metallic green body, "FORD" is now left off the front of the tractor, "FORD" remains on the baseplate.

46-G Hot Chocolate   2-13/16"   1972
Metallic brown front lid and sides, black roof, rear and fenders, flat black painted metal baseplate with hole center of rear axle cover, chrome plated plastic engine, exhaust pipes and interior, pearl gray tempa stripes on roof and rear, five spoke accent front wheels, large five spoke rear wheels, "Made In Hong Kong" on baseplate. (formerly SF43-3).

1. Amber plastic windows, red plastic body support bar.

47-A 1 Ton Trojan Van   2¼"   1958
Red body, no windows, with & without silver grille, headlights, black baseplate, green leaf decal on side doors, white lettered black outlined "BROOKE BOND TEA" in three lines on sides.

1. Metal wheels, knobby treads, crimped axles, red grille.
2. Same as 1, dark gray wheels.
3. Same as 2, silver grille.
4. Same as 3, rounded axles.
5. Same as 4, gray plastic wheels.

47-B Commer Ice Cream Canteen   1963
Metallic blue, blue or cream body, cream or white plastic interior with man holding ice cream cone, with short legs or no legs, clear windows,

body colors vary from dark to light colors. Man holding ice cream cone with and without model. Three different sets of decals.

Decal—1: large square roof decal in five colors, maroon square with 'Lions Maid' on long 3 colored strip on sides.
Decal—2: short square roof decal in five colors, maroon square with 'Lions Maid' on long 3 colored strip on sides.
Decal—3: oval shaped roof decal in yellow & black with maroon background 'Lions Maid' in white, white background maroon lettering on sides.

1. Metallic blue body, cream interior, black wheels, knobby treads, decal—1, snap-in baseplate.
2. Same as 1, white interior.
3. Same as 2, dark blue body.
4. Same as 3, gray wheels, decal—2.
5. Same as 4, black wheels.
6. Same as 5, fine treads.
7. Same as 6, light blue body.
8. Same as 7, dark blue body, front rivet baseplate.
9. Same as 8, light blue body.
10. Same as 9, dark blue body, decals—2 & 3.
11. Same as 10, decals—1 & 3.
12. Same as 11, cream body, decal—2.
13. Same as 12, decal—3.
14. Light blue body, white interior, gray wheels, fine treads.

47-C DAF Tipper Container Truck   3"   1968
Aqua or silver cab & chassis, yellow tipper box with light gray or dark gray plastic roof, green windows, red plastic grille & front baseplate, 6 black plastic wheels on 3 axles, with & without tow slot, with & without small brace at back of tipper. Models 1, 2 & 3 have a plain rear base under rear axle where later models contain a raised brace in front of the letter "A".

1. Aqua cab & chassis, light gray roof, plain baseplate, without rear brace.
2. Same as 1, silver cab and chassis.
3. Same as 2, tow slot baseplate.
4. Same as 3, dark gray roof.
5. Same as 4, with rear brace.
6. Same as 5, small tow slot baseplate.

47-D DAF Tipper Container Truck   3"   1970
Silver cab & chassis, yellow box, gray removable roof, red baseplate & grille, green windows, five spoke thin wheels.

1. No "Pat number" on front baseplate.
2. With "Pat number" on front baseplate.

47-E Beach Hopper   2-5/8"   1974
"Rolamatic" dark metallic blue body, hot pink splattered over body, bright orange interior, tan driver (pops up & down) five spoke racing wheels.

1. Clear windshield, yellow sunburst label on hood, hot pink painted base.
2. Clear windshield, yellow sunburst label on hood, silver/gray baseplate.
3. Clear windshield, yellow sunburst label on hood, hot pink painted base, braces front of baseplate. (see page 221 of March Bulletin).
4. No windshield, new body casting forming wind screen front of driver, yellow sunburst label on hood, hot pink painted baseplate, braces on base.
5. Windscreen front of driver, yellow sunburst label on hood, hot pink painted baseplate, braces on base, bright yellow interior.
6. Windscreen front of driver, yellow sunburst label on hood, hot pink painted baseplate, braces on base, orange interior, pinkish tan driver.
7. Windscreen front of driver, yellow sunburst label on hood, hot pink painted baseplate, braces on base, bright yellow interior, pinkish tan driver.
8. Windscreen front of driver, yellow sunburst label on hood, pinkish lavender painted baseplate, braces on base, orange interior,

tan driver.
9. Windscreen front of driver, yellow sunburst label on hood, salmon pink painted baseplate, braces on base, orange interior, tan driver.
10. Same as 8, Pat. App. 12174/72 replaced by Pat. No. 1424808.
11. Same as 10, unpainted metal baseplate.
12. Same as 11, unpainted metal baseplate, pale orange interior.
13. Same as 10, pinkish lavender painted baseplate, yellow sunburst on light brown circular label on hood.
14. Same as 11, unpainted metal baseplate, yellow sun-burst on light brown circular label on hood.

47-F Pannier Tank Loco   3"   1979
Green body, black plastic under carriage, rear tow hook and front tow ring, black metal insert baseplate, six large thin plastic wheels.

1. Red accentuated gold 'G W R' on green labels on each side tank, two hand rails rear top of coal bin.
2. Same as 1, no hand rails rear top of coal bin.
3. Same as 1, metallic brown metal insert baseplate.
4. Same as 1, charcoal gray painted metal insert baseplate.

47-G Jaguar SS 100   1982
(Preproduction shown)

48-A Meteor Sports Boat & Trailer   2-3/8"   1958
Metal boat with tan deck and blue hull, black metal trailer with tow bar, small hole in base of trailer.

1. Length of trailer 1-7/8", metal wheels, crimped axles, round circle tow bar hole.
2. Length of trailer 2", metal wheels, crimped axle, flat tow bar hole.
3. Same as 2, gray plastic wheels.
4. Same as 3, round axles.
5. Same as 4, silver plastic wheels.

48-B Sports Boat & Trailer (2-5/8")   boat 2-3/8"   1961
Plastic boat with red or white deck, red, white or cream hulls, motors are gold or silver (unplated) metal, trailers are light or dark blue metal with two wheels, front tow bar has round & reinforced circle. The plastic boats can be changed from one trailer to another, thereby tripling the number of variations. Listed are those known to be authentic.

1. White deck, red hull, silver motor, dark blue trailer, flat tow bar, gray plastic wheels.
2. Same as 1, black wheels.
3. Same as 2, gold motor.
4. Same as 3, round tow bar.
5. Same as 4, light blue trailer.
6. Same as 5, red deck, cream hull.
7. Red deck, white hull, silver motor, dark blue trailer, round tow bar, black wheels.
8. Same as 7, gold motor.
9. Same as 8, light blue trailer.
10. Same as 9, dark blue trailer, reinforced tow bar.
11. Same as 10, light blue trailer.
12. White deck, red hull, gold motor, light blue trailer reinforced tow bar, black wheels.

48-C Dumper Truck   3"   1966
Red body, green tinted windows, silver plastic grille & baseplate, 3 round axles, 2 front, 4 rear black plastic wheels. Model changed to Superfast wheels.

1. Full length baseplate.
2. Full length baseplate, with tow slot.
3. Three-fourths inch baseplate, with tow slot.

48-D Dumper Truck   3"   1970
Bright blue cab & chassis, yellow body, green windows, silver plastic baseplate & grille. "Pat App.' which appears at the rear of the baseplate comes with small or large lettering.

1. Five spoke thin wheels.
2. Four spoke front wheels, 8 spoke rear wheels.
3. Four spoke wide wheels.

Matchbox 1-75 Series /Superfast

4. 'Blue' painted cab & chassis, not metallic blue.

48-E Pi-eyed Piper   2-7/8"   **1972**

Metallic blue body, amber windows, silver motor in hood, silver grille, metal baseplate & exhaust pipes, red, white & blue label on roof with yellow No. 8, small fron wheels, large rear wheels, clover leaf design.
1. Amber windows.
2. Amber windows, inside body casting supports under rear windows.
3. Blue windows, inside body casting supports.
4. White painted body, black painted baseplate, black plastic windows, exhaust pipes and front grille, silver plastic motor with black plastic intake stacks, red and yellow "POW" tempa imprint on trunk, red and yellow stripes tempa imprint on front fenders, red and yellow "spark design" tempa imprint on roof, small clover leaf front wheels, large clover leaf rear wheels, baseplate now reads, "No. III White Lightening".
5. Red body, silver plastic engine and air scoop, 'BIG BANGER' labels, body engine and labels are from SF 26-2, blue windows, unpainted metal baseplate (SF 48-2) and silver plated side exhaust pipes, clover leaf front wheels, large clover leaf rear wheels, this unique variation was found in several stores in the Special Issue display in "VII Brown Sugar" blister packs.
6. Same as 4, off-white painted body.
7. Same as 4, black plastic windows, gray plastic exhaust pipes and front grille.

48-F Sambron Jacklift   3-1/16"   **1977**

Yellow body, black painted baseplate with black plastic insert, no window. Numbers 1, 2, and 3 variations may also be found with a combination of yellow fork and yellow/orange boom or yellow/orange fork and yellow boom.
1. Yellow plastic fork, four spoke large wheels.
2. Yellow/orange plastic fork, four spoke large wheels.
3. Yellow/orange plastic fork, large five spoke accent wheels.
4. Yellow plastic fork, large five spoke accent wheels.
5. Same as 3, large five spoke accent wheels, metallic brown painted baseplate with black plastic insert.
6. Same as 4, large five spoke accent wheels, metallic brown painted baseplate with black plastic insert, yellow plastic fork.
7. Same as 3, large five spoke accent wheels, charcoal gray painted baseplate with black plastic insert, yellow/orange plastic fork.
8. Same as 7, large five spoke accent wheels, charcoal gray painted baseplate with black plastic insert, yellow plastic boom, black plastic fork.
9. Yellow body, black painted metal baseplate with black plastic insert, no windows, yellow plastic forks, yellow "SAMBRON" on narrow red tempa stripe on left side door, large five spoke accent wheels.

48-G Red Rider   2-7/8"   **1972**

Red body, flat black painted metal baseplate, grille and bumpers, chrome plated plastic engine protruding from hood, white tempa flames on roof and rear deck, white tempa "RED RIDER" and flames on sides, small cloverleaf front wheels, large cloverleaf rear wheels, "Made In Hong Kong" on baseplate. (formerly SF48-2).
1. Red plastic windows, black plastic side exhaust pipes.

49-A M3 Personnel Carrier   2½"   **1958**

Olive green body, white star inside circle decal on hood, 3 axles, gray rubber treads.
1. Large metal front wheels, metal rollers, crimped axles.
2. Dark gray plastic wheels, metal rollers, crimped axles.
3. Dark gray plastic wheels, metal rollers, round axles.
4. Light gray plastic wheels, metal rollers, round axles.
5. Light gray plastic wheels, large gray plastic rollers.
6. Large fine tread gray plastic wheels, large silver plastic rollers.
7. Large knobby black plastic wheels, large black plastic rollers.
8. Black plastic wheels, small black plastic rollers.
9. Black plastic wheels, small black plastic rollers, with rivet behind front axle in baseplate.

10. Small black plastic wheels, small black plastic rollers, with rivet behind front axle in baseplate.

49-B Mercedes Unimog   2½"   **1967**

Silver grille, 4 black plastic tires, yellow wheels, spare tire mounted on left side behind cab under bed, 2 axles, small brace under each axle, large brace in front of front axle, tow slot & tow hook, green windows.
1. Tan cab & bed, green chassis & baseplate, large support behind rear axle.
2. Tan cab & bed, green chassis & baseplate, without rear support.
3. Blue cab & bed, red chassis & baseplate.
4. Blue cab & bed, red chassis & baseplate, longer brace under rear of bed.

49-C Mercedes Unimog   2-3/8"   **1970**

Green windows, red baseplate, red or black axle covers, 8 spoke wheels.
1. Blue body, balloon tires.
2. Blue body, balloon tires, silver grille.
3. Blue/green body, wide wheels.
4. Metallic light blue body, balloon tires.
5. Metallic light blue body, balloon tires, silver grille.
6. Bright blue body, wide wheels.
7. Metallic light blue body, wide wheels.
8. Olive green body, green tinted windows, olive green painted baseplate with black plastic insert, no number 49 on baseplate, small green and white star round label on hood, multi-spoke wide wheels, no hub caps, spare wheel removed from under carriage and space filled. 8 is found with a bright green star label and no shell box in TP-13 along with SF-73-3 Weasel.
9. Same as 8, white "A" on square blue and red label on hood, tan plastic shell box containing four shells in rear of truck. (TP-13).
10. Same as 8, olive green and white star on round label on hood, tan plastic shell box containing four shells in rear of truck. 10 is found with a dull olive green star label, has a shell box in TP-13 along with SF 32-3 Field Gun. (TP-13).

49-D Chop Suey Motorcycle   2-3/4"   **1973**

Metallic red body, chrome yellow bulls head on front handle bars, silver plastic motor, exhaust & baseplate, wide black body. Handle bars are various shades of red.
1. Silver handle bars.
2. Red plastic handle bars.
3. Orange plastic handle bars.
4. Red plastic handle bars, closed opening between exhaust pipes.
5. Same as 4, black plastic handle bars, closed opening between exhaust pipes.

49-E Crane Truck   2-15/16"   **1976**

Yellow body and rotating crane truret, black plastic baseplate and grille, extendable yellow plastic boom, red plastic hook, six five-spoke accent wheels.
1. Dark green side windows, dark green frosted windshield.
2. Dark green side windows, dark green frosted windshield, six multi-spoke wheels.
3. Red body and rotating turret, black plastic baseplate and grille, extendable yellow plastic boom, red plastic hook, clear side windows, clear frosted windshield, six five-spoke accent wheels, (Sold in Germany only?)
4. Same as 1, light yellow rotating crane and turret, dark green side windows, dark green frosted windshield, five spoke accent wheels.
5. Same as 3, dark green side windows, dark green frosted windshield.
6. Same as 1, light green side windows, light green frosted windshield.
7. Same as 4, light green side windows, light green frosted windshield.
8. Same as 1, yellow body, yellow/orange extendable boom, dark green windows, dark green frosted windshield, five spoke accent wheels.

9. Same as 4, multi-spoke wheels.
10. Same as 1, yellow body, black plastic extendable boom, red plastic hook, dark green windows, dark green frosted windshield, five spoke accent wheels.
11. Yellow body, black plastic extendable boom, red plastic hook, red plastic side windows, red frosted plastic windshield, black plastic baseplate, five spoke accent wheels.
12. Yellow body, black plastic expendable boom, red plastic hook, purple plastic side windows, purple frosted plastic windshield, black plastic baseplate, five spoke accent wheels.

50-A Commer Pick-up Truck   2½"   **1958**

With & without silver grille & bumpers, black baseplate with front rivet, 2 axles, 4 wheels.
1. Dark tan body, metal wheels, crimped axles.
2. Same as 1, light tan body.
3. Same as 2, dark gray plastic wheels.
4. Same as 3, light gray plastic wheels.
5. Dark tan body, dark gray plastic wheels, rounded axles.
6. Same as 5, light tan body.
7. Dark tan body, silver plastic wheels, rounded axles.
8. Same as 7, red/white body color.
9. Same as 8, red/gray body color.
10. Same as 9, light gray plastic wheels.
11. Same as 10, black plastic wheels.

50-B John Deere Tractor   2-1/8"   **1964**

Green body & tow hook, silver radiator, yellow plastic wheels, and steering wheel.
1. Gray plastic tires.
2. Black plastic tires.

50-C Kennel Truck   2¾"   **1969**

Metallic green body, clear or blue tinted canopy, smooth or textured bed, white plastic or silver grille, black base, 2 axle, 4 black plastic wheels, 4 white plastic dogs, wheels turn by 'autosteer'. The metallic green body comes in several shades. Model changed to Superfast.
1. Clear canopy, smooth bed, white grille.
2. Tinted canopy, smooth bed, white grille.
3. Tinted canopy, textured bed, white grille.
4. Tinted canopy, textured bed, silver grille.

50-D Kennel Truck   2¾"   **1970**

Green windows, light blue tinted canopy, rough bed, four white plastic dogs, five spoke wheels.
1. Metallic green body, silver grille, black baseplate, thin wheels.
2. Dark green metallic body, silver grille, black baseplate, thin wheels.
3. Metallic green body, silver grille, dark yellow baseplate, wide wheels.
4. Metallic green body, silver grille, light yellow baseplate, wide wheels.
5. Metallic green body, silver grille, charcoal baseplate, wide wheels.
6. Metallic green body, silver grille, gray baseplate, wide wheels.
7. Light green body, silver grille, black baseplate, wide wheels.
8. Light green body, silver grille, charcoal baseplate, wide wheels.
9. Light green body, silver grille, gray baseplate, wide wheels.
10. Light green body, white plastic grille, charcoal baseplate, wide wheels.
11. Light green body, white plastic grille, black baseplate, wide wheels.
12. Metallic green body, silver grille, black baseplate, wide wheels.
13. Light green body, white plastic grille, gray baseplate, wide wheels.
14. Light green body, white plastic grille, unpainted metal baseplate, wide wheels.

50-E Articulated Truck   2¾"   **1973**

Black baseplate & grille, purple tinted windows, small wide wheels, clover leaf design (on cab) light blue dumper with yellow stripe plastic bottom, five spoke wide wheels, dark blue & yellow label on dumper. Cab and dumpers are interchangeable with SF number 63.

1. Yellow cab.
2. Light yellow cab.
3. Yellow cab, no label on dumper.
4. Yellow cab, no label on dumper, no rivet on axle cover under dumper.
5. Yellow cab, no label, no rivet on axle cover, small five spoke wheels on cab.
6. Yellow cab, no label, no rivet on axle cover, clover leaf wheels on cab, thin five spoke wheels on dumper.
7. Yellow cab, dark bright blue and yellow label, no rivet on axle cover, small clover leaf wheels on cab, wide five spoke wheels on dumper.
8. Yellow cab, no label, no rivet on axle cover, wide clover leaf wheels on cab and dumper.
9. Same as 4, wide raised line around cab, black plastic baseplate, parellel lines replacing arrow like lines on rear axle cover, raised lip at rear horizontal edge of blue dumper.
10. Same as 9, red tinted plastic windows, circular hole (3/32'') and reinforcements above rear license plate with number removed, raised lip at rear horizontal edge of blue dumper.
11. Same as 10, red tinted plastic windows, orange/yellow plastic base on trailer.
12. Light yellow cab, black baseplate and grille, purple tinted plastic windows, blue dumper, yellow plastic base with black plastic insert over rear axle, clover leaf wheels on cab, five spoke wide wheels on dumper, white plastic hook rear of dumper. The square box rear of dumper where the white plastic tow hook is inserted has been modified and is now with rear face perpendicular to the ground instead of being at an angle as in model 50-B-10. (TP-16).
13. Same as 12, red tinted plastic windows. (TP-16).
14. Same as 10, light yellow cab, yellow plastic base on dumper, purple tinted plastic window. Combinations of cab variations and dumper variations can easily be created and therefore will not be listed.
15. Same as 10, light yellow cab, yellow plastic base on dumper, red tinted plastic windows.
16. Same as 10, light yellow cab, yellow plastic base on dumper, purple tinted plastic windows, multi-spoke wheels on cab, five spoke wide wheels on dumper.
17. Same as 10, light yellow cab, yellow plastic base on dumper, purple tinted plastic windows, five spoke accent wheels on cab, five spoke wide wheels on dumper.
18. Red cab, blue dumper with red plastic bottom, black plastic baseplate on cab, yellow rear axle cover on dumper, red plastic windows, wide clover leaf wheels on cab, five spoke wheels on dumper.
19. Same as 18, purple tinted plastic windows.
20. Same as 18, gray dumper.

50-F Articulated Trailer   1980
Blue dumper, yellow plastic base with black plastic insert over rear axle, five spoke rear wheels, five spoke accent front wheels.
1. Light yellow front metal hitch assembly, black plastic cover over front wheel axle.

50-G Harley Davidson Motorcycle   2-11/16''   1980
Metallic silver/brown frame, gas tank and rear fender, chrome plated motor and exhaust pipes, black plastic handle bars, front wheel suspension and fender, with brown rider.
1. Black plastic seat, chrome spoke wheels with black tires.

51-A Albion Chieftan   2½''   1958
Yellow body, tan & light tan bags, silver grille, small round decal on doors, 'Blue Circle Portland Cement' decal on sides, 2 axles, 4 wheels, black base, body color subject to shades, the tan bags can be found in various colors.
1. "Portland Cement" in two lines on sides, metal wheels, crimped axles.
2. "Blue Circle Portland Cement" in two lines on sides, metal

wheels, crimped axles.
3. Large dark gray plastic wheels, crimped axles.
4. Small dark gray plastic wheels, crimped axles.
5. Small dark gray plastic wheels, round axles.
6. Small light gray plastic wheels, round axles.
7. Large silver plastic wheels, round axles.
8. Small silver plastic wheels.
9. Small light gray plastic wheels, dark tan bags.
10. Small black plastic wheels, dark tan bags.

51-B John Deere Trailer   2-5/8''   1964
Green tipping body with tow bar, 2 small yellow wheels, 3 yellow plastic barrels.
1. Gray plastic tires.
2. Black plastic tires.

51-C 8-Wheel Tipper   3''   1969
Blue tinted windows, plastic grille & partial base from bumper to 2nd axle, tilting tailgate, 4 axles, 8 black plastic wheels, labels on each side of tipper body, silver tipper.
1. Orange body, Douglas label, white plastic base and grille, with tow slot, thin rear support.
2. Same as 1, yellow body, silver base and grille.
3. Orange body, Douglas label, silver base and grille, without tow slot, thick rear support.
4. Same as 3, yellow body.
5. Same as 4, orange body, with tow slot.
6. Same as 4, yellow body.
7. Yellow body, Pointer label, silver base and grille, without tow slot, thick rear support.
8. Same as 7, with tow slot.
9. Orange body, Pointer label.

51-D 8-Wheel Tipper Truck   3''   1970
Yellow cab & chassis, silver/gray tipper, blue windows, five spoke thin wheels.
1. Silver grille & baseplate, dark green "Pointer" labels.
2. Silver grille & baseplate, light green "Pointer" labels.
3. Silver grille & baseplate, no labels. (G-4 gift set).
4. Gray grille & baseplate, light green labels.
5. Gray plastic grille & baseplate, no label on tipper.
6. Gray plastic grille & baseplate, dark green labels.

51-E Citroen SM   3''   1972
Metal baseplate, clear windows, frosted rear window, five spoke wheels, tow hook.
1. Orange interior & tow hook, bronze body, no patent number on front axle.
2. Cream interior & tow hook, bronze body, with patent number on front axle.
3. Cream interior, bronze body, no patent number on front axle.
4. Cream interior & tow hook, bronze body, patent number on front axle cover, silver/gray painted baseplate.
5. Cream interior & tow hook, dark metallic reddish bronze body, patent number on front axle, unpainted metal baseplate.
6. Yellow interior & tow hook, dark metallic reddish bronze body, patent number on front axle, unpainted metal baseplate.
7. Light yellow interior & tow hook, dark metallic reddish bronze body, patent number on front axle, unpainted metal baseplate.
8. Light tan interior and tow hook, bronze body, patent number on front axle, unpainted metal baseplate.
9. Metallic turquoise blue body, light tan interior and tow hook, patent number on front axle, unpainted metal baseplate.
10. Metallic turquoise blue body, orange/yellow interior and tow hook, unpainted metal baseplate, no number 51 on baseplate, red 'STP' logo, black 'Shell' and black 'YAMAHA' on yellow and white label on hood, multi-spoke wheels, black plastic tire rack on roof. (TP-21).
11. Streaker metallic turquoise blue body, white & red racing stripes front to rear, white number 8 on roof, white arrows on hood, clear windows, Light tan interior, unpainted metal baseplate

and grille.
12. Yellow interior, unpainted metal baseplate and grille.
13. Ivory interior, unpainted metal baseplate and grille.
14. Ivory interior, unpainted metal baseplate, streaker design ends in fish tail on trunk lid. The modification in streaker design transfer appears to have come about because of a crack showing in the design for several months, model can be found showing such damaged design.
15. Yellow (lemon) interior, unpainted metal baseplate, streaker design ends in fish tail, five spoke wheels.
16. Yellow (lemon) interior, unpainted metal baseplate, streaker design ends in fish tail, multi-spoke wheels.
17. Yellow/orange interior, unpainted metal baseplate, streaker design ends in fish tail, multi-spoke wheels.
18. Light tan interior, unpainted metal baseplate, streaker design ends in fish tail, five spoke wheels.

51-F Combine Harvester   2¾''   1978
Red body, black painted metal baseplate, yellow plastic grain shute and intake reel.
1. Large black plastic non-superfast front wheels, small black plastic non-superfast wheels. May be found with or without two parallel recessed areas on base next to the two slots for the intake reel.
2. Same as 1, large black four spoke Superfast like front wheels with yellow painted hub designs. Found only with recessed areas on base next to the two slots for the intake reel.
3. Same as 1, large black four spoke front wheels, no hub caps, orange/yellow plastic intake reel.
4. Red body, redesigned casting, no baseplate, model identification and number part of casting under intake reel, orange/yellow intake reel and grain shute, large Superfast like four spoke front wheels, with yellow painted hub design, small non-superfast rear wheels.
5. Same as 4, large Superfast like front wheels, no hub caps, small non-superfast rear wheels.

51-G Midnight Magic   1972
Black body, silver pearl gray painted metal baseplate, front bumper and rear panel, silver tempa stripes on hood, roof and rear engine lid, silver tempa stripes on sides, five spoke front wheels, clover leaf rear wheels. (formerly 53-E).
1. Clear plastic windows, chrome plastic interior and rear engine.

52-A Maserati 4CL T/1948   2-3/8''   1958
Red or yellow body, cream or white driver with & without circle on left shoulder, with & without silver trim & with & without numbered decals on sides of racer body, black base, 2 axle, 4 wheels.
1. Red body, no decal number, cream driver, without shoulder circles, wheels solid black, crimped axles.
2. Same as 1, number 52 decal.
3. Same as 2, rounded axles.
4. Same as 3, wire black wheels.
5. Same as 4, yellow body.
6. Same as 5, number 5 decal.
7. Same as 6, number 52 decal, with shoulder circle.
8. Same as 7, white driver.
9. Same as 8, number 5 decal.
10. Same as 9, number 3 decal.
11. Same as 10, yellow/green body, number 52 decal.
12. Same as 11, number 5 decal.

52-B BRM Racing Car   2-5/8''   1965
Blue or red body, white plastic driver, decal or labeled number '5' on hood & side, rear metal motor, exhaust pipes & base, yellow wheels, small front and large rear black plastic tires. Blue and red body colors vary in shades.
1. Blue body, decals, no support over rear tail pipes.
2. Blue body, decals, with support over rear tail pipes.
3. Blue body, labels.
4. Red body, decals.
5. Red body, labels.

52-C Dodge Charger 2-7/8" 1970
Clear windows, black interior & rear grille, green baseplate & front grille, five spoke wide wheels. Baseplate comes in as many as five shades of green. Most models come with number 5 labels from G-3 gift sets.
1. Light pinkish/red body.
2. Light red body.
3. Dark red body.
4. Dark red body, yellow/black label on hood.
5. Magenta.
6. Dark purple.
7. Lime green body, red baseplate.
8. Lime green body, bright red baseplate.
9. Lime green body, unpainted metal baseplate.
10. Lime green body, red baseplate, tow box. (tow hole filled in).
11. Light red body, green baseplate, tow hole, black number 5 on white labels on roof and sides. (G-3 gift sets).
12. Dark red body, green baseplate, tow hole, black number 5 on white labels on roof and sides. (G-3 gift sets).
13. Lime green body, green baseplate, tow hole, black number 5 on white labels on roof and sides. (G-3 gift sets).
14. Lime green body, red baseplate, tow box, "Castrol" red and green round logo on square white label on hood.
15. Metallic red/purple body, black plastic interior and rear panel, metallic green painted baseplate and front grille, tow box (hole filled in), five spoke wide wheels. (sold in Japan in special black box numbered J-8).

52-D Police Launch 3" 1976
White deck, blue plastic hull and police officers, silver fog horns, small thin wheels in hull.
1. Dark blue windows, white 'Police' and orange stripes side labels.
2. Same as 1, dark blue windows, white "POLICE" and orange stripes side labels, light blue hull (same color as basic police officers).
3. Same as 1, dark blue windows, white "Police" on orange stripes side labels, blue plastic hull, casting top of cabin modified, metal fog horns eliminated.
4. Same as 3, blue opaque plastic windows. (windows are of same color as the plastic hull and could possibly be an intergral part of the hull.
5. Same as 3, dark blue plastic hull.
6. White upper structure, red tempa cabin roof and rear deck, red plastic hull, yellow plastic fire fighters, blue plastic windows, white "4 LOS ANGELES CITY FIRE DEPARTMENT 4" on red stripe side labels, small thin black plastic wheels in hull. (Code Red Issue).

52-E BMW MI 2-15/16" 1981
Metallic silver gray body, gray plastic lid on hood, red plastic interior, rear louvers and rear bumper, black tempa "52" and three black stripes on sides, five spoke accent wheels.
1. Clear plastic windows, glossy black painted metal baseplate.
2. Clear plastic windows, flat black painted metal baseplate.

53-A Aston Martin DB2 Saloon 2½" 1958
Metallic light green, with & without silver grille, headlights, with & without red painted tail lights, black base, 2 axles, 4 wheels. The green and red models vary in shades.
1. Silverish green body, metal wheels, crimped axles.
2. Same as 1, metallic green body.
3. Same as 2, large dark gray wheels.
4. Same as 3, rounded axles.
5. Same as 4, large light gray wheels.
6. Same as 5, metallic red body.
7. Same as 6, large knobby black wheels.

53-B Mercedes Benz 220SE 2¾" 1963
Silver grille, with & without silver headlights, bumpers, clear windows, ivory interior, black baseplate, 2 axles, 4 wheels.
1. Maroon body, light gray plastic wheels.

2. Maroon body, knobby silver plastic wheels.
3. Maroon body, finer silver plastic wheels.
4. Red body, light gray plastic wheels.
5. Red body, black plastic wheels.
6. Red body, black plastic wheels, patent number on front of baseplate.

53-C Ford Zodiac MK IV 2¾" 1968
Metallic silver blue body, metal grille, headlights & baseplate, clear windows, ivory interior, with tow slot on front of baseplate, 2 axles, 4 black plastic wheels, silver motor under hood with spare wheel. The metallic color varies in shades. Model changed to Superfast wheels.
1. Narrow tow slot.
2. Wide tow slot.

53-D Ford Zodiac 2¾" 1970
Clear windows, ivory interior, metal baseplate & grille, silver motor, five spoke wheels.
1. Metallic light blue body, thin wheels.
2. Metallic light green body, thin wheels.
3. Metallic dark green body, thin wheels.
4. Metallic dark green body, thin wheels, wide wheel wells.
5. Metallic dark green body, wide wheels, wide wheel wells.
6. Light green body, wide wheels, wide wheel wells.

53-E Tanzara 3" 1972
Orange body, silver interior, motor in rear, metal baseplate, small front wheels, larger rear wheels, clover leaf design.
1. Green tinted windows.
2. Amber tinted windows.
3. Light amber windows.
4. Streaker white body, blue & red stripes on hood & roof, red number 53 on hood, silver interior & rear motor, small clover leaf front wheels, large clover leaf rear wheels, amber windows, & unpainted metal baseplate & grille.
5. Same as 4, silver gray painted metal baseplate.

53-F CJ6 Jeep 2-15/16" 1977
Red body, unpainted metal baseplate, front bumper and winch, five spoke reverse accent wheels.
1. Orange plastic interior and tow hook, tan plastic roof cover.
2. Same as 1, silver gray painted metal baseplate.
3. Same as 1, unpainted metal baseplate now reads "JEEP CJ6" on raised metal part.
4. Same as 1, orange plastic interior and tow hook, tan plastic roof cover, no hub caps.
5. Same as 3, "JEEP CJ6" on baseplate, lighter yellow/orange plastic interior.
6. Same as 3, light tan plastic roof cover.
7. Same as 3, "JEEP CJ6" on baseplate, black plastic interior & tow hook.
8. Metallic green body, unpainted metal baseplate, front bumper winch, light yellow/orange plastic interior and tow hook, tan plastic roof cover, five spoke reverse accent wheels.
9. Same as 8, black plastic interior and tow hook.
10. Yellow body, flat black painted metal baseplate, front bumper and tow winch, black plastic interior and tow hook, brown textured plastic roof cover, brown "CJ6", brown and orange stripes tempa imprint on sides, five spoke reverse accent wheels.
11. Same as 3, "JEEP CJ6" on baseplate, light yellow/orange plastic interior and tow hook, pinkish tan plastic roof cover.
12. Same as 8, yellow/orange plastic interior and tow hook, pinkish tan roof cover.
13. Same as 8, black plastic interior and tow hook, pinkish tan plastic roof.

53-G Flareside Pick-up 1982
Medium blue body, white interior, grille, exhaust pipes, and bars in back. Clear plastic windshield and dome light, 8-spoke wheels with bounce black bumpers & tow bar, white letters on top "B.F. Goodrich", "Baja Bouncer" on hood, and black "326" in white oval on hood and doors.

54-A Saracen Personnel Carrier 2¼" 1958
Olive green body, small rotating gun turret, 3 axles, 6 black plastic wheels, 3 small steps cast on upper body, 2 on left side, 1 on right front side.
1. Large knobby black plastic wheels, crimped axles.
2. Large knobby black plastic wheels, crimped axles, with brace at rear of baseplate behind gas tank.
3. Large knobby black plastic wheels, rounded axles, with brace at rear of baseplate behind gas tank.
4. Large fine tread black plastic wheels, rounded axles, with brace at rear of baseplate behind gas tank.
5. Large fine tread black plastic wheels, rounded axles, with brace at rear of baseplate behind gas tank, no step on right upper side of body.

54-B S & S Cadillac Ambulance 2-7/8" 1965
White body, red dome & top lights, blue tinted windows, white interior, red cross decal or label on front doors, black baseplate, 2 axles, 4 black plastic wheels. Changed to Superfast wheels.
1. Small red cross decal on doors.
2. Small red cross decal on doors, with small flat support over rear axle.
3. Small red cross label on doors, with small flat support over rear axle.
4. Large red cross label on doors, with small flat support over rear axle.

54-C Cadillac Ambulance 2-3/8" 1970
White body, white interior, blue tinted windows, red dome lights, red cross label on sides, black baseplate, silver grille.
1. Five spoke thin wheels.
2. Five spoke thin wheels, off-white body & grille, large red cross label on sides.
3. Five spoke thin wheels, white body & grille, large red cross label on sides.
4. Five spoke thin wheels, white body, silver painted grille and headlights, large red cross label on sides.

54-D Ford Capri 3" 1971
Ivory interior & tow hook, clear windows, metal baseplate & grille, silver motor, five spoke wide wheels.
1. Dark orange body, black mat hood.
2. Light orange body, black mat hood.
3. Metallic purple body.
4. Metallic light purple body, white interior, five spoke slicks.
5. Metallic light purple body, ivory interior, five spoke wide wheels.
6. Metallic light purple body, ivory interior, five spoke slicks.
7. Metallic light purple body, ivory interior, five spoke wide wheels, silver gray painted baseplate.
8. Orange body & hood, unpainted metal baseplate, baseplate extended under tow hook, five spoke slicks, ivory interior. (TP-5).
9. Metallic purple body, unpainted metal baseplate, baseplate extends under tow hook, five spoke slicks, ivory interior.
10. Metallic purple body, unpainted metal baseplate, no extention under tow hook, ivory interior and tow hook, clover leaf slicks.

54-E Personnel Carrier 3" 1976
Military olive green body, black painted metal baseplate and grille, large wide multi-spoke wheels.
1. Tan plastic men and benches, tan plastic cab roof mounted machine gun, dark green windows.
2. Same as 1, large multi-spoke wheels, no hub caps.
3. Same as 2, blueish/green plastic windows.

54-F Mobile Home 3½" 1980
Ivory painted body, dark brown plastic door and door closing trigger, orange plastic interior, multi-spoke wheels.
This first 1890 model now displays the model scale on the baseplate. It will now be listed on the UPGRADE when available. The word SUPERFAST has dissappeared from the baseplate, and new details such as transmission shaft and spare tire have been added.
1. Clear plastic windows and sky-lights, charcoal gray painted metal

baseplate, grille and bumpers.
2. Clear plastic windows and sky-lights, flat black painted metal baseplate, grille and bumpers.
3. Same as 1, cream painted body, charcoal gray painted metal baseplate.
4. Same as 2, cream painted body, flat black painted metal base-plate.
5. Same as 4, cream painted body, flat black painted metal base-plate, chocolate brown plastic door and door closing trigger.
6. White body, light brown plastic side door and door closing trigger, orange plastic interior, smoke tinted plastic windows and skylights, charcoal gray painted metal baseplate, grille and bumpers, multi-spoke wheels.
7. White body, dark brown plastic side door and door closing trigger, orange plastic interior, smoke tinted plastic windows and skylights, charcoal gray painted metal baseplate, grille and bumpers, thin brown stripe each side of roof line, wider brown stripe each side below windows, multi-spoke wheels.
8. Same as 3, charcoal brown painted metal baseplate, chocolate brown plastic door and closing trigger.
9. Same as 6, charcoal brown painted metal baseplate.
10. Same as 6, charcoal gray painted metal baseplate, dark brown plastic side door and closing trigger.
11. Same as 6, glossy black painted metal baseplate, light brown plastic side door and closing trigger.
12. Same as 6, glossy black painted metal baseplate, dark brown plastic side door and closing trigger.
13. Same as 7, brown stripes on sides, charcoal gray painted metal baseplate, light brown plastic side door and closing trigger.
14. Same as 7, brown stripes on sides, charcoal brown painted metal baseplate, light brown plastic side door and closing trigger.
15. Same as 7, brown stripes on sides, charcoal brown painted metal baseplate, dark brown plastic side door and closing trigger.

54-G N.A.S.A. Tracking Vehicle   1982
White body with silver radar screen on top, red tinted windows, blue letters "Space Shuttle Command Center" on sides, red "N.A.S.A" on roof.

55-A D.U.K.W.   2¾''   1958
Olive green body, black baseplate, 2 axles, 4 wheels.
1. Metal wheels, crimped axles.
2. Gray plastic wheels, crimped axles.
3. Gray plastic wheels, rounded axles.
4. Black plastic wheels, rounded axles.

55-B (Ford Fairlane) Police Car   2-5/8''   1963
Silver grille, with & without silver bumpers, red interior, ivory interior, clear windows, large clear decal on hood with black 'Police' and blue/red/white shield, clear decal on doors with shield, 2 axles, 4 plastic wheels, black baseplate.
1. Dark blue body, knobby black wheels.
2. Blue body, smaller knobby wheels.
3. Blue body, smaller finer wheels.
4. Blue body, gray plastic wheels.

55-C (Ford Galaxie) Police Car   2-7/8''   1966
White body, ivory interior & driver & tow hook, clear windows, red or blue dome light, metal grille and baseplate with tow slot, clear decal or labels on hood & doors, 2 axles, 4 black plastic wheels, 55/59 on baseplate.
1. Blue dome light, with decals.
2. Red dome light, with decals.
3. Red dome light, with labels.

55-D Mercury Police Car   3''   1968
White body, ivory interior with 2 figures, clear windows, red or blue dome light, red or blue dome light on hood & doors, metal grille & baseplate, 2 axles, 4 silver wheels with black plastic tires, "Mercury" on raised casting on baseplate, 'No. 55 or 73'. Model changed to Superfast wheels.
1. Red dome light.
2. Blue dome light, '1968 Mercury' on base.

3. Blue dome light.

55-E Mercury Police Car   3''   1970
White body, ivory interior, two occupants, clear windows, five spoke thin wheels, metal baseplate, black lettered "Police" label & shield on hood, shield label on side doors, NOTE: the word "Mercury" on the baseplate is on a raised platform and comes in three positions, near the base, close to the base and connected to the base.
1. Blue dome light.
2. Red dome light.

55-F Mercury Police Stationwagon   3''   1971
White body, ivory interior, no occupants, clear windows, five spoke wide wheels, black lettered "Police" label & shield label on hood, shield label on doors, metal baseplate & grille.
1. Police label & shield labels.
2. Red & yellow Police label on hood.
3. Red & yellow Police label on hood, silver/gray painted base & grille.
4. Red & yellow police label on hood, black 'Police' on red & yellow arrow shaped labels on doors, unpainted metal baseplate.
5. Red & yellow police label on hood, black 'Police' on red & yellow arrow shaped label on doors, silver/gray baseplate.

55-G Hellraiser   3''   1975
White body, unpainted metal baseplate, grille & rear panel, silver plated plastic rear engine, five spoke accent front slicks, multi-spoke rear slicks.
1. Clear windows, red stripe on white & white stars on front label on hood, red interior, five spoke reverse accent front slicks, multi-spoke rear slicks.
2. Clear windows, red stripe on white and white stars on label on hood, red interior, multi-spoke wheels front and rear, five spoke reverse accent front slicks, multi-spoke rear slicks.
3. Metallic blue body, unpainted metal baseplate, grille and rear panel, silver plated plastic rear engine, five spoke reverse accent front slicks, multi-spoke rear slicks, clear windows, ivory interior, red stripe on white and white stars on blue hood label.
4. Same as 3, silver/gray painted metal baseplate, may be found without label on hood.
5. Same as 4, silver/gray painted metal baseplate, red interior.
6. Same as 4, silver/gray painted metal baseplate, black "3" and black/yellow and orange stripes label on hood. (label from SF 3-2)

55-H Ford Cortina   3-1/16'' 1979
Metallic goldish green body, unpainted metal baseplate, bumpers and grille, wide multi-spoke wheels.
1. Clear windows, red plastic interior and tow hook, no patent number on baseplate.
2. Clear windows, red plastic interior and tow hook, Patent no. 983558 rear of back wheels on baseplate.
3. Bright metallic greenish/gold body, unpainted metal baseplate, bumpers and grille, Pat. no. on baseplate, clear plastic windows, red plastic interior and tow hook, wide multi-spoke wheels.
4. Same as 3, light yellow plastic interior and tow hook.
5. Metallic red body, bright yellow plastic interior and tow hook, unpainted metal baseplate, bumper and grille, clear plastic win-dows, wide multi-spoke wheels.

55-I Ford Cortina   1982
Metallic tan body, light yellow plastic interior, thick and thin dark blue racing stripes on left side of hood, top & trunk, and on sides.

56-A London Trolley Bus   2-5/8''   1958
Red body, with two trolly poles on top of roof, black base, 3 axles, 6 wheels, small front, rear and rear right upper sides, white long decal upper sides "Drink Peardrax" The white side decals are subject to turn-ing yellow.
1. Black trolly poles, metal wheels, crimped axles.
2. Red trolly poles, metal wheels, crimped axles.
3. Small dark gray wheels, crimped axles.
4. Small dark gray wheels, rounded axles.
5. Small light gray wheels, rounded axles.
6. Small silver plastic wheels, rounded axles.

7. Small black plastic wheels, rounded axles.

56-B Fiat 1500   2½''   1965
Silver grille, with & without silver bumpers, red interior & tow hook, brown or tan luggage on roof, clear windows, black plastic baseplate, 2 axles, 4 black plastic wheels. Although the roof luggage has been found in reverse position, and either color on any model, they are not being listed as variations due to the plastic luggage being pulled off and changed around.
1. Green body, brown luggage.
2. Green body, tan luggage.
3. Red body, tan luggage. (Found only in the Gift set of G-1-1969.)

56-C BMC 1800 Pininfarina   2¾''   1970
Clear windows, ivory interior, metal baseplate & grille, five spoke wheels, NOTE: models can be found in G-3 Gift sets with "Gulf" label & No. 17. Most models may be found with small or large rear view mirror.
1. Light metallic gold body, thin wheels.
2. Butterscotch body, thin wheels.
3. Butterscotch body, thin wheels, wide wheel wells.
4. Butterscotch body, wide wheels, wide wheel wells.
5. Butterscotch body, wide wheels, wide wheel wells, silver/gray baseplate.
6. Light orange body, wide wheels, wide wheel wells, metal baseplate.
7. Light metallic gold body, thin wheels, small wheel wells, "Gulf" labels on hood, no label on sides. (G-3 Gift set).
8. Light metallic gold body, thin wheels, small wheel wells, "Gulf" label on hood, small black No. 17 on white labels on sides. (G-3 Gift set).
9. Butterscotch body, thin wheels, small wheel wells, "Gulf" label on hood, small black No. 17 on white labels on sides. (G-3 sets).
10. Butterscotch body, thin wheels, wide wheel wells, "Gulf" label on hood, small black No. 17 on white labels on sides. (G-3 sets).
11. Light orange body, thin wheels, small wheel wells, unpainted metal baseplate.

56-D Hi-Tailer   3''   1974
Team Matchbox Racer, white body, silver engine and windshield, wide five spoke front wheels, wide clover leaf rear wheels, black No. 5 MB, white 'Team Matchbox' letterings, blue and orange stripes on white label covering car from front to rear engine, black "Superfast MB" lettering, blue & orange stripes on white label on rear air foil. May also be found without any label on air foil.
1. Unpainted metal baseplate, blue driver.
2. Unpainted metal baseplate, blue driver, small 'MB' on rear air foil label.
3. Unpainted metal baseplate, yellow/orange driver, small "MB" on rear air foil label.
4. Same as 3, red painted metal baseplate.
5. Same as 4, red painted metal baseplate, white "MARTINI RAC-ING" on blue and white U-shaped stripes, black "7" and red, yel-low and black "DUNLOP" logo on large white label covering car from front to rear engine, white "MARTINI" and blue and red stripe on white label on air foil. (K-7) aslo found in blister pack.
6. Same as 5, light yellow plastic driver.

56-E Mercedes 450SEL   3''   1979
Metallic blue body, unpainted metal baseplate and grille, wide multi-spoke wheels.
1. Clear windows (plastic) light tan plastic interior and tow hook.
2. Clear plastic windows, red plastic interior and tow hook.

56-F Mercedes Taxi   3''   1980
Unpainted metal baseplate, grille and bumpers, dark tan plastic interior and tow hook, clear plastic windows, red plastic "TAXI" sign protrud-ing through roof, small multi-spoke wheels.
1. Manilla tan plastic interior and tow hook, (almost same color as body).
2. Tan plastic interior and tow hook, clear plastic supports above seats, part of window unit to support 'TAXI' sign.
3. Same as 1, manilla tan plastic interior and tow hook, clear plastic supports above seats, part of window unit, to support 'TAXI' sign.

56-G   Peterbuilt ® Tanker   **1982**
Blue cab, white tank with red letters in box "Milk's the One", white decals on door and side of hood, silver plastic grille, gas tank, vertical exhaust pipes, and fender. 6 wheels.

57-A   Wolseley 1500   **2-1/8"   1958**
With & without grilles, rear tail lights & bumpers painted, black baseplate, 2 axles, 4 wheels.
1. Pale yellow/green body, gold grille, dark gray plastic wheels, crimped axles.
2. Plae yellow/green body, silver grille, dark gray plastic wheels, crimped axles.
3. Pale green body, silver grille, dark gray plastic wheels, crimped axles.
4. Pale green body, silver grille, dark gray plastic wheels, rounded axles.
5. White body, silver grille, gray plastic wheels.

57-B   Chevrolet Impala   **2¾"   1961**
Pale blue roof, metallic blue body, green tinted windows, with & without silver grilles, bumpers, with & without red painted tail lights, 2 axles, 4 wheels, with tow hook, metallic blue bodies and blue baseplate, subject to various shades.
1. Knobby gray plastic wheels, black baseplate and tow hook.
2. Same as 1, finer gray plastic wheels.
3. Knobby silver plastic wheels, black baseplate and tow hook.
4. Finer silver plastic wheels, black baseplate and tow hook.
5. Same as 4, dark blue baseplate & tow hook.
6. Fine black plastic wheels, black baseplate and tow hook.

57-C   Land Rover Fire Truck   **2½"   1966**
Red body, blue tinted windows & dome light, white plastic ladder on roof, gray plastic baseplate & rear section of hose reel, small square window in base in various plastic colors, 2 axles, 4 wheels, "Kent Fire Brigade" decals or labels on upper flat or lined sides, red & yellow decal or label shield on middle doors, two sizes of wide or narrow rear booster reel. Model changed to Superfast wheels.
1. Large fine tread gray plastic wheels, decal outlined, plain baseplate.
2. Black fine tread plastic wheels, decal outlined, plain baseplate.
3. Black fine tread plastic wheels, decal outlined, extended axle braces.
4. Black fine tread plastic wheels, label not lined, extended axle braces.

57-D   Land Rover Fire Truck   **2½"   1970**
Red body, white plastic removable ladder, blue tinted windows, silver front bumper, five spoke thin wheels, blue dome light, gray plastic baseplate & rear, shield labels on side doors, "Kent Fire Brigade" labels on upper side panels in various shades.
1. Small rear booster hose reel.
2. Larger rear booster hose reel.

57-E   Eccles Trailer Caravan   **3"   1970**
Orange roof, green plastic interior, five spoke thin wheels, red or black axle covers.
1. Without (R) on baseplate, cream body.
2. Cream body with (R) on baseplate, maroon stripe on sides, short overhang on rear.
3. Cream body, long overhang.
4. Cream body, flower label at end of maroon stripe, long overhang.
5. Cream body, flower label at end of maroon stripe, short overhang.
6. Light yellow body, long overhang.
7. Light yellow body, short overhang.
8. Bright yellow body, white interior, red roof, red dot on yellow stripe label on each side, small hubless accent wheels, black riveted axle cover, no number (57) on base.
9. Bright yellow body, white interior, red roof, black stripe label with red and yellow flower on each side, small hubless accent wheels, black riveted axle cover, no number (57) on base. Side labels may be found with flower to the front or flower to the rear. (TP-4).
10. Same as 9, butterscotch tan body, no number 57 on baseplate (TP-4).
11. Same as 10, butterscotch tan body, no number 57 on baseplate,

white bird silhouette and orange and red stripes on elongated side labels, (labels are same as SF 31-3). (TP-4)
12. White body with orange 'Sun set' label with stripe and palm tree against yellow sun on sides.

57-F   Wild Life Truck   **2¾"   1973**
Yellow body, red windows, light tinted blue canopy, orange background label on hood with 'white elephant' & black lettered 'Ranger', dark tan 'lion' revolved by "Rola-matic" wheels, vie spoke wide wheels.
1. Unpainted metal baseplate & grille.
2. Unpainted metal base & grille, red tinted canopy.
3. Red tinted canopy, silver/gray baseplate & grille. (all No. 57-3's may be found in the four variations of the pat. app. line on baseplate.
4. Clear canopy, unpainted metal baseplate & grille. (all 4 base variations).
5. Frosted canopy, unpainted metal baseplate & grille.
6. Blue tinted canopy, unpainted metal baseplate and grille, patent no. at rear of baseplate now reads 1424808 instead of 12174/72.
7. Same as 6, light brown plastic lion.
8. Same as 7, light brown plastic lion, clear tintless canopy.
9. Same as 7, light brown plastic lion, dark amber/orange plastic windows.
10. White body, black zebra stripe tempa print on sides, unpainted metal baseplate & grille, dark amber/orange plastic windows, dark tan plastic lion on yellow plastic turn table on truck bed, smoky gray plastic canopy, five spoke wide wheels. May be found with either blue tinted, smokey gray tinted or clear plastic canopy, and may also be found with either tan or reddish brown plastic lion.
11. Same as 10, red plastic windows, clear canopy.
12. Same as 10, purple plastic windows, clear canopy.

57-G   Carmichael Commando
White body, black top, 6 wheels, "Police Rescue" on side.

57-H   4x4 Mini Pick-up   **1982**
Red body, large wheels, black roll bar.

58-A   BEA Coach   **2½"   1958**
Blue body, with & without silver grille, headlights, black base, 2 axles, 4 wheels, "British European Airways" on rear of sides. Blue body subject to all shades, all wheels have small knobby treads.
1. Clear decal "British European Airways" gray plastic wheels, crimped axles, decal—red square with white lettering, "BEA" on all other models.
2. "BEA" decal faces front, gray plastic wheels, crimped axles.
3. Same as 2, "BEA" faces rear.
4. Same as 3, "BEA" faces front, rounded axles.
5. Same as 4, "BEA" faces rear.
6. Same as 5, "BEA" faces front, silver plastic wheels.
7. Same as 6, "BEA" faces rear.
8. Same as 7, "BEA" faces front, black plastic wheels.
9. Same as 8, "BEA" faces rear.

58-B   Drott Excavator   **2-5/8"   1962**
Red or orange body, with or without silver motor & baseplate, movable front shovel, with & without closed triangle behind blade on arms, 2 open axles, 4 rollers, green rubber treads.
1. Red body, silver motor & baseplate, metal rollers, crimped axles.
2. Red body, silver motor & baseplate, metal rollers, rounded axles.
3. Red body, silver motor & baseplate, silver plastic rollers, rounded axles.
4. Red body, silver motor & baseplate, black plastic rollers, rounded axles.
5. Orange body, silver motor & baseplate, black plastic rollers, rounded axles.
6. Orange body orange motor & baseplate, black plastic rollers, rounded axles.

58-C   D.A.F. Girder Truck   **3"   1968**
Light cream body of various shades, green tinted windows, red plastic grille & short base, 3 axles, 6 black plastic wheels, red plastic girders. Model changed to Superfast wheels.

1. Rivet holds windows to roof.
2. Pin holds windows to roof.
3. Pin holds windows to roof, tow slot.

58-D   D.A.F. Girder Truck   **2-7/8"   1970**
Red plastic girders, black plastic holders, green windows, red plastic baseplate & grille, five spoke thin wheels.
1. Cream cab & chassis, without patent no. on front baseplate.
2. Metallic greenish/gold body, without patent no. on front baseplate.
3. Cream body, with patent no. on front baseplate.
4. Metallic greenish/gold body, with patent no. on front baseplate.

58-E   Woosh-n-Push   **2-7/8"   1972**
Yellow body, red interior, silver plastic motor in rear, small front wheels, larger rear wheels, clover leaf design, metal baseplate, black no. 2 label on rear roof.
1. Labeled no. 2.
2. Light & dark orange flower labels.
3. Black "2" label on roof, light yellow interior.
4. Metallic magenta red body, light yellow interior, yellow no. 8 and white stars on red/white/blue label on roof. (label is same as SF 48-2).
5. Metallic magenta red body, light yellow interior, black no. 8 label on roof.
6. Metallic red body, light yellow interior, black no. 2 label on roof.
7. Yellow body, red interior, black no. 2 label on roof, small five spoke front wheels.
8. Yellow body, red interior, red flower labels, small five spoke wheels.

58-F   Faun Dump Truck   **2-7/8"   1976**
Yellow cab and dumper, black plastic baseplate and front bumper. Body may be found in tones from dark yellow to bright light yellow.
1. No window, large wide heavy duty tread clover leaf wheels.
2. Light yellow cab and dumper, no window, large heavy duty tread clover leaf wheels.
3. Same as 2, two vertical braces connecting back of cab to chassis.
4. Same as 3, red painted dumper.

59-A   Ford Thames Van   **2-1/8"   1958**
Silver grille, with & without silver headlights & bumper, black base, 2 axles, 4 plastic knobby wheels, red large "S" on doors, with & without casting lines on doors, red "SINGER" decals at upper rear of body panel.
1. Light green library, without door lines, light red door decal, gray wheels, crimped axles.
2. Same as 1, with door lines.
3. Same as 2, rounded axles.
4. Same as 3, silver wheels.
5. Same as 3, dark red door decal.
6. Same as 5, silver wheels.
7. Same as 6, kelly green.
8. Same as 7, gray wheels.

59-B   Ford Fairlane Fire Chief's Car   **2-5/8"   1962**
Red body, white dome light, ivory interior, clear windows, black base, 2 axles, 4 plastic wheels, silver grille, with & without silver bumpers, yellow "Fire Chief" decal on hood & sides.
1. Gray plastic wheels.
2. Silver plastic wheels.
3. Black plastic wheels, knobby treads.
4. Black plastic wheels, fine treads.

59-C   Ford Galaxie Fire Chief's Car   **2-7/8"   1966**
Red body, blue dome light, ivory interior, driver & tow hook, clear windows, metal grille & base, 2 axles, 4 black plastic wheels, "FIRE CHIEF" decals or labels on hood, shield decal or label on front doors, with tow slot. Model changed to Superfast wheels.
1. '55/59' on baseplate.
2. '59' on raised square on baseplate.

59-D   Ford Galaxie Fire Chief's Car   **2-7/8"   1970**
Red body, ivory interior & tow hook, one occupant, blue dome light, clear windows, metal baseplate, five spoke thin wheels, "Fire Chief"

label on hood in various shades, shield label on doors.
1. Decal on hood, label on sides.
2. Label on hood & sides.
3. No label on hood, labels on sides.

59-E   Mercury Fire Chief's Car   3"   1971
Red body, two occupants, ivory interior, five spoke wide wheels, clear windows, blue dome light, No. 59 or 73 on baseplate, "Mercury" on baseplate in three different positions.
1. Fire Chief label on hood, shield on doors.
2. Fire helmet & crossed axes on hood, shield on doors.
3. Fire helmet & crossed axes on hood & doors.
4. Fire helmet & crossed axes on hood & doors, silver/gray base & grille.
5. Fire helmet & crossed axes label on hood, no labels on doors, unpainted metal baseplate.
6. Helmet & crossed axes label on hood, no label on doors, long braces over axle channels on unpainted metal baseplate.
7. Fire chief label on hood, fire helmet label on doors, long braces over axle channels on unpainted baseplate.
8. Helmet & crossed axes label on hood and doors, long braces over axle channels on unpainted metal baseplate.
9. Helmet and crossed axes labels on hood and doors, long braces over axle channels, no. 59 only on unpainted metal baseplate.
10. Helmet and axe labels on sides, 'Fire Chief' yellow and red label on hood, long braces over axle channels, No. 59 only on unpainted metal baseplate. (TP 7-b).
11. Helmet and crossed axes labels on sides and hood, long wide braces over axle channel, word 'Superfast' removed from front axle channel, no No. 59 on unpainted metal baseplate, multi-spoke wide wheels. (TP-7).
12. Same as 11, ivory interior, driver and passenger are now removed from front seat.
13. Red body, rectangular blue plastic roof lights, ivory interior, clear windows, no driver or passenger, unpainted metal baseplate, bumpers and grille, black "FIRE" and shield, red star and stripe on yellow side labels, multi-spoke wide wheels, no number on baseplate. (TP-12).
14. White body, rectangular blue plastic roof lights, ivory interior no driver or passenger, unpainted metal baseplate, bumpers and grille, black "POLICE" and shield on white side labels, clear windows, multi-spoke wide wheels, no number on baseplate. (TP-2).
15. Same as 13, purple tinted windows. (TP-12).
16. White body, rectangular blue plastic roof lights, unpainted metal baseplate, bumpers and grille, no number 59 on baseplate, blue plastic windows, white plastic interior, white "201" on black tempa covering hood, white "POLICE" on black tempa covering trunk lid, white "LOS ANGELES POLICE DEPARTMENT" on black tempa covering doors on sides, black tempa "201" on roof, multi-spoke wheels. (Code Red Issue).
17. Red body, rectangular blue plastic roof lights, unpainted metal baseplate, bumpers and grille, no number 59 on baseplate, clear plastic windows, white tempa "CHIEF" on sides rear of front wheels, white "LOS ANGELES CITY FIRE DEPARTMENT" on side doors and on hood, white "1 CHIEF 1" on hood and roof, multi-spoke wheels. (Code Red Issue).
18. White body, rectangular blue plastic roof lights, unpainted metal baseplate, bumpers and grille, no number 59 on baseplate, blue plastic windows, white plastic interior, blue tempa covering side of front and rear fenders, black tempa "POLICE" and shield on doors each side, (tempa design from SF 10-3) multi-spoke wheels.
19. Same as 18, blue plastic windows, ivory plastic interior.
20. Same as 18, purple plastic windows, ivory plastic interior.
21. Same as 18, clear plastic windows, white plastic interior.

59-F   Planet Scout   2¾"   1975
Metallic green top half of body, lime green painted bottom half of body and baseplate, silver plated plastic grille, interior, rear panel and roof panel and ornaments, black plastic insert front to back center of base-

plate holding wheels, five spoke ac ent slicks, large multi-spoke rear wheels.
1. Amber windows and dome lights.
2. Amber windows and dome lights, unplated brown plastic rear panel.
3. Amber windows and dome light, five spoke accent slicks front and rear.
4. Light amber (pinkish) windows and dome light, five spoke reverse accent front wheels, large multi-spoke rear wheels.
5. Amber windows and dome light, large multi-spoke wheels front and rear.
6. Metallic red top half of body, light tan bottom half of body, silver plated plastic grille, interior, rear panel and roof panel and ornaments, black plastic insert front to back center of baseplate holding wheels, five spoke reverse accent front slicks, large multi-spoke rear wheels.
7. Light avocado green top half, dull black bottom half of body, silver plated plastic grille, interior, rear panel, roof panel and roof ornaments, purple plastic windows, black plastic insert front to back center of baseplate holding wheels, five spoke reverse accent front slicks, large multi-spoke rear wheels.
8. Same as 1, apple green painted bottom half of body and baseplate.
9. Same as 7, amber windows. (K-2005)
10. Same as 6, two parallel reinforcement over each axle cover on black plastic base insert.
11. Same as 7, two parallel reinforcement over each axle cover on black plastic base insert.
12. Same as 6, five spoke reverse accent wheels front and rear.
13. Metallic blue top half of body, black painted bottom half and baseplate, black plastic insert center of baseplate, silver plated plastic windows and dome lights, five spoke reverse accent front wheels, large multi-spoke rear wheels. (found in 3-pack sold in the U.K.).

59-G   Porsche 928   3"   1980
Metallic light brown body, black painted metal baseplate and rear registration plate, wide five spoke accent wheels.
1. Yellow plastic interior, clear windows, glossy black baseplate.
2. Yellow plastic interior, clear windows, flat black baseplate.
3. Brown plastic interior, clear windows, glossy black baseplate.
4. Brown plastic interior, clear windows, flat black baseplate.
5. Dark tan plastic interior, amber windows, glossy black baseplate.
6. Dark tan plastic interior, amber windows, flat black baseplate.
7. Metallic tan body, dark tan plastic interior, amber windows, glossy black baseplate.
8. Metallic tan body, dark tan plastic interior, amber windows, flat black baseplate.
9. Metallic light brown body, ivory plastic interior, clear windows, glossy black baseplate.
10. Metallic light brown body, brown plastic interior, amber windows, glossy black baseplate.
11. Metallic light brown body, brown plastic interior, amber windows, metallic brown baseplate.
12. Metallic light brown body, dark tan plastic interior, amber windows, metallic brown baseplate.
13. Metallic light brown body, brown plastic interior, amber windows, flat black painted baseplate.
14. Metallic tan body, brown plastic interior, clear plastic windows, glossy black baseplate.
15. Metallic gold body, brown plastic interior, clear plastic windows, glossy black baseplate.
16. Metallic gold body, brown plastic interior, amber plastic windows, glossy black painted baseplate.
17. Metallic brown body, brown plastic interior, cloudy amber plastic windows, glossy black painted baseplate.
18. Metallic bronze body, brown plastic interior, clear plastic windows, charcoal gray painted baseplate.
19. Metallic light brown body, brown plastic interior, clear plastic windows, charcoal gray painted baseplate.

20. Metallic blue body, dark tan plastic interior, clear plastic windows, glossy black painted metal baseplate.
21. Metallic light brown body, brown plastic interior, amber plastic windows, charcoal gray painted baseplate.
22. Metallic light brown body, brown plastic interior, cloudy amber plastic windows, charcoal gray painted baseplate.
23. Metallic blue body, brown plastic interior, clear plastic windows, glossy black painted baseplate.
24. Metallic blue body, brown plastic interior, clear plastic windows, charcoal gray painted baseplate.
25. Metallic blue body, brown plastic interior, clear plastic windows, silver gray painted baseplate.
26. Metallic blue body, dark tan plastic interior, clear plastic windows, silver gray painted baseplate.
27. Metallic blue body, brown plastic interior, amber plastic windows, glossy black painted metal baseplate.
28. Black body, red interior, Porsche shield on hood & white stripe on sides, hood and top.

60-A   Morris J2 Pick-Up   2¼"   1958
Blue body, open windshield & side door windows, with & without rear open window, with & without silver grilles, bumpers, black base, 2 axles, 4 plastic wheels, with large red "BUILDERS" decal on sides with white or black letters:—"SUPPLY COMPANY" on 2nd line.
1. Red & black decal, dark gray plastic wheels, crimped axles.
2. Red & white decal, dark gray plastic wheels, crimped axles.
3. Red & white decal, dark gray plastic wheels, rounded axles.
4. Red & white decal, light gray plastic wheels, rounded axles.
5. Red & white decal, small gray plastic wheels, rounded axles.
6. Knobby silver plastic wheels.
7. Finer silver plastic wheels.
8. Knobby black plastic wheels.
9. Fine black plastic wheels.
10. Fine black plastic wheels, without rear window .

60-B   Site Hut Truck   2½"   1966
Blue body, blue windows, silver plastic grille & baseplate with 2 rivets, 2 axles, 4 black plastic wheels, yellow plastic hut with green plastic roof, Hut is removable from truck body, with or without tow slots. Model changed to Superfast wheels.
1. Recessed brace behind cab lower than back of bed.
2. Brace behind cab even with back of bed.

60-C   Site Hut Truck   2½"   1970
Blue cab & chassis, blue windows, silver plastic baseplate & grille, five spoke thin wheels, yellow removable hut with green roof.
1. Pat. App. at rear of baseplate reads same as lettering, one rivet at rear of baseplate.
2. Pat. App. at rear of baseplate reads in reverse of baseplate lettering, one rivet at rear of baseplate.
3. Pat. App. at rear of baseplate reads same as lettering, two rivets, one at rear, one in middle of baseplate.
4. Pat. App. at rear of baseplate reads in reverse of baseplate lettering, two rivets, one at rear, one in middle of baseplate.

60-D   Lotus Super Seven   2-7/8"   1971
Butterscotch body, clear windshield, black interior & trunk, metal baseplate, four spoke wide wheels.
1. Black figured label in red fire on hood.
2. Black figure in red flame label on hood, yellow body.
3. Streaker yellow body, red checkerboard stripes on hood & rear fenders, no. 60 in red oval on hood, blue spear on hood, small blue square between seat & truck, large four spoke wide wheels, unpainted metal baseplate, grille & exhaust pipes.

60-E   Holden Pick-up   3"   1977
Unpainted metal baseplate, amber windows, black "500" on white with yellow, black and red checkers label on hood, small multi-spoke wheels.
1. Red painted body, yellow plastic interior and tow hook.
2. Metallic maroon red painted body, yellow plastic interior and tow hook.
3. Metallic maroon red painted body, orange plastic interior and tow

hook.
4. Red painted body, yellow plastic interior and tow hook, bright yellow plastic cycles.
5. Same as 1, red painted body, yellow plastic interior and tow hook, clear plastic windows.
6. Same as 1, amber plastic windows, yellow plastic interior and tow hook, shield shaped label on hood, white star on red background, white borders and blue wavy stripes above. (label from Adventure 2000 units).
7. Same as 1, red body, red plastic interior and tow hook, amber plastic windows, yellow plastic cycles.
8. Same as 1, red body, red plastic interior and tow hook, amber plastic windows, olive green plastic cycles.
9. Metallic blue body, unpainted metal baseplate, amber plastic windows, yellow plastic interior and tow hook, orange/yellow plastic cycles, label on hood with black "RALLYE–81–PARIS–DAKAR" on yellow background at the top, two rows of black and white checkers at the center and black "PARIS–MATCH" on white background at the bottom, small multi-spoke wheels. (sold in France).
10. Red body, unpainted metal baseplate, grille & bumpers, red plastic interior and tow hook, amber plastic windows, olive green plastic cycles, yellow on blue sunburst label on hood. (label from SF47-2) small multi-spoke wheels.
11. Cream body, unpainted metal baseplate, grille and bumpers, red plastic interior and tow hook, amber plastic windows, red or yellow/orange plastic cycles, black "SUPERBIKE", blue, yellow and black stripes on white labels on sides, small multi-spoke wheels.
12. Same as 11, tan plastic interior and tow hook, yellow/orange or red plastic cycles.

60-F Piston Popper   1982
Yellow body with red plastic windows, silver engine in front, labels on top & sides, large back wheels, small front wheels.

61-A Ferret Scout Car   2¼"   1959
Olive green, tan driver in various shades facing front or back, 2 axles, 4 black plastic wheels, with spare wheel mounted on left side, black metal base with 3 or 4 lines of print excluding the words "MATCHBOX" Series", with or without blocks in all four corners.
1. Knobby black wheels, crimped axles, 3 line base.
2. Knobby black wheels, rounded axles, 3 line base.
3. Knobby black wheels, rounded axles, 4 line base.
4. Fine black treads, 4 line base.

61-B Alvis Stalwart   2-5/8"   1966
White body, yellow plastic removable canopy, green windows, 3 axles, 6 plastic tires, green or yellow wheels, "BP" EXPLORATION" decal or labels on sides, smooth or ribbed bed.
1. Smooth bed, green wheels, decals.
2. Ribbed bed, green wheels, decals.
3. Ribbed bed, green wheels, labels.
4. Ribbed bed, green wheels, labels, "BP" at rear of label.
5. Ribbed bed, yellow wheels, labels.

61-C Blue Shark   3"   1971
Metallic dark blue, white driver, clear glass, silver motor, black exhaust pipes, 4 spoke wide wheels, metal base.
1. Orange label with no. 86 with red arrows on hood.
2. Orange label with no. 86 with red arrows on hood, metal reinforcement behind driver.
3. Orange label with no. 86 & red arrows on hood, metal reinforcement behind driver, silver/gray baseplate.
4. Yellow/orange/black label no. 69 (same as no. 69-2), metal reinforcement behind driver, metal unpainted baseplate, amber tinted windshield.
5. Yellow, orange & black no. 69 label, reinforcements behind driver, unpainted metal baseplate, clear windshield.
6. Red and black on white Scorpion round label, reinforcement behind driver, unpainted metal baseplate, clear windshield.
7. Red and black on white Scorpion round label, reinforcement

behind driver, unpainted metal baseplate, amber windshield.
8. Orange label with no. 86 and red arrows on hood, metal reinforcement behind driver, unpainted metal baseplate, amber windshield.
9. Yellow, orange & black no. 69 label, reinforcements behind driver, silver/gray baseplate, amber windshield.
10. Orange label with no. 86 & red arrow on hood, no metal reinforcement behind driver, straight casting edge at rear of motor well, metallic medium blue body, clear windshield.
11. Orange label with no. 86 with red arrow on hood, reinforcement behind driver, clear windshield, off-white driver, casting raised on on hood front of driver.
12. Yellow/orange and black no. 69 label, reinforcement behind driver, silver/gray painted baseplate, clear windshield.
13. Same as 8, clear frosted windshield.

61-D Ford Wreck Truck   3"   1978
Red painted body, flat black painted metal baseplate and grille, frosted amber plastic windows and dome light, five spoke reverse accent wheels.
1. White plastic hoists with zig-zag designs, red plastic hooks.
2. Same as 1, frosted blue plastic windows.
3. Same as 1, charcoal gray painted metal baseplate and grille.
4. Same as 1, charcoal gray painted metal baseplate and grille, red plastic hoists with zig-zag designs, red plastic hooks.
5. Same as 1, black painted metal baseplate, white plastic hoists, black plastic hooks.
6. Yellow body, flat black painted metal baseplate and grille, frosted amber plastic windows and dome lights, red plastic hoists, red plastic hooks, five spoke reverse accent wheels.
7. Same as 7, flat black painted metal baseplate and grille, green plastic hoists, red plastic hooks.
8. Same as 6, flat black painted metal baseplate and grille, green plastic hoists, black plastic hooks.
9. Same as 6, charcoal gray painted metal baseplate and grille, green plastic hoists, red plastic hooks.
10. Same as 6, charcoal gray painted metal baseplate and grille, green plastic hoists, black plastic hooks.
11. Same as 6, charcoal gray painted metal baseplate and grille, white plastic hoists, red plastic hooks.
12. Same as 6, charcoal gray painted metal baseplate and grille, green plastic hoists, black plastic hooks.
13. Same as 6, charcoal gray painted metal baseplate and grille, red plastic hoists, black plastic hooks.
14. Same as 1, charcoal gray painted metal baseplate and grille, white plastic hoists, black plastic hooks.
15. Same as 1, flat black painted metal baseplate and grille, red plastic hoists, red plastic hooks.
16. Same as 7, glossy black painted metal baseplate and grille, green plastic hoists, black plastic hooks.
17. Same as 6, glossy black painted metal baseplate and grille, green plastic hoists, red plastic hooks.
18. Same as 6, glossy black painted metal baseplate and grille, red plastic hoists, black plastic hooks.
19. Same as 6, unpainted metal baseplate and grille, red plastic hoists, black plastic hooks.
20. Same as 6, unpainted metal baseplate and grille, pinkish/red plastic hoists, black plastic hooks.
21. Red body, flat black painted metal baseplate and grille, white tempa "RADIO DISPATCHES" 24 HOUR" "TOWING" and two thin white stripes each side, frosted amber plastic windows and dome lights, white plastic hoists and red plastic hooks, five spoke reverse accent wheels.
22. Same as 21, flat black painted metal baseplate and grille, red plastic hoists, black plastic hooks.
23. Same as 21, flat black painted metal baseplate and grille, white plastic hoists, black plastic hooks.

61-E Peterbilt ®Wrecker   1982
Red body, two black tow arms and hooks, silver grille & stack.

62-A General Service Lorry   2-5/8"   1959

Olive green body, with & without silver headlights & bumper, with tow hook, 3 axles, 6 black plastic wheels.
1. Knobby treads, crimped axles.
2. Knobby treads, rounded axles.

62-B T.V. Service Van   2½"   1963
Cream body, green tinted windows with roof window, 2 axles, 4 plastic wheels, with & without front rivet in base, small hole in roof for red plastic antenna, red plastic ladder & 3 T.V. sets, with & without silver grille, bumpers.
1. Red "RENTASET" decals, knobby gray plastic wheels.
2. Red "RENTASET" decals, fine tread gray wheels.
3. Red "RENTASET" decals, knobby black wheels.
4. Red "RENTASET" decals, fine black tread wheels.
5. Red "RENTASET" decals, rivet front base.
6. Green "RADIO RENTALS" decal, knobby tread gray wheels, rivet front base.
7. Green "RADIO RENTALS" decals, fine tread gray wheels, rivet front base.
8. Green "RADIO RENTALS" decals, fine tread black wheels, rivet front base.
9. Red "RENTASET" decals, fine tread gray wheels, rivet base.

62-C Mercury Cougar   3"   1968
Metallic lime/green body in various shades, metal grille & baseplate with tow slot, red plastic interior & tow hook, clear windows, autosteer silver wheels, black plastic tires. Model changed to Superfast wheels.

62-D Mercury Cougar   3"   1970
Red interior & tow hook, clear windows, five spoke thin wheels, metal baseplate & grille.
1. Metallic lime/green body.
2. Metallic yellow/green body.

62-E Mercury Cougar "Rat Rod"   3"   1970
Silver motor in hood, red interior & tow hook, clear windows, metal baseplate & grille, small five spoke front wheels, larger five spoke wide rear wheels, square hole in front baseplate.
1. Open front motor mounts, wide or narrow hood vent space, five spoke wheels.
2. Closed front motor mounts, wide or narrow framed vents, four spoke rear wheels.
3. Lime/green, closed front motor mounts, wide or narrow hood vents, four spoke rear wheels. May be found with the plastic window assembly mounted backward, the windshield with the rear-view mirror is at the rear.
4. Lime/green, closed front motor mounts, wide or narrow hood vents, four spoke rear wheels, silver/gray painted base & grille.
5. Lime/green, closed front motor mounts, wide or narrow hood vents, four spoke rear wheels, unpainted baseplate & grille, yellow-tan wildcat label (same as no. 8-2g).
6. Open front motor mounts, light green body, wide hood vent space, four spoke wheels. (same as a).

62-F Renault 17TL   3"   1974
White interior, green tinted windows, green no. 9 in black bordered white circle and yellow, green and red stripes on white label on left side of hood, wide five spoke wheels. Baseplate may be found with or without dot under number of patent number or with thick or thin wall front of tow box. Also may be found with the no. 9 label upside down on hood looking like a no. 6 label.
1. Deep cherry red body, black baseplate, top field of slashes on baseplate (/////////).
2. Deep cherry red body, black baseplate, top field of slashes on baseplate.
3. Orange red body, black baseplate, top field of slashes on baseplate.
4. Orange red body, black baseplate, top field of slashes on baseplate.
5. Orange red body, black painted baseplate, slashes on base going from left to right, wide clover leaf front wheels, small clover leaf rear wheels.
6. Orange red body, black painted baseplate, wide five spoke wheels, black shield and red 'FIRE' on yellow side labels (same as 22-3),

(found in G-12).

62-G Chevrolet Corvette   1979
Metallic dark red body, unpainted metal baseplate and side exhaust pipes, gray plastic interior, five spoke accent front wheels, five spoke reverse accent rear wheels.

1. Clear plastic windows, white tempa accent design on hood and doors.
2. Same as 1, clear plastic windows, white tempa imprint on hood only.
3. Same as 1, clear plastic windows, five spoke accent wheels front and rear.
4. Same as 1, black plastic interior, white tempa accent designs on hood and doors.
5. Same as 2, black plastic interior, white tempa accent designs on hood only.
6. Same as 1, tan plastic interior, white tempa accent designs on hood and doors, no numbers on license plates front and rear, no "CORVETTE" on trunk lid.
7. Same as 2, clear plastic windows, white tempa imprint on hood only, white plastic interior.
8. Black body, unpainted metal baseplate and exhaust pipes, orange and yellow tempa stripes on roof and hood, gray plastic interior, five spoke accent front wheels, five spoke reverse accent rear wheels.
9. Same as 8, orange and greenish/yellow tempa stripes on hood and roof.
10. Same as 8, orange and yellow tempa stripes on hood and roof, silver painted metal baseplate.

63-A Ford Service Ambulance   2½"   1959
Olive green body, 4 plastic wheels, round white circle on sides with red cross, with & without silver grille, bumpers, with & without hole in base under rear axle.

1. Black knobby wheels, crimped axles.
2. Black knobby wheels, rounded axles.
3. Black knobby wheels, rounded axles, with hole under rear axle.
4. Black fine tread wheels, rounded axles, with hole under rear axle.

63-B Foamite Crash Tender   2¼"   1964
Red body, silver painted grille, silver base & rear section, 3 axles, 6 black plastic wheels, white plastic hose & ladder on roof, white plastic lettering on sides, gold foam nozzle on front roof.

1. Plastic springs under 1st & 2nd axle. One small brace on sides of base between 1st & 3rd axle.
2. Plastic springs under 1st & 2nd axle, 4 small braces on base between axles.
3. Without plastic springs, leaving 2 square holes under 1st & 2nd axle.
4. Angled brace under front axle, square hole under 3rd axle.
5. Angled front brace, filled in hole under rear axle.

63-C Dodge Crane Truck   3"   1968
Yellow body, green windows, black plastic grille & base, 3 axles, 6 black plastic wheels, rotating crane cab, with & without brace inside, single cable plastic hook. Model changed to Superfast wheels.

1. Red plastic hook.
2. Red plastic hook, tow slot.
3. Red plastic hook, tow slot, brace inside crane cab.
4. Yellow plastic hook, tow slot, brace inside crane cab.

63-D Dodge Crane Truck   2¼"   1970
Yellow body, green windows, black baseplate & grille, four spoke wide wheels, yellow plastic hook, red or black axle covers, hooks facing in or out.

1. Yellow hook.
2. Light yellow hook.

63-E Freeway Gas Truck   3"   1973
Red cab, black baseplate & grille, purple tinted windows, small wide wheels on front, clover leaf design, white tank with red plastic bottom, five spoke wide wheels.

1. "Burmah" labels on tanker in red/white & blue on white background, black lettered "Burmah" at rear of label.
2. Red lettering on white background "Castrol" label on sides.
3. Red, white & blue Burmah labels on tanker, five spoke wheels on cab and tanker.
4. Red, white and blue "Burmah" labels on sides, small clover leaf wheels on cab, five spoke wheels on tanker, no rivet on axle cover under tanker, 3/8" braces each side of base from axle housing to center of baseplate.
5. 15/16" braces each side of base from axle housing to rivets front of baseplate.
6. Red, white and blue "Burmah" labels on sides, blue on top or small "Burmah", small clover leaf wheels on cab, five spoke wheels on tanker, no rivet, 3/8" braces. May be found with blue top "Burmah" label on one side and red on top on the other side.
7. Red, white and blue "Burmah" labels on sides, blue on top of small "Burmah", small clover leaf wheels on cab, five spoke wheels on tanker, no rivets, 15/16" braces. May be found with blue top "Burmah" label on one side and red on top on the other side.
8. Red, white and blue "Burmah" labels on sides, red on top, small clover leaf wheels on cab and tanker, no rivet, 3/8" braces.
9. Military olive green cab and tankers, "95 HIGH OCTANE K" olive green, white and red side labels, black plastic baseplates on cab and tanker, small clover leaf wheels on cab, five spoke wheels on tanker no hub caps. (TP-14).
10. Same as 9, small clover leaf wheels on cab and tanker. (TP-14).
11. Military olive drab cab and tanker, French flag side labels, black plastic baseplate on cab and tanker, small clover leaf wheels on cab, five spoke wheels on tanker, no hub caps.
12. Red, white, and blue "BURMAH" side labels, small clover leaf wheels on cab, five spoke wheels on tanker, no rivet on axle cover, circular hole (3/32") and reinforcements above rear license plate. May be found with side labels reading "95 HIGH OCTANE//K" on both sides or with '95 HIGH OCTANE//K' on right side and 'K//95 HIGH OCTANE' on left side.
13. Same as 12, numbers removed from license plate.
14. Same as 9, circular hole (3/32") and reinforcements above rear license plate with numbers removed. May be found with side labels reading '95 HIGH OCTANE//K' on both sides or with '95 HIGH OCTANE//K' on right side and 'K//95 HIGH OCTANE' on left side.
15. Blue cab, black plastic baseplate on cab, purple tinted windows, blue plastic bottom half of tanker, white painted metal top half of tanker, blue and white 'ARAL' labels, small clover leaf wheels on cab, five spoke wheels on tanker, circular hole (3/32") and reinforcements above rear license plate with number removed.
16. Same as 12, number removed from license plate, white plastic hook inserted in hole at rear of tanker. (TP-12).
17. Same as 12, black "CHEVRON" with red and blue chevrons on white side labels, numbers removed from rear license plate, circular hole and reinforcements above rear license plate.
18. Same as 17, white plastic hook inserted in hole at rear of tanker.
19. Same as 17, wide raised line on axle cab, black plastic baseplate, parallel lines replacing arrow like lines on rear axle cover.
20. Same as 19, white plastic hook inserted in hole at rear of tanker.
21. White cab, yellow plastic base with black plastic insert, purple tinted windows, white painted metal top half of tanker, yellow plastic bottom half of tanker, red and yellow shell logo on white stripe label each side of tanker, four clover leaf wheels on cab, two five spoke wheels on tanker, hole for tow hook at rear. (Shell tanker may be found with long or short braces on baseplate under tanker.)
22. Same as 21, red tinted plastic windows.
23. Same as 22, red tinted plastic windows, orange/yellow plastic insert over rear axle.
24. Same as 21, orange/yellow plastic half bottom of tanker.
25. Same as 21, white plastic hook inserted in hole rear of tanker.
26. White cab, black plastic base with black plastic insert, purple tinted plastic windows, white painted metal top half of tanker, white plastic bottom half of tanker, red "EXXON" in white rectangle bordered in blue on red stripe side label, four clover leaf wheels on cab, five spoke wheels on tanker.
27. White cab, yellow plastic base with black plastic insert, purple tinted plastic windows, white painted metal top half of tanker, yellow plastic bottom half, black plastic insert over rear axle, red "EXXON" on white rectangle bordered in blue on red stripe side labels, four clover leaf wheels on cab, five spoke wheels on tanker.
28. White cab, black plastic base with black plastic insert, purple tinted plastic windows, white painted metal top half of tanker, green plastic bottom half, black plastic insert on rear axle, green and yellow "BP" logo and red "BP SUPER" on white stripe side labels, four clover leaf wheels on cab, five spoke wheels on tanker.

63-F Freeway Gas Tank Trailer   1978
Red painted metal front wheel carriage and trailer hitch, five spoke accent front wheels, white painted metal top half of tanker, red plastic bottom half portion of tanker five spoke rear wheels. The trailer was achieved by removing the cab of SF 63-2 and replacing it by a metal front carriage and hitch.

1. Black "BURMAH" and red, blue and black "BURMAH" logo on white labels each side of tanker. (TP-12).
2. Same as 1, black "CHEVRON" with red and blue chevrons on white side labels. (TP-12).
3. Same as 2, black "CHEVRON" with red and blue chevrons on white side labels, parallel lines replacing arrow like lines on rear axle cover. (TP-12).
4. Same as 3, red "SHELL" and red and yellow Shell logo on white stripe label each side of tanker, yellow bottom half of tanker, black plastic insert over rear axle. (TP-17).
5. Same as 4, red "SHELL" and red and yellow Shell logo on white stripe label each side of tanker, orange/yellow bottom half of tanker, black plastic insert over rear axle. (TP-17).

63-G Dodge Challenger   2-7/8"   1980
Pale green body, black painted metal baseplate, bumpers and grille, no number 63 on baseplate, (Made in Hong Kong), clear plastic windows.

1. Ivory plastic interior, large dark green tempa stripe on sides front to rear, large white tempa "2" on side doors and on hood, two thin dark green and one thin white tempa stripes on hood and roof, dark green tempa covering trunk lid, old baseplate with "MATCH-BOX" SUPERFAST and "GALANT/ETERNA", clover leaf wheels.
2. Same as 1, five spoke wheels.
3. Dark green plastic interior, large green tempa "2" on side doors and on hood, two thin dark green and one thin black tempa stripes on hood and roof, dark green tempa covering trunk lid, new baseplate with "MATCHBOX", Dodge Challenger", five spoke wide wheels.

63-H Snorkle Fire Engine   1982
Red body with black interior, white extending ladder and bucket, white letters on sides "Los Angeles City Fire Dept.".

64-A Scammel Breakdown Truck   2½"   1959
Olive green, double cable hook, 3 axles, 6 black plastic wheels.

1. Green metal body, flat rivet holds hook to crane, knobby black treads, crimped axles.
2. Green metal body, flat rivet holds hook to crane, knobby black treads, rounded axles.
3. Green metal body, crimped rivet holds hook to crane, knobby black treads, rounded axles.
4. Gray plastic hook, rounded rivet holds hook to crane, knobby black treads, crimped axles.
5. Silver metal body, crimped rivet holds hook to crane, knobby black treads, rounded axles.
6. Gray plastic hook, rounded rivet holds hook to crane, fine black

64-B MG 1100 2-5/8" 1966
Green body, ivory interior, driver, dog & tow hook, clear windows, metal grille and baseplate, 2 axles, 4 black plastic wheels. Model changed to Superfast wheels.

64-C MG 1100 2-5/8" 1970
Ivory interior & tow hook, one occupant & dog, clear windows, metal baseplate & grille, five spoke thin wheels.
1. Green body.
2. Metallic dark blue body.
3. Metallic light blue body.

64-D Slingshot Dragster 3" 1971
Pink body, white driver, silver plastic motors, black exhaust pipes, five spoke thin front wheels, 8 spoke wide rear wheels, black baseplate.
1. No. 9 on hood in black on yellow background with flame label.
2. Orange body, black exhaust pipes, same as the first no. 38 Honda cycle.
3. Metallic blue body, black exhaust pipes.
4. Metallic blue body, red exhaust pipes.
5. Metallic blue body, red exhaust pipes, unpainted metal baseplate.
6. Orange body, red exhaust pipes, unpainted metal baseplate.
7. Metallic blue body, red exhaust pipes, black painted baseplate, white star inside blue circle and flame label on hood.
8. Metallic blue body, red exhaust pipes, black base, no. 3 black on yellow stripe label on hood.
9. Metallic blue body, red exhaust pipes, black baseplate, no. 9 black and yellow flame label on hood, wide front wheels.

64-E Fire Chief's Car 3" 1976
Red body, unpainted metal baseplate, dark blue tinted windows and dome light, silver plastic air scoops on hood, interior and rear panel, small front five spoke accent wheels, larger rear five spoke reverse accent wheels.
1. Black 'FIRE' letters and red star on red and yellow label each side.
2. Black 'FIRE' letters and red star on red and yellow label each side, with black outline of shield and lower edge of label.
3. Same as 2, five spoke accent wheels front and rear.
4. Same as 2, large five spoke reverse accent wheels front and rear.

64-F Caterpillar Tractor 2-5/8" 1979
Yellow body, unpainted metal baseplate engine and tow hook, yellow plastic blade, tan plastic cab.
1. Base reads "Caterpillar Tractor", black rubber traction treads, orange plastic rollers.
2. Base reads "Caterpillar Tractor", black rubber traction treads, light yellow plastic rollers.
3. Base reads "[c]Caterpillar D-9 Tractor", black rubber traction treads, orange plastic rollers.
4. Base reads "[c]Caterpillar D-9 Tractor", black rubber traction treads, light yellow plastic rollers.
5. Same as 1, yellow/orange plastic rollers.
6. Same as 3, yellow/orange plastic rollers.
7. Light yellow body, unpainted metal baseplate, engine and tow hook, "Caterpillar D9 Tractor" on baseplate, black rubber treads, orange/orange plastic rollers, yellow plastic blade, tan plastic cab.
8. Yellow body, unpainted metal baseplate, engine and tow hook, "Caterpillar D-9 Tractor" on baseplate, black rubber treads, yellow/orange plastic rollers, yellow plastic blade, light tan (putty) plastic cab.
9. Same as 8, with black plastic cab.

65-A Jaguar 3.4 Litre Saloon 2½" 1959
Silver grille, with & without silver headlights, bumpers, with & without red painted tail lights, black painted baseplate, bumpers silver or black, 2 axles, 4 gray plastic wheels.
1. Metallic blue body of various shades, crimped axles.
2. Blue painted body, crimped axles.
3. Metallic blue body, round axles.
4. Blue painted body, round axles.

65-B Jaguar 3.8 Litre Sedan - 2-5/8" 1962

Red body of various shades, green tinted windows, silver motor & baseplate with tow hook, with & without silver grille, headlights & bumpers, 2 axles, 4 plastic wheels.
1. Red painted body, large gray plastic wheels, fine treads.
2. Metallic red body, large knobby silver plastic wheels.
3. Red painted body, large knobby silver plastic wheels.
4. Red painted body, large black plastic wheels, fine treads.

65-C Claas Combine Harvester 3" 1967
Red body, yellow plastic rotating blades & front wheels, black plastic front tires and rear sold wheels, with & without small hole in base, with 4 or 5 lettered lines on base, with & without "MATCHBOX Series & No. 65" on 3 line raised plate on base.
1. Dark red body, no hole in base, 5 line lettering, open bottom step in ladder.
2. Dark red body, with small hole in base, 4 lettered line with raised plate above, closed step in ladder.
3. Brighter red body.

65-D Saab Sonnet 2¾" 1973
Metallic blue body, amber windows, light orange interior & hood, pale blue rear trunk, five spoke wide wheels.
1. Metal baseplate, light blue body.
2. Metal baseplate, dark blue body.
3. Unpainted metal baseplate, light amber windows.
4. Black painted metal baseplate and grille, amber windows.
5. White body, unpainted metal baseplate, amber windows. (MP-1)

65-E Airport Coach 3" 1977
Metallic blue bottom half of body, white plastic top half and roof, amber windows and sun roofs, unpainted metal baseplate, yellow plastic interior, multi-spoke wide wheels.
1. Red, white and blue "American Airlines A A" side labels.
2. Red, white and blue 'BRITISH AIRWAYS' side labels, dark amber windows.
3. White, orange, black and blue 'LUFTHANSA' side labels.
4. Red, white and blue 'AMERICAN AIRLINES A A' side labels, dark amber windows and sun roofs.
5. Red, white and blue 'BRITISH AIRWAYS' side labels, dark amber windows and sun roofs.
6. Red, white and blue 'AMERICAN AIRLINES A A' side labels, clear windows and sun roofs.
7. Red, white and blue 'BRITISH AIRWAYS' side labels, clear windows and sun roofs.
8. White, orange, black and blue "LUFTHANSA" side labels, clear plastic windows and sun roofs. (found at some K-Mart in the USA).
9. Red, white and blue "British Airways"side labels, clear plastic windows and sun-roof, ivory plastic interior.
10. Red, white and blue 'AMERICAN AIRLINES' side labels, amber plastic windows and sun roofs, ivory plastic interior.
11. Red, white and blue 'AMERICAN AIRLINES' side labels, clear plastic windows and sun roofs, ivory plastic interior.
12. White, orange, black and blue "LUFTHANSA" side labels, amber plastic windows, ivory plastic interior.
13. Red, white and blue "AMERICAN AIRLINES" side labels, amber plastic windows, yellow plastic interior, unpainted metal baseplate with deep well front of front wheels now filled.
14. Red, white and blue "BRITISH AIRWAYS" side labels, amber plastic windows, yellow plastic interior, unpainted metal baseplate with deep well front of front wheels now filled.
15. White, orange, black and blue "LUFTHANSA" side labels, amber plastic windows and sun roofs, yellow plastic interior, unpainted metal baseplate with deep well front of front wheels now filled.
16. Metallic red bottom half of body, white plastic top half and roof, amber plastic windows and sun roofs, yellow plastic interior, red "TWA" and two red stripes on white side labels, multi-spoke wheels.
17. Same as 16, white "QANTAS" and logo on red side labels.
18. Orange bottom half of body, white plastic top half and roof, amber plastic windows and sun roofs, yellow plastic interior,

unpainted metal baseplate and grille, black "SCHULBUS" on orange and black silhouette of two children in black bordered white rectangle side labels, multi-spoke wheels. (Sold in Germany).
19. Same as 16, white "QANTAS" and logo on red side labels, cloudy amber windows and sun roofs.

65-F Tyrone Malone Bandag Bandit 1982
Black body, white letters "Bandag Bandit" on hood, yellow and white stripes on hood & sides, large recessed hub back wheels, small recessed hub front wheels.

66-A Citroen D.S. 19 2½" 1959
Light or dark yellow body, with & without silver painted grille, headlights, bumpers, black baseplate, 2 axles, 4 plastic wheels.
1. Dark gray plastic wheels, crimped axles.
2. Dark gray plastic wheels, rounded axles.
3. Light gray plastic wheels, rounded axles.
4. Knobby tread silver plastic wheels.

66-B Harley Davidson Motorcycle & Sidecar 2-5/8" 1962
Metallic bronze body, sidecar attached to cycle with 2 flat braces with raised lines on base, 3 wire wheels, black plastic tires.

66-C Greyhound Bus 3" 1967
Silver body, white plastic interior, with clear or dark amber windows, black baseplate with 2 small rivets at rear of base, with & without tow slot, 3 axles, 6 black plastic wheels, decal or label:—'GREYHOUND' lettering with greyhound dog at either end of lettering and dog facing front or back. Model changed to Superfast wheels.
1. Clear windows, blue decal, plain base.
2. Amber windows, blue decal, plain base.
3. Amber windows, blue decal, tow slot.
4. Amber windows, gray label, plain base.
5. Amber windows, gray label, tow slot.

66-D Greyhound Bus 3" 1970
Silver body, white interior, amber windows, five spoke thin wheels, gray lined label on sides.
1. Black baseplate.
2. Dark yellow baseplate.
3. Light yellow baseplate.
4. Pink baseplate.

66-E Mazda RX 500 3" 1971
Orange body, purple windows, silver motor in rear, five spoke wide wheels.
1. Metal baseplate.
2. Cream baseplate.
3. White baseplate.
4. White baseplate, dark orange body.
5. White baseplate, light orange/yellow body.
6. Red body, white painted baseplate, 'CASTROL' red & green round logo on square white label on roof.
7. Orange body, white baseplate, amber windows.
8. Red body, white painted baseplate, tan plastic interior and motor, five spoke accent wheels, cut out between exhaust pipes squared off. (MP-1).
9. Dark green body, silver pearl gray painted metal baseplate and rear panel, green and yellow tempa stripes on roof, hood and rear engine lead, yellow "66" each side of rear engine lid, chrome plated plastic interior and rear engine, five spoke accent wheels, "Made In Hong Kong" on baseplate.
10. Streaker red body, no. 77 in white shield on hood, white RX500 and simulated headlights on front, green stripe over front fenders, two white no. 77 on green on roof, STP—TOTAL on green on rear motor lid, silver interior and motor, five spoke wheels. Purple windows, and white painted baseplate.
11. Same as 10, amber windows.
12. Same as 10, light amber (pinkish) windows.
13. Same as 10, amber windows, five spoke accent wheels, cut out between exhaust pipes on base is now squared off.
14. Amber windows, five spoke accent wheels, same as 10.
15. Same as 13, tan plastic interior and motor.

66-F Ford Transit   2¾"   1977
Orange body, light yellow plastic interior and tow hook, unpainted metal baseplate and grille, green tinted windows and windshield, small multi-spoke slicks.

1. Tan plastic crate cargo with black 'FRAGILE' "SPARES" on white and brown side labels. (Labels on cargo may be found in either light or dark brown.)
2. Same as 1, thick rear panel.
3. Same as 2, light blueish green windows.
4. Same as 2, tan interior.
5. Same as 2, dark green windows.
6. Same as 2, light brown plastic crate cargo with black 'FRAGILE' and "SPARES" on white and brown side labels.
7. Same as 2, light yellow plastic interior, amber plastic windows.
8. Same as 4, tan plastic interior, amber plastic windows, light tan plastic crate cargo with black "FRAGILE" and "SPARES" on white and brown side labels.
9. Same as 4, tan plastic interior and tow hook, cloudy amber plastic windows, light tan plastic cargo.
10. Same as 2, olive green plastic interior and tow hook, green plastic windows, light tan plastic cargo.
11. Same as 2, olive green plastic interior and tow hook, amber plastic windows, light tan plastic cargo.
12. Light orange body, light yellow plastic interior and tow hook, black painted metal baseplate and grille, green tinted plastic windows, light tan plastic cargo, small multi-spoke slicks.

66-G Tyrone Malone Super Boss   1982
67-A Saladin Armoured Car   2½"   1959
Olive green body, rotating gun turret, 3 axles, 6 black plastic wheels.

1. Knobby black plastic wheels, crimped axles.
2. Knobby black plastic wheels, rounded axles.
3. Black plastic wheels, fine treads, rounded axles.

67-B Volkswagen 1600 TL   2¾"   1967
Ivory interior, metal grille & baseplate with tow slot, 2 axles, 4 black plastic tires, silver plastic wheels. Model changed to Superfast wheels.

1. Red painted body.
2. Red painted body, with maroon plastic roof rack. (found in gift set 6-4, 1969.)
3. Metallic purple body. (Canadian market only).

67-C Volkswagen 1600 TL   2-5/8"   1970
Ivory interior, clear windows, metal baseplate & grille, five spoke wheels.

1. Red body, thin wheels.
2. Metallic purple body, thin wheels.
3. Dark purple body, thin wheels.
4. Medium purple body, thin wheels.
5. Light purple body, thin wheels.
6. Hot pink body, thin wheels.
7. Hot pink body, wide wheels, wide wheel wells.

67-D Hot Rocker   3"   1973
Metallic lime/green body, (variations from lime to light yellow green), white interior & tow hook, silver popping motor by "Rola-matic" wheels, five spoke wide wheels, clear windows.

1. Metal baseplate & grille.
2. Silver/gray baseplate & grille.
3. Unpainted metal baseplate and grille, extended baseplate braces at rear of each side of front and rear axle housings.
4. Unpainted metal baseplate and grille, extended baseplate braces wide five spoke 'Rolamatic' front wheels, large wide clover leaf rear wheels, (same as 10-B).
5. Orange/red body, unpainted metal baseplate & grille, extended baseplate braces, five spoke wide wheels.
6. Same as 5, Pat. no. 12174/72 replaced by Pat. no. 1424808.

67-E Datsun 260 Z 2+2   3"   1978
Metallic burgundy painted body, flat black painted metal baseplate, grille and bumpers, light yellow plastic interior and tow hook, multi-spoke wheels.

1. Clear plastic windows.

2. Same as 1, metallic blue body.
3. Same as 1, dark yellow plastic interior.
4. Same as 2, light blue metallic body, light yellow plastic interior. (TP-21).
5. Same as 1, clear plastic windows, glossy black painted metal baseplate.
6. Same as 1, clear plastic windows, light yellow plastic interior, charcoal gray painted metal baseplate.
7. Same as 6, smoky gray plastic windows.
8. Same as 4, dark yellow plastic interior.
9. Silver gray body, charcoal gray painted metal baseplate and bumpers, light yellow plastic interior and tow hook, clear plastic windows, multi-spoke wheels.
10. Same as 9, red plastic interior and tow hook.
11. Same as 9, black painted metal baseplate, red plastic interior and tow hook.
12. Metallic blue body, charcoal brown metal baseplate and bumpers, red plastic interior and tow hook, clear plastic windows, multi-spoke wheels.
13. Same as 11, white interior.

68-A Austin MK II Radio Truck   2-3/8"   1959
Olive green body, with & without silver painted grille, headlights & bumper, 2 axles, 4 black plastic wheels.

1. Knobby treads, crimped axles.
2. Knobby treads, rounded axles.
3. Fine treads, rounded axles.

68-B Mercedes Coach   2-7/8"   1965
White plastic top half, white plastic interior, clear windows, open or closed axles, thin or thick axle supports, high or low seats, 2 axles, 4 black plastic wheels.

1. Green bottom half of body, open axles, thin supports.
2. Orange bottom half of body, open axles, thin supports.
3. Orange bottom half of body, closed axles, thin supports.
4. Orange bottom half of body, closed axles, thick supports.

68-C Porsche 910   2-7/8"   1970
Amber windows, ivory interior, five spoke wheels, metal baseplate & exhaust pipes, no. 68 label on hood. (G-3 sets have no. 68 on sides also.)

1. Metallic red, thin wheels.
2. Metallic red, wide wheels.
3. White body, wide wheels, (produced for the European market).
4. Metallic red, wide wheels, clear windows.
5. Metallic red, wide wheels, amber windows, square no. 45 label on hood, (same as 45-A 4).
6. Metallic red, wide wheels, no. 68 label on hood, deep orange windows.
7. Metallic red, wide wheels, square no. 45 label on hood, clear windows.
8. Metallic red body, thin wheels, black no. 68 on white label on hood, small black no. 68 on white labels on sides. (G-3 sets).
9. Metallic red body,wide wheels, black no. 68 on white label on hood, small black no. 68 on white labels on sides. (G-3 sets).

68-D Cosmobile   2-7/8"   1975
Metallic blue top half body, yellow painted bottom half of body and baseplate, silver plated plastic interior, headlights, side ornaments and roof horns, black plastic insert front to back center of baseplate holding model, five spoke accent slicks front and rear. (larger back slicks).

1. Amber windows, small five spoke accent front wheels, large five spoke reverse accent wheels.
2. Amber windows, small five spoke accent front and rear wheels.
3. Amber windows, large reverse accent wheels front and rear.
4. Amber windows, five spoke accent rear wheels, large five spoke reverse accent rear wheels, extended divider between silver plastic air intakes on roof.
5. Same as 4, white interior, headlights, side ornaments, silver plastic air intakes on roof with extended divider.
6. Same as 4, five spoke accent wheels front and rear.

7. Same as 5, large five spoke accent wheels front and rear.
8. Metallic red top half of body, light tan bottom half of body, white plastic interior, headlights and side ornaments, black plastic insert front to back center of baseplate, extended divider on silver plated plastic air intakes on roof, five spoke accent front wheels, large five spoke reverse accent rear wheels.
9. Same as 8, five spoke accent wheels front and rear.
10. Light avocado green top half, dull black bottom half of body, white plastic interior, headlights and side ornaments, black plastic insert front to back, center of baseplate, extended divider on silver plated plastic air intakes on roof, purple plastic windows, five spoke accent front wheels, large five spoke reverse accent rear wheels. (K-2005).
11. Same as 8, silver plated interior, headlights and side ornaments.
12. Same as 10, silver plated interior, headlights and side ornaments.
13. Same as 10, amber windows. (K-2005).
14. Same as 11, five spoke accent wheels front and rear.
15. Same as 8, large five spoke reverse accent wheels front and rear.
16. Same as 12, five spoke accent wheels front and rear.
17. Metallic blue top half of body, black painted bottom and baseplate, black plastic insert center of baseplate, (same as 59-C) silver plated plastic interior, ornaments and headlights, purple plastic windows, five spoke accent front wheels, five spoke reverse accent rear wheels, (found in 3-pack sold in U.K.)

68-E Chevy Van   3"   1979
Orange body, unpainted metal baseplate and grille, reverse accent front wheels, large multi-spoke rear wheels.

1. Light blue tinted (almost clear) windows and skylights, red and blue tempa print stripes each side, blue stripe design starts forward of front wheel well.
2. Blue plastic windows and roof lights, red and blue tempa print stripes each side, blue stripe design starts rear of front wheel well.
3. Blue plastic windows and skylights, white and blue tempa print stripes each side, blue stripe starts rear of front wheel well.
4. Blue plastic windows and skylights, black and red tempa print stripes starts rear of front wheel well.
5. Same as 2, large multi-spoke wheels front and rear.
6. Same as 3, large multi-spoke wheels front and rear.
7. Same as 2, light blue tinted (almost clear) windows and skylights.
8. Same as 2, small reverse accent front and rear.
9. Red plastic windows and skylights, black and red tempa imprint, stripes each side, red stripe design starts rear of front wheel well.
10. Same as 4, large multi-spoke wheels front and rear.
11. Green plastic windows and skylight, black and red tempa imprint stripes each side, black stripe design starts rear of front wheel well.
12. Same as 9, dark amber/orange plastic windows, black and red tempa imprint stripes each side.
13. Same as 9, no plastic window insert, black and red tempa imprint striped each side.
14. White body, unpainted metal baseplate and grille, blue plastic windows and skylights, blue "USA—1" over two red flowing stripes and vertical blue stripe with three white stars rear of van, side tempa imprint, five spoke reverse accent front wheels, large multi-spoke rear wheels.
15. Orange body, unpainted metal baseplate and grille, blue plastic windows and skylight, red, yellow and black "MATCHBOX COLLECTORS CLUB" on sides, five spoke reverse accent front wheels, large multi-spoke rear wheels. (promotional Lesney U.K. Club).
16. White body, unpainted metal baseplate and grille, blue plastic windows and skylight, blue tempa three lines "ADIDAS" "DIE WELTMARE MIT" "DEN3 STREIFEN" and large name logo on sides, five spoke reverse accent front wheels, large multi-spoke rear wheels. (sold in Germany).
17. Green body, unpainted metal baseplate and grille, blue plastic windows and skylights, black "CHEVY" on brown and black stripes each side, five spoke reverse accent front wheels, large

18. Same as 17, green body, black "CHEVY" on yellow and black stripes each side.
19. Bright orange body, unpainted metal baseplate and grille, blue plastic windows and skylights, red and blue tempa print stripes each side, five spoke reverse accent front wheels, large multi-spoke rear wheels.
20. Silver body with side "Vampire" over black, red & blue stripes.

69-A   Commer 30 CWT Van   2¼"   1959
Silver grille, with & without silver painted headlights & bumpers, sliding left side door, black baseplate, 2 axles, 4 plastic wheels, yellow "NES-TLES'S" decal on upper rear panel.
1. Maroon body, dark gray plastic wheels, crimped axles.
2. Maroon body, dark gray plastic wheels, rounded axles.
3. Maroon body, light gray plastic wheels.
4. Dark red body, light gray plastic wheels.
5. Red body, light gray plastic wheels.

69-B   Hatra Tractor Shovel   3"   1965
Orange or yellow movable shovel arms, with 2 rivets in base or single hole over rear axle, 2 axles, 4 plastic tires, orange, red or yellow wheels, with & without brace behind front bucket.
1. Orange body, orange wheels, gray tires, 2 baseplate rivets, without brace, orange shovel.
2. Same as 1, but red wheels and black tires.
3. Same as 2, yellow wheels.
4. Same as 3, with brace.
5. Same as 3, baseplate with single hole.
6. Yellow body, red wheels, black tires, baseplate with single hole, with brace. Yellow shovel.
7. Same as 6, yellow shovel.
8. Same as 6, yellow shovel.

69-C   Rolls Royce Silver Shadow Coupe   3"   1969
Amber tinted windshield, metal grille, five spoke wheels.
1. Blue body, tan interior, light brown boot, black baseplate, thin wheels, narrow wheel wells.
2. Same as 1, dark yellow baseplate.
3. Same as 1, light yellow baseplate.
4. Same as 1, metallic gold body, tan baseplate.
5. Same as 4, dark yellow baseplate.
6. Same as 5, metallic gold body.
7. Same as 5, wide wheel wells.
8. Same as 7, wide wheel wells.
9. Same as 7, black baseplate, wide wheels.
10. Same as 9, narrow wheel wells.
11. Same as 9, silver baseplate.
12. Same as 11, narrow wheel wells.
13. Same as 10, black boot.
14. Same as 9, dark gold body, black boot.
15. Same as 11, black boot.
16. Same as 14, silver baseplate.
17. Same as 15, charcoal baseplate.
18. Same as 15, charcoal baseplate.
19. Same as 14, metallic gold body, ivory interior.
20. Same as 19, charcoal baseplate.
21. Same as 19, silver baseplate.
22. Same as 20, dark gold body.
23. Same as 20, gray baseplate.
24. Same as 19, lime/gold body.
25. Same as 24, charcoal baseplate.
26. Lime/gold body, tan interior, black boot, charcoal baseplate.
27. Metallic gold body, tan interior, black boot, silver baseplate, wide wheels, wide wheel wells.
28. Metallic gold body, tan interior, black boot, light yellow baseplate, thin wheels, narrow wheel wells.
29. Lime/gold body, ivory interior, black boot, charcoal baseplate, wide wheels, wide wheel wells.

69-D   Turbo Fury   3"   1973

Metallic red, white driver, clear window, cream rear propellers (Rola-matic) five spoke wide wheels, black baseplate.
1. Yellow/orange/black label no. 69.
2. Red arrow on orange no. 86 label on hood, black baseplate.
3. Yellow/orange/black no. 69 label, black baseplate, amber wind-shield.
4. Red & black on white round "Scorpion" label on hood, black baseplate, clear windshield.
5. Red & black on white round "Scorpion" label on hood, black baseplate, clear windshield, four spoke wide wheels. (no Rola-matic action).
6. Red arrow on orange no. 86 label on hood, black baseplate, clear windshield, four spoke wide wheels. (No Rola-matic action).
7. Same as 1, Pat. App. 12174/72 replaced by Pat. No. 1424808.

69-E   Armored Truck   2-13/16"   1978
Red painted body, white plastic roof, silver/gray painted metal base-plate and grille, wide five spoke reverse accent wheels.
1. Dark blue tinted plastic windows and dome light, white tempa imprints on sides, logo and on two lines "WELLS FARGO", A Division of Baker Industries" on cab body, on three lines "Wells Fargo", Armored Services" and "Corporation" on side doors, "732–2031" on front fenders.
2. Same as 1, light blue tinted plastic windows and dome light.
3. Same as 2, light blue tinted windows and dome light, no tempa imprint on sides.
4. Same as 2, light blue tinted windows and dome light, five spoke accent wheels.
5. Same as 1, telephone number on fenders above front wheels now reads "QZ–2031".
6. Dark green body, white plastic roof, silver gray painted baseplate and grille, blue plastic windows and dome lights, light gray tempa "DRESDNER BANK" on sides, wide five spoke reverse accent wheels. (sold in Germany)

69-F   1933 Willy's Street Rod   1982
Preproduction, used for picture purpose.

70-A   Ford Thames Estate Car   2-1/8"   1959
Yellow upper half of body, bluish/green lower half, and with variations, with & without silver painted grille, headlights, & bumpers, black base-plate, 2 rounded axles, 4 plastic wheels, with or without plastic win-dows, clear or light tinted green.
1. Without windows, gray plastic wheels.
2. With clear windows, gray plastic wheels.
3. With green tinted windows, gray plastic wheels.
4. With clear windows, silver plastic wheels.
5. With green tinted windows, silver plastic wheels.
6. With green tinted windows, black plastic wheels.

70-B   Grit Spreader Truck   2-5/8"   1966
Dark red cab & chassis, metal grille & short baseplate with lettering near front or near axle, green tinted windows, rear of body contains plastic pull which, when pulled, allows sand to leave the inside body dropping through an opening in the baseplate, 2 axles, 4 black plastic wheels. Model changed to Superfast wheels.
1. Light yellow body, black plastic pull.
2. Light yellow body, gray plastic pull.
3. Bright yellow body, gray plastic pull.

70-C   Grit Spreader Truck   2-5/8"   1970
Red cab & chassis, yellow body, green windows, metal baseplate, gray plastic rear pull.
1. Four spoke thin wheels, short brace on baseplate.
2. Five spoke thin wheels, short brace on baseplate.
3. Five spoke thin wheels, long braces on baseplate.
4. Five spoke thin wheels, long braces on baseplate.

70-D   Dodge Dragster   3"   1971
Pink body, clear windows, silver interior, five spoke wide front wheels, four spoke wide rear wheels, red plastic lifter.
1. Dark yellow baseplate.
2. Light yellow baseplate.

---

3. Tan baseplate.
4. Metallic green baseplate.
5. Dark purple baseplate.
6. Unpainted metal baseplate.
7. Black baseplate.
8. Black painted baseplate, five spoke wide front wheels (same as 5-A), large four spoke wide rear wheels.
9. Black painted baseplate, "Rat Rod" labels on sides, five spoke wide front wheels (same as 5-A), four spoke wide rear wheels.
10. Black painted baseplate, yellow and tan 'Wild Cat' labels on sides, five spoke wide front wheels, (same as 5-A), four spoke wide rear wheels.
11. Black painted baseplate, "Snake" labels on sides, five spoke wide wheels front and rear (same as 5-A).
12. Black painted baseplate, new "Snake" labels (white around mouth-brighter colors), five spoke wide front wheels (same as 5-A), large four spoke wide rear wheels.
13. Black painted baseplate, white star in blue circle and flame label on hood (same as 40-A), five spoke wide front wheels, large four spoke wide rear wheels.
14. Yellow body, black painted baseplate, chrome plastic interior, motor and grille, red plastic body lifter, red tinted windows, the following tempa imprint are located on each side of the body from front to rear, 2 black stripes, black "HOT SMOKER" above red and black "GOOD YEAR" logo and black "STP" logo, large black "19" in red outline square, red and black "CHAMPION" logo, black "VALVOLINE" logo, black "DODGE" and black "CHRYSLER" logo in solid red rectangle, small five spoke front wheels, large four spoke wide rear wheels, baseplate now reads: "No. V Hot Smoker."
15. Same as 12, 'Snake' labels, charcoal painted baseplate.
16. Same as 12, black painted baseplate, "CASTROL", red and green round logo on square white label on hood, five spoke wide front wheels, large four spoke wide rear wheels.

70-E   Self-Propelled Gun   2-5/8"   1976
Military olive green body and baseplate, 'Rolamatic' action, small black plastic front rollers, large black plastic rear rollers.
1. Black plastic gun barrel, tan rubber traction treads.
2. Black plastic gun barrel, black rubber treads.
3. Military olive drab body and baseplate, black plastic gun barrel, tan traction rubber treads.

70-F   Ferrari 308 GTB   2-15/16"   1981
Red body, red painted metal base, one piece black plastic interior, front grille, rear bumper, rear deck air louvers, and side stripe between base and top of body, wide five spoke accent wheels.
1. Smokey gray tinted windows.

71-A   Austin 200 Gallon Water Truck   2-3/8"   1959
Olive green body, with & without silver painted bumper & headlights, 2 axles, 4 black plastic wheels, spare wheel mounted behind cab, small hole in top of baseplate, with square or curved rear corners in base.
1. Square corners in base, black knobby treads.
2. Curved corners in base, black knobby treads.
3. Curved corners in base, black fine treads.

71-B   Jeep Gladiator Pick-Up Truck   2-5/8"   1964
Red body, clear windows, green or white interior, silver painted grille, with & without silver painted headlights & bumper, metal or plastic door springs, black baseplate with & without patent number, with & without brace inside hood over front axles, 2 axles, 4 black plastic wheels, fine treads.
1. Green interior, plastic door springs, large wheels, without patent number, without brace.
2. Same as 1, white interior.
3. Same as 2, small wheels.
4. Same as 2, with patent number.
5. Same as 5, metal door springs.
6. Same as 5, metal door springs.
7. Same as 6, with brace.

71-C Ford Heavy Wreck Truck　　　3″　　　**1968**
Red cab, white bumper, chassis, body & baseplate, amber or green windows, 3 axles, 6 black plastic wheels, red plastic single cable hook, white label with red letters (large or small) "ESSO" inside blue circle. Model changed to Superfast wheels.
1. Amber windows & dome light, plain flat front base, no lettering, smooth bed.
2. Amber windows & dome light, lettered front base, textured bed.
3. Amber windows & dome light, lettered front base, yellow plastic hook, textured bed.
4. Green windows & dome light, lettered front base, red plastic hook, textured bed.
5. Green windows & dome light, with brace in corners of rear body.

71-D Ford Heavy Wreck Truck　　　3″　　　**1970**
Red cab, white body, baseplate & grille, green windows & dome light, four spoke wide wheels.
1. Light blue outlined label "Esso" on sides, red plastic hook.
2. Dark blue outlined label "Esso" on sides.
3. Military olive green body, green tinted windows and dome light, black plastic hook, red and white triangle and white "3LGS64" on olive green side labels, four spoke wide wheels, no hub caps, riveted axle covers, no number 71 on baseplate. (TP-16).
4. Same as 3, four spoke wide wheels, with chrome hub caps: (found in 3-pack sold in U.K.).
5. Dark blue body, green plastic windows and dome light, black plastic hook, four spoke wide wheels, riveted black plastic axle covers, no number 74 on baseplate, (MPI-UK).

71-E Jumbo Jet Motorcycle　　　2¾″　　　**1973**
Dark metallic blue body, red elephant head on handle bars, silver motor & exhaust pipes, wide wheels.
1. Dark blue plastic handle bars.
2. Light blue plastic handle bars.

71-F Cattle Truck　　　3″　　　**1976**
Metallic bronze body and chassis, yellow/orange cattle carrier, unpainted metal baseplate and grille, large wide reverse accent wheels.
1. Dark green windows, two black plastic cows in carrier.
2. Dark green windows, two black plastic cows in carrier silver/gray painted metal baseplate.
3. Blue windows, two black plastic cows in carrier, unpainted metal baseplate.
4. Blue windows, two black plastic cows in carrier, silver/gray painted baseplate.
5. Blue windows, two black plastic cows in carrier, silver/gray painted metal baseplate, modified portion at rear of body no longer covers rear end of baseplate.
6. Same as 5, red body and chassis, cream cattle carrier, black plastic tow hook rear of carrier, hornless black plastic cows. (TP-19)
7. Same as 6, black painted metal baseplate. (TP-19).
8. Same as 4, small multi-spoke front wheels, large reverse accent rear wheels. (TP-19).
9. Same as 4, yellow plastic cattle carrier, hornless black plastic cows.
10. Same as 6, yellow cattle carrier, hornless black plastic cows.
11. Same as 6, large reverse accent front wheels, small multi-spoke rear wheels.
12. Same as 5, yellow/orange plastic carrier, hornless black plastic cows, light blueish/green windows.
13. Same as 6, red body and chassis, bone white plastic cattle carrier, black plastic tow hook rear of carrier, hornless black plastic cows. (TP-19).
14. Same as 5, yellow/orange plastic carrier, hornless black plastic cows, purple tinted plastic windows.
15. Same as 5, yellow/orange plastic carrier, light blueish green plastic cattle, purple tinted plastic windows.
16. Same as 5, light yellow/orange plastic carrier, hornless black plastic cattle, light blueish/green plastic windows.
17. Same as 5, orange/yellow plastic carrier, hornless brown plastic cattle, dark amber/orange plastic windows.

18. Metallic bronze body and chassis, yellow cattle carrier, silver gray painted baseplate and grille, blue plastic windows, black plastic tow hook rear of carrier, hornless black plastic cattle, large wide five spoke reverse accent wheels.
19. Metallic green body and chassis, cream plastic cattle carrier, silver gray painted metal baseplate and grille, amber plastic windows, hornless brown plastic cattle, large wide five spoke reverse accent wheels.
20. Same as 19, yellow/orange plastic cattle carrier.
21. Red body and chassis, yellow/orange plastic cattle carrier, silver gray painted metal baseplate and grille, amber plastic windows, black plastic hook rear of carrier, hornless brown plastic cattle, large five spoke reverse accent wheels. (TP-10).
22. Same as 19, yellow plastic cattle carrier.
23. Metallic lime green body and chassis, cream plastic cattle carrier, silver gray painted metal baseplate and grille, amber plastic windows, hornless brown cattle, large wide five spoke reverse accent wheels.
24. Same as 23, yellow/orange cattle carrier.
25. Metallic green body and chassis, yellow/orange plastic cattle carrier, silver gray painted metal baseplate and grille, red plastic windows, hornless brown or black cattle, large wide five spoke reverse accent wheels.
26. Same as 15, purple plastic windows, brown or black hornless cattle.
27. Same as 23, yellow/orange plastic cattle carrier, red plastic windows.
28. Red body and chassis, yellow/orange plastic cattle carrier, silver gray painted metal baseplate and grille, red plastic windows, no hook rear of carrier, hornless black plastic cattle, large five spoke reverse accent wheels.
29. Same as 27, purple plastic windows.

71-G 1962 Corvette　　　　　　**1982**
Preproduction, see for pictures.

72-A Fordson Tractor　　　2″　　　**1959**
Blue body with tow hook, silver painted grille with blue middle bar, 2 axles, spread rivet at rear of base with thin raised casting.
1. Large front knobby gray plastic wheels, orange rear wheel with large gray tires without treads.
2. Large front knobby black wheels, orange rear wheels with large black tires without treads.
3. Large front fine tread black wheels, orange rear wheels with large black tires without treads.
4. Large front fine tread black wheels, orange rear wheels with knobby tread black tires.
5. Yellow wheels front & back, black fine tread front tire, knobby black rear tires.
6. Orange wheels front & back, black fine tread front tire, knobby tread black rear tires.
7. Orange wheels front & back, black fine tread front tire, knobby tread black rear tires, large flat raised brace around spread rivet.
8. Orange wheels front and back, gray treads.
9. Yellow wheels front and back, gray treads.

72-B Jeep CJ5　　　2-3/8″　　　**1966**
Yellow body, red plastic interior & tow hook, black baseplate, front bumper & small step on each side under door opening, 2 axles, 4 yellow wheels with black plastic tires, black spare tire mounted at rear. Model changed to Superfast wheels.
1. Without brace inside hood.
2. With brace inside hood.

72-C Jeep CJ5　　　2-3/8″　　　**1970**
Red interior & tow hook, black baseplate & grille, red or black axle covers, 8 spoke wheels.
1. Yellow body, balloon tires.
2. Yellow/orange body, balloon tires.
3. Yellow/orange body, balloon tires, two braces behind rear axle.
4. Yellow/orange body, wide wheels, two braces behind rear axle.

5. Bright yellow body, wide wheels, two braces behind rear axle.

72-D Hovercraft　　　　　　**1972**
White body, black bottom & baseplate, red top propellers, black labeled SR N6.
1. Blue windows.
2. Blue windows, dark red propellers.
3. Blue windows, no. 72 & 2 on black baseplate.
4. Blue windows, no. 72 & 2 on black baseplate, dark red propeller.
5. Blue windows, black plastic baseplate reads: "No. 72 Hovercraft" without "SRN6" or "2".
6. No windows, No. 72 & 2 on black plastic baseplate, red propeller. May be found without side labels. (MP-2).

72-E Bomag Road Roller　　　2-15/16″　　　**1979**
Mustard yellow body and metal baseplate, large black plastic front roller, large accent wheels with yellow painted hub design.
1. Red plastic interior and motor.
2. Red plastic interior and motor, large accent wheels with chrome hub caps.

72-F Maxi Taxi　　　　　3″　　　**1973**
Yellow body, flat black painted metal baseplate, bumpers and grille, chrome plated plastic engine protruding from hood with "Rolamatic" action, black tempa "MAXI TAXI" diagonally on roof, two rows of black and white checkers on sides, black tempa bordered rectangle with fare rates on doors, five spoke wheels, "Made In Hong Kong" on baseplate. (formerly SF 67-2).
1. Clear plastic windows, tan plastic interior and tow hook.
2. Same as 1, black tempa "MAXI TAXI" on roof is lined up with front left corner of roof to rear right corner instead of rear left corner to front right corner.
3. Same as 1, clear plastic windows, dark tan plastic interior.

72-G Dodge Delivery Truck　　　　　　**1982**
Preproduction used for picture purposes, released in all countries but the U.S.A.

73-A 10 Ton Pressure Refueller　　　2-5/8″　　　**1959**
Bluish gray body, 3 axles, 6 gray plastic wheels, light & dark, with & without silver bumper, decal on cab roof with blue outside circle, white inside with red circle. The first issued models contained broken off rear base sections called "open end" which were then strengthened.
1. Flat brace between compartment & tank, "open end" base on some.
2. Round brace between compartment & tank, "open end" base on some.
3. Full cast brace between compartment & tank.

73-B Ferrari F1 Racing Car　　　2-5/8″　　　**1962**
Red body (light & dark), plastic driver, black baseplate & grille, metal exhaust pipes, wire wheels & axles, black plastic tires, No. 73 decal on sides in white with yellow crest.
1. Gray plastic driver.
2. White plastic driver.

73-C Mercury Station Wagon　　　3-1/8″　　　**1968**
Metallic lime green of varying shades on body, ivory interior with dogs in rear, metal grille & baseplate with tow slot, no. 55 or 73 cast on baseplate, 2 axles, 4 silver plastic wheels with black plastic tires. Model changed to Superfast wheels.
1. 1968 "MERCURY" on baseplate.
2. "MERCURY" on raised casting on baseplate.

73-D Mercury Station Wagon　　　3″　　　**1970**
Ivory interior with two dogs, clear windows, metal baseplate & grille, five spoke wheels, "Mercury" on a platform on baseplate comes in different positions.
1. Metallic lime green, thin wheels.
2. Metallic lime green, thin wheels, wide wheel wells, no gas tank cover.
3. Metallic lime green, wide wheels, wide wheel wells, no gas tank cover.

73-E Mercury Station Wagon　　　3″　　　**1972**
Red body, ribbed rear roof, ivory interior with two dogs, clear windows,

five spoke wide wheels, "Mercury" on a platform on baseplate comes in different positions.
1. With gas tank cover, label on hood.
2. Without gas tank cover, with label on hood.
3. Spotted brown cat face label on hood.
4. Spotted brown cat face label on hood, silver/gray painted baseplate.

73-F Weasel   2-7/8"   1974
Metallic green body, metallic green painted metal baseplate with green plastic center insert, large five spoke slicks, "Rolamatic".
1. Black plastic turret and gun.
2. Military olive green body, metallic green painted baseplate with green plastic center insert, black plastic turret and gun, large five spoke slicks, no hub caps.(TP-13).
3. Same as 1, Pat. App. 12174/72 replaced by Pat. No. 1424808.
4. Same as 2, Pat. App. 12174/72 replaced by Pat. No. 1424808.
5. Military olive green body, military olive green painted baseplate with green plastic center insert, black plastic turret, large five spoke slicks with chrome hub caps, Pat. no. 1424808.
6. Same as 2, military olive drab body. (MM-2)
7. Same as 6, large five spoke wheels, no hub caps.
8. Same as 7, black plastic insert on baseplate.

73-G Model "A" Ford   3"   1979
Off white body, dark green spare wheel cover, running boards and fenders, black plastic baseplate, five spoke wide wheels.
1. Green plastic windows, chrome plastic grille, head lamps and front bumper.
2. Green plastic windows, chrome plated plastic grille, head lamps and front bumper, dark green solid spare wheel/cover on left front fender.
3. No plastic windows, chrome plated plastic grille, head lamps and front bumper, no spare wheel/cover on left front fender.
4. Same as 1, five spoke reverse accent wheels front and rear.
5. Same as 1, light green plastic windows.
6. Light metallic green body, dark green fenders and running boards, black plastic baseplate, chrome plated plastic grille, headlamps, and front bumpers, no windows, five spoke reverse accent front wheels, large multi-spoke rear wheels.
7. Same as 6, dark green plastic windows.
8. Same as 6, light green plastic windows.
9. Tan body with black roof panel, black running boards & fenders, front small five spoke reverse accent wheels and back large five spoke wheels.

74-A Mobile Refreshment Canteen   2-5/8"   1959
Cream, white, or silver body, with upper side door that opens to expose interior utensils, 1 axle, 2 plastic wheels, spread rivet or one round rivet at front of baseplate, with tow bar with 2 open windows above, thin or thick hinges on open bar door with 2 braces or 1 inside brace, 2 tow bar castings, "REFRESHMENT" decals on front side, doors are interchangeable.
1. White body, blue spread rivet base & interior, thin double brace door hinges, dark gray plastic wheels.
2. Pinkish cream body, blue spread rivet base & interior, thin double brace door hinges, dark gray plastic wheels.
3. Silver body, aqua spread rivet base & interior, thin double brace door hinges, silver plastic wheels.
4. Silver body, blue spread rivet base & interior, thin double brace door hinges, silver plastic wheels.
5. Silver body, blue spread rivet base & interior, thin double brace door hinges, knobby gray plastic wheels.
6. Silver body, blue spread rivet base & interior, thick single brace door hinges, smooth gray plastic wheels.
7. Silver body, blue round rivet base & interior, thick single brace door hinges, smooth gray plastic wheels, reinforced tow bar.
8. Silver body, pale blue round rivet base & interior, thick single brace door hinges, smooth gray plastic wheels, reinforced tow bar.
9. Silver body, dark blue round rivet base & interior, thick single

brace door hinges, smooth gray plastic wheels, reinforced tow bar.

74-B Daimler Bus   3"   1966
Double deck white plastic interior, 2 axles, 4 black plastic wheels, decal or label on upper sides, "Esso" in red letters inside blue circle of various shades, "ESSO EXTRA PETROL" in white letters on red background. Model changed to Superfast wheels.
1. Cream body, decals.
2. Cream body, labels.
3. Green body, labels.
4. Red body, labels.

74-C Daimler Bus   3"   1970
White plastic interior, "Esso" labels on sides in various shades, five spoke thin wheels.
1. Green body.
2. Red body.
3. Red body, florescent red baseplate.
4. Florescent body, red baseplate.
5. Florescent baseplate & body.
6. Same as 2, "Inn on the Park" label.

74-D Toe Joe   2¾"   1972
Metallic lime green body, yellow interior, amber dome lights, green hoist, red hooks, metal baseplate & grille, five spoke wide wheels.
1. Amber windows, yellow interior, no raised line around windshield, square opening top of crane.
2. Amber windows, yellow interior, raised line around windshield, square opening top of crane.
3. Amber windows, yellow interior, raised line around windshield, notched opening top of crane.
4. Amber windows, light yellow interior, raised line around windshield, notched opening top of crane.
5. Amber windows, yellow interior, raised line around windshield, notched opening top of crane, silver/gray painted baseplate.
6. Light amber windows, raised line around windshield notched opening top of crane, unpainted metal baseplate.
7. Amber windows, yellow interior, light green hoist, unpainted baseplate, small clover leaf wheels.
8. Amber windows, yellow interior, green hoist, unpainted metal baseplate, no patent number on baseplate, wide five spoke accent wheels.
9. Yellow body, yellow interior, amber windows & dome light, red hoist, black hooks, unpainted metal baseplate, wide five spoke accent wheels, (TP-6) also found in blister packs).
10. Yellow body, yellow interior, amber windows and dome light, green hoist, black hooks, unpainted metal baseplate, wide spoke accent wheels. (TP-6)
11. Metallic lime green, yellow plastic interior, amber windows and dome lights, green plastic hoist, red tow hooks, flat black painted metal baseplate, wide five spoke accent wheels.
12. Same as 9, flat black painted metal baseplate.
13. Same as 11, dark metallic green body, flat black painted metal baseplate.
14. Same as 13, dark metallic green body, flat black painted metal baseplate, zig-zag designs on green plastic hoists.
15. Same as 12, flat black painted metal baseplate, zig-zag designs on red plastic hoists.
16. Same as 12, red painted body, flat black painted metal baseplate, zig-zag design on red plastic hoists. (TP-6)
17. Same as 15, five spoke wide wheels front and rear.
18. Same as 15, small wide multi-spoke wheels.
19. Yellow/orange body, light yellow plastic interior, amber plastic windows and dome lights, red plastic hoists zig-zag designs, black plastic tow hooks, unpainted metal baseplate, wide five spoke accent wheels. (TP-6).
20. Same as 12, red painted body, flat black painted baseplate, green plastic hoists, zig-zag designs, black plastic tow hooks. (TP-6).
21. Same as 9, unpainted metal baseplate, red plastic hoists zig-zag designs, black plastic tow hooks. (TP-6).

22. Metallic lime green body, yellow plastic interior, amber plastic windows and dome lights, red plastic hoists with zig-zag designs, black plastic tow hooks, wide five spoke accent wheels.
23. Same as 22, light amber plastic windows, white plastic hoists, black plastic hooks. (MP1).

74-E Cougar Villager   3-1/16"   1978
Metallic light or dark lime green painted body, unpainted metal baseplate, grille and bumpers, yellow plastic interior, multi-spoke wide wheels.
1. Clear plastic windows, green plastic tail gate.
2. Same as 1, orange/yellow plastic interior.
3. Metallic green body, unpainted metal baseplate, grille and bumpers, deep orange/yellow plastic interior, green plastic tail gate, clear plastic windows, multi-spoke wide wheels.
4. Metallic blue body, unpainted metal baseplate, grille and bumpers, orange/yellow plastic interior, blue plastic tail gate, clear plastic windows, multi-spoke wide wheels.
5. Same as 4, deep orange/yellow plastic interior.
6. Same as 3, light yellow plastic interior.

74-F Orange Peel   3"   1971
White body, flat black painted metal baseplate, wide orange tempa stripe with thin black border and black "ORANGE PEEL" each side, orange tempa racing stripes on hood and trunk lid, orange tempa circle with white "70" on roof, five spoke accent wheels, "Made in Hong Kong" on baseplate.
1. Clear plastic windows, chrome plated interior motor and grille, red plastic body support bar, hole on baseplate over rear axle.
2. Same as 1, no hole on baseplate.

75-A Ford Thunderbird   2-5/8"   1960
Cream top half, pink bottom half, green tinted windows, silver painted grille, headlights, red painted tail lights, 2 axles, 4 plastic wheels, tow hook.
1. Gray plastic wheels, black baseplate.
2. Silver knobby tread wheels, black baseplate.
3. Silver knobby tread wheels, dark blue baseplate.
4. Silver finer tread wheels, dark blue baseplate.
5. Silver finer tread wheels, bluish/green baseplate.
6. Black plastic wheels, black baseplate.

75-B Ferrari Berinetta   3"   1965
Metallic green body of various shades, clear windows, ivory interior & tow hook, metal baseplate with tow slot, 2 axles, 4 wire or silver plastic wheels with black tires, silver painted grille, with & without silver painted headlights. Model changed to Superfast wheels.
1. Wire wheels, black plastic tires, gray painted base.
2. Wire wheels, black plastic tires, metal base.
3. Silver plastic wheels, black tires.
4. Red body, silver wheels, black tires.

75-C Ferrari Berinetta   2¾"   1970
Ivory interior, clear windows, metal baseplate, five spoke thin wheels, all models come with or without stick shift between front seats.
1. Dark green body.
2. Light green body.
3. Dark red body, silver grille.
4. Dark red body, red grille.

75-D Alfa Carabo   3"   1971
Pink body, ivory interior, clear windows, black trunk, five spoke wide wheels.
1. Dark yellow baseplate.
2. Unpainted metal baseplate.
3. Bright canary yellow baseplate.
4. Yellow painted baseplate, small five spoke wide wheels (same as SF 40-1).
5. Hot pink body, (no streaker design), yellow painted baseplate, five spoke wide wheels.

75-E Alfa Carabo   3"   1975

Streaker hot pink body, black rear motor lid, yellow and green designs front to rear, ivory interior, five spoke wide wheels.

1. Yellow painted baseplate, clear windows.
2. Yellow painted baseplate, clear windows, small five spoke wide wheels. (same as 5-A).
3. Red body, streaker designs, yellow painted baseplate, clear windows, five spoke wide wheels.
4. Same as 3, five spoke accent wheels, (sold in Japan in special black box numbered J-7). This model may also be found in the US in ''MATCHBOX'' Roar and Stunt Sets.

75-F   Seasprite Helicopter   1977

White body, red plastic baseplate, black rotor blades, small black non-superfast plastic wheels. Thin parts of blade near rotor hub have been strenghtened making this part slightly thicker. The strenghtened blade may be found with both blue and green windows.

1. Dark blue windows, blue ''RESCUE'' with red and blue bull's eye on white side labels.
2. Green plastic windows, blue ''Rescue'' with red and blue bull's eye on white side labels.
3. Purple tinted plastic windows, blue ''RESCUE'' with red & blue

bull's eye on white side labels.
4. Red plastic windows, blue ''RESCUE'' with red and blue bull's eye on white side labels.

75-G   Helicopter   1982

White body with black rotors & skis, no wheels, blue ''MBTV NEWS'' on side.

1. Light orange baseplate.
2. Dark orange baseplate.

The Limited Edition Series which was released in 1978 is comprised of reissues of older Superfast models with new colors, decor, name and numbered baseplates.

I	Silver Streak	1978	V	Hot Smoker	1978	VIII	Black Widow	1978
II	Sleet-n-snow	1978	VI	Lady Bug	1978	IX	Flaming Manta	1978
III	White Lightening	1978	VII	Brown Sugar	1978	X	Golden ''X''	1978
IV	Flying Beetle	1978						

Another set of Limited Edition toys was released without numbers. The first six were discontinued 1-75 series toys. The last four were previous Japanese issue toys which later were released in the 1-75 series.

Unnumbered Limited Editon Name	Previously No.	Became No.
Bush Wacker	18	
Cobra Mustang	44	
Viper Van	46	
Pizza Van	23	
Can Cracker	9	
Hot Popper	10	
Boulevard Blaster	Japanese 5	31
Sun Burner	J-21	25
Phantom Z	Japanese 2	24
Hot Points Challenger	J-22	63

Japanese issue Superfast toys were released in 1979 in conjunction with a special Japanese catalog. In general, these were discontinued toys from the 1-75 series packaged in special boxes. The first nine were found primarily in black boxes, and the rest in white or colored boxes with Japanese writing. The toys were identified in the catalog by J and numbers 1 to 12, 14, 21 and 22. The latter two were the only ones made with J-numbers cast into the baseplates. A 2 and a 5 were also issued without the "J" preceeding their numbers for the Japanese market only.

Japanese Issue Superfast

J-1   33 Lamborghini Muira
Packed in black box or colored box with 38 printed as issued in 1979.
J-2   5 Lotus Europa
Packed in black box with gold JPS (John Player Special) printing, ivory interior, in black box or rarely in colored box.
J-3   14 Iso Grifo
Pale blue body, white interior, in black box or rarely in colored box.
J-4   24 Rolls Royce Silver Shadow
Gold body, ivory interior, in black box.
J-5   41 Ford G.T.
White body, red interior in black box.
J-6   15 Volkswagen 1500
Off-white body, ivory interior, in black box or rarely in colored box.
J-7   75 Alfa Carabo Streaker
Red body, in black box.
J-8   52 Dodge Charger MK3
Magenta body, black interior, in black box or rarely in white box.

J-9   27 Mercedes 230 SL
Yellow body, black base, in black box or in colored box with 31 printed as issued in 1979.
J-10   7 V.W. Golf
Yellow body, in white box.
J-11   45 BMW Polizei
White body with 'Polizei' labels, in white box. (Also released in German market).
J-12   32 Maserati Bora
Burgundy body with 8 label in white box.
J-13   Never issued.
J-14   27 Lamborghini
Red streaker body, in white box.
J-15   Never issued.
J-16   Never issued.
J-17   Never issued.
J-18   Never issued.

J-19   66 Mazda RX500
Rare in white box.
J-20   Never issued.
J-21   Toyota Celica
Red or cream body, baseplate cast J-21, in white box with J-21 or 47 numbers.
J-22   Galant Eterna
Red or yellow body, baseplate cast J-22, in white box with J-22 or 70 numbers.
No. 2   Datsun 280Z
Baseplate cast with 2, packed in colored box, issued 1981. This toy was later issued for the American market with different numbers.
No. 5   Mazda RX7
Baseplate cast with 5, packed in colored box, issued 1981. This toy was later issued for the American market with different numbers.

Australian Issue Superfast

76-A   Mazda RX 7   1981
       (Australian issue)
Shown with box.
77-A   Toyota Celica   1981

       (Australian issue)
Shown with box.
78-A   Datsun 280Z   1981
       (Australian issue)

Shown with box.
79-A   Galant Eterna   1981
       (Australian issue)
Shown with box.

Models of Yesteryear

A new series of toys was introduced in 1956 by the release of four replicas of Antique cars in a slightly larger scale than the Matchbox 1-75 series. These new toys were designated "Models of Yesteryear", and the name was registered by Lesney as a trademark. The series has grown through the years with the introduction of new toys so that currently there are 23 different models of Yesteryear in the series. As with the 1-75 series, Lesney personnel have discontinued toys of each number periodically and replaced them with new issues.

Each toy is enclosed in a specially designed box showing the toy and number in this series. The sizes and designs on the boxes have been modified through the years. The first all-Yesteryear catalog was put out in 1958. In it were illustrations of the nine Yesteryear toys available that year.

When Mattel's "Hot Wheels" toys were brought out in 1969, the

Models of Yesteryear

Lesney people realized the vulnerability of the toy market as their sales decreased dramatically. They responded not only by redesigning their wheels in the 1-75 series to create "Superfast" toys, but they also looked for ways to diversify, widen their product line, to better weather future challenges to their toy business. Therefore, in 1970 Lesney acquired a company called AMT which made plastic model kits, and marketed other products related to the toy business. During the period of these diversifications, Lesney's efforts were drawn away from the Yesteryear line which was their least popular at the time, and eventually the series was discontinued for two years.

From 1970 through 1972 the models of Yesteryear were available as long as the pre-1970 supply lasted and in gift sets G-5 and G-7 of four toys boxed together. Then, gradually, additions were once again made to this series. The Lesney catalog for 1972 listed the new Y-16-A 1928 Mercedes SS for the first time, and the catalog for 1973 introduced the Y-11-C 1938 Lagonda Drophead Coupe and the Y-17-A Hispano Suiza as new toys. That year older models appeared in different colors, wheel styles and packaging and with minor variations which can be thought collectively as using up some old parts. Plastic components such as interiors also appeared more frequently from 1974.

Silver and gold plated Yesteryear bodies have been made from selected Yesteryear toys since 1964. The process is technically called vacuum plating with a gold or silver finish, but these have come to be known as "plated."

These toys were originally made to be mounted on pen stands, ash trays, or other presentation items. Therefore, the baseplates of these toys were made to incorporate two holes for the attachments.

Models of Yesteryear

Y-1-A   **1925 Allchin Traction Engine**   2-2/3"   **1956**
Green body of varying shades with dark red wheels and unpainted rear treads, copper colored boiler door, crimped axles, cab floor unpainted with nine slats, gold trim.
1. Straight rear wheel treads.
2. Diagonal rear wheel treads.
3. Rear wheel treads painted dark red.
4. Front wheels & rear spokes & treads painted bright red.
5. Same as 4, but rear wheel treads unpainted.
6. Front wheels & rear spokes painted dark red, rear wheel treads unpainted, gold painted boiler door.
7. Same as 6, but rear wheel treads painted dark red.
8. Same as 7, but boiler door painted gold.
9. Same as 5, but boiler door painted gold.
10. Same as 6, but rivetted axles and no gold trim on bottom chimney flange, back end of crosshead, or top of gear cover on right side of cab.
11. Same as 10, but rear wheel treads painted dark red.
12. Same as 10, but front wheels, rear wheel spokes and treads painted bright red.
13. Same as 10, but front wheels and rear wheel spokes painted bright red.
14. Same as 13, but eleven floor slats in cab.
15. Same as 14, but boiler door painted silver.

Y-1-B   **1911 Model "T" Ford**   3"   **1964**
Red body, base, and fenders, black seats, grille and smooth roof, red metal steering wheel, gold metal wheels, red roof support and one control lever, minor variations exist on headlamps, grille, front & rear license plate, and back axle housing strut.
1. Two holes in the baseplate & two control levers.
2. Two holes in the baseplate and the backhoe is closer to the front.
3. No hole in the baseplate.
4. Same as 3, but black plastic steering wheel.
5. Same as 4, but with small gold metal wheels, (like those found on Y-8-C Stutz models).
6. Same as 4, but with dark red grille.
7. Same as 4, but with textured black roof.
8. Same as 4, but with textured black roof.
9. Cream body with black &/or red seats & grille, black textured roof and steering wheel, silver plastic wheels with 12 spokes & wider tire (and occasionally 24 spokes), silver front roof support.
10. Same as 9, but dark red seats and grille.
11. Same as 9, but textured dark red roof.
12. Same as 10, but textured dark red roof.
13. Same as 12, but with gold front roof support.
14. Same as 12, but white body.
15. Same as 13, but textured light red roof.

Y-1-C   **1936 Jaguar SS100**   3-7/8"   **1977**
White body with black interior, white baseplate, running boards and fenders, silver horn headlights and grille, silver spoke wheels with black tires and spare wheel at back.
1. Small headlights on fenders, and thin brace from back of license plate to front axle.
2. Large headlights on fenders, and thick brace from back of license plate to front axle.
3. Same as 2, with white wall tires.
4. Same as 2, but light metallic blue fenders.
5. Same as 4, with ribbed bottom of running boards.
6. Same as 5, with white wall tires.
7. Same as 6, but 12-spoke silver wheels.

Y-2-A   **1911 "B" Type London Bus**   2-2/3"   **1956**
Red body with silver radiator, black or blue driver (the blue ones ranging in shade from light, medium and dark), sides with decals "General", "Oakey" or "Dewars", unpainted underside of the upper deck, gray metal wheels, crimped axle, and eight small upper side windows.
1. Only four upper side windows, black driver.
2. Same as 1, but blue driver.

3. Black driver.
4. Blue driver.
5. Same as 3, but red radiator.
6. Same as 5, but blue driver.
7. Same as 5, with rivetted axles.
8. Same as 7, with blue driver.
9. Same as 5, with tan painted underside of upper deck.
10. Same as 6, with tan painted underside of upper deck.
11. Same as 8, with tan painted underside of upper deck.
12. Same as 7, with tan painted underside of upper deck.
13. Same as 11, with black metal wheels and an occasional very dark brown driver.
14. Same as 12, with black metal wheels.

Y-2-B   **1911 Renault Two-Seater**   3"   **1963**
Light to dark green body with green metal steering wheel & post (in 3 various shades of green), silver or gold metal wheels, unpainted or gold spare tire brace with 4 prongs (3 variations of the prongs), no back fender brace, and with a top molding on the windshield.
1. Unpainted headlamp, windshield, & dashboard supports, & spare tire carrier, silver metal wheels.
2. Gold headlamp, windshield, & dashboard supports, spare tire carrier & wheels.
3. Same as 1, but also side windshield moldings.
4. Same as 2, but also side windshield moldings.
5. Same as 3, with back fender brace.
6. Same as 4, with back fender brace.
7. Same as 6, with 3-prong spare tire carrier, (2 variations of the prongs).
8. Same as 7, but black plastic steering wheel & post.

Y-2-C   **1914 Prince Henry Vauxhall**   3½"   **1970**
Red or blue body with white seats, red or black grille, gold or copper full tank, gold metal wheels, side lamps with or without strengthening bracket.
1. Dark red body and red grille, gold fuel tank, no side lamp bracket.
2. Same as 1, but lighter red body, (windwheld & side lamp sometimes backward.)
3. Same as 2, with side lamp bracket.
4. Same as 2, but copper fuel tank.
5. Same as 4, with side lamp bracket.
6. Same as 5, with black grille.
7. Blue body with red seats, black grille, copper fuel tank, silver plastic wheels with wider tires, with side lamp bracket.
8. Same as 7, white seats.
9. Same as 8, with a floor brace behind front seat.
10. Same as 8, with gold metal wheels.
11. Same as 10, with gold fuel tank.
12. Same as 11, with a floor brace behind front seat.

Y-3-A   **1907 London "E" Class Tram Car**   3-1/8"   **1956**
Red body with cream roof and gray thick cow catcher, silver or gold head lamps & control panels, gray metal or black plastic wheels, with access to the top deck.
1. Thin gray cowcatcher, silver head lamps and control panels, gray metal wheels, open space under stairs.
2. Same as 1, but thick cowcatcher.
3. Same as 2, with gold head lamps & control panels.
4. Same as 2, but space under stairs closed.
5. Same as 2, but space under stairs closed.
6. Same as 4, but red cowcatcher.
7. Same as 4, but white roof.
8. Same as 4, but black plastic wheels & partially filled in space under stairs.
9. Same as 7, but white roof, black plastic wheels & partially filled in space under stairs.
10. Same as 8, with closed access to top deck.
11. Same as 9, but white roof and closed access to top deck.
12. Same as 11, but white cowcatcher.

Y-3-B   **1910 Benz Limousine**   3½"   **1966**

Cream body with dark green roof, green seats and grille, cream metal steering wheel, two holes in base, high or low headlamps, with or without side lamp bracket, open or closed back fender braces, gold metal wheels.
1. High head lamps, no side lamp bracket, open back fender braces.
2. Same as 1, but low head lamps.
3. Same as 2, but maroon slats and grille.
4. Same as 1, with closed back fender braces.
5. Same as 3, with closed back fender braces.
6. Same as 3, with closed back fender braces.
7. Same as 5, but chartreuse roof.
8. Same as 6, but chartreuse roof.
9. Same as 5, but body and steering wheel pale green.
10. Same as 9, with chartreuse roof.
11. Same as 10, with braced side lamp bracket.
12. Same as 11, but slats and grille maroon.
13. Same as 12, but braced side lamp bracket.
14. Same as 13, with black roof.
15. Same as 14, but black plastic steering wheel.
16. Same as 13, but dark green body and black plastic steering wheel.
17. Same as 16, but black roof.
18. Same as 17, but no holes in base.

Y-3-C   **1934 Riley MPM**   3-7/8"   **1974**
Combinations of differently colored bodies, fenders and baseplates exist among the four colors, with white seats and grilles and silver plastic wheels with 24 spokes. This was the first Yesteryear issued with a plastic radiator, windshield and dashboard assembly.
1. Purple body and fenders.
2. Purple red body and fenders.
3. Dark red body and fenders.
4. Same as 3, with 12-spoke wheels.
5. Orange red body and fenders.

Y-3-D   **1912 Model "T" Ford Petrol Tanker**   **1982**

Y-4-A   **Sentinel Steam Wagon**   2¾"   **1956**
Dark to medium blue body with black baseplate, blue or gold square tank on right side, yellow or orange letters on decals (with light or dark blue backgrounds, and thickness and shade of red border variations in various combinations), gray metal wheels & crimped or rivetted axles. Models were made without a cast center windshield support, especially on models with gray metal wheels and rivetted axles.
1. Blue tank on right side, orange decal letters, crimped axles.
2. Same as 1, but gold tank on right side.
3. Same as 2, with yellow decal letters.
4. Same as 2, with rivetted axles.
5. Same as 3, with rivetted axles.
6. Same as 5, but with wider back wheel diameter.
7. Same as 4, with black plastic wheels.

Y-4-B   **Shand-Mason Horse Drawn Fire Engine**   3½"   **1960**
Red body with gold or silver boiler and/or pump, pulled by horses, and with firemen riding the engine.
1. Gold boiler and pump (usually, but could be one silver), gray horses with white mane & tail, Kent decal with ribs above & below, firemen's helmets gold, horse bar with semi-circular plate and one rivet to vase of engine, back platform perforated & with narrow braces connecting back platform with red plate beneath boiler.
2. Same as 1, but white horses with gray mane and tail.
3. Same as 2, but London decal with blue border.
4. Same as 3, but no ribs near decal and black decal border.
5. Same as 4, but black horses with white mane and tail.
6. Same as 4, but tow rivets on horse bar with rectangular plate joining base of engine.
7. Same as 6, but slots in back platform partially filled in on right side and wide braces on back platform.
8. Same as 7, but black horses with white mane and tail.
9. Same as 8, but silver boiler and pump (one could be gold).

10. Same as 8, with black firemen's helmets.
11. Same as 9, with black firemen's helmets.
12. Same as 8, with gold border on decal.
13. Same as 10, with gold border on decal.
14. Same as 11, with gold border on decal.
15. Same as 13, with redesigned wide tapered braces at right angles to the rear platform.

Y-4-C   1909 Opel Coupe   3-1/8"   1966
White body & baseplate with maroon on red seats and grille. Smooth tan roof without windows attached to the body or seat, rounded or rectangular control levers, gold metal wheels, flat baseplate with two holes and lettered "Models of Yesteryear".
1. Maroon seats and grille, roof fitted to body, and rounded control levers.
2. Same as 1, with rectangular control levers.
3. Same as 1, but red grille.
4. Same as 3, with rectangular control levers.
5. Same as 3, but red seats.
6. Same as 4, but red seats.
7. Same as 6, with raised letters on baseplate "Matchbox ® Model of Yesteryear".
8. Same as 7, but roof fitted to seats.
9. Same as 8, but no holes in baseplate where raised letters read "1909 Opel" above "Coupe".
10. Same as 9, with small gold metal wheels.
11. Same as 9, but textured tan roof with window.
12. Same as 11, but orange body of various shades from dark to light, matt or shiny black baseplate, maroon seats, white grille, textured tan roof with windows, silver plastic wheels with wide tires.

Y-4-D   1930 Duesenberg Model "J" Town Car   4½"   1976
White body with red/orange baseplate, fenders & trunk, text and roof, silver plastic wheels, windshield, grille, horns & bumpers.
1. Yellow roof, seats and floor.
2. Red body, baseplate, fenders & trunk, black roof, seats and floor.
3. Light green body with metallic green baseplate, fenders & trunk and black roof, white walled tires.

Y-5-A   1929 LeMans Bentley   3-1/8"   1958
Green body of slightly varying shades with back end gray or green, black No. 5 decals, red seats, silver or gold radiator with silver or green grille, wheels and steering wheel copper or silver, crimped or riveted axle, black baseplate and fenders.
1. Gray end of body, silver radiator and grille, copper metal wheels and steering wheel with crimped axles.
2. Same as 1, but green grille.
3. Same as 2, but gold radiator.
4. Same as 3, with some variation in No. 5 decals, green back of body, and combinations of silver or copper steering wheel and/or wheels.
5. Same as 4, but rivetted axles.
6. Same as 5, but silver metal wheels.
7. Same as 6, but silver metal steering wheel.
8. Same as 7, with dark red seats.

Y-5-B   1929 4½ Litre "S" Bentley   3½"   1962
Dark green body or shades varying dark to medium, with dark green baseplate of 3 types (flat or raised lettering and with or without holes), silver radiator grille & silver or green radiator which is fixed to the body or separate, green or red slats and back of body, numbered decal, fuel tank free or joining back springs.
1. Metallic green body over flat baseplate without holes, silver green radiator fixed to the body, dark green seats and back, black 5 decal, gas tank free from back springs.
2. Same as 1, but dark green body.
3. Same as 2, but 2 holes in baseplate.
4. Same as 3, but dark red seats and back.
5. Same as 3, but silver radiator separate from the body, with red seats and back.

6. Same as 5, but fuel tank joined to back springs.
7. Same as 6, but red 6 decal.
8. Same as 6, but black 3 decal.
9. Same as 8, but raised lettering on baseplate with no holes.
10. Same as 9, with red 6 decal.
11. Same as 9, with black 5 decal.

Y-5-C   1907 Peugeot   3-2/3"   1969
Yellow body, base & fenders of various shades or gold body with black base and fenders, black or gold roof, orange windows of varying shades, red or black seats & grille, gold metal wheels, body with beading on side panel, spare tire holders wide apart or close and filled in.
1. Yellow body, base & fenders, black roof, dark orange windows, red seats & grille, no beading on side panel, spare tire arms wide apart.
2. Same as 1, with beading on side panel.
3. Same as 2, but pale orange windows.
4. Same as 2, but clear windows.
5. Gold or orange variations body & roof with black base and fenders, pale orange windows, red and/or black seats & grille, black grille and spare tire holders close and filled in.
6. Same as 5, but seats more commonly both black.
7. Same as 6, but silver plastic wheels with larger tire and black roof.
8. Same as 7, but gold or orange roof.

Y-5-D   1927 Talbot Van   3-2/3"   1978
Green body, black baseplate, fenders, steering wheel and seats, silver radiator, grille, and windshield frame, gold tool box top, green plastic 12-spoke wheels and black tires, spare wheel mounted, back doors open.
1. Sides labelled "Lipton Tea" and English Royal Cypher.
2. Same as 1, with silver 12-spoke wheels.
3. Same as 1, but 4 silver 12-spoke wheels and green spare wheel.
4. Same as 1, but silver 24-spoke wheels.
5. Same as 1, but four silver 24-spoke wheels and green spare wheel.
6. Same as 1, but Royal Cypher replaced by "City Road, London, E.C.I." with company crest.
7. Same as 6, with silver 12-spoke wheels.
8. Same as 6 with 4 silver 12-spoke wheels and green spare wheel.
9. Same as 6, with silver 24-spoke wheels.
10. Same as 6, with four silver 24-spoke wheels and green spare wheel.
11. Same as 1, but blue body with yellow lettering "Chocolate Menier" decal on the sides, and silver 24-spoke wheels.
12. Same as 11, but white lettering.
13. Same as 11, but silver 12-spoke wheels.
14. Same as 1, but yellow body and baseplate, red 12-spoke wheels, white walled tires, sides lettered "Taystel old fashioned enriched bread" decal in white, red and black on sides.
15. Same as 14, but maroon plastic wheels.
16. Same as 1, but side labels "2nd Annual I.A.M Inc. Convention Toy Show, Harrisburg, Pa. May 27, 28, 1978".
17. Same as 1, but beige body and roof, with side labels "Chivers & Son. Ltd. Jams, Jellies, Marmalades".

Y-6-A   1916 A.E.C. "Y" Type Lorry   2¾"   1958
Gray body of varying shades with matching or silver hood handles, side decal "Osram Lamps" in light or dark red, (silver radiator) gray metal wheels, crimped or riveted axles.
1. Pale gray body with silver handles, crimped axles.
2. Same as 1, but handles match body color.
3. Same as 2, with pale blue/gray body.
4. Same as 2, but pale blue/gray body.
5. Same as 1, but blue/gray body.
6. Same as 2, with blue/gray body.
7. Dark gray body and handles, riveted axles.
8. Same as 7, with a black outline on lettering of the decal.
9. Same as 7, with orange/red decal border.

Y-6-B   1923 Type 35 Bugatti   3-1/8"   1961
Blue or red body, with a red 6 decal, gold steering wheel & radiator, red or white dashboard and floor, and gold control levers, & wheels.
1. Blue body, red dashboard and floor, gold wheels with wide rims

and gray knobby tires.
2. Same as 1, but black knobby tires.
3. Same as 1, but black fine tires & gold or silver wheels.
4. Same as 3, but gold or silver control levers and/or wheels.
5. Same as 4, but narrow wheel rims.
6. Same as 3, but narrow wheel rims.
7. Same as 6, but silver steering wheel.
8. Same as 6, but blue radiator & no gold trim.
9. Same as 6, but white dashboard and floor, no gold trim.
10. Same as 9, but red body.
11. Same as 10, but decal upside down.
12. Same as 10, but red radiator.

Y-6-C   1913 Cadillac   3-3/8"   1967
Gold or green body, each with various shades, with or without holes in baseplate, long or short sump, gold metal or silver plastic wheels.
1. Gold body with maroon or dark red smooth roof, red grille and seats, gold metal wheels, shallow holder for the spare tire, two holes in the baseplate, short sump.
2. Same as 1, but only 1 hole in the back of the baseplate.
3. Same as 1, but no holes in the baseplate.
4. Same as 1, but no baseplate holes and the first 1 missing from the "1913" date there, also longer sump.
5. Same as 4, but full "1913" date.
6. Same as 4, but 2 baseplate holes.
7. Same as 4, but roof is textured dark red.
8. Same as 7, but silver plastic wheels with wider tires and deeper holder for the wider spare tire.
9. Green body with black textured roof, yellow grille and seats, gold metal wheels with deeper holder for the spare tire, two baseplate holes and longer sump.
10. Same as 9, but silver plastic wheels and the shallower spare tire holder.
11. Same as 10, but red textured roof.
12. Same as 10, but no hole in baseplate.
13. Same as 10, but with deeper spare tire holder.

Y-6-D   1920 Rolls Royce Fire Engine   6-2/3"   1977
Red body and baseplate, black plastic seats and steering wheel, gold radiator, windshield & ladder supports, brown plastic ladder with yellow letters "Borough Green & District".
1. Baseplate has Y7.
2. Same as 1, but ridges on sides to mark labels.
3. Same as 2, with ladder with rounded ends.
4. Same as 3, but baseplate reads "Y6 & Y7".
5. Same as 4, but with red 12-spoke wheels.
6. Same as 4, but with gold 24-spoke wheels.
7. Same as 4, but with silver 24-spoke wheels.

Y-7-A   4-Ton Leyland Van   2¾"   1957
Brown body of 3 different shades with off-white roof, unpainted on the under-side, silver or body-colored radiator with silver grilles, gray metal wheels & rivetted or crimped axles. Decal reading "W & R. Jacob & Co. Ltd./by Royal Appointment to His Majesty the King/Biscuit Manufacturers".
1. Clear white roof, silver radiator, crimped axles.
2. Same as 1, but off-white roof.
3. Same as 2, but second line of decal omitted.
4. Same as 2, but body lighter red/brown, radiator matches body.
5. Same as 4, but rivetted axles.
6. Same as 5, but under-side of roof painted off-white.

Y-7-B   1913 Mercer Raceabout   3¼"   1961
Lilac or yellow body (each with shade variations), black seats, baseplates and fenders as body color, with any combination of 3 steering wheels and 4 types of black tires with knobby or fine treads on gold or silver wheels. The front fender brace can be open with a separate brace forming a triangle, with the triangle filled in and a ridge at the brace, or with a smooth triangle.
1. Lilac body with no baseplate holes, gold wheels with knobby tires, an open front fender brace, no axle brace, and a short spotlight.

2. Same as 1, but a brace attaching the front fender.
3. Same as 2, but silver wheels.
4. Same as 2, but two baseplate holes with a different baseplate lettering position, and an axle housing brace.
5. Same as 4, but a filled in front fender brace with a ridge.
6. Same as 4, but a smooth filled in fender brace.
7. Same as 6, but fine tire treads.
8. Same as 7, but silver wheels.
9. Same as 6, but long spotlight.
10. Same as 7, but yellow body.
11. Same as 10, but long spotlight.

Y-7-C 1912 Rolls Royce 3¾" 1968
Silver or gold body and hood with red or gray roof, red or black seats and/or grille, gold or copper fire extinguisher, gold or silver wheels, two or no baseplate holes, and shallow spare tire holder or deeper one to accommodate the thicker tires with silver plastic wheels.
1. Silver body & hood with red seats, grille, and smooth roof, gold fire extinguisher and wheels, two base holes & shallow spare tire holder.
2. Same as 1, with smooth gray roof.
3. Same as 1, with ribbed gray roof.
4. Same as 1, with ribbed red roof.
5. Same as 4, but silver plastic wheels & deeper spare tire holder.
6. Same as 4, but gold body, black seats & copper fire extinguisher.
7. Same as 4, but gold body & hood.
8. Same as 7, but copper fire extinguisher.
9. Same as 7, but silver plastic wheels & deep spare tire holder.
10. Same as 9, but black seats & grille.
11. Same as 10, but copper fire extinguisher.

Y-8-A 1926 Morris Cowleg "Bullnose" 2½" 1958
Light or dark tan body with dark brown baseplate and fenders, copper or silver colored wheels, crimped or rivetted axles, and large or small pins to hold the Dicky seat.
1. Copper wheels with crimped axles & large seat pins.
2. Same as 1, with silver wheels.
3. Same as 2, but rivetted axles.
4. Same as 3, but small seat pins.

Y-8-B 1914 Sunbeam Motorcycle and Milford Sidecar 2-2/3" 1962
Silver plated motorcycle with black seat and sidecar with green seat, plain or silver wheels.
1. Silver wheels.
2. Plain wheels.

Y-8-C 1914 Stutz 3-3/8" 1969
Metallic blue or red body with green seats & grille, tan or black roof, gold or copper fuel tank, gold or silver wheels with thick or thin windshield supports.
1. Red body, green seats & grille, smooth tan roof, gold fuel tank, gold metal wheels.
2. Same as 1, but copper fuel tank.
3. Same as 2, but textured roof.
4. Light or dark blue body, white seats, textured black roof, copper fuel tank, silver plastic wheels.

Y-8-D 1945 MG TC 3-7/8" 1978
Green or red body with tan roof, red seats, 24-spoke silver wheels, white circle label with number 3 or 6 on side doors.
1. Green body, tan seats, number 3 label.
2. Same as 1, but number 6 label.
3. Same as 1, but label inverted to read 9.
4. Same as 1, but with 12-spoke silver wheels.
5. Same as 1, but with 12-spoke red plastic wheels.
6. Red body, black seats, tan roof, 12-spoke silver wheels, no labels.

Y-9-A 1924 Fowler "Big Lion" Showmans Engine 3¼" 1958
Dark maroon varying to red body with white roof sometimes shaded to cream, copper, gold or silver boiler door with the name plate the same color as the body, maroon or black. The roof supports and braces had several variations in color (gold, white or silver) and in shades. The baseplate is either square or T-ended. The wheels are found in shades of yellow and orange. Other less important variants exist in the wheel designs, roof castings & baseplates.
1. Copper boiler door, body colored name plate, gold cylinder block, gold roof supports with white braces.
2. Same as 1, but gold boiler door, and body colored cylinder door.
3. Same as 2, but black name plate, and gold roof supports & braces colored alike.
4. Same as 2, but white roof supports & braces.
5. Same as 2, but maroon nameplate and white roof supports and braces.
6. Same as 2, but silver boiler door.
7. Same as 6, but also silver roof supports & braces.
8. Same as 2, but silver roof supports and braces.

Y-9-B 1912 Simplex 3¾" 1968
Yellow, green, gold or red body with matching or contrasting fenders and baseplate. Roof tan, black, or red with red or yellow seats in several shades. Maroon or yellow grille, with gold or silver wheels and round or square axle hole.
1. Yellow/green body with matching fenders & baseplate, tan roof, red seats, maroon grille, gold metal wheels, and round axle holes.
2. Same as 1, but green body and square axle holes.
3. Similar to 1, but gold body, brown fenders & baseplate, black roof.
4. Same as 3, but square axle holes.
5. Dull gold body with orange fenders and baseplate, black roof, yellow seats & grille. Silver plastic wheels, & square axle holes.
6. Same as 5, but red seats.
7. Same as 5, but red body, baseplate & fenders.
8. Same as 7, but black baseplate & fenders, yellow roof & seats, red plastic wheels.

Y-10-A 1908 "Grand Prix" Mercedes 2-7/8" 1958
White body with copper, silver, or unplated wheels and knobby black plastic tires. The exhaust pipes, chain drives, steering wheel and spare tire holder can be found in combinations of copper, silver, and unplated finishes. The oil pump, dashboard instruments, gas cap and radiator cap can be found gold, silver, or unpainted. The seat originally had a thin side brace which was redesigned thicker.
1. Copper wheels with crimped axles with a thin chassis cross bar, and thin side brace for the seat.
2. Same as 1, but thick side brace for the seat.
3. Same as 2, but silver wheels.
4. Same as 2, but rivetted axles.
5. Same as 3, but rivetted axles.
6. Same as 5, but unplated wheels.
7. Same as 5, but thick rear chassis cross bar.
8. Same as 6, but thick rear chassis cross bar.

Y-10-B 1928 Mercedes Benz 36/220 3¾" 1963
White body, baseplate & fenders with red seats and tan dashboard and floor, silver metal wheels, black plastic tires, two or no holes in the baseplate, one or two spare tires.
1. Two baseplate holes, two spare tires.
2. Same as 1, one spare tire.
3. Same as 1, but the front fender brace strengthened.
4. Same as 3, but one spare tire.
5. Same as 3, but no baseplate hole.
6. Same as 4, but no baseplate hole.

Y-10-C 1906 Rolls Royce Silver Ghost 3-2/3" 1969
Metallic lime/green body with brown baseplate and fender, red or maroon seats & floor, red grille, gold metal wheels, spare tire holder with wide arms.
1. Small front spring assembly plate.
2. Large front spring assembly plate and a triangular brace added to front springs & baseplate.
3. Same as 2, but white body with maroon baseplate & fenders, red seats & floor, black grille, silver plastic wheels and redesigned spare tire holder with narrow arms.
4. Same as 3, but black seats & floor.
5. Same as 4, but red baseplate and fender.
6. Same as 2, but silver body, silver baseplate & fenders. Yellow seats & floor, and red plastic wheels.

Y-11-A 1920 Aueling & Porter Steam Roller 3-1/8" 1958
Green body & canopy of varying shades, with black or green long or short canopy supports, brown or black flywheel assembled with hub showing or reversed, gold or green steering rods, green makers' name plate. Variations in the diameters of the rollers and lengths of the hubs exist.
1. Black canopy supports, brown flywheel, gold steering rods and name plate.
2. Same as 1, but green name plate.
3. Same as 2, but black matt or glossy flywheel.
4. Same as 3, but green shorter canopy supports.
5. Same as 4, but green steering rods.
6. Same as 5, but brown flywheel.

Y-11-B 1912 Packard Landaulet 3¼" 1964
Dark red body with silver, gold, or unplated radiator, front floor, head lamps, spare tire prongs, steering wheel (also black plastic) and wheels. Combinations of these plated and unplated exist. Two holes in baseplate, black seats, hood, and shield–shaped door decal. The spare tires were held by varieties of 4 and 1 , 3-prong spare tire holders.
1. 4-prong silver spare tire holder and silver wheels.
2. Gold 4-prong spare tire holder and gold wheels.
3. Gold 4-prong spare tire holder and silver wheels.
4. Same as 2, but black steering wheels and 3-prong gold spare tire holder.
5. Same as 4, but lighter red body.

Y-11-C 1938 Lagonda Drophead Coupe 4-3/8" 1973
Gold body with varying shades of red and gold baseplate and fenders, black seats, grille and luggage trunk, gold metal or silver plastic wheels.
1. Purple baseplate and fenders and short back of the the chassis.
2. Maroon baseplate and fenders and revised longer back chassis with an additional brace at the back of the luggage truck.
3. Same as 2, but bright red baseplate and fenders.
4. Same as 2, but red body and gold baseplate & fenders.
5. Same as 4, with silver plastic wheels.
6. Similar to 5, but beige body, black baseplate, brown seats and brown luggage trunk.

Y-12-A 1899 London Horse-drawn Bus 3½" 1959
Red body with tan seats, deck & driver with black hat, brown horses, black wheels with rivetted axles. The horse collar has a continuous gold line around early models & shor line later. Variations in the horse bar fitting have 1 rivet or are redesigned with a plate and 2 rivets. Some slight variations exist in the length of the "Victoria & Kings Cross" decals.
1. Horse collar with continuous gold line, the horse bar fitting has 1 rivet, and the decal is short.
2. Same as 1, but the decal is longer.
3. Horse collar with continuous gold line, horse bar with plate & 2 rivets, and long decal.
4. Same as 3, with short gold line on horse collar.
5. Same as 4, with pink tone to body.

Y-12-B 1909 Thomas Flyabout 4" 1967
Blue body, baseplate & fenders of varying tones with yellow or dark red seats and grille, tan or black roof, gold or silver windshield, and wheels. Baseplate flat or with raised square area, with 2 or no holes. Roof fitted to the body or the seats, side lamp bracket long or short. Spare tire holder wide or redesigned to hold the silver plastic wheels.
1. Yellow seats and grille, tan roof, gold windshield and wheels, flat baseplate with 2 holes, roof fitted to body, long or short side lamp bracket, and wide spare tire holder.
2. Same as 1, but dark red seats & grille, tan roof, silver windshield.
3. Same as 2, but gold windshield and roof fitted to the seats.
4. Same as 3, but redesigned square area on baseplate and no holes.
5. Same as 4, but white seats and black roof.

6. Same as 5, but dark red body, dark red seats, black grille & roof, silver plastic wheels & redesigned narrow spare tire holder.
7. Same as 6, but black seats.
8. Same as 7, but red body.

Y-12-C   1912 Model "T" Ford Truck   3½"   1979
Yellow body, black roof, seats, chassis, & baseplate, gold radiator, grille, & windshield, "Coleman's Mustard" decal on each side.
1. 12-spoke red plastic wheels.
2. Same as 1, but maroon plastic wheels.
3. Same as 1, but 12-spoke silver wheels.
4. Same as 1, but 24-spoke silver wheels.
5. Same as 1, but white body with "Coca-Cola" decal on each side.
6. Same as 5, but a vertical line added to body from the wheel arch to the lower panel.
7. Same as 5, but 12-spoke silver wheels.
8. Same as 5, but 24-spoke silver wheels.
9. Same as 1, but "Taystel Old Fashioned Enriched Bread" decal on each side.
10. Same as 1, but "Suze a la Gentiane" decal on each side.
11. Same as 10, but with 24-spoke silver wheels.
12. Same as 1, but blue body and "Birds' Custard Powder" decal on each side.

**Y-13-A   1862 American "General" Locomotive   3-1/3"   1959
"Santa Fe"**
Green body varying dark to lighter shades, with black baseplate and wheels, rivet on baseplate maroon or green, headlight lens silver or maroon, gold boiler door and trim on smokestacks, large driving wheels thick or thin, and small wheels square edged or curved.
1. Baseplate rivet maroon, silver headlight lens, driving wheels thick, and small wheels square edged, gold trim on walkway.
2. Same as 1, but walkway edge green, and maroon headlight lens.
3. Same as 2, but green baseplate rivet, silver headlight lens and small wheels edges curved.
4. Same as 3, but thin driving wheels.
5. Same as 4, but silver boiler door.
6. Same as 2, but back smokestack without gold, thin driving wheels, and curved edge on small wheels.
7. Same as 6, but front stack also without gold, and squared edge on small wheels.

Y-13-B   1911 Daimler   3-1/3"   1966
Yellow body of varying shades with black or dark red seats, black or red grille, gold metal wheels, steering wheels with 4 or 5 spokes (the five-spoked ones also have a hand throttle).
1. Black seats, black grille, 5-spoke steering wheel, and baseplate with 2 holes, 2-line model description, and rivet on end of pan.
2. Same as 1, but red seats.
3. Same as 1, but 4-spoke steering wheel.
4. Same as 2, but 4-spoke steering wheel.
5. Same as 4, but no baseplate holes.
6. Same as 5, but 3-line model description on baseplate.
7. Same as 6, but 1 baseplate hole and back rivet on pan closer to middle.
8. Same as 7, but two baseplate holes.
9. Same as 7, but red grille and no baseplate hole.
10. Same as 9, but one baseplate hole.

Y-13-C   1918 Crossley R.A.F. Tender   3-7/8"   1973
Gray/blue body with maroon or white seats, tan or green grille & canopies of varying shades, "R.A.F." decals, silver plastic 24-spoke wheels, and two baseplate styles.
1. Maroon seats, tan canopies & grille, flat baseplate.
2. Same as 1, but white seats.
3. Same as 2, but an additional brace on front fender.
4. Same as 3, with recast baseplate with 2 circles, the back one smudging "Ltd."
5. Same as 4, but green canopies & grille.
6. Red body, black baseplate, fenders, seats, & coal sacks, "Coal & Coke" labels, red plastic 12-spoke wheels.

7. Same as 6, with 12-spoke silver wheels.
8. Same as 6, with 24-spoke silver wheels.

Y-14-A   1903 "Duke of Connaught" Locomotive·3"   1959
Green body with brown tool boxes, gold trim on parts of the body in varying combinations, right tool box cast separately or joined to body.
1. Gold tool boxes and right one cast separately.
2. Brown tool boxes and right one joined to body.
3. Same as 2, but silver boiler door.

Y-14-B   1911 Maxwell Roadster   3¼"   1965
Turquoise body, red or brown seats, black roof, copper fuel tank, and fire extinguisher. Black or red grille, gold or silver windshield, dashboard, radiator shell and headlights, two baseplate holes, gold metal wheels, or no baseplate holes.
1. Black grille, gold fuel tank.
2. Black grille, copper fuel tank.
3. Same as 2, but red grille.
4. Same as 2, but silver fire extinguisher.
5. Same as 2, but silver windshield and dashboard and no baseplate hole.
6. Same as 5, but gold windshield and dashboard.
7. Same as 6, but red grille.
8. Same as 5, but no ridges for holes in the baseplate.
9. Same as 8, but redesigned larger spring bars.

Y-14-C   1931 Stutz Bearcat   4-2/5"   1974
Green metallic body with dark green baseplate and fenders, red seats and grille, silver plastic wheels, base dated 1973. The back bumper in early models is missing the left support, then the bumper was redesigned with 4 thick supports.
1. Back bumper missing left support.
2. Same as 1, but back bumper redesigned.
3. Same as 1, but baseplate dated 1974.
4. Same as 2, but baseplate dated 1974.
5. Same as 4, but emerald green baseplate.
6. Red & white body, red fender, baseplate. Black seats & grille, silver plastic wheels, base dated 1974 and redesigned back bumper supports.
7. Same as 6, but green & white body, green fenders & baseplate, black seats, and red grille.

Y-15-A   1907 Rolls Royce Silver Ghost   3¼"   1960
Silver/green body with black seats, silver or gold wheels with gray or black tires with knobby or fine treads. The side panels of the running boards were extended in later models. The baseplates of early models have a dome-shaped projection at the back which was changed to a flat disc. Variations exist in the number of holes in the baseplate, & the castings of the windshield, spare tire holders, steering wheels, and fender braces.
1. Silver back license plate, red back lights, silver wheels with gray knobby tires, short side of the running boards, baseplate with no holes and a dome-shaped projection at the back.
2. Same as 1, but back light is body colored.
3. Same as 2, but back license plate is body colored.
4. Same as 3, but gold wheels.
5. Same as 4, but black knobby tires.
6. Same as 5, but gray knobby tires and a front baseplate hole.
7. Same as 6, but black knobby tires.
8. Same as 6, but a disc shaped projection at the back of the base-plate.
9. Same as 7, but a disc shaped projection at the back of the base-plate.
10. Same as 9, but fine tire treads.
11. Same as 10, but two holes in baseplate.
12. Same as 11, but silver wheels.
13. Same as 12, but sides of running boards are long.
14. Same as 13, but gold wheels.
15. Same as 14, but green seats.
16. Same as 15, but green seats has no holes and is extended to join the cross brace.

17. Same as 16, but black seats.

Y-15-B   1930 Packard Victoria   4½"   1969
Gold body shaded brown or green, with dark brown fenders and base-plate, red, maroon, or black textured roof and trunk, brown or dark red seats, red grille, gold metal or silver plastic wheels. Early models have a vertical brace cast into the baseplate at the back wheel well.
1. Gold/brown body, maroon roof and trunk, brown seats, gold metal wheels.
2. Same as 1, but dark red seats.
3. Same as 2, but red roof and trunk.
4. Same as 2, but black roof and trunk.
5. Same as 3, but silver plastic wheels.
6. Same as 3, but silver plastic wheels.
7. Same as 4, but silver plastic wheels.
8. Same as 7, but gold/green body.
9. Same as 5, but gold/green body.
10. Same as 6, but gold/green body.
11. Same as 7, but gold/green body.
12. Same as 2, but black baseplate and fender, and tan roof with maroon trunk.
13. Maroon body, black baseplate and fenders, white roof, black trunk, maroon seats, black grille, silver plastic wheels.

Y-16-A   1904 Spyker   3-1/3"   1961
Yellow body shaded light to dark color, gold or body colored radiator shell, green seats, gold side lights, gold metal wheels with gray or black tires, with a spare tire holder of silver, copper, or gold with 3 thin or thick spokes. The front license plate had thin braces on early models and thick with strengthening bars on later models.
1. Gold radiator shell, gray knobby tires, gold bent control levers, no baseplate holes.
2. Same as 1, but black knobby tires.
3. Same as 1, but black fine tread tires.
4. Same as 1, but silver bent control levers.
5. Same as 3, but one front baseplate hole.
6. Same as 5, but two baseplate holes.
7. Same as 5, but radiator shell colored as the body.
8. Same as 7, but two baseplate holes.

Y-16-B   1928 Mercedes Benz SS Coupe   4½"   1972
Models vary in color from silver gray with red baseplate and fenders with green baseplate & fenders to white or to blue. Most models have black seats, grille, roof and luggage rack. The wheels are gold metal or silver plastic.
1. Silver gray body with red baseplate and fenders, with gold metal wheels, and a gearbox on the baseplate which is cast on both sides of the back axle.
2. Same as 1, but no gearbox on the baseplate.
3. Lime green body with dark green baseplate and fenders, and silver plastic wheels, no gearbox on baseplate.
4. Same as 3, but light green baseplate and fenders.
5. Same as 3, but dark green roof and luggage trunk.
6. Same as 3, but white body, baseplate & fenders.
7. Same as 3, but light blue body with dark blue baseplate and fenders.

Y-17-A   1938 Hispano Suiza   4-2/5"   1973
Red or blue body with black baseplate, fenders, seats, grille, and roof. Silver plastic wheels. An experimental nylon was used to cast the windshield, headlights, radiator, and front and back bumpers instead of the usual metal.
1. Dark red body.
2. Same as 1, but yellow roof and seats.
3. Same as 1, but dark red roof and seats.
4. Same as 1, but white roof and seats.
5. Same as 1, but green roof and seats.
6. Light blue body with black roof and seats.

Y-18-A   1937 Cord 812   4¾"   1979
Red body, fenders and baseplate, white roof and seats, silver fenders, windshield and exhaust pipes, baseplate numbered unusually YY18

Models of Yesteryear

1. Silver plastic wheels.
2. Red plastic wheels.
3. 24-spoke silver plastic wheels.

Y-19-A   1933 Auburn 851   4½"   1980
Light tan body, brown baseplate and fenders, red plastic seats, silver grille, windshield, fenders, & exhaust pipes.
1. Silver plastic wheels.
2. Red plastic wheels.

3. Same as 2, but black plastic seats.
4. Same as 2, but maroon plastic seats.

Y-20-A   1937 Mercedes Benz 540-K   5"   1981
Silver-gray body, black baseplate and fenders, red seats, silver fenders, windshield, exhaust pipes, and wheels with white walled black tires.

Y-21-A   1929 Woody Wagon   1981
Yellow body with brown roof extending over the sides, red interior and silver plastic wheels.

Y-22-A   1930 Model "A" Ford Van   1982
Red with black roof, baseplate and fenders. Sides lettered "OXO"—It's Meat & Drink To You", white sided tires, clear windows, spare tire.

Y-23-A   1922 A.E.C. "S" Type Bus   1982
Red body, red upper deck, dark brown seats, black baseplate, silver grille with black inserts, red wheels with black plastic tires.

Plated Models of Yesteryear

Plated   Y-1-B   1911 Model T Ford   3"   1964
Silver body.
1. Black roof, red seats and grille, silver metal steering wheel.
2. Same as 1, red roof.
3. Same as 2, black plastic steering wheel.
4. Black roof, black seats and grille, black plastic steering wheel.

Plated   Y-2-B   1911 Renault   3"   1964
Silver body and red seats.
1. Four pronged spare tire holder.
2. Three pronged spare tire holder.

Plated   Y-2-C   1914 Prince Henry Vauxhall   3½"   1970
Silver or gold body and maroon seats.
1. Gold body, bright red grille.
2. Gold body, maroon grille.
3. Silver body, maroon grille.

Plated   Y-3-B   1910 Benz Limousine   3¼"   1966
Silver body, black roof, maroon seats.

Plated   Y-3-C   1934 Riley   3-7/8"   1974
Silver body.
1. Red seats.
2. Black seats and grille, red base and fenders.

Plated   Y-4-C   1909 Opel Coupe   3-1/8"   1966
Silver or gold body, red roof, seats and grille.
1. Silver body.
2. Gold body.

Plated   Y-5-B   1929 4½ litre Bentley   3½"   1962
Silver body, no. 5 decal and flag on each side.
1. Green tonneau cover and seat.
2. Red tonneau cover and seat.

Plated   Y-5-C   1907 Peugeot   3-2/3"   1969
Silver body with black roof and red seats and grille.

Plated   Y-6-B   1923 Type 35 Bugatti   3-1/8"   1961
Silver body, black seats.

Plated   Y-6-C   1913 Cadillac   3-3/8"   1967
Silver or gold body with maroon seats and smooth or textured maroon roof.

1. Silver body, smooth roof.
2. Gold body, smooth roof.
3. Gold body, textured roof.

Plated   Y-7-B   1913 Mercer Raceabout   3¼"   1961
Silver body with black seats.

Plated   Y-7-C   1912 Rolls Royce   3¾"   1968
Silver or gold body and smooth or ribbed roof.
1. Silver body with gray ribbed roof.
2. Silver body with gray smooth roof.
3. Gold body with red ribbed roof. (Also found in golden Veterans set).

Plated   Y-8-C   1914 Stutz   3-3/8"   1969
Silver body with tan roof and green seats.

Plated   Y-9-B   1912 Simplex   3¾"   1968
Silver body with black textured roof, & maroon seats and radiator.

Plated   Y-10-B   1928 Mercedes Benz 36/220   3¾"   1964
Silver body, red seats, one or two spare wheels and tires.
1. Silver body, two spare tires.
2. Silver body, one spare tire.
3. Gold body, one spare tire.

Plated   Y-10-C   1906 Rolls Royce Silver Ghost   3-2/3"   1969
Silver or gold body, red seats and grille.
1. Silver body.
2. Gold body.

Plated   Y-11-B   1912 Packard Landaulet   3¼"   1964
Silver body with black seats.

Plated   Y-12-B   1909 Thomas Flyabout   4"   1967
Silver or gold body with smooth or textured tan roof and red seats.
1. Silver body, smooth roof.
2. Gold body, smooth roof.
3. Silver body, textured roof.
4. Gold body, textured roof.

Plated   Y-13-B   1911 Daimler   3-1/3"   1966
Silver or gold body, maroon seats, black grille with two or three lines of writing on base.
1. Silver body, two lines on base.

2. Gold body, two lines on base.
3. Silver body, three lines on base.
4. Gold body, three lines on base.

Plated   Y-13-C1   1918 Crossley R.A.F. Tender   3-7/8"   1973
Gold body, red seats, black canopy, red cross decals, black or tan grille.
1. Tan grille.
2. Black grille.

Plated   Y-13-C6   1918 Crossley Coal & Coke Truck   1973
Gold body, red seat, black grille, brown front canopy, red or maroon labels.
1. Maroon label.
2. Red label.

Plated   Y-14-B   1911 Maxwell Roadster   3¼"   1965
Silver or gold body, with red or maroon seats, roof and radiator.
1. Gold body, maroon seats, roof and radiator.
2. Silver body, maroon seats, roof and radiator.
3. Gold body, red seats, roof and radiator.

Plated   Y-15-A   1907 Rolls Royce Silver Ghost   3¼"   1960
Silver or gold body with green or black seats.
1. Silver body, black seats.
2. Gold body, black seats.
3. Silver body, green seats.
4. Gold body, green seats.

Plated   Y-15-B   1930 Packard Victoria   4½"   1969
Gold body, maroon seats, maroon or red trunk, maroon or red roof.
1. Maroon trunk, maroon roof.
2. Maroon trunk, red roof.
3. Red trunk, red roof.

Plated   Y-16-A   1904 Spyker   3-1/3"   1961
Silver body, green seats, long or short side panels.
1. Short side panels.
2. Long side panels.

Plated   Y-17-A   1938 Hispano Suiza   4-2/5"   1973
Silver body.

Accessories

In the late 1950's the Lesney personnel began thinking about producing non-vehicular items associated with the Matchbox 1-75 series toys. Three accessories were brought out in 1957 and the following year the group were called "Accessory Packs". These first three were a set of fuel pumps and sign (A1-A), a car transporter truck

(A2-A), and a small one-car garage (A3-A).

At various times since, the series has been expanded to include road signs, a small store, a fire station called Matchbox Fire Station and designated MF1, and three service garages called Matchbox Garages and designated MG.

The latest accessory is a plastic handle to which an elastic string attaches a toy car (from the 1-75 series). By pulling the handle, a car quickly can be sent ahead and travel quite fast.

A1-A	Petrol Pumps and Sign - Esso	4½"	1957
A1-B	Petrol Pumps and Sign - BP	4½"	1963
A1-C	Service Ramp	4½"	1970

Lifts a car up for repair work, "Castrol" lettering on back wall.

A2-A	Bedford Car Transporter	6½"	1957
A3-A	Metal Lock-up Garage	3"	1957
A3-B	Brroomstick (or Zingomatic)		1971

Usually has an orange handle with elastic string, and one of a number of different car toys.

A4-A	Road Signs	1960

Black painted metal signs indicating:

Round about	Bend
School	Cross Roads
Cattle	Level Crossing
Hospital	Double Bend

A5-A	Home Store	3"	1961
MF1-A	Matchbox Fire Station	9¾"	1963

Also part of the G10, then G5 Gift Sets.
1. Red Roof.
2. Green Roof.

MG1-A	Matchbox Garage	1959

One-story plastic garage made under contract for Lesney Products by LRL Company. A raised ramp is on the left side of the platform.
1. Red base, yellow building, red clock.
2. Yellow base, red building, yellow clock.
3. Same as 2, but lettering in center of base reads "Made in England".

MG1-B	Matchbox Garage	9¾"	1961

Two-story garage with removable ramp at the back of the building.
1. Esso labels in red and white.
2. BP labels in green and white.

MG1-C	Matchbox Garage	1968

One-story garage with BP sign, pumps, and shelter in front of the garage. After the garage had been released, an associated cardboard base was issued which was printed with spaces for the pumps and sign. Later in 1970, a second board was issued with a space for the A/C Service Ramp. The garage and boards were also available in the G1-B Service Station gift set with three vehicles.

MG2	Service Station	1979

Flat white base with 2 filling pumps, car wash, elevator, and service ramp.

MG3	Garage	1979

Texaco sign, 2 pump islands, and two separate buildings: one a Texaco gas station with attached ramp and roof car park, the other a restaurant with roof sign of man holding hamburger and coke.

MG4	Super Garage	1981

Large 3 level building in a V-shape around a pump island.

Major Packs

The Major Packs were introduced as a new series in 1957 being a slightly larger size than the Matchbox 1-75 series. That year, two Majors (as they are generally called) were released, the (M1-A) Caterpillar Earth Scraper and the (M2-A) Bedford Ice Cream Truck. In successive years, additions were made to this series until there were ten different toys, with five replacement numbers issued. These fifteen toys were all discontinued in 1966, for by then the King size series was well instated and replaced the Majors in popularity. Some of the Major toys were issued as King size toys after the Major Pack series was discontinued (for example M4-B became K4-B, and M6-B became K5-B).

Major Packs

M-1-A Caterpillar Earth Scraper 4½" 1957
Yellow body, silver metal wheels & black plastic tires. A tan version, possibly a pre-production model, was reported by U.K. "Matchbox".

M-1-B BP Autotanker 4" 1961
Yellow & green body, silver trim, yellow/green/white "BP" decal on front, rear, & each side. Black plastic wheels. Discontinued in 1966.

M-2-A Bedford Ice Cream Truck 4-1/3" 1957
Light blue tractor, silver trim, off-white trailer, blue & red "WALL'S ICE CREAM" decals on each side of trailer. Gray metal or plastic wheels.
　1. Gray metal wheels.
　2. Gray plastic wheels.

M-2-B Bedford Tractor & York Trailer 4-5/8" 1961
Orange or silver tractor body, silver trim on tractor & trailer, silver or reddish/brown trailer body with 3 door colors. Red/white/black "YORK FREIGHT MASTER" decal on front of trailer, "DAVIES TYRES" or "LEP" decals on each side of trailer & gray or black wheels. Discontinued in 1966.
　1. Orange tractor, silver trailer with orange doors, "DAVIES TYRES" decals & gray plastic wheels.
　2. Same as 1, but black plastic wheels.
　3. Silver tractor, reddish/brown trailer & trailer doors, "LEP" decals & black plastic wheels.
　4. Same as 3, but black trailer doors.

**M-3-A Thorneycraft Antar with Sanky 50-ton 4½" 1959
　　tank transporter and Centurion MKIII tank.**
Dark olive green body, 3 various rollers on tank, gray rubber tracks on tank & black plastic wheels. Earlier models may have silver trim. Discontinued in 1966.
　1. Tank has gray metal rollers.
　2. Tank has gray plastic rollers.
　3. Tank has black plastic rollers.

M-4-A Ruston Bucyrus Power Shovel 3-7/8" 1959
Maroon body, yellow floor & shovel assembly, red or yellow side decals ≡≡ 22.RB ≡≡, "Taylor Woodrow" rear decal in black & white, gray metal rollers with green or gray tracks. Rear decals came in 2 sizes & were often omitted entirely.
　1. Red side decals & green rubber tracks.
　2. Same as 1, but black side decals.
　3. Same as 2, but gray rubber tracks.

M-4-B GMC Tractor & Fruehauf Hopper Train 11¼" 1964
Dark red tractor, silver trim, 2 silver hopper trailers, red and white "FRUEHAUF" on each side of hoppers. Major Pack no. M-4 on tractor baseplate, red plastic wheels, & black plastic tires. Changed to K-4-B in 1966.

M-5-A Massey Ferguson Combine Harvester 4-5/8" 1960
Red body, yellow grain reel, tan driver, black & white "MASSEY FERGUSON" on each side & rear. Black plastic tires with various wheels. Came with silver or red metal steering wheel or yellow plastic steering wheel. Discontinued in 1966.
　1. Silver plastic front wheels, black plastic wheels on rear.
　2. Same as 1, but orange plastic front wheels.
　3. Same as 1, but yellow plastic front wheels.
　4. Orange plastic wheels front & rear.
　5. Yellow plastic wheels front & rear.

M-6-A Pickfords 200 Ton Transporter 11" 1960
Blue tractor, silver trim, blue dollies at each end of maroon or red lowboy trailer, white "PICKFORDS" decal on each side of tractor & both dollies. Black plastic wheels.

M-6-B Racing Car Transporter 5-1/8" 1965
Green body, silver tailgate & inside ramp, black/white/yellow "BP" & "RACING TRANSPORTER" decals on each side. "MATCHBOX" Major Pack no. M-6 on baseplate & red plastic wheels with black plastic tires. Changed to K-5-B in 1966.

M-7-A Jennings Cattle Truck 4¾" 1960

Red tractor, silver trim, tan trailer, tan or red tailgate & gray or black plastic wheels. Discontinued in 1964.
　1. Tan tailgate & gray plastic wheels.
　2. Same as 1, but red tailgate.
　3. Same as 2, but black plastic wheels.

M-8-A Mobilgas Petrol Tanker 3-7/8" 1960
Red body, silver trim, blue & white "MOBILGAS" decal on each side of trailer. Blue/red/white "MOBIL" decal on rear of trailer & gray or black plastic wheels.
　1. Gray plastic wheels.
　2. Black plastic wheels.

M-8-B Guy Warrior Car Transporter 8¼" 1964
Blue/green tractor, silver trim & orange trailer. Black on white block lettering or white Roman-type lettering with black outlines "FARNBOROUGH MEASHAM CAR AUCTION COLLECTION" decals on each side of trailer. Orange plastic wheels with gray plastic tires.
　1. Black lettering. (no serifs on letters).
　2. White lettering. (letters have serifs).

M-9-A Interstate Double Freighter 11-1/8" 1962
Blue tractor & silver trailer. Silver or gray trailers with yellow or orange "COOPER—JARRET" decal on each side & front of both trailers, black plastic wheels and recessed (1 wheel) or standard (2 wheels) rear wheels. Early models had blue trailer doors but all later models had doors the same color as the trailer body. The dolly connecting the trailers usually came painted blue but was often left unpainted. Discontinued in 1967.

M-10-A Dinkum Dumper 4½" 1962
Yellow body, red steering wheel, black & white "D.D 70" decal on each side of dump body. Black plastic tires & silver metal wheels or red plastic wheels. Discontinued in 1966.
　1. Silver metal wheels.
　2. Red plastic wheels.

King Size/Super Kings/Speed Kings/Adventure 2000

The success of the Major Pack series from 1957 to 1960 encouraged Lesney personnel to produce an even larger scale toy, and this they called the King Size series. The first group was issued in 1960 and included construction, transportation and large farm vehicles. As certain toys in this series were discontinued, they were replaced with new toys in that number position. In 1966, when the Major Pack series was discontinued, the most popular Majors toys were incorporated into the King Size series with new numbers.

When the Superfast wheels were designed in 1969 for the Matchbox 1-75 series, larger wheels of each design were also made for the

King Size/Super Kings/Speed Kings/Adventure 2000

King Size toys, and when these were released in 1970, the new toys were known as Super Kings. (The description of Superfast wheels is in the section on the Matchbox 1-75 series.)

The King Size automobiles were introduced in 1971 as a separate series called "Speed Kings" and numbered from K-21 on consecutively. The designation "Speed King" continued through 1978 after which the toys were merged into the Super King series. The Super Kings series has grown gradually over the years to include 93 toys currently.

K-1-A   Weatherhill Hydraulic Shovel   3-7/10"   1960
Yellow body & shovel with silver grille, "Weatherhill Hydraulic" decals on front & back, black metal wheels with gray plastic tires.
K-1-B   8-wheel Tipper Truck   4¼"   1964
Red cab & bed with silver trim, orange dumper with "Hoveringham" black lettering on each side. Red plastic wheels with black plastic tires.
K-1-C   O & K Excavator   4-7/8"   1970
Red body with silver shovel and arms, labels "M46" on the arms.
1. Amber windows, 2 red & white "O & K" labels on the back, red plastic wheels with black plastic tires.
2. Same as 1, but 1 label on back and Super King wheels.
3. Same as 1, but Super King wheels.
4. Same as 3, but clear windows.
K-2-A   Muir Hill Dumper   3"   1960
Red body, silver grille, black metal seat & steering wheel, decal "Muir Hill 14B" over grille, black decal on left front side, black & white decal "Muir Hill" on sides of dumper.
1. Black metal wheels with gray plastic tires.
2. Green metal wheels with black plastic tires.
K-2-B   K.W. Dump Truck   5-2/3"   1964
Yellow body with red & white decal "KW-DART" on both sides of dumper, red plastic wheels with black plastic tires.
K-2-C   Scammel Heavy Wreck Truck   4¾"   1969
Red tow arms and box, white plastic tow cables, red, white & blue label "Esso" on doors, silver exhaust stack & horns.
1. White body, silver base, red grille, green windows, silver hooks & red plastic wheels with black plastic tires.
2. Same as 1, but amber windows.
3. Same as 2, but gold body.
4. Same as 3, but Super King wheels.
5. Same as 4, but red base.
6. Same as 5, but black grille.
7. Same as 5, but gold grille.
8. Same as 7, but black hooks.
9. Same as 7, but clear windows.
10. Same as 9, but gold hooks.
K-2-D   Car Recovery Vehicle   4¾"   1977
Green or body with white interior, amber windows, and Super King wheels. Included with this was the K-37 Sand Cat or K-59 Capri.
1. Body labeled "Car Recovery" with red ramps. The included model K-37 Sand Cat has a red body with green base, black seats, gray roof, and No. 3 label.
2. Same as 1, but the included K-37 model has gray seats.
3. Same as 2, but the included K-37 model has a black roof.

4. Same as 2, but the included K-37 model has an orange base.
5. Same as 2, but the label on the recovery vehicle reads "24-hour Breakdown Service" and the ramps are black.
6. Same as 5, but the ramps are red.
7. Metallic blue body on recovery vehicle with label reading "24-hour Breakdown Service", and black ramps. The included model is K-59 Capri with a yellow body.
8. Same as 7, but the recovery vehicle has a gray interior and clear windows.
K-3-A   Caterpillar Bulldozer   3-1/3"   1960
Yellow body with red engine, decal on top of the blade reading "Cat. D9" in black lettering.
1. Gray metal rollers, with a blade.
2. Gray metal rollers, without a blade.
3. Red plastic rollers, with a blade.
4. Red plastic rollers, without a blade.
5. Yellow plastic rollers, with a blade.
6. Yellow plastic rollers, without a blade.
K-3-B   Hatra Tractor Shovel   5-9/10"   1965
Orange body & shovel with red plastic wheels and black plastic tire. The side decal lettering is black reading "Hatra" in either short or tall slanted letters.
1. Short letters.
2. Tall slanted letters.
K-3-C   Massey Ferguson Tractor and Trailer   8"   1970
Red tractor body with gray engine and white grille, yellow plastic wheels and black plastic tires. The red trailer has a yellow tow bar and axle bed with yellow plastic wheels and black plastic tires.
K-3-D   Mod Tractor and Trailer   7¾"   1974
Tractor with metallic blue or dark blue/green body, red or yellow seat and/or grille, chrome engine, and white steering wheel, red plastic wheels and black tires. The trailer has a yellow upper half and the lower half matches the tractor with Super King wheels and either a stars & stripes label or none.
1. Tractor with metallic blue body with red seat and grille. Trailer with stars & stripes label.
2. Same as 1, with yellow seat.
3. Same as 1, but with yellow grille.
4. Same as 2, with yellow grille.
5. Same as 4, but the tractor is dark blue/green and the trailer has no label.
K-3-E   Grain Transporter   11-7/8"   1980
Red or green body with black interior & grille, clear windows, white headlights, "Bedford" on grille, white wind deflector above cab, white

trailer & tank with black top strip & silver lids, black removable hoses with silver nozzles, & Super King wheels.
1. Red cab & trailer chassis, & tank labeled "Kellogg's-The Best To You Each Morning".
2. Green cab & white trailer chassis & tank labeled "Heidelberger Zement", released in West Germany.
K-4-A   International Tractor   2-4/5"   1960
Red body with decals on each side reading "McCormick International" in white letters, and "B 250" in red letters on white circle, with black plastic tires.
1. Green metal wheels.
2. Red metal wheels.
3. Red plastic wheels.
4. Orange plastic wheels.
K-4-B   G.M.C. Tractor with Fruehauf Hopper Train   11¼"   1967
Dark red cab with silver trim. The two silver hoppers have red and white labels "Fruehauf" on the sides. The base is marked "King Size No. K-4".
1. Red plastic wheels with black plastic tires.
2. Red plastic wheels with gray plastic tires.
K-4-C   Leyland Tipper   4½"   1969
Cab, chassis & tipper of varying colors. The tipper is labeled variously, & there are red plastic wheels with black plastic tires or Super King wheels.
1. Dark red cab & chassis with silver tipper labeled "LE transport", resting on red plastic wheels with black plastic tires.
2. Same as 1, but label "W. WATES".
3. Same as 2, but yellow/green cab, chassis and tipper.
4. Same as 3, but orange/red cab and chassis.
5. Same as 4, but metallic green tipper.
6. Same as 5, but Super King wheels.
7. Blue cab & chassis, silver tipper with label of miner & cave, resting on Super King wheels.
K-4-D   Big Tipper   4-2/3"   1974
Red or metallic purple cab with yellow tipper bearing labels either of 3 red stripes or "Liang", and resting on Super King wheels.
1. Metallic purple cab, 3 red stripes on dumper, & with a Press-A-Matic mechanism which adjusts the angle of the dumper.
2. Same as 1, but dumper labeled "Liang".
3. Same as 1, but red cab.
4. Same as 2, but red cab.
5. Same as 1, but no Press-A-Matic.
6. Same as 2, but no Press-A-Matic.
7. Same as 3, but no Press-A-Matic.
8. Same as 4, but no Press-A-Matic.

King Size/Super Kings/Speed Kings/Adventure 2000

K-5-A   Foden Tipper Truck   4¼"   1961
Yellow cab, chassis and tipper with silver grille, red "Foden" on sides of hood, black plastic tires.
1. Silver metal wheels.
2. Red plastic wheels.

K-5-B   Racing Car Transporter   5"   1967
Green body with silver back door and inside ramp. Side decals of black, white, yellow, and green. Base marked "Matchbox" King Size No. K-5. Red plastic wheels and black plastic tires.

K-5-C   Muir Hill Tractor and Trailer   9½"   1972
Yellow bodies and red tow bar and trailer chassis, with silver grille and engine, removable front blade, red plastic wheels and black plastic tires. The trailer tires can be large or small.
1. Driver is blue and flesh colored, amber windows, and trailer labels read "Muir Hill".
2. Same as 1, but white driver and clear windows.
3. Same as 2, but white windows.
4. Same as 3, but blue and red bodies and trailer labels read "Hock & Tief Bauunternekmen". (German release)

K-6-A   Allis-Chalmers Earth Scraper   5-7/8"   1961
Orange body with red engine, two springs joining the scraper, side decals "260" on white and "Allis-Chalmers" in black, with black plastic tires.
1. Silver metal wheels.
2. Red plastic wheels.

K-6-B   Mercedes Benz Ambulance   4-1/8"   1967
White body with silver grille, blue dome light, opening doors, white plastic stretcher & man with red plastic blanket, "Autosteer" working steering, and base marked K-6.
1. Red plastic wheels with black plastic tires.
2. Silver wheels with black plastic tires.

K-6-C   Cement Mixer   5¾"   1971
Blue cab with tan or black box on top, red chassis & pouring spout, amber or clear windows, black & yellow door labels, yellow plastic barrel with matt or metallic red stripes, & 8 Super King tires.
1. Tan box on van, amber windows, matt red barrel stripes.
2. Same as 1, but black box.
3. Same as 2, but metallic red barrel stripes.
4. Same as 3, but clear windows.

K-6-D   Motorcycle Transporter   4¾"   1976
Metallic blue body with open hood or closed hood with a variety of labels, yellow tail gate, amber dome light & windows, Super King wheels. The transporter carries a no. 18-G Hondarora motorcycle.
1. Open hood exposing a chrome engine. Carrying a red motorcycle.
2. Same as 1, carrying an orange motorcycle.
3. Same as 1, with closed hood & "Arrow" design label as found on 52-C Dodge Charger.
4. Same as 3, with closed hood & "Arrow" design label.
5. Same as 3, with "Chain-link" design label as found on K-6-C Cement Truck.
6. Same as 4, with "Chain-link" design label.
7. Same as 3, with "Flying Wind" design Honda label.
8. Same as 4, with "Flying Wind" design Honda label.
9. Closed hood with "Flying Wind" design label, blue dome light and cab windows, clear canopy window, and red motorcycle.
10. Same as 1, with green motorcycle.

K-7-A   Curtiss Wright Rear Dumper   5¾"   1961
Yellow body with red engine, dumper with red "Curtiss-Wright CW D-321" and black "CW" decals on sides, gray metal wheels and black plastic tires.

K-7-B   Refuse Truck   4-3/5"   1967
Red or blue cab & chassis, 2-part tipper box with "Cleansing Service" label on sides, red plastic or Super King wheels.
1. Red cab & chassis, all-silver tipper box, red plastic wheels with black plastic tires.
2. Same as 1, with Super King wheels.

3. Same as 2, but back part of tipper box is red.
4. Dark blue cab & chassis, all-orange tipper box w/yellow, black & white side label, & Super King wheels.

K-7-C   Racing Car Transporter   6-1/8"   1973
Yellow body with red rear gate, black or blue interior, amber or clear windows, silver headlights and grille, opening doors, side labels "Team Matchbox" (with variations) and Super King wheels. Various racer models are included in the transporter.
1. Black interior transporting a pink no. 34-D Formula 1 racer.
2. Same as 1, transporting a green no. 24-D Team "Matchbox" racer.
3. Same as 1, transporting a red no. 24-D Team "Matchbox" racer.
4. Same as 1, transporting a yellow no. 34-D Formula 1 racer.
5. Same as 4, but transporter has a blue interior.
6. Same as 5, but clear cab windows.
7. Same as 5, but clear canopy windows.
8. Same as 1, transporting a red no. 36-E Formula 5000 racer.
9. White body with blue rear gate, black interior, amber windows, side labels "Martini Racing" and "Dunlop" transporting a white no. 56-D Hi-Tailer racer with labels "Martini Racing" and "7".
10. Same as 9, but cab with red top.

K-8-A   Prime Mover & Transporter with   12½"   1962
          Caterpillar Crawler Tractor
Prime mover & transporter with orange bodies and silver metal or red plastic wheels with black plastic tires. Prime mover door with black & white decal "Civil Engineering Contractors". Transporter with thick or thin "LIANG" lettering on side decal. Yellow caterpillar tractor with red motor, gray, red, yellow, or orange plastic rollers, green rubber treads, & no. 8 on base.
1. Prime mover & transporter with silver metal wheels, transporter with thick "LIANG" lettering, tractor with gray metal wheels.
2. Same as 1, but transporter has also a decal reading "Civil Engineering Contractors".
3. Same as 1, but transporter has thin "LIANG" lettering.
4. Same as 3, but tractor has red plastic rollers.
5. Same as 4, but prime mover and trailer have red plastic wheels.
6. Same as 5, but tractor rollers are orange plastic.
7. Same as 1, but tractor rollers are yellow plastic.

K-8-B   Guy Warrior Car Transporter   8¼"   1967
Blue/green or yellow cab with orange or red wheels and gray or black plastic tires. Orange or yellow trailer with "Farnborough Measham/Car Auction Collection" decals on the sides, and "King Size K-8" on base.
1. Blue/green cab with orange wheels and gray tires. The trailer is orange.
2. Same as 1, but black tires.
3. Same as 2, but red wheels.
4. Same as 3, but the trailer is yellow.
5. Same as 4, but the cab is also yellow.

K-8-C   Caterpillar Traxcavator   4-1/8"   1970
Yellow body of various shades with blue and/or white driver & label at back "Caterpillar 977-K Traxcavator". The arms & shovel are yellow or orange & the body rests on yellow or black rollers with green or black rubber treads.
1. Yellow body, arms, shovel & rollers with green treads.
2. Light yellow body and rollers, orange arms & bucket & green treads.
3. Same as 2, but black rollers.
4. Same as 3, but body is yellow/orange.
5. Same as 4, but body is black treads.
6. Same as 5, but body is silver.

K-8-D   Animal Transporter   12-1/3"   1980
Orange tilt-forward cab with white interior & white wind deflector on top with brown animal design. Trailer with dark brown chassis, beige body, white roof with clear windows & side "Anitran" labels, 3 opening doors, & mag wheels. Inside are 6 animals & a man.

1. Trailer with brown doors.
2. Trailer with green doors.

K-9-A   Diesel Road Roller   3¾"   1962
Green body with red & white decal on sides & red metal rollers.
1. Gray driver.
2. Red driver.

K-9-B   Claas Combine Harvester   5½"   1967
Green or red body with red or yellow movable blade, "Claas" circular label on sides, & red or yellow plastic wheels with black plastic tires. Some models have a driver.
1. Green body with red blade, green & white "Claas" labels, & red plastic wheels. No driver.
2. Same as 1, with a white driver.
3. Red body with yellow blade, green & white "Claas" label, & yellow plastic wheels, with tan driver.
4. Same as 3, with red & white "Claas" label.
5. Same as 4, with no driver.

K-9-C   Fire Tender   6-1/8"   1973
Red body with silver metal ladder and gray, black or white extension, amber or clear windows, side labels reading "Denver" & "Fire Dept.", with Super King wheels.
1. Gray extension ladder & amber windows.
2. Gray extension ladder & clear windows.
3. Black extension ladder & amber windows.
4. White extension ladder & amber windows.

K-10-A   Aveling-Barford Tractor Shovel   4-1/8"   1963
Blue/green or ming green body, red seat & steering wheel, with or without air cleaner on right side, round decal on front and "Aveling-Barford" decals on sides, silver metal or red plastic wheels with black plastic tires.
1. Blue/green body with air cleaner & silver metal wheels.
2. Same as 1, but red plastic wheels.
3. Same as 2, but no air cleaner.
4. Same as 3, but mint green body.

K-10-B   Pipe Truck   8"   1967
Variously colored body & trailer, black plastic grille, green tinted windows, 6 pipes of varying colors supported by silver vertical bars, 2 types of wheels.
1. Yellow body & trailer, gray plastic pipes, red plastic wheels with black plastic tires.
2. Pinkish–purple body & trailer, gray plastic pipes, & Super King wheels.
3. Metallic purple body & trailer, yellow plastic pipes and Super King wheels.
4. Same as 3, but orange plastic pipes.

K-10-C   Car Transporter   10½"   1976
Red cab & trailer with silver loading ramp and chassis, amber or clear windows and dome light, chrome interior & engine, unpainted horns, & 3 various trailer labels.
1. Amber windows & dome light, trailer with "Auto Transport" labels.
2. Same as 1, but clear windows.
3. Amber windows & dome light, trailer with label of horse with striped border (same label as K-60-A Mustang).
4. Amber windows & dome light, trailer with white label reading "4" in black border.

K-10-D   Bedford Car Transporter   10-1/3"   1981
Metallic blue upper cab & trailer, white loading ramp & chassis, clear windows, black grille, & interior & coiled hares, white wind deflector above cab, labels reading "Bedford" on cab, "Courier" on door & trailer sides, "Courier" on wind deflector.

K-11-A   Fordson Tractor & Farm Trailer   6¼"   1963
Blue tractor with silver grille & headlights, silver or blue steering wheel, & side decals "Fordson Super Major". Trailer with blue chassis and gray tipper, orange or red wheels and black plastic tires.
1. Silver steering wheel & orange metal wheels.
2. Same as 1, but orange plastic wheels.

3. Same as 2, but blue steering wheel.

K-11-B   D.A.F. Car Transporter   9"   1969
Metallic blue or yellow cab with unpainted or metallic red grille & blue or clear windows, transporter with variously colored body, black or red car wheel blocks on top, D.A.F. or striped labels, & 2 kinds of wheels.
1. Metallic blue cab with unpainted grille, blue windows; trailer gold with black car wheel blocks, D.A.F. labels & red plastic wheels with black plastic tires.
2. Same as 1, but yellow cab and reddish yellow trailer.
3. Same as 2, but red car wheel blocks.
4. Same as 3, but Super King wheels.
5. Same as 4, but clear windows.
6. Same as 5, but metallic red grille.
7. Same as 6, but orangish/yellow trailer.
8. Same as 7, but orange & white striped labels.

K-11-C   Tow Truck   5"   1976
Yellow or red body with red hooks and white tow arms, unpainted or black base, black box & back gate, chrome grille, 3 various door labels & Super King wheels.
1. Yellow body, unpainted base, door label "AA".
2. Same as 1, but black base.
3. Same as 2, but door label "Shell Recovery".
4. Red body, black base, & door panel "Falck Zonen". This was a Scandinavian promotional and "Matchbox" collectors' club offer.
5. Same as 4, but door label "Shell Recovery".

K-11-D   Dodge Delivery Van   5-1/3"   1981
Yellow or light blue body, chrome grille, cream interior, side decal "Michelin" or "Frankfurter Allgemeine", & clear windows & mag wheels.
1. Yellow body & "Michelin" decal.
2. Light blue body & "Frankfurter Allgemeine" decal.

K-12-A   Heavy Breakdown Wreck Truck   4¾"   1963
Green body with yellow tow crane, silver grille, clear windows, side decals "BP", and "Matchbox Service Station", & "Head Office Eastway London"; & red decal "Matchbox BP Service". Black plastic tires.
1. No roof light, with silver metal wheels.
2. No roof light, with red plastic wheels.
3. With roof light & red plastic wheels.

K-12-B   Scammel Crane Truck   6"   1969
Various colored body & chassis & base. Silver headlights & bumpers, white interior, clear windows in cab, green tinted windows in crane cab, white cable with silver hook, yellow/black "Laing" label on crane sides & red plastic wheels with black plastic tires or Super King wheels.
1. Yellow cab & chassis, unpainted base & red plastic wheels with black plastic tires.
2. Orange cab & chassis, unpainted base & Super King wheels.
3. Same as 2, but silver/gray base.
4. Silver, red big MX model crane cab & arm, red base & Super King wheels.

K-12-C   Hercules Mobile Crane   6-1/8"   1975
Various body colors & hook. Amber windows & dome lights, 2 different labels, black extending crane arm & support legs, black hydraulic sleeves, silver/gray base & Super King wheels.
1. Yellow & black body, yellow hook & black & yellow "Laing" labels.
2. Same as 1, but with a yellow & red body.
3. Same as 2, but with a red hook.
4. Same as 3, but a dark blue/pale blue or red body, "Hoch & Tief Bauunternehmen" label. (released in Germany).

K-13-A   Ready Mix Concrete Truck   1963
Various shades of orange body & black base & pouring pan. Silver grille, green windows, rotating READYMIX or RMC barrel, silver metal or red plastic wheels with black plastic tires.
1. White background on door signs, READYMIX barrel & silver metal wheels.
2. Same as 1, but red plastic wheels.

3. Same as 2, but RMC barrel.
4. Same as 3, but orange background on door signs.

K-13-B   Building Transporter   5¾"   1971
Shades of green body & chassis, white interior, red plastic frame on flat bed & various colors of side tanks & grille. Yellow, blue & clear parts that snap together to make a building, blue tinted or clear cab windows & Super King wheels.
1. Metallic green body & chassis, silver side tanks & grille, blue tinted cab windows.
2. Same as 1, but red side tanks & grille.
3. Same as 2, but clear cab windows.
4. Same as 3, but yellow side tanks & grille.
5. Same as 4, but lime green body & chassis.

K-13-C   Aircraft Transporter   8"   1976
Red or silver/gray body, yellow base, 3 various cab labels, amber or clear cab windows & white or gray cab interior. Jet & bombs are white or tan with 2 different labels & black or red jet holder.
1. Red body, yellow base, white interior, amber cab windows & black & white "X4" cab label. Jet & bombs are white, labels on jet & wing are red, yellow, blue & white, "10" labels on jet are black & white, black jet holder.
2. Same as 1, but gray cab interior.
3. Same as 2, but clear cab windows.
4. Same as 1, but tan jet & bombs.
5. Same as 1, but large yellow "12" on red background cab label.
6. Same as 1, but silver/gray body, red jet holder, red tempa stripes on cab & blue "F10" with red stripes on wings of jet & red tempa stripes on jet.

K-14-A   Taylor Jumbo Crane   5"   1964
Yellow body & crane, green tinted windows, black plastic hydraulic sleeve, white plastic cable & silver hook on crane. Yellow or red boom box, white & black "TAYLOR JUMBO CRANE" decal on boom box, decal or label on bumper & red plastic tires with black plastic tires.
1. Yellow boom box & red, white & black decal on bumper.
2. Same as 1, but red boom box.
3. Same as 2, but orange, white & black label on bumper.

K-14-B   Freight Truck   5½"   1971
Metallic blue body, silver or gray base, bumper & headlights. White interior, clear windows, white roof, copper box sides, sliding box doors, black & silver "LEP INTERNATIONAL TRANSPORT" labels on box sides & Super King wheels.
1. Silver headlights, base & bumper.
2. Gray headlights, base & bumper.

K-14-C   Heavy Breakdown Truck   5-1/8"   1977
White cab, chassis & interior, clear or amber windows, red rear boom box & hook, silver tow crane, white, yellow, blue & red "SHELL RECOVERY" labels on sides & Super King wheels.
1. Clear windows & white interior.
2. Same as 1, but amber windows.

K-15-A   Merryweather Fire Engine   6"   1964
Metallic red or red body, silver grille, green windows & gold control panel & bells on cab roof. Gray or silver plastic extension ladder, red, white & black no. 15 on cab doors, red & yellow "KENT FIRE BRIGADE" on sides & red plastic wheels with black plastic tires or Super King wheels.
1. Red body, gray ladder & red plastic wheels with black plastic tires.
2. Same as 1, but Super King wheels.
3. Same as 2, but silver ladder.
4. Same as 3, but metallic red body.
5. Same as 4, but big MX model.

K-15-B   The Londoner   4¾"   1973
Red or silver body, various colored interior, clear windows, gold or silver doors, opening doors, with or without bell, various labels & Super King wheels.
1. Red body, yellow interior, gold doors, bell underneath & "SWINGING LONDON CARNABY STREET LONDON TRANSPORT"

labels by doors & "PRAED ST. KENSINGTON" label on front.
2. Same as 1, but no bell.
3. Same as 2, but white interior.
4. Silver body & doors, red interior, no bell & "SILVER JUBILEE 1952–1977 1952 E//R 1977" label on front. ("Matchbox" collectors Club & U.K. release).
5. Same as 3, but "ENTER A DIFFERENT WORLD—HARRODS LONDON TRANSPORT" labels by doors & red, white, blue & black "HACKNEY 30" label on front. (U.K. promotional).
6. Same as 5, but "Hamleys, the finest toy shop in the world London transport" labels by doors.
7. Same as 6, but "TOURIST LONDON—BY BUS LONDON TRANSPORT" labels by doors. (Heritage series model).
8. Same as 3, but all-white "London Transport" insignia by doors.
9. Same as 8, but yellow interior.
10. Same as 9, but "Visit The London Dungeon" labels.
11. Same as 10, but "London Dungeon Museum" labels & all-white "London Transport" insignia by doors. "London Bridge No.48" label on front.
12. Bright silver body & doors, light blue interior, no bell, "The Royal Wedding 1981" labels & Prince of Wales crest by doors & "St. Paul's Cathedral" on front.
13. Same as 12, but yellow interior & "1979 Royal Visit" labels.

K-16-A   Dodge Tractor with Twin Tippers   11-7/8"   1966
Green or yellow cabs & beds, silver headlights & bumper, yellow or blue tipper with red & white "Dodge Trucks" on sides & red plastic wheels with black plastic tires or Super King wheels.
1. Green cab & bed, yellow tipper & red plastic wheels with black plastic tires.
2. Yellow cab & beds, blue tipper & Super King wheels.

K-16-B   Petrol Tanker
White tank on trailer, "Long Vehicle" on rear, chrome exhaust stacks, black or gray grille, and Super King wheels. There are 8 major label variations of different petroleum companies, and within each one, many model variations.
1. TEXACO
   Red cab, silver frame, red tank bottom, chrome or black tank top filling strip, "TEXACO" door labels, green or clear windows, and chrome engine & interior. A special "Matchbox" collectors club offer model has green cab & tank bottom, & no door label.
2. QUAKER STATE
   This is a special Canadian promotional with green cab and tank bottom, silver frame, chrome tank top filling strip, no door labels, green windows & chrome engine & interior.
3. SHELL
   White cab, yellow frame & tank bottom, chrome tank top filling strip, shell door label, green or clear windows, chrome engine & interior.
4. EXXON
   White cab, frame & tank bottom, chrome or black tank top filling strip, "EXXON" door labels, green or clear windows, chrome or black engine & interior.
5. ARAL
   3 types of door & 3 types of rear labels exist. Dark or light blue cab & tank bottom, silver or light blue frame, chrome tank top filling strip, engine & interior, and green or clear windows.
6. TOTAL
   White cab with red or orange frame & tank bottom, chrome or black tank top filling strip, "TOTAL" door labels, green or clear windows, and chrome engine & interior.
7. BP
   White cab, yellow frame & tank bottom, chrome tank top filling strip, engine & interior, "BP" door labels, & green windows.
8. LEP International Transport
   Metallic red cab, silver frame, red tank bottom, chrome tank top filling strip, engine, & interior, "LEP International Transport" door labels, green windows.

9. CHEMCO
Dark green cab, yellow tank & chassis, "Chemco" with red & black side stripes, white hose.

K-17-A   Low Loader and Bulldozer   9½"   1967
3 various colors of cab, silver grille, green windows, red dome light, shades of green low bed, various colors of tractor & "Laing" or "Taylor Woodrow" decals. Red, yellow or blue rollers, green or black treads & black plastic tires or Super King wheels.
1. Green & yellow low bed & treads, red & dark yellow tractor, "Laing" decals, red rollers & black plastic tires.
2. Same as 1, but "Taylor Woodrow" decals & yellow rollers.
3. Same as 2, but light green cab & low bed, orange & yellow tractor, black rollers & Super King wheels.
4. Same as 3, but Florentine tractor.
5. Same as 4, but blue treads.

K-17-B   Articulated Container Truck   9-7/8"   1974
4 various colors of cab & cab roof, yellow cab interior, clear windows, blue, silver or black cab chassis, 4 various colors of trailer chassis & chrome or black exhaust stacks. Yellow, orange or white container sides & various colored container roof & doors. "Gentransco" labels, Super King wheels & black plastic wheels on front of trailer.
1. Metallic red cab with silver chassis, trailer has red chassis, yellow side on container & blue roof & doors on container. Chrome exhaust stacks.
2. Same as 1, but the container has light blue roof & doors.
3. Same as 1, but container has orange sides.
4. Same as 3, but container has light blue roof & doors.
5. Same as 4, but container has orange roof & doors.
6. Same as 1, but container has white sides.
7. Same as 6, but container has light blue roof & doors.
8. Same as 6, but container has orange roof & doors.
9. Same as 6, but container has black roof & doors.
10. Same as 6, but container has red roof & doors.
11. Same as 6, but trailer chassis is dark blue.
12. Same as 11, but blue cab chassis.
13. Yellow cab & container sides, roof & doors. Black cab chassis & trailer chassis, chrome exhaust stacks & DBP (West German Post Office) labels.
14. Same as 13, but black exhaust stacks.
15. Same as 6, but blue trailer chassis.
16. Same as 6, but white trailer chassis.
17. Same as 16, but black cab roof, blue cab chassis, & "PPPick up a Penguin" labels. (U.K. release).
18. White cab & white container sides with green trailer chassis & container roof, 7-up labels on doors of cab and sides of container.

K-18-A   Articulated Horse Box   6½"   1966
Red cab with green windows, silver horns, & silver or gray grille & base. Red & white horse's head on sides of cab, tan or orange trailer, & green,

yellow, & white "Ascot Stables" on sides of trailer. Clear windows in trailer, white plastic interior in front of trailer & various colored rear interior of trailer. 2 opening silver door ramps on trailer, 4 white plastic horses & red plastic wheels with black plastic tires or Super King wheels.
1. Tan trailer, silver grille & base, gray rear interior of trailer & red plastic wheels with black plastic tires.
2. Same as 1, but green rear interior of trailer.
3. Same as 1, but red rear interior of trailer.
4. Same as 1, but brown rear interior of trailer.
5. Same as 1, but multi-color interior at rear of trailer.
6. Same as 2, but Super King wheels.
7. Same as 6, but orange trailer.
8. Same as 7, but gray grille & base.

K-18-B   Articulated Tipper Truck   8"   1974
Various cab colors, green windows & silver, red or black frame. Black, red or blue-dark rear chassis & yellow, silver or light blue tipper. Chrome exhaust stacks, black plastic tipping gate at rear, various labels on cab & tipper, Super King wheels & black plastic wheels on front of trailer.
1. Red cab, silver frame, black rear chassis, yellow tipper & red & yellow stripe labels on cab & tipper.
2. Same as 1, but metallic red cab.
3. Same as 2, but no label on cab.
4. Silver cab & tipper, red frame & rear chassis & red & yellow stripes labels on tipper.
5. Same as 4, but black & yellow "TARMAC" labels on tipper & black & silver door labels.
6. Yellow cab & tipper, black frame & rear chassis & black & yellow "US Steel" on cab & tipper.
7. Light blue cab & tipper, red frame, dark blue rear chassis, & "Hoch & Tief Bauunternehmen" labels.

K-19-A   Scammell Tipper Truck   4¾"   1967
Red or metallic red cab & chassis, green windows, silver bumper & base, yellow or orange & yellow tipper, black or red grille & red plastic wheels with black plastic tires or Super King wheels.
1. Red cab & chassis, orange & yellow tipper, black grille & red plastic wheels with black plastic tires.
2. Same as 1, but yellow tipper.
3. Metallic red cab & chassis, orange & yellow tipper, red grille & Super King wheels.
4. Same as 3, but yellow tipper & black grille.

K-19-B   Security Truck   12-7/8"   1979
White cab, shell & rear door, green windows, & gold & black lattice label on side windows. Black bumper & combination dials, yellow, orange or red roof with "Group 4" or "FORT KNOX" labels. White & gold cart and blue, white & flesh colored man. Super King wheels, treaded on rear & black plastic wheels on cart.
1. Yellow roof with "GROUP 4" labels.
2. Orange roof with "FORT KNOX" labels.

3. Same as 2, but "GROUP 4" labels.
4. Same as 2, but red roof.

K-20-A   Tractor Transporter   9"   1968
4 various colors of cab & side tanks. Silver grille, green windows & red dome light on cab. Red, yellow or silver trailer, yellow plastic snap-in rack holding 3 no. 39 Ford tractors on transporter. Blue or orange tractors & red plastic wheels with black plastic tires or Super King wheels.
1. Red & yellow cab & side tanks, red trailer, blue tractors & red plastic wheels with black plastic tires.
2. Same as 1, but red cab & tank sides.
3. Florentine cab & side tanks, yellow trailer, blue tractors & Super King wheels.
4. Same as 3, but blue cab & side tanks & orange tractors. (Big MX model).
5. Same as 4, but silver trailer.

K-20-B   Cargo Hauler and Pallet Loader   7½"   1973
2 shades of green cab & chassis, various colors of side tanks & grille & clear windows. Yellow or blue barrels, red or orange loading ramp, pallets & holder. Rubber-plastic black tires on pallet, 15-5 Fork Lift Truck included, chrome or olive engine & Super King wheels.
1. Metallic green cab & chassis, red side tanks & grille & yellow barrels. Red loading ramp, pallets & holder, & chrome engine.
2. Same as 1, but yellow side tanks & grille.
3. Same as 1, but black side tanks & grille.
4. Same as 1, but olive side tanks & grille.
5. Same as 2, but lime green body.
6. Same as 5, but blue barrels.
7. Same as 5, but blue side tanks & grille.
8. Same as 5, but red side tanks & grille.
9. Same as 5, but orange loading ramp, pallets & holder.
10. Same as 5, but olive colored engine.

K-20-C   Peterbilt Wrecker   6-1/3"   1979
White or dark green cab & white rear body. White, dark green or unpainted air conditioner on top of cab & red twin winches with silver tow hooks. Chrome grille, bar lights on roof, plastic extending supports on sides. Gold or unpainted crane hooks with white, tan, yellow or black cords. Unpainted horns on top of cab, amber dome lights & red, white & black labels. "HEAVY DUTY RECOVERY DAY & NIGHT ROAD SERVICE" labels, mag wheels & separate black plastic or molded red plastic tow trailer wheels.
1. Dark green cab, white rear, white air conditioner on top of cab & separate black plastic tow trailer wheels.
2. Same as 1, but dark green air conditioner.
3. Same as 1, but unpainted air conditioner.
4. Same as 3, but molded red plastic tow trailer wheels.
5. Same as 4, but white cab.

Super Kings

K-21-A   Mercury Cougar   4-1/8"   1968
Metallic gold body, unpainted base, clear windows, white or red interior & black plastic wheels.
1. White interior.
2. Red interior, with or without hole under grille.

K-21-B   Cougar Dragster   4-1/8"   1971
Various body colors, unpainted base, clear windows, white interior, & "Dinamite" or "Bender" labels.
1. Light pink body & "Dinamite" label.
2. Same as 1, but dark pink body.
3. Same as 1, but purple body.
4. Same as 1, but burgundy body.

5. Same as 3, but "Bender" label.

K-21-C   Tractor Transporter   6-3/8"   1974
Blue body, yellow interior, amber windows, silver/gray painted base. Yellow, red, & black label on doors of cab, yellow plastic removeable ramp & support section. With two 25-B Mod Tractors in purple with red or yellow seats, & Super Fast wheels.

K-21-D   Ford Transcontinental   13-1/3"   1979
Blue or yellow cab, white or yellow chassis, white or green tarp, "Santa Fe" or "Continental" logo. Clear, amber, or blue dome lights & maltese cross wheels or wide mag wheels.
1. Blue cab, white chassis & tarp, clear dome lights, maltese cross wheels, & "Santa Fe" logo trailer.

2. Same as 1, but amber dome lights.
3. Same as 1, but blue dome lights.
4. Yellow body & chassis, green tarp, "Continental" logo, amber dome lights & maltese cross wheels.
5. Same as 4, but wide mag wheels.

K-22-A   Dodge Charger   4½"   1969
Blue body with pale blue interior, unpainted base, clear windows, & black plastic tires.

K-22-B   Dodge Dragster   4½"   1971
Body in various shades of orange, unpainted base, clear windows, white interior & "Bender" or "Dinamite" labels.
1. Pinkish orange body & "Bender" label.

2. Same as 1, but orange body.
3. Same as 1, but light orange body.
4. Same as 2, but "Dinamite" label.

K-22-C   SRN6 Hovercraft   5"   1974
Blue or white upper deck, white or black lower deck, white or red window section, "SRN6" or "Calais—Ramsgate" upper label, & "Seaspeed" or "Hoverlloyd" lower label.
1. Blue upper deck, white lower deck & window section, "SRN6" upper label & "Seaspeed" lower label.
2. White upper deck, black lower deck, red window section, "Calais—Ramsgate" upper label & "Hoverlloyd" lower label.
3. Same as 1, but "SRN6" upper label & "Seaspeed" lower label.
4. Same as 1, but white upper deck.

K-23-A   Mercury Police Commuter   4-3/8"   1969
White body, unpainted base, red interior, clear windows, blue dome lights & BPT (black plastic tires) or Super Fast wheels.
1. Black plastic tires.
2. Super Fast wheels.

K-23-B   Lowloader and Bulldozer   9-7/8"   1974
Various cab colors, silver/gray or red base, yellow or black interior, various colors on trailer body, base & blade.
1. Metallic blue cab, silver/gray base, yellow interior, base & blade. Gold trailer & red body, may be found with black or yellow trailer coupling.
2. Dark blue cab & body, red base & blade, black interior & pale blue trailer, red painted roof & "Hoch & Tief" labels.
3. Orange cab & trailer, silver/gray base & blade, black interior & yellow body.

K-24-A   Lamborghini Miura   4"   1969
White interior, body in various shades of red or dark/yellow. Yellow, silver/gray, or unpainted base, with or without hood label or tow hook, clear or amber windows & black plastic spiro, or 5-spoke wheels.
1. Metallic red body, unpainted base, no hood label or tow hook, clear windows & black plastic tires.
2. Same as 1, but with mag wheels.
3. Same as 1, but bronze red body and (spiro) narrow type Super Fast wheels.
4. Same as 3, but with tow hook.
5. Same as 4, but amber windows & 5-spoke wheels.
6. Same as 4, but burgundy body colors & with hood label.
7. Same as 6, but amber windows.
8. Same as 6, but yellow base.
9. Same as 8, but no hood label.
10. Same as 7, but blue/yellow body.
11. Same as 8, but yellow body.
12. Same as 11, but amber windows.
13. Same as 11, but 5-spoke wheels.
14. Same as 12, but 5-spoke wheels.
15. Same as 14, but unpainted base.
16. Same as 13, but silver/gray base.

K-24-B   Scammell Container Truck   5¼"   1976
Red cab & chassis, silver/gray base, white or orange container, red, orange or blue container roof & various labels.
1. Red cab & chassis, red container roof, silver/gray base, white container & "Crowe" labels.
2. Same as 1, but orange container roof.
3. Same as 1, but orange container & "Michelin" label.
4. Same as 3, but "Bauknecht Kemplettkuchen" label.
5. Same as 1, but "Gentransco" label.
6. Same as 5, but blue container roof.

K-25-A   Powerboat and Trailer   6"   1971
Orange or red deck, white hull, yellow trailer, white, red or blue prop & "Seaburst" or "Chrysler" side labels. "Super 70" or "Chrysler" outboard labels.
1. Orange deck, white hull & prop, yellow trailer, "Seaburst" side labels & "Super 70" outboard labels.

2. Same as 1, but red prop.
3. Same as 2, but red deck & "Chrysler" side labels.
4. Same as 3, but orange deck & "Chrysler" outboard label.
5. Same as 4, but "Seaburst" side labels.
6. Same as 4.
7. Same as 4.
8. Same as 4, but blue prop.

K-25-B   Digger and Plough   5-1/8"   1977
Amber windows, red or orange body, base & plough, red interior, white driver, silver digger section with white "MH6" on red background label on sides & red "Muir Hill 161" with black stripes on white background labels over engine. Tires are black plastic with red hubs.
1. Red body, base & plough.
2. Orange body, base and plough.

K-26-A   Mercedes Benz "Binz" Ambulance 4-1/8"   1971
White body & interior, black base, light blue or blue windows. Blue dome light, red cross on white background hood label, blue "Ambulance" on white background labels on side of roof. Super Fast wheels.
1. Blue windows.
2. Light blue windows.

K-26-B   Cement Truck   4"   1978
Yellow or blue body, black or red base & barrel stripes, gray or blue barrel, clear or amber windows & "McAlpine" or "Hoch & Tief" labels.
1. Yellow body, black base, gray barrel with red barrel stripes, clear windows & "McAlpine" labels.
2. Same as 1, but black barrel stripes.
3. Blue body & barrel, red base & barrel stripes, clear windows, "Hoch & Tief" labels.
4. Same as 1, but red base.
5. Same as 2, but amber windows.

K-27-A   Camping Cruiser   4-3/8"   1971
Yellow body, amber, light amber, or clear front & rear window, orange roof, unpainted base & cream interior.
1. Yellow body, amber front & rear window, orange roof, unpainted base & cream interior.
2. Same as 1, but clear front window.
3. Same as 2, but clear rear window.
4. Same as 1, but light amber rear & front window.

K-27-B   Boat Transporter   10-1/8"   1978
Various colors on cab, with or without roof lines, amber or clear windows, orange or red trailer ramp, amber or blue boat windshield & various labels.
1. White cab, no roof lines, amber windows & boat windshield, red trailer ramp & "Embassy" labels.
2. Same as 1, but 5 roof lines & red cab.
3. Same as 1, but 5 roof lines.
4. Same as 3, but orange trailer ramp & "Benihana" labels.
5. Same as 4, but red cab.
6. Same as 4, but orange/white cab.
7. Same as 4, but orange cab.
8. Same as 2, but clear windows & blue boat windshield.
9. Same as 4, but orange cab & blue boat windshield.
10. Same as 9, but amber boat windshield.
11. Same as 2, but "Matchbox" labels.

K-28-A   Drag Pack   10"   1971
Mercury body in various shades of green. Red rack. Dragster in light pink, dark pink, or purple body with "Dinamite" labels. Yellow base on trailer with yellow or yellow/orange platform.
1. Mercury body is lime color with red rack, Dragster body is light pink with "Dinamite" labels. Trailer has a yellow base & platform.
2. Same as 1, but Mercury body is metallic green.
3. Same as 1, but Dragster body is purple.
4. Same as 3, but metallic green body on Mercury & orange/yellow platform on trailer.
5. Same as 4, but yellow platform on trailer.
6. Same as 4, but Mercury has dark lime body & Dragster has dark pink body.

K-28-B   Skip Truck   4-1/3"   1978

Orange or blue cab & orange or red skip arms, yellow or blue body, yellow or light blue container, black or red base & "Hales" or "Hoch & Tief" labels.
1. Orange cab & skip arms, yellow body & container, black base & "Hales" labels.
2. Blue cab & red skip arms, blue body, light blue containers, red base & "Hoch & Tief" labels.

K-29-A   Miura Seaburst Set   10"   1971
Bronze & red, burgundy or blue & yellow body, unpainted or yellow base, with or without hood label, clear windows, tow hook & spiro wheels. Boat & trailer have orange or red deck, white hull, yellow trailer, red prop, "Seaburst" or "Chrysler" side labels & "Super 70" outboard labels.
1. Bronze red body, unpainted base, no hood label & clear or amber windows, tow hood & spiro or 5-spoke wheels. Powerboat & trailer has orange deck, white hull, yellow trailer, red prop, "Seaburst" side labels & "Super 70" outboard labels.
2. Car is same as 1, but burgundy body color, clear or amber windows, with or without hood label. Boat & trailer same as 1, but unpainted or yellow base, red deck & "Chrysler" side labels.
3. Car is same as 1, but with blue/yellow body, unpainted or yellow base. Boat & trailer are same as 2.

K-29-B   Ford Delivery Van   4-1/3"   1978
Orange/white, red or white cab, white or dark green base, gray, red or lime container, five or no roof lines, various labels.
1. Orange/white cab, white base, gray container, 5 roof lines, & "U-Haul" labels.
2. Red cab & container, white base, 5 roof lines & "Avis" labels.
3. Same as 2, but no roof lines.
4. White cab, dark green base, lime container, five roof lines & "Mr. Softy" labels.
5. Same as 4, but white base.
6. Same as 2, but white cab.
7. Blue cab, white chassis, white container with side "Jelly Babies" labels.

K-30-A   Mercedes C III   4"   1972
Various body, base & window colors, black or gold headlight covers & with or without "3" label.
1. Gold body, red base, purple windows, black headlight covers & no label. Battery compartment instead of engine. Early models with horizontal switch on base, and later models with vertical switch on base.
2. Lime body, gold base & headlights covers, amber windows & no label.
3. Same as 2, but with black headlight covers.
4. Blue body, white base, amber windows, black headlight covers & black no. 3 on yellow label.
5. Same as 2, but purple windows.
6. Same as 5, but pale amber windows.
7. Same as 6, but clear windows.
8. Same as 6, but orange base.
9. Same as 7, but dark lime body.
10. Gold body, red base, purple windows, black headlight covers & no label.

K-30-B   Unimog and Compressor   7¼"   1978
Yellow, beige or gray body, brown or black base, red interior, amber windows, & brown or red compressor.
1. Beige body.
2. Gray body.
3. Yellow body, black base, & red compressor.

K-31-A   Bertone Runabout   4"   1972
Orange body, lime base, black interior, serpent hood label.
1. Green windows.
2. Clear windows.

K-31-B   Peterbilt Refrigerator Truck   11-7/8"   1978
Red or white cab, hood, roof & sleeper. White or unpainted air conditioner & blue, red or black base. Trailer is blue, red or black, contain-

er is white or red, roof is white or black & labels are varied.
1. Cab, hood, roof, sleeper & air conditioner are white. Base is blue. Trailer is blue with white container & roof, "Iglo Langnese" label.
2. Same as 1, but "Christian Salvesan" label.
3. Same as 1, but red cab & base, red trailer & container & "Coca-Cola" label.
4. Same as 1, but unpainted air conditioner & "Glaces Gervais" label.
5. Same as 1, but blue roof on trailer & "Pepsi-Cola" label.
6. Same as 1, but white roof on cab, black trailer, & "Burger King" label.
7. Same as 3, but red hood on cab.
8. Same as 7, but red roof on cab.
9. Same as 8, but red sleeper & unpainted air conditioner.
10. Same as 4, but "Christian Salvesan" label.
11. Same as 6, but "Iglo Langnese" label.

K-32-A   Shovel Nose   4"   1972
Yellow body, black or yellow base & interior, clear or amber windows, no. K-32 or K-32/40 on base & no. 2 or 4 label.
1. Yellow body, black base & interior, clear windows, no. K-32 on base & no. 2 label.
2. Same as 1, but no. K-32/40 on base & no. 4 label.
3. Same as 1, but amber windows.
4. Same as 2, but amber windows.
5. Same as 2, but yellow base & interior.

K-32-B   Farm Unimog and Trailer   8-7/8"   1978
Unimog—gray body, dark brown base, red interior & grille, amber windows, brown or yellow plastic insert in cab bed. Trailer—gray body & ramp, dark brown base, brown fence stakes, white tow hook, plastic farmer & sheep & dog.
1. Brown plastic insert in cab bed.
2. Yellow plastic insert in cab bed.

K-33-A   Citroen SM   4½"   1972
Magenta body, silver/gray base & green windows. With or without tow hook & heater lines.
1. With tow hook & no heater lines.
2. Same as 1, but with heater lines.
3. Same as 2, but no tow hook.

K-33-B   Cargo Hauler
Blue cab, white or orange base, blue container and decal.
1. White base & "U.S. Steel Corporation" decal.
2. Orange base & "Gauntlet International" decal.

K-34-A   Thunderclap   1972
Various body colors.
1. Yellow body.
2. Black body.
3. White body.
4. Red body.

K-34-B   Pallet Truck and Forklift   5-5/8"   1979
White body with dark blue painted roof & white interior. Dark blue base, grille & side tanks, clear windows, blue tarps with "K" labels with white or yellow background or "MW" labels on tarp. 3 gray plastic crates with brown, dark brown, or light brown tops. No. 15 Forklift in red with long red pallet, unpainted or black base.
1. Light or dark brown or brown crate tops.
2. "MW" labels on tarp.

K-35-A   Lightning   4¼"   1972
Red or white body, unpainted base. Various hood, side & spoiler labels.
1. Red body, hood label "Team 35 Matchbox" and side label "35" on wedge shape, and "STP -----30-50" spoiler label.
2. White body, hood label "STP 35 -----", side label "35" on rectangle, spoiler label "Texaco".
3. Same as 2, but hood label "Team 35 Matchbox" and spoiler label "STP ....
4. Same as 1, but all labels "Flame out".
5. Same as 1, but white body.

K-35-B   Massey Ferguson Tractor and Trailer   8-7/8"   1979
Tractor—red body, silver/gray base, white plastic canopy, white steering

wheel, & black exhaust stack & grille. Silver plated engine. "MF 595" labels in black on white background. Trailer—red body (cast K-35) with silver/gray base (cast K-32). Brown plastic stakes, six straw colored hay bales, & white tow hook.

K-36-A   Bandalero   4½"   1972
Blue body, red or black base, white or yellow interior, clear or amber windows, white steering wheel & no. K-36 or K-36/41 on base.
1. Blue body, red base, white interior & steering wheel, amber windows & no. K-36 on base.
2. Same as 1, but no. K-36/41 on base.
3. Same as 2, but clear windows.
4. Same as 3, but yellow interior.
5. Same as 4, but amber windows.
6. Same as 5, but black base.
7. Same as 6, but white interior.

K-36-B   Construction Transporter   6-3/8"   1978
Dark yellow body, yellow interior, silver/gray painted base & amber windows. Black "Laing" on yellow background side labels. Black or yellow plastic ramp & support section. With no. 26, no. 29 shovel of varying colors or no. 48 Sambron or lime K-28-A (Mercury Commuter).
1. Black plastic ramp & support section.
2. Yellow plastic ramp & support section.
3. Same as 1, but no. 29 shovel replaced with no. 48 Sambron.
4. Same as 1, both no. 26 & no. 29 replaced by lime K-28-A Mercury Commuter.

K-37-A   Sand Cat   3-3/8"   1973
Orange, red or gold plated body, green or orange base, black or gray roof & interior, various labels & with or without green spatter.
1. Orange body & base, black roof & interior, tiger type hood ornament & green spatter.
2. Red body, green base, gray base, gray roof & interior, no. 3 label & no spatter.
3. Same as 1, but gold plated body, stripes label & no spatter.
4. Same as 2, but black roof.

K-37-B   Leyland Tipper   4-1/3"   1979
Yellow cab & chassis, white painted roof, red tipper, silver/gray painted base & grille & amber windows. "Laing" labels on tipper sides. "Laing" & "Leyland" imprinted on front of cab. Black plastic hydraulic lift sleeves.

K-38-A   Gus's Gulper   4¼"   1973
Black base, white steering wheel, silver plated engine & exhaust & Stars & Stripes hood & roof labels. "Gulper" side labels and "STP/Firestone/20-50" spoiler labels. Pink or dark pink body & yellow or light yellow interior. Yellow, light yellow, or orange roll bar & clear windows.
1. Pink body, yellow interior & roll bar. Clear windows.
2. Dark pink body, light yellow interior & roll bar. Clear windows.
3. Pink body, orange interior & roll bar. Clear windows.

K-38-B   Dodge Ambulance   5-1/3"   1980
White body, white plastic roof, orange painted hood & side stripes & black plastic base. White interior, blue windows, amber dome & side lights & mag wheels. Silver plated beacon, antennae, etc., reversed "Ambulance" hood label & ambulance labels over windshield and on roof sides. Blue & white medical cross on sides.

K-39-A   Milligan's Mill   4½"   1973
Light or dark green body, orange or yellow interior & roll bar, A or B roof & spoiler labels & clear or blue windows. Black base, white steering wheel, silver plated engine & exhaust & "Milligan's Mill" labels on hood & sides.
1. Light green body, orange interior & roll bar, "A" roof & spoiler labels & clear windows.
2. Same as 1, but dark green body.
3. Same as 1, but yellow interior.
4. Same as 3, but yellow roll bar.
5. Dark green body, orange interior & roll bar, "B" roof & spoiler labels & clear windows.
6. Same as 5, but "A" roof & spoiler labels & blue windows.

K-39-B   Simon Snorkel Fire Engine   8¼"   1980

Red body & base, black interior & amber windows & dome lights. Silver painted roof & body panels, red supports & white lift section with 2 red knobs & 2 red ladders. Red lift platform, black "Simon Snorkel" on lift, "County Fire Department" labels & 4 dark blue firemen. (May be found with lead man in pale blue).

K-40-A   Blaze Trailer   4"   1973
Red body, yellow or black base, orange or yellow interior, clear or amber windows, orange, yellow or black antennae, white steering wheel & blue or amber dome lights.
1. Yellow base, orange interior & antennae, amber windows, white steering wheel & blue dome lights.
2. Yellow base, interior & antennae, clear windows, white steering wheel & blue dome lights.
3. Same as 1, but clear windows.
4. Same as 2, but black base.
5. Same as 2, but black antennae.
6. Same as 5, but amber windows.
7. Same as 5, but amber dome lights.

K-40-B   Pepsi Delivery Truck   5-1/3"   1980
White cab with painted red or blue roof, white plastic container with blue roof & red or blue base. White plastic tarp sides with "Pepsi" emblem. "Pepsi" emblem at rear with "Pepsi-Cola" on front of container & blue base.
1. Red cab roof & red base.
2. Blue cab roof & base.

K-41-A   Fuzz Buggy   4½"   1973
White body, black or red base & clear or amber windows. White, yellow or yellow/orange interior, blue or amber dome lights & black, yellow or white steering wheel, orange lift-up door, silver plated engine with black plastic engine attachment, "Police" labels on top & sides of door & "K-36/41" label.
1. Black base, amber windows, yellow interior, blue dome lights & black steering wheel.
2. Same as 1, but amber dome lights & yellow steering wheel.
3. Same as 2, but yellow/orange interior & white steering wheel.
4. Same as 3, but clear windows & white interior.
5. Same as 4, but yellow interior & blue dome lights.
6. Same as 5, but white interior.
7. Same as 5, but white steering wheel.
8. Same as 7, but clear windows.
9. Same as 7, but red base.
10. Same as 8, but red base.

K-41-B   Brabham BT 44B   4¼"   1977
Red body, base & spoiler, white driver, black windscreen, & silver plated engines. No labels, "Martini—Brabham", "7" & stripes imprint markings. "Goodyear" or "IΔVΔ///∠" on front airfoils.
1. "Goodyear" on front airfoils.
2. "IΔVΔ///∠" on front airfoils.

K-41-C   JCB Excavator   9-7/8"   1981
Yellow body, base, excavator arm & extension. Red scoop, white lift-up cab unit, "808" labels, opening engine compartment, black treads & white driver.

K-42-A   Nissan 270X   4"   1973
Orange body, green base, yellow interior, green or clear windows, "8" labels.
1. Orange body, green base, yellow interior, green windows & "8" label.
2. Same as 1, but clear windows.

K-42-B   Traxcavator Road Ripper   5½"   1979
Yellow body, base, shovel, shovel arms & rear ripper. Black plastic roof with "1" label on top. White driver, black treads, black rollers, & black exhaust stack.

K-43-A   Cambuster   4-3/8"   1973
Yellow body & black or yellow base. Green, clear or amber windows & small or large exhaust. Silver plated interior, engine & exhausts, white steering wheel & "Cambuster" labels on sides & roof.
1. Yellow body, black base, green windows & small exhaust.

2. Same as 1, but clear windows.
3. Same as 1, but amber windows.
4. Same as 1, but large exhaust.
5. Same as 4, but yellow base.
6. Same as 5, but black base.
7. Same as 3, but yellow base.

K-43-B   Log Transporter   12-2/5"   1981
K-44-A   Bazooka   4-3/8"   1973
Red body, yellow or black base, amber, light amber & green windows, "Bazooka" or "Firestone" side labels.
1. Red body, yellow base, amber windows, "Bazooka" side labels.
2. Same as 1, but "Firestone" labels.
3. Same as 1, but light amber windows.
4. Same as 1, but black base.
5. Same as 4, but green windows.
6. Same as 5, but black base.
7. Same as 2, but black base.

K-44-A   Surtees Formula I   4¼"   1977
White body, base, driver & spoiler. Red airfoil, silver plated engine, & amber windshield. "Chesterfield, 18, Goodyear" and "Benrus" labels on hood, sides & spoiler.

K-44-C   Bridge Layer   13-1/8"   1981
K-45-A   Marauder   4-1/8"   1973
Bergundy or red body, amber windshield, green or black base, orange or yellow interior & airfoil. "7" or "Cibie" labels, & white or tan driver.
1. Burgundy body, green base, orange interior & airfoil, "7" label & white driver.
2. Same as 1, but yellow interior & airfoil.
3. Same as 1, but orange interior.
4. Same as 1, but yellow airfoil.
5. Same as 2, but tan driver.
6. Same as 2, but amber windshield.
7. Red body, black base, yellow interior & airfoil, "Cibie" labels & white driver.
8. Same as 7, but with "Super Kings" cast on base.

K-46-A   Racing Car Pack   10¼"   1973
Yellow or lime body, no. K-23 or K-46 on base, red or maroon roof rack, various racers in pack, white base & blue or black platform.
1. Yellow body on car & no. K-23 on base with red roof rack. No. 34-A1 racer & trailer with yellow base & blue platform.
2. Same as 1, but no. 34-A2 racer.
3. Same as 1, but no. 34-A3 racer.
4. Same as 1, but no. 35-A2 racer.
5. Same as 4, but no. K-46 on base of car.
6. Same as 5, but no. 35-A3 racer.
7. Same as 6, but no. 35-A1 racer.
8. Same as 7, but no. 34-A3 racer.
9. Same as 8, but no. 35-A3 racer & black trailer platform.
10. Same as 1, but lime body on car.
11. Same as 5, but maroon roof rack.

K-47-A   Easy Rider   4¾"   1973
Blue body & seat, silver handlebars, various colored rider, & flame label.
1. Blue body & seat, silver handlebars, tannish/brown rider & flame label.
2. Same as 1, but orange rider.
3. Same as 1, but white rider.
4. Same as 1, but "Super Kings" on base & no tank labels.

K-48-A   Mercedes 350 SLC   4-1/8"   1973
Bronze body, silver/gray base, yellow interior, clear or amber windows & no. K-48 or K-61/48 on base.
1. Clear windows & no. K-48 on base.
2. Same as 1, but amber windows & no. K-61/48 on base.

K-49-A   Ambulance   4-3/8"   1973
Red or white body & interior, red or cream roof, black or cream base, various colored windows, blue or clear dome light, & "Ambulance" or "Malteser" labels.
1. White body, red roof & interior, black base, clear windows, blue

dome light & "Ambulance" label.
2. Same as 1, but white interior.
3. Red body, cream roof & base, white interior, pale blue windows, blue dome light & "Malteser" labels.
4. Same as 1, but amber windows.
5. Same as 3, but dark blue windows & clear dome light.

K-50-A   Street Rod   4"   1973
Various body, base & fender colors, no. K-50/53 or K-50 on base, with or without "Hot T" labels & black roof interior.
1. Lime body, dark green base & fenders, no. K-50/53 on base, "Hot T" label & black roof & interior.
2. Orange body, gold plated base & fenders, no. K-50/53 on base, no labels & black roof & interior.
3. Same as 1, but pine green base & fenders & no. K-50 on base.
4. Same as 1, but dark green body.

K-51-A   Barracuda   4¼"   1973
Blue, dark blue or white body & black base. Yellow, orange or white interior & orange, yellow, or lemon airfoil. Clear or amber windshield, no. 5 or 14 label & white driver.
1. Blue body, black base, yellow interior, orange airfoil, clear windshield, no. 5 label & white driver.
2. Same as 1, but yellow airfoil.
3. Same as 2, but orange interior.
4. Same as 3, but dark blue body & yellow interior.
5. Same as 4, but amber windshield & white driver with red hat.
6. Same as 5, but white body & interior. No. 14 label.
7. White body & driver, "Super King" cast on black base, yellow interior & airfoil, amber windshield & No. 14 label.
8. Same as 1, but lemon colored airfoil.

K-52-A   Datsun Rally Car   4-1/8"   1974
Various body & hood colors, black base, various labels, clear windows, with or without base hole.
1. Yellow body, black base with no hole, red hood, clear windows, & no. 52 label with red background color.
2. Same as 1, but silver body & no. 52 label with black background color.
3. Same as 2, but no. 52 label with red background color.
4. Same as 3, but red hood.
5. Same as 4, but no. 52 label with black background color.
6. Same as 2, but with hole in base.
7. Green body, black base with hole, white hood, clear windows, & "Cibie" label.

K-53-A   Hot Fire Engine   3-7/8"   1976
Red body & base, black interior, black or blue riders with various colored helmets.
1. Red body & base, black interior & riders with gold helmets.
2. Same as 1, but riders have white helmets.
3. Same as 2, but riders are blue.
4. Same as 3, but riders helmets are blue.

K-54-A   AMX Javelin   4¼"   1976
Burgundy or red body, silver/gray base, yellow interior, various window shades & various labels on roof, hood & sides.
1. Burgundy body, silver/gray base, yellow interior, green windows, & no. 7 roof, hood & side labels.
2. Red body, silver/gray base, yellow interior, dark green windows, no roof or hood labels, & no. 24 label on sides.
3. Same as 2, but clear windows, no. 24 roof label & stripe hood label.
4. Same as 1, but dark windows.
5. Same as 3, but black body & no labels.

K-55-A   Corvette Caper Cart   4¼"   1976
Blue or red body, blue or black roof & yellow or orange/yellow interior. Clear windows, silver gray base, with or without no. 55 label.
1. Blue body & roof, yellow interior, clear windows, silver/gray base & no. 55 labels.
2. Same as 1, but red body, black roof & no labels.

3. Same as 1, but orange/yellow interior.

K-56-A   Maserati Bora   4"   1976
Silver or gold body, red or gold base & yellow or orange interiors. Clear or amber windows, with or without labels.
1. Silver body with labels, red base, yellow interior & clear windows.
2. Same as 1, but orange interior.
3. Same as 2, but amber interior.
4. Same as 3, but yellow interior.
5. Gold body with no labels, gold base, orange interior & clear windows.
6. Same as 5, but red body.

K-57-A   Javelin Drag Race Pack   9¾"   1976
Various shades of no. 54A Javelin hauling no. 39-A in various shades on yellow trailer.
1. Javelin is no. K-54-A1, race car is "Milligan's Mill" no. K-39-A1 & trailer is yellow.
2. Same as 1, but Javelin is no. K-54-A2 & race car is no. K-39-A3.
3. Same as 2, but race car is no. K-39-A4.
4. Same as 3, but race car is no. K-38-A1 "Gus's Gulper".
5. Same as 1, but Javelin is no. K-54-A3 & race car is no. K-39-A3.

K-58-A   Corvette Powerboat Set   10-1/8"   1976
Various shades of K-55-A Corvette & K-25-A Boat & Trailer.
1. No. K-55-A1 Corvette with no. K-25-A3 Boat & Trailer.
2. Same as 1, but Corvette is no. K-55-A2.
3. No. K-55-A3 with no. K-25-A4 Boat & Trailer.
4. Same as 3, but no. K-55-A1 Corvette.
5. Same as 4, but no. K-25-A7 Boat & Trailer.

K-59-A   Ford Capri II   4-1/8"   1976
White & beige body, various colors on roof, black base, clear windows, with or without "Capri II labels.
1. White body, black roof & base, clear windows & "Capri II" labels.
2. Same as 1, but beige body.
3. Same as 2, but beige roof & no labels.
4. Same as 2, but white roof.
5. Same as 2, but dark brown roof.

K-60-A   Ford Mustang II   4¼"   1976
Blue body with white interior & black plastic base. Black steering wheel, green windows & silver plated side exhausts & rear parachute case. 2 windows cast on each side & Mustang & "20" labels on hood, roof & sides.

K-60-B   Cobra Mustang   4¼"   1978
White body & interior, no hood or side exhausts, green windows, black steering wheel & black plastic base. Silver plated license plate instead of parachute case. One window cast on each side. 2nd "window" is cast as part of the body as a louvre. Cobra decals on hood, roof & sides and "Speed Kings" or "Super Kings" cast on base.
1. "Speed Kings" cast on base.
2. "Super Kings" cast on base.

K-61-A   Mercedes Police Car   4¼"   1976
White body, white or green hood & doors, yellow or bright yellow interior, amber windows, no. K-48 or K-61/48 cast on base, "Police" or "Polizei" door labels & various wheel patterns.
1. White body, hood & doors, yellow interior, amber windows, no. K-61/48 on base, "Police" door labels & 5-spoke wheel pattern.
2. Same as 1, but mo. K-48 on base & "Polizei" door labels.
3. Same as 1, but no. K-61/48 on base.
4. Same as 3, but green hood & doors.
5. Same as 4, but with no. K-48 on base.
6. Same as 4, but with "Police" door labels.
7. Same as 4, but bright yellow interior.
8. Same as 6, but bright yellow interior.
9. Same as 1, but 5-arch wheel pattern.
10. Same as 4, but 5-arch wheel pattern.
11. Same as 4, but with wide 5-spoke wheel patterns.

K-62-A   Doctor's Emergency Car   4½"   1977
White body, silver/red or gray base, amber windows & dome light, white steering wheel & "Doctor" labels.

1. Silver/gray base.
2. Red base.

K-63-A Mercedes Benz "Binz" Ambulance 4-1/8" 1977
White or cream body, white interior, black base, dark or pale blue windows & dome & "Speed Kings" or "Super Kings" on base.
1. White body & interior, black base, dark blue windows & dome & "Speed Kings" on base.
2. Same as 1, but paler blue windows & dome & "Super Kings" on base.
3. Same as 2, but cream body.

K-64-A Range Rover Fire Engine 4-1/8" 1978
Red body, black base & interior, amber dome light, yellow ladder, "Fire" or "Falck" labels & various colored firemen & hats.
1. Red body, black base & interior, amber dome light, yellow ladder, "Fire" labels & black firemen with gold hats.
2. Same as 1, but firemen have white hats.
3. Same as 1, but with "Falck" labels.
4. Same as 1, but with turcuoise/blue firemen.
5. Same as 1, but with white ladder.

K-65-A Plymouth Trail Duster 4½" 1979
Red or green body, white base, interior & canopy, amber windows & "Emergency Rescue" or "Bergrettungwacht" labels.
1. Red body & "Emergency Rescue" labels.
2. Green body & "Bergrettungwacht" labels.

K-66-A Jaguar XJ12 Police Patrol 4¾" 1979
White body & base. Various colored interior & dome lights. No. 1, 2, 3, or 4 side labels & maltese cross wheels or mag wheels.
1. White body & base, brown interior, pale dome lights, single blue stripe label, & maltese cross wheels.
2. Same as 1, but 2 blue stripes with central orange stripe label.
3. Same as 2, but clear dome lights.
4. Same as 2, but dark blue dome lights.
5. Same as 4, but black interior.
6. Same as 4, but 2 blue stripes without orange stripe label.
7. Same as 4, but County Police & Checkered design label.
8. Same as 7, but ivory interior & mag wheels.

K-67-A Dodge Monaco Fire Chief Car 4½" 1978
Red or yellow body & interior, red or black base, red or white roof, amber windows, blue or red dome light & "Fire Chief" or "Hackensack" decals.
1. Red body & base, white roof, yellow interior, amber windows, blue dome light & "Fire Chief" decals.
2. Yellow body, black base, white roof, red interior & dome light, amber windows & "Hackensack" decals.
3. Same as 1, but red roof.

K-68-A Dodge Monaco and Trailer 8¼" 1979
Beige body & base, dark brown roof & red interior on Monaco. Beige body & beige or black canopy on trailer.
1. Beige canopy on trailer.
2. Black canopy on trailer.

K-69-A Jaguar Sedan and Europa Caravan 10-2/3" 1980
Jaguar has red or blue body & base & brown or ivory interior, with or without mag wheels. Caravan has white or beige body & base. White, beige, & unpainted gas cover, with or without maltese cross wheels.
1. Blue body on Jaguar with brown interior. Caravan has a white body & gas cover & a beige base.
2. Same as 1, but Jaguar has a red body & base with ivory interior.
3. Same as 2, but with mag wheels on Jaguar & Caravan.
4. Blue body & base with brown interior on Jaguar and beige body. White base & gas cover.
5. Same as 3, but beige gas cover on Caravan & mag wheels on Jaguar & Caravan.
6. Same as 5, but unpainted gas cover on Jaguar & Caravan.
7. Same as 6, but with maltese cross wheels on Caravan.

K-70-A Porsche Turbo 4-5/8" 1979
Dark green or lime body, lime base, dark green trunk, black interior & clear windows.

1. Dark green body.
2. Lime body.

K-71-A Porsche Polizei Patrol 7-7/8" 1980
White body & base, black interior, blue dome light & dark green doors, hood & trunk. Clear windows, "K-70" cast on base & "Polizei" & "1705" labels.

K-72-A Brabham BT 44B 4¼" 1980
Silver plated engine, no labels, black windscreen. "Martini–Brabham", "7" and stripes imprint markings. Base cast "K-72". This was originally no. K-41-B.
1. Red body, base & spoiler, white driver.
2. Green body, white spoiler & tan driver.

K-73-A Surtees Formula I 4¼" 1980
Amber windshield, red airfoil & silver plated engine. "Chesterfield, 18, Goodyear" & "Benrus" labels on hoods, side & spoiler. "K-73" cast on base. Originally K-44-B.
1. White body, base & spoiler & white driver.
2. Same as 1, but black spoiler & tan driver.

K-74-A Volvo Estate 5-3/8" 1980
Dark red body, black base, white interior, black plastic front & rear bumpers, white plastic tow hook & mag wheel. With or without black rectangular roof label toward front.
1. With roof label.
2. Without roof label.

K-75-A Airport Fire Tender 5-1/3" 1979
Yellow body, red base, white interior, amber windows & various labels.
1. "Airport Fire Tender" label.
2. "Securite Aeroport" label.
3. "Flughafen-Feurwehr" label.

K-76-A Volvo Rally Set 10-5/8" 1980
Volvo has a white body & black base. Hood & door labels & a dark brown or tan plastic roof rack & accessories. The Datsun has a green body, black base & white hood. "Cibie" labels, plastic tow assembly & 3 blue plastic figures.
1. Tan plastic roof rack & accessories.
2. Dark brown plastic roof rack & accessories.

K-77-A Highway Rescue Vehicle 5-1/3" 1979
White body & plough, orange base, white interior, amber windows & various labels.
1. "Highway Rescue System" labels.
2. "Secours Routier" labels.
3. "Strassen Service" labels.

K-78-A Gran Fury Police Car 5-3/8" 1980
Blue & white or black body. Black base, blue or white interior, clear windows & "Police" or "Polizei" side decals.
1. Blue & white body, black base, blue interior, clear windows & "Polizei" side decals.
2. Same as 1, but "Police" side decals.
3. Same as 2, but black body & white interior.
4. Same as 3, but blue interior.

K-79-A Gran Fury U.S. Taxi 5-3/8" 1981
Yellow body, black plastic base, red interior, black roof mount, clear windows, mag wheels, silver plastic grille & assorted labels on sides, hood & trunk.

K-80-A Dodge Custom Van 5-1/3" 1980
Light & dark blue body, black base, clear windows & white flowered or white plain interior.
1. Light blue body, black base, white flowered interior & clear windows.
2. Same as 1, but white plain interior.
3. Same as 2, but dark blue body.

K-81-A Suzuki Motorcycle 4-1/3" 1981
K-82-A BMW Motorcycle 4-1/3" 1981
Silver body, black seat, front & side assemblies. Silver plated exhausts, wheel assembly & mag wheels. Black plastic tires & blue or red plastic rider with white helmet & black gloves & boots. "BMW" label on side tanks & clear windshield.

1. Blue driver.
2. Red driver.

K-83-A Harley Davidson Motorcycle & Rider 1982
White plastic body & fenders, black plastic seats & luggage racks, light tan gas tank, chrome engine, chrome handlebars, amber windshield, & blue driver. Gray mag wheels with black plastic tires, red tail lights, "Police" and "83" labels.

K-84-A Peugeot 305 1981
Blue or white body with black or white interior. Clear windows, black plastic base & grille, amber head lights, and mag wheels.
1. Blue body with white interior.
2. Same as 1, but with black interior.
3. White body with black interior, and red & blue decals with stripes, "Expo" and "14".

K-85-A not issued.

K-86-A V.W. Golf 1981
Black body with white interior, clear windows, black base & grille, side decal orange, red, & yellow. White plastic gas pump.

K-87-A Tractor and Rotary Rake 1981
Red tractor with silver/gray base, white plastic canopy & steering wheel, black plastic exhaust stack & grille, silver plated engine, & labels "MF 595" Rake is orange with yellow plastic rakes, black & yellow striped label on a shield, and black plastic tires.

K-88-A Money Box 1981
White body with blue painted roof, and white container with blue roof cast with coin slot. Black windows and back door, black base cast K-19. Labels blue, white & orange reading "Volksbank Raiffeisenbank".

K-89-A Forestry Range Rover & Trailer 1982
Yellow Range Rover with green roof rack, brown ladder and clear dome light & windows. Brown interior, gray grille, black base with K-64 cast. Decals read "Kellder Forest". Yellow trailer with black base & brown stakes, light brown tree trunk, dark green stand, and green fronds, with blue man.

K-90-A Matra Rancho 1982
Red body & base with white painted roof. Black windscreen, window trim & side molding, grille, & tow hook. Clear windows, decal on hood reads "Trans Globe Couriers".

K-91-A Motorcycle Racing Set 1982
Metallic silver Plymouth automobile with red interior and tow hook, clear windows. Decals on hood: red "Speed", blue "Track", black "Champion". On trunk: blue "MH", red "Racing". On roof: black "48". On sides: red, black, blue & white "Castle", "4", "Motor cycle racing", "Radio Eastside", and "Seutron Bikes". Red trailer with two 33-D Cycles with white bodies, red seats and wind guard. Labels "4", chrome engine, and mag wheels.

K-92-A Helicopter Transporter 1982
K-93-A Lamp Maintenance Set 1982
Unimog truck, yellow body with orange arm & yellow plastic bucket. Red interior and grille, clear windows, black plastic base cast "K-93," red & yellow striped label on sides, "Autoroute Services" on hood. Separate white plastic lamp in green stand, white man in bucket.

K-94-A Not isssued.

K-95-A Audi Quattro 1982
White body with black and red racing paint job, black interior.

K-96-A Not issued.

K-97-A Not issued.

K-98-A Forestry Unimog 7¼" 1979
Unimog has a dark green body & red base, interior, & grille. Amber windows, tan plastic canopy, "K-30" cast on base & "Forstamt" & striped labels. Trailer has a dark green body, straw-colored hay bales, "K-30" cast on base & striped label.

K-99-A Range Rover Polizei Set 4-1/8" 1979
Cream body, green interior, mount, & side panels. Green painted hood & side stripes & dark green tailgate. Black base, blue dome lights & "Polizei" labels.

Adventure 2000

This series was introduced in the 1977 catalog with the following opening remarks:

> The year—2000 A.D. Aliens attack earth!
> Disaster on the Antarctic!
> 'Adventure 2000' the new range of all action packed
> vehicles from "MATCHBOX" to the rescue.

For the first time in Lesney Products history the toys were of imaginery design. Their outer-space military orientation followed the popularity of the Battle Kings (1974) and Two Packs (1976) which also carry out military themes. By 1982 there were six toys in this series. Cast plastic soldiers were also packaged with the toys by 1981. The Adventure 2000 series was not included in the 1982 Matchbox catalog.

K2001	Raider Command, in two parts	6-1/3"	1977	
K2002	Flight Hunter	4-3/5"	1977	
K2003	Crusader Tank	4-3/8"	1977	
K2004	Rocket Striker	4-3/8"	1978	
	(Same as Battle King 111 Missile Launcher in different colors)			
K2005	Command Force		1977	
	(Including: No. 68 Cosmobile, No. 59 Planet Scout, No. 2 Hovercraft, and K2004)			
K2006	Shuttle Launcher		1982	

Gift Sets

Groups of toys related by their theme were packaged together in sets in 1967 to create a new series called "Gift Sets". These proved to be quite successful and have been continued with notable variations to the present. In 1970 the name of the series changed to "Super Sets" to reflect the use of "Superfast" toys with "Superfast" wheels, but gradually the term "Gift Set" was restored and is used currently. Out of the variety of Matchbox 1-75 toys, Accessories, Yesteryear series, and Skybusters, groups of from three to ten toys are grouped and boxed together. These gift sets include service and fire stations, car transport groups, farm and construction equipment, racing sets, and airplanes.

G1-A   Service Station Set   1967
Contains: MG1-B Two story garage, with vehicles 13, 31, 64, and A1-B (BP) pumps (was G10 in 1964).

G1-B   Service Station Superset   1970
Contains: MG1-C One-story garage and pumps, with 3 vehicles.

G1-C   Car Transporter Set   1979

G2-A   Car Transporter Set   1967
Contains: No's. 22, 28, 36, 75, and K8.

G2-B   Transporter Superset   1970

G2-C   Big Mover Transporter Set   1973
Includes Transport Truck and five cars.

G2-D   Railway Set   1979

G3-A   Vacation Set   1967
Contains: 12, 23, 27, 42, 45, 56, 68, and Sports Boat on trailer.

G3-B   Farm Set   1968

G3-C   Superfast Racing Specials   1970

G3-D   "Wild Ones" Set   1973
Includes five Mod cars.

G3-E   Racing Car Set   1979

G4-A   Racetrack Set   1967
Contains: No's. 13, 19 (green), 19 (orange), 29, 41 (white), 41 (yellow), 52 (blue), 52 (red), 54, K5 and R-4.

G4-B   Race-n' Rally Set   1968

G4-C   Truck Superset   1970

G4-D   Team "Matchbox" Set   1973
Includes racing car transporter and 4 racing cars. In 1976 was called "Superfast Champions".

G4-E   Military Assault Set   1979

G4-F   Convoy Set   1982
Includes 10G Police Car, 61E Peterbilt Wreck Truck and 3 Convoy Series toys, CY3, CY7, and CY8.

G5-A   Fire Station Set   1967
Contains MF1 Fire Station and cars No's 29, 54, and 59.

G5-B   Famous Cars of Yesteryear Set   1968
Contains four Yesteryear toys.

G5-C   Construction Set   1979

G6-A   Commercial Truck Set   1967
Contains: No's. 16, 17, 25, 26, 30, 69, 70, and 71.

G6-B   Drag Race Set   1972
Includes a Launching Track and six cars.

G6-C   Farm Set   1979

G7-A   "Models of Yesteryear" Set   1967
Contains Y1, Y3, Y11, and Y14.

G7-B   Ferry Boat and four cars   1972

G7-C   Emergency Set   1979

G8-A   King Size Set   1967
Contains K1, K11, K12, and K15.

G8-B   Thunder Jets   1979

G9-A   Commando Task Force   1976

G10-A   Fire Station and 4 vehicles   1964
Station is MF1 Accessory and vehicles are 14C, 59B, and two 9B's.

G10-B   Thunder Jets   1976
Includes four Skybusters airplanes.

G11-A   Strike Force   1976

G12-A   Rescue Set   1976

G13-A   Construction Site   1976

G14-A   Grand Prix Set   1976

G15-A   Car Transporter Set   1976

G16-A   Sky Giants   1978
Includes four civilian airplanes.

G17-A   Car Ferry   1977
Includes four cars and the ferry boat.

G18-A   Sky Giants   1979

G100   Twin Thunderbolt Launcher Set   1976

Skybusters

Military and civilian airplanes were released in 1973 by Lesney Products as a series called "Sky Busters". Sixteen toys were shown in the first advertisements, and the series has grown to twenty-eight planes so far. A few new toys have been issued to replace discontinued planes.

SB-1-A   Learjet   4-1/16"   1973
Yellow upper fuselage and tail. White lower fuselage and wings. Dark blue window insert. Three wheels on wire supports. A sticker on top of each wing with small black, orange & yellow striped block and D-ILDE in black letters on white background.

SB-2-A   Corsair A7D   4-1/16"   1973
Metallic emerald green upper fuselage, wings and vertical tail section. White lower fuselage and horizontal tail section. Clear window insert. Three wheels on wire supports. A sticker on top of each wing with white star in 3/8" blue circle on white-red-white striped 21/32" rectangle with thin blue border. Top point of white star points to forward edge of wing. One on each side of tail, vertical trapezoidal, with large white 'LA' and small white '282' on green background. Wing stickers exist in shades of light to dark blue. White lettering on tail stickers varies slightly in size.

1. Model numbered 'SP-2'. Window insert either clear or tinted light blue.
2. Same as 1, but light blue tinted window insert. Two wheels under nose on short axle. Two wheels under wings on long axle. Reinforcing ridges on underside tip ends of wings and horizontal tail sections.
3. Same as 2, but blue upper fuselage.

SB-3-A   A300B Airbus   4-9/64"   1973
White upper fuselage and vertical tail section. Silver lower fuselage, wings, and horizontal tail section. Three wheels on wire supports. Stickers—one on each side of fuselage, 1-5/32" long, over wings with small red square, small dark blue square, and small "AIR France" on white background. V-shaped emblem sticker on each side of tail.

1. No tail stickers. Casting lettering on underside of fuselage and wings. Model numbered 'SP-3'. 2-1/16" rivet spacing.
2. Four-sided dark blue and white tail stickers. Casting lettering on underside of fuselage and wings. Model numbered 'SP-3'. 2-1/16" rivet spacing.
3. Five-sided blue tail stickers. Casting lettering on underside of fuselage and wings. Model numbered 'SP-3'. 2-1/16" rivet spacing.
4. Five-sided blue tail stickers. Casting lettering on underside of wings. 1-5/8" rivet spacing. Two wheels on rounded end axle in black plastic axle housing. Two wheels under wings on rounded end axle in black plastic axle suspension.
5. Five-sided blue tail stickers. No fuselage stickers. Casting letters on underside of fuselage and wings. Model numbered 'SP-3'. 2-1/16" rivet spacing. The small red and blue squares on the fuselage stickers can appear to the left or the right of the lettering on either side of fuselage in variations 1 to 5.
6. Casting lettering on underside of wings. 1-5/8" rivet spacing. Two wheels on short axle under nose. Two wheels on long axle under wings. No stickers. Imprint markings as follows: Steel blue window stripe with white windows, both sides of fuselage. Steel blue 'Lufthansa' and small 'D-AXJ1' above window panel, both sides. Gold emblem circle on steel blue panel, both sides of tail.
7. Casting lettering on underside of wings. 1-5/8" rivet spacing. Two wheels on short axle under nose. Two wheels on long axle under wings. No stickers. Imprint markings as follows: Steel blue windows with two lengthwise tapered end stripes below windows, both sides of fuselage. Blue or pale blue (two shades) 'Air France' above windows, both sides. Two steel blue chevrons on each side of vertical tail section.

SB-3-B   NASA Space Shuttle   4"   1980
White with black wheels. Gray nose and lower wings, black rocket exhaust pipes. "NASA United States" and flag on sides.

SB-4-A   Mirage F1   4-11/32"   1973
Metallic scarlet fuselage, wings and tail. Clear window insert. Three wheels on wire supports. Stickers—one on each wingtop, 7/16 ' multicolored bullseye. One on each side of tail, 1/2" vertical trapezoidal.

1. Small orange circle on white on blue on yellow bullseye on wing stickers. Orange, white, & blue vertical stripes on tail stickers. Model numbered 'SP-4'.
2. Large light orange circle on white on blue on yellow bullseye on wing stickers. Light orange, white, & blue vertical stripes on tail

stickers. Model numbered 'SP-4'.

3. Stickers same as 2, smoky tinted window insert. Two wheels under fuselage on rounded end axle. Two wheels under wings on long rounded end axle. Reinforcing ridges on underside of tip ends of wings and horizontal tail sections.

4. Same as 3, except tail stickers are 1/4'' tall.

SB-5-A Starfighter 4-17/64'' 1973
White upper fuselage and tail. Silver lower fuselage and wings. Blue window insert. Three wheels on wire supports. A sticker on top of each wing, 3/8'' circular with red maple leaf on white circle on dark blue circle. One on each side of tail, rectangular, with red maple leaf on white background with vertical blue stripe borders.

1. Stem of leaf on wing stickers points to rear edge of wing. Tail sticker, 3/8'' long, has wide white background.

2. Stem of leaf on wing stickers points to rear edge of wing. Tail sticker, 5/16'' long has narrow white background.

3. Stem of leaf on wing stickers points to front edge of wing. Tail sticker, 5/16'' long has narrow white background. Window inserts and wing stickers exist in shades of light to dark blue.

SB-6-A MIG 21 4¼'' 1973
Metallic blue (several shades) upper fuselage, wings, and tail. White lower fuselage. Clear window insert. Three wheels on wire supports. A sticker on top of each wing, 15/32'' star shaped with red star and thin white edging. Top point of stars points to forward edge of wing. One on each side of tail, 11/32'' star shaped with red star and thin white edging.

1. No tail stickers. Model numbered 'SP-6'.

2. With tail stickers. Model numbered 'SP-6'.

3. Stickers on wingtops and each side of tail are 13/32'' star shaped. Model numbered 'SP-6'.

4. Stickers on wingtops and each side of tail are 13/32'' star shaped. Two wheels under nose on short rounded end axle. Two wheels under wings on long rounded end axle. Reinforcing ridges on underside of tip ends of wings and horizontal tail sections.

5. As 4, except stickers on wingtops and each side of tail are 7/16'' circular with white outlined red star on blue background.

SB-7-A Junkers 87B 3-5/32'' 1973
Metallic shades varying from yellow/green to green fuselage, wings and tail. Clear window insert. Two wheels on wire supports under wings. One thin wheel at rear in fuselage. Single three blade black propeller with rounded blade ends. A sticker on top of each wing, 7/16'' cross-shaped, black cross with white edging. One on each side of tail with black swastika on 1/4'' square white background.

1. Swastika measures 7/32''. Model numbered 'SP-7'.

2. Swastika measures 3/16''. Model numbered 'SP-7'.

3. Swastika measures 3/16''. Model numbered 'SP-7'. Black upper fuselage and tail. Silver lower fuselage and wings.

4. Model numbered 'SP-7'. Stickers on sides of tail are 7/32'' cross-shaped, black cross with white edging.

5. Stickers as 2, two wheels under wings on long axle.

SB-8-A Spitfire 3-25/64'' 1973
Metallic green (several shades) upper fuselage and tail. Metallic gold lower fuselage and wings, very light blue window insert. Two wheels on wire supports under wings. One thin wheel at rear in fuselage. Single three blade black propeller with rounded blade ends. A sticker on top of each wing, 9/16'' circular with orange circle on dark blue circle. On each side of tail, 1/4'' tall, vertical trapezoidal with red/orange, white and blue vertical stripes.

1. Dark brown upper fuselage and tail. With tail stickers. Model numbered 'SP-8'.

2. Basic model as described. No tail stickers. Model numbered 'SP-8'.

3. Basic model as described. Model numbered 'SP-8'.

4. Dark brown upper fuselage and tail, with tail stickers. Model numbered 'SP-8'. Clear window insert.

5. Basic model as described, with tail stickers, model numbered 'SP-8'. Clear window insert.

6. Two wheels under wings on long axle. Model numbered 'SP-8'. With or without tail stickers.

SB-9-A Cessna 402 3-7/16'' 1973
Metallic yellow/green upper fuselage and tial, white lower fuselage & wings. Very light blue window insert, no window insert at side windows. Two 3-blade black propellers with squared ends. 3 wheels on wire supports. A sticker on each engine top with orange, white & black stripes. One on each side of tail, 6-sided offset chevron shaped with orange, white and black chevrons.

1. Engine top stickers square cut at front end, model no. 'SP-9'. Rivet spacing, 1-19/32''.

2. Engine top stickers rounded at front end, light orange, white, & black stripes & chevrons, model no. 'SP-9'. Rivet spacing, 1-9/32''.

3. Stickers as 2, rivet spacing 1½'', two wheels on short axle under nose, two wheels on long axle under wings.

4. 1½'' rivet spacing, 2 wheels on short axle under nose, 2 wheels on long axle under wings. No stickers, imprint markings as follows: -black 'N7873Q' on right top wing. Red U-shaped design with thin black 'Cessna 402' below it on each engine top.

SB-10-A Boeing 747 4-11/32'' 1973
White upper fuselage & vertical tail section, dark metallic blue lower fuselage, wings and horizontal tail section, 3 wheels on wire supports. A stickers on each side of fuselage, 31/32'' long, positioned over front edge of wing with a small red, white and blue British flag & dark blue 'BOAC' on a white background. One on each side of tail, vertical trapezoidal (except that the longest side is slightly curved at the lower end to follow the vertical tail section profile) with a small yellow/orange irregular shaped emblem on dark blue.

1. Basic model as described. Model no. 'SP-10'.

2. Stickers on fuselage, 1-3/16'' long, have dark blue irregular shaped emblem at front of sticker, both sides and dark blue 'British Airways' on white background. Tail stickers, four sided, primarily red with white and dark blue straight edged triangular pattern on lower section. Model no. 'SP-10'.

3. Stickers as 2, two wheels on short axle under nose, two wheels on long axle under wings.

4. Two wheels on short axle under nose, two wheels on long axle under wings, no stickers. Imprint markings as follows: Blue window and door stripe with white windows, both sides of fuselage. Blue 'British Airways' above window stripe. Red and blue 4-sided emblem on each side of vertical tail section similar to tail stickers on 2 & 3.

5. Two wheels on short axle under nose, two wheels on long axle under wings, no stickers. Imprint markings as follows: Red window and door stripe with black windows, both sides of fuselage. Red 'Qantas' in large letters and red 'Australia' in smaller letters above window stripe, both sides. Row of blue dots above a portion of 'Qantas' lettering, both sides. White stylized kangaroo-inflight emblem on red panel, both sides of tail.

6. Plated gold and mounted in flight on ashtray. White upper fuselage and vertical tail section. Gold plated lower fuselage, wings and horizontal tail section. ''British Airways'' stickers on fuselage and tail same as SB-10-A2. Model numbered ''SP-10'' on underside of fuselage. Mounting support attached to underside of fuselage near tail.

7. Silver wings & lower fuselage, labels: United States of America over windows, blue stripe by windows, American flag on tail.

SB-11-A Alpha Jet 4-13/32'' 1973
Vermillion upper fuselage, wings and vertical tail section. White lower fuselage and horizontal tail section. Three wheels on wire supports. A sticker on top of each wing, 13/32'' maltese cross, black with white edging. One on each side of tail, 7/32'' long horizontal striped rectangle with black, red, and yellow stripes.

1. Basic model as described. Model no. 'SP-11'.

2. 2 wheels on short axle under nose, two wheels on long axle under wings. Models exist with the black stripe on tail sticker either at top or bottom.

3. 2 wheels on short axle under nose, 2 wheels on long axle under

wings, tail stickers, vertical trapezoidal with similar stripes.

SB-12-A Douglas Skyhawk 4'' Long 1973
Dark metallic blue upper fuselage & tail, white lower fuselage & wings, clear window insert, 3 wheels on wire supports. A sticker on top of each wing with white star in 5/16'' blue circle on white, red, and white striped 5/8'' rectangle with thin blue border, top point of white star points to rear edge of wing. One on each side of tail, 7/16'' long rectangle, with 'Navy' in black on white background, with or without 'Navy' stickers on tail.

1. Basic model as described, model no. 'SP-12'.

2. Top point of white star on singtop stickers points to forward edge of wing, model no. 'SP-12'.

3. 2 wheels under fuselage on short axle, 2 wheels on long axle under wings.

4. 2 wheels under fuselage on short axle, 2 wheels on long axle under wings, no stickers, imprint markings as follows: White star in 1/4'' blue circle on white, red, and white striped 17/32'' rectangle with thin blue border, left wing. 'Marines' in blue, right wing. Four red bars on trailing edge, both sides.

SB-12-B Pitts Special 3-2/3'' 1980
Red top and white lower fuselage, wings checker-board, red and white, white pilot, black propeller.

SB-13-A DC-10 4-5/16'' 1973
White upper fuselage and vertical tail section, red lower fuselage, wings, and horizontal tail section, three wheels on wire supports. A sticker on each side of front end of fuselage, 1-5/32'' long, with a small red swept-winged arrow & black 'Swissair' on a white background. One on each side of tail, vertical trapezoidal, with 11/64'' white cross on red background.

1. Basic model as described, model no. 'SP-13'.

2. No stickers, imprint markings as follows: Red window stripe with white windows, both sides of fuselage. Red swept-winged arrow and black 'Swissair' above window panel, both sides. White cross on red panel, both sides of tail. Model no. 'SP-13'.

3. No stickers, imprint markings as 2, silver lower fuselage, wings and horizontal tail section. Model no. 'SP-13'.

4. No stickers, imprint markings as 2, silver lower fuselage, wings and horizontal tail section, 2 wheels on short axle under nose, 2 wheels on long axle under fuselage.

5. No stickers, imprint markings as follows: Red window stripe with blue windows above blue stripe, both sides of fuselage. Blue and red 'U' emblem and red 'United' above window stripe, both sides. Blue and red 'U' emblem, both sides of tail.Small red 'DC-10' both sides at rear. Silver lower fuselage, wings and horizontal tail section. 2 wheels on short axle under nose, 2 wheels on long axle under wings.

6. No stickers, imprint 'Swissair' markings as 2, two wheels on short axle under nose, 2 wheels on long axle under wings.

SB-14-A Cessna 210 3-35/64'' 1973
Orange upper fuselage & vertical tail section, white lower fuselage, wings & horizontal tail section, clear front window insert. No window insert at 2 side windows on each side, single two blade black propeller with rounded blade ends, 3 wheels on wire supports. A sticker on each side of top of wing, mirror image J-shaped, with narrow black & white stripes & wide orange strope with wide orange strope nearest to rear edge of wing. One on each side of tail, similarly curved to those on wingtops with white, black, orange, and white stripes of varying widths. Model no. 'SB-14'.

1. Basic model as described.

2. Orange/yellow upper fuselage and vertical tail section.

3. 2 wheels on short axle under nose, 2 wheels on long axle under wings. Models exist with/without wing stickers.

4. 2 wheels on short axle under nose, 2 wheels on long axle under wings, no stickers, imprint markings as follows: Black 'N94209' on right wingtop. Four wide red/orange stripes, each with 2 thin black outlined stripes, on wingtops. Outermost black outline stripes include 'Cessna' in black, wide stripes vary from light to

Skybusters

dark red/orange.

SB-15-A Phantom F4E   4-9/32″   1975
Metallic scarlet upper fuselage & tail, white lower fuselage & wings, very
light blue window insert, 2 wheels under nose on rounded end axle in
black plastic axle housing, 2 wheels under wings on rounded end axle
in black plastic axle suspension.
1. A sticker on each wingtop, 7/16″ circular, with red on white on
   dark blue bullseye. One on each side of tail, 5/16″ rectangle with
   vertical red, white, and dark blue stripes.
2. Wingtop stickers, 3/8″ circular with red on white on dark blue on
   yellow bullseye (same as SF 14-B Mini Ha Ha).
3. Tail stickers 1/2″ rectangular with similar striping.

SB-16-A Corsair F4U   3-15/32″   1975
Metallic blue fuselage, wings & tail, clear window insert, 2 wheels on
rounded end axle in black plastic axle suspension, 1 thin wheel at rear
in fuselage, single 3-blade black propeller with rounded blade ends.
1. A sticker on top of each wing with white star in 3/8″ blue circle
   on white, red, and white striped 13/16″ rectangle. Top point of
   white star points to forward edge of wing. One on each side of
   tail with blue star in 9/32″ white circle.
2. A sticker on top of right wing with white star in 5/16″ blue circle
   on white, red, and white striped 5/8″ rectangle with thin blue
   border. One on top of left wing, 25/32″ rectangle with 'Navy' in
   black letters & red dashes on white background.
3. Same as 2, but orange fuselage.

SB-17-A Ram Rod   3-5/16″   1976
Red upper fuselage & tail sections, white lower fuselage & wings, clear
window insert, 2 wheels under wings on rounded end axle, 1 thin wheel
at rear in fuselage, single 2-blade black propeller with rounded blade
ends, silvered engine parts. A sticker on each wingtop with 3 yellow-
outlined red "lightening" stripes on irregular shaped background.

SB-18-A Wild Wind   3-3/16″   1976
Apple green upper fuselage, wings & vertical tail section, white lower
fuselage, horizontal tail section & wheel coverings. Open cockpit with
plastic windshield, 2 wheels under fuselage on rounded end axle, 1 thin
wheel at rear in fuselage, single 2-blade propeller with rounded blade
ends, silvered radial engine parts. The 1977 U.S. Dealer's catalog lists
this model as the 'SB-17' Wild Wind and pictures it with colors and
stickers as issued. This model has been reported as bearing 'SB-17' cast-

in numbering and without stickers. A sticker on left wingtop with
'WILD', one on right wingtop with 'WIND'. Both have orange lettering
on black with dark blue, light blue, and white multi-shaped irregular
shaped background. One on each side of tail, 5/16″ diameter, with
black '7' on white circle with orange outline.

SB-19-A Piper Commanche   3-17/32″   1977
Red upper fuselage & tail sections, yellow lower fuselage & wings, clear
window insert, front & side windows, silvered interior, 2 wheels on
short axle under nose, 2 wheels on long axle under wings, single 2-blade
black propeller with rounded blade ends, silvered engine parts, 2 silvered
inserts in underside, 1 adjacent to each wheel housing. A sticker on each
wingtop, 1-1/32″ long rectangular with 'N 246 P' in black on yellow
background.

SB-20-A Helicopter   4-1/16″   1977
Clear window inserts, front & side windows, white interior, 2 wheels on
short axle under nose, 2 wheels on long axle under fuselage, silvered
engine components on roof, 4-blade black rotor on roof, 2-blade black
stabilizer on left side of tail.
1. Military olive/green body with a sticker on each side of fuselage,
   irregular shaped, with white star in blue circle on red, white &
   blue striped rectangle & white 'ARMY' on military olive/green
   background. Sticker background color varies from light to dark.
2. White upper fuselage with light blue base. A sticker on each side
   of fuselage, irregular shaped, with white star in blue circle on red,
   white & blue striped rectangle, small black and white Coast
   Guard emblem on wide slanted red stripe, narrow slanted blue
   stripe & black 'Coast Guard' on white background.
3. White upper fuselage with red base. A sticker on each side of fuselage, irregular shaped with narrow red stripe across top edge, black
   'Police' and black and red winged circle emblem on white background.

SB-21-A Lightning   4-9/32″   1977
Military olive/green upper fuselage, wings & vertical tail section, light
gray lower fuselage & horizontal tail section, smoky tinted window
insert, with frosted inside surface. 1 red plastic missile on each side of
fuselage under forward edge of wing, 2 wheels on short axle under nose,
2 wheels on long axle under fuselage. A sticker on top of each wing,
13/32″ circular, with red circle on dark blue circle. One on each side
of tail, 5/8″ tall, vertical trapezoidal, with short red & dark blue slant-

ed bars & black, red & white circular serpent monogram on green background.

SB-22-A Tornado (M.R.C.A.)   4-7/8″   1978
Slate gray upper fuselage, wings & tail with light gray camouflage pattern on top flat surfaces. White lower fuselage, clear window insert
with fronsted inside surface, 2 red plastic missiles on each side of fuselage under forward edge of wing, 2 wheels on short axle & 2 wheels on
long axle under fuselage. The slate gray upper fuselage, wings & tail;
the light gray camouflage pattern; & slate gray sticker backgrounds all
exist in varying shades.
1. A sticker on top of each wing, 5/16″ octagonal, with white outlined black maltese cross on slate gray background. One on each
   side of tail, 1/4″ tall, 5-sided with black, red & yellow horizontal
   stripes.
2. A sticker on each side of tail, 19/32″ tall, 5-sided with black, red,
   & yellow horizontal stripes & white outlined black '01' on dark
   slate gray background.

SB-23-A SST (Super sonic transport)   5½″   1979
White fuselage, wings and tails. Decals on side.
1. Air France decal.
2. Singapore Airlines decal.
3. MEA decal (Mid-East Airlines).

SB-24-A F.16   4½″   1979
White body, red wings, lower fuselage, various label changes on side, F-
16 on tail, 4 tires.

SB-25-A Rescue Helicopter   4¼″   1979
Black rotars, skids and tail propellar, black and white interior.
1. Rescue version, yellow body.
2. Code Red version, white body.

SB-26-A Cessna 210 Float Plane   1981
Red and white fuselage and wings, black pontoons.

SB-27-A Harrier Jet   1981
Red lower fuselage, white upper fuselage. Horizontal sticker on tail,
stickers red and blue.

SB-28-A A300 Airbus   1981
Same as no. SB-3-A. BOAC stickers. (Not issued.)

Plated Skybuster HS212 (from Heritage Series)
Gold Concorde mounted on pen stand, no markings, and a completely
different casting from SB-23-A Super Sonic Transport. (SST).

Matchbox Military

The fore-runner of the "Battle Kings" was a test market series of
two military toys which were issued in South Africa and Germany in
1973. These were called "Matchbox Military" toys and were not
included in any catalog. These were King size toys packaged in a
design which now is associated with the fronts of the Military Two
Packs packages.

MM1-A Articulated Petrol Tanker   1973
Similar to K16 but dark green in color, black engine, grille, hoses, and
plain wheels. Orange cover on back axle, gold cover on tanker trailer
axles.

1. Black figure 8 label with red and yellow sections on sides and
   back of tanker.
2. White five-pointed star label in white circle lettered "Armored
   Div." on sides and back of tanker.

MM2-A Armoured Car Transporter   1973
Similar to K20 Cargo Hauler, but dark green color, black loading ramp,
white "7" label on doors. Carries a brown engine and 73 Weasel in dark
green.

Battle Kings

"Armoured fighting vehicles" the 1974 catalog called them on their introduction by Lesney to the King size group of toys—and they were named the "Battle Kings" series. The first eight Battle Kings are drab Army green colored vehicles of military use. Additions have been made to increase the series to eighteen different toys. Tan cast plastic soldiers were packaged with the Battle kings in some cases. The Battle Kings series was not included in the 1982 catalog.

BK101	Sherman Tank	3-5/8"	1974
BK102	M48-A2 Tank	4-5/8"	1974
BK103	Chieftan Tank	4¾"	1974
BK104	King Tiger Tank	4½"	1974
BK105	Hover Raider	4-7/8"	1974
BK106	Tank Transporter with M48-A2 Tank	10½"	1974
BK107	155mm Self-propelled Howitzer Gun	4¼"	1974
BK108	M3-A1 Half Track Truck	3-7/8"	1974
BK109	Sheridan Tank	4-1/8"	1976
BK110	Recovery Vehicle	5-1/8"	1976
BK111	Missile Launcher	4-3/8"	1976
BK112	DAF Ambulance	3¾"	1977
BK113	Military Crane Truck (Army version of K12)	6-1/8"	1977
BK114	Army Aircraft Transporter (Army version of K13)	8"	1977
BK115	Army Petrol Tanker (Army version of K16)	9"	1977
BK116	Troop Carrier and Howitzer	8-7/8"	1977
BK117	Self-propelled "Hawk" Rocket Launcher	4-1/8"	1977
BK118	Kaman Seasprite Army Helicopter	5-7/8"	1978

Two-Packs [900-Range]

In 1976, Lesney Products released a new series of toys packaged two together and called the series "Two Packs". That year, 8 different sets of Two Packs were shown in the catalog. The following year, 1977, six new Two Packs were issued, all Military vehicles.

The series was renamed "Matchbox 900 Range" in 1979 including both the civilian and military toys. Toys have been added each year to bring this series up to 32 toys.

TP1-A	Mercedes Truck and Trailer	1976
TP2-A	Mod Tractor and Hay Trailer (No. 25 Mod Tractor and No. 40 Hay Trailer)	1976
TP2-B	Police Car and Fire Engine (No. 59 Police Sedan and, either No. 35 Fire Engine or No. 22 Blaze Buster.)	1979
TP2-C	Articulated Petrol Tanker, Exxon	1981
TP3-A	Weekender, Javelin and Pony Trailer (Car No. 9 or No. 53)	1976
TP4-A	Holiday Set (A variety of cars pulling No. 57 Caravan)	1976
TP5-A	The Weekender (Car towing No. 9 Boat & Trailer. Many variations in the car)	1976
TP5-B	2 black Lotus John Player Special Cars.	
TP6-A	Breakdown Set Wrecker (74 Toe Joe or 61) and car (29 Racing Mini, 15 VW 1500, 65 Saab, or 20 Police)	1976
TP6-B	J.6 Volkswagen 1500	
TP7-A	Emergency Set (No. 46 Stretcha Fetcha & No. 59 or 64 Fire Chief Car)	1976
TP7-B	Jeep and Glider Set (No. 38 Jeep & No. 7 Jeep Glider Trailer)	1978
TP7-C	Escort and Glider Trailer	1982
TP8-A	Transporter Set (No. 17 Londoner Bus & No. 72 Hovercraft)	1976
TP8-B	Field Car and Motorcycle Trailer (No. 18 Field Car and Honda cycle)	1977

Two-Packs [900-range]

TP9-A	Field Car and Racing Car	1978
	(No. 18 Field Car & No. 24 Team Matchbox racing car)	
TP10-A	Mercedes Ambulance and Fire Chief Car	1978
TP11-A	Military Jeep and Motorcycle	1977
	(No. 2 or 38 Jeep & No. 18 Motorcycle)	
TP11-B	Tractor and Hay Trailer	1979
TP12-A	Military Police Patrol and Field Car	1977
	(No. 20 or 23 Patrol car & No. 18 Field Car)	
TP12-B	Military VW Ambulance and Field Car	1978
TP13-A	Military Scout and Armoured Car	1977
	(No. 28 Scout & No. 73 Armoured car)	
TP13-B	Military Unimog and Weasel Field Gun	1978
	(No. 49 Unimog & No. 32 Gun)	
TP14-A	Military Tanker and Radar Truck	1977
TP14-B	Military Ambulance (No. 3) and Staff Car (No. 46)	1978

TP15-A	Military Mercedes Truck & Trailer	1977
	Truck is No. 1 and Trailer is No. 2.	
TP16-A	Military Dump Truck and Bulldozer	1977
	Truck is No. 28.	
TP16-B	Military Wrecker and Alvis Stalwart	1979
	Wrecker No. 71 and Alvis Stalwart No. 61.	
TP16-C	Articulated Truck No. 50 and Trailer	1980
TP17-A	Tanker & Trailer	1979
	(SF 63 Modified)	
TP18-A	Water Sporter	1979
	(No. 7 V.W. & No. 5 Seafire)	
TP19-A	Cattle Truck and Trailer	1980
	(No. 71 Truck)	
TP20-A	Shunter and Side Tipper	1980
	(No. 24 Shunter)	

TP21-A	Motorcycle Transporter set	1980
	(Car No. 21, 51, or 67, pulling trailer & 3 Plastic	
	motorcycles)	
TP22-A	Double Container Truck	1980
TP23-A	Covered Container Truck	1980
TP24-A	Box Container Truck	1980
TP25-A	Pipe Truck	1980
TP26-A	Boat Transporter	1981
TP27-A	Steam Loco and Caboose	1981
TP28-A	Cortina and Caravan	1982
TP29-A	Flareside and Boat Trailer	1982
TP30-A	Datsun 260Z and Speed Boat	1982
TP31-A	Citroen and Motorcycle Trailer	1982
TP32-A	Wreck Truck and Dodge Challenger	1982

Sea Kings

A new series of King size fighting ships was introduced by Lesney Products in 1976 and called "Sea Kings". Each toy has movable gun turrets and wheels just below the waterline. Eight toys were issued initially, with two additions in 1978 to bring the series to ten in all. Sea Kings were not included in the 1982 catalog.

SK301	Frigate	8-5/8"	1976	SK305	Submarine Chaser	7-7/8"	1976	
SK302	Corvette	7-7/8"	1976	SK306	Convoy Escort	7-7/8"	1976	
SK303	Battleship	8½"	1976	SK307	Helicopter Carrier	8¼"	1976	
SK304	Aircraft Carrier	8¾"	1976	SK308	Guided Missile Destroyer	8-1/3"	1976	

SK309	Submarine	8-1/8"	1978
SK310	Anti-aircraft Cruiser	8-1/8"	1978

Walt Disney Characters

Lesney Products produced a series of six Walt Disney Productions inspired toys in 1971 for the pre-school market which was not popular. They made three Space series cars and three Hot Rod cars, each driven by Mickey Mouse or Donald Duck.

Hoping for better success with different designs, they again brought out Disney Characters in 1979, and these have proved to be quite popular. There are now twelve members of the Walt Disney Characters series.

SPACE SERIES		about 5" long	1971
W1	Astrocar (Donald)		1971
W2	Astrotracker (Mickey)		1971
W3	Astrocat (Mickey)		1971
HOT ROD SERIES			
W7	Hotcar (Donald)		1971
W8	Draggin Waggin (Mickey)		1971
W9	Fun Bug (Donald)		1971

WD1-A	Mickey Mouse Fire Engine	2-7/8"	1979
WD2-A	Donald Duck Beach Buggy	2-7/8"	1979
WD3-A	Goofy Beetle	2-7/8"	1979
	1. Ears not attached to shoulders.		
	2. Ears attached to shoulders.		
WD4-A	Minnie Mouse Lincoln	2-7/8"	1979
WD5-A	Mickey Mouse Jeep	2-7/8"	1979
	1. "M.M." on hood with blue and white flowers.		

	2. "Mickey's Mail Jeep" on hood.		
WD6-A	Donald Duck Jeep	2-7/8"	1979
WD7-A	Pinnochio's Travelling Theatre	2-7/8"	1979
WD8-A	Jiminy Cricket's Old Timer	2-7/8"	1979
WD9-A	Goofy's Sports Car	2-7/8"	1979
WD10-A	Goofy's Train	2-7/8"	1980
WD11-A	Donald Duck's Ice Cream Van	2-7/8"	1980
WD12-A	Mickey Mouse Corvette	2-7/8"	1980

Popeye Series

Following the success of the twelve Walt Disney Characters, Lesney Products introduced three toys in 1981 inspired by the Popeye group of characters. These are numbered consecutively after the Disney group and appear to be the beginning of comic book character-related toys by Matchbox. Unlike any previous toy groups, these are related by the personalities of the drivers rather than by the designs of the vehicles themselves.

CS13-A	Popeye's Spinach Wagon	1981
CS14-A	Bluto's Road Roller	1981
CS15-A	Olive Oyl's Sports Car	1981

Glo-Racers

"Glo-Racers", introduced in 1982, are die-cast plastic toys which glow in the dark. The first twelve represent only six body styles but twelve different paint jobs.

They are packaged with a glo-launcher which powers the racers and can house the racer. The launcher is desinged to be hung from a belt and carried.

GR1-A	Light Beamer	1982
GR2-A	Speed Blazer	1982
GR3-A	Flamin' Vette	1982
GR4-A	Streak Ray	1982

GR5-A	Twilight TR	1982
GR6-A	Quicksilver	1982
GR7-A	Burnin' 280	1982
GR8-A	Sizzlin' ZX	1982

GR9-A	Turbo Flash	1982
GR10-A	Dark Rider	1982
GR11-A	Flash Fire	1982
GR12-A	Night Bird	1982

Gifts, Souvenirs, & Heritage Series

Through the years, Lesney Products has made groups of gift items which may include Matchbox toys as part of their ornament, but which themselves are souvenirs or useful articles.

In 1976, Lesney introduced the Heritage Series of silver plated miniature figurines comprised of:

12 British Inn signs,

6 Pips (dogs),

12 Regimental badges,

1 Silver Jubilee crest, and

8 Landmark paperweights.

Silver plated British Inn Signs   2½"

701	The Lion
702	The Pig and Whistle
703	The Cock
704	Elephant and Castle
705	George and Dragon
706	The Unicorn
707	The Swan
708	Sherlock Holmes
709	Rose and Crown
710	The Bull
711	Dick Turpin
712	The Volunteer
713	The Mermaid
714	The Spread Eagle
715	Brittania
716	Prince of Wales
717	The Smugglers
718	The Dolphin
780	Pack A includes signs No. 701, 702, 707, 708, 716, & 718.
781	Pack B includes signs No. 703, 704, 709, 711, 715, & 717.
782	Pack C includes signs No. 705, 706, 710, 712, 713, & 714.

Silver plated Pips

601	Labrador Retriever
602	French Poodle
603	Alsatian
604	Scottie
605	Rough Collie
606	Cocker Spaniel
610	Pack A includes signs No. 601 to 606.

Regimental Badges

551	Royal Marines
552	Coldstream Guards
553	17th/21st Lancers
554	Black Watch
555	Royal Artillery
556	Argyll and Sutherland Highlanders

Magnetic Board Games

801	Draughts
802	Chess
803	Solitaire
804	Nine Men's Morris
805	Noughts and Crosses (Tic-Tac-Toe)
806	Backgammon
807	Mini Chinese Checkers

Souvenirs

005	Green ceramic tray and London bus.
105	Flock lined stainless box and antique pistol.
106	Flock lined stainless box and Concorde decoration.
107	Flock lined stainless box and "Tower Bridge" decoration.
121	Decorated wood cigarette box and Rolls Royce car.
123	DeLuxe wood cigarette/trinket box and Packard car.
124	DeLuxe wood cigarette/trinket box and antique pistol.
126	Luxury soft-top cigarette/trinket box and "George Washington' antique pistol.
127	DeLuxe wood cigarette box/trinket box and 1922 London bus.
302	Wood double pipe rack and Rolls Royce car.
500	Londoner bus in tourist souvenir pack.
501	City of London Coat of Arms paperweight.
502	London scene paperweight—Tower Bridge.
503	London scene paperweight—Big Ben.
504	London scene paperweight—St. Paul's Cathedral.
505	Rolls Royce Vintage car double gift pack.
453	Single wood bookend and antique pistol.
004	Green ceramic tray and Rolls Royce car.
016	Gray ceramic ash tray and Boeing 747 airplane.
018	Gray ceramic ash tray and Rolls Royce car.
019	Brown ceramic "Tidy" and Rolls Royce car.
020	Stainless tray and Thomas Flyabout car.
150	Brown ceramic tray and George and Dragon.
007	Ceramic occasional tray double gift pack.
014	Blue ceramic ash tray and Rolls Royce car.
024	Stainless ash tray and Rolls Royce car.
152	Brown ceramic occasional tray and The Mermaid.
205	Green simulated onyx single penstand and Boeing 747 airplane.
206	Green simulated onyx single penstand and Crossley Coal Truck.
211	Blue ceramic penstand and Spitfire airplane.
212	Blue ceramic penstand and Concorde airplane.
221	Green simulated onyx double penstand and Packard car.
222	Green simulated onyx double penstand and Concorde airplane.
224	Green simulated onyx double penstand and George Washington antique pistol.
621	Perpetual calendar single penstand with street Rod car on blue ceramic base.
623	Perpetual calendar single penstand with Concorde airplane on blue ceramic base.
624	Perpetual calendar single penstand with Rolls Royce car on blue ceramic base.

Code Red ™

A series of eight vehicles relating to the "Code Red" ABC—television series was issued by Lesney in 1981. These toys represent apparatus of the Los Angeles, California fire fighting team as they are represented in weekly episodes. Numbers have not been assigned to these toys.

Code Red Fire Chief's Car	1981	Code Red Pumper	1981
Code Red Police Car	1981	Code Red Fire Boat	1981
Code Red Motorcycle and Policeman	1981	Code Red Snorkle Truck	1981
Code Red Ambulance	1981	Code Red Helicopter	1981

Convoy Series

A new series of small scale models of Peterbilt® and Kenworth® long-haul trucks was introduced in 1982. Originally advertised as the "Highway Express" Series, it was actually issued as the "Convoy" Series.

CY1-A	Kenworth® Car Transporter	1982	CY6-A	Kenworth® Horsebox Transporter	1982
CY2-A	Kenworth® Rocket Transporter	1982	CY7-A	Peterbilt® Petrol Tanker	1982
CY3-A	Peterbilt® Double Container Truck	1982	CY8-A	Kenworth® Box Truck	1982
CY4-A	Kenworth® Boat Transporter	1982	CY9-A	Kenworth® Conventional/Box Truck-	
CY5-A	Peterbilt® Covered Truck	1982		Midnight Express	1982

Pocket Catalogs

The first commercial catalog of Matchbox toys was made in 1957. In this one-page, fold up sheet printed on both sides, the cover of the then-current No. 1 Road Roller box was duplicated in large size to fill the cover. Inside, 42 toys are illustrated. The following year, 1958, a booklet style catalog was issued, showing a picture of the then-new No. 44 Rolls Royce Silver Cloud emerging from its box on the cover. Since those first catalogs, new pocket-size ones have been issued yearly and in increasing numbers of languages. As the distribution of Matchbox toys grew, separate catalogs for the foreign countries were produced for the United States, general International use, Germany, Japan, France, Italy, Spain, Holland, Scandinavia and Canada.

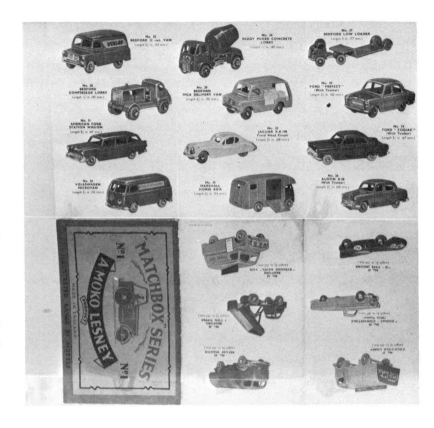

MATCHBOX POCKET CATALOGS CHECKLIST

	1982/83	1981/82	1980/81	1979/80	1978	1977	1976	1975	1974	1973	1972	1971	1970	1969-2	1969-1**	1968-B*	1968-A*	1967	1966	1965	1964	1963	1962	1961	1960	1959-2	1959-1	1958	1957
American	X	X	X	X	X	X	X	X	X	X	X	X	X	X	X	X	X	X	X	X	X	X	X	X	X		X	X	
English	X	X	X	X	X	X	X	X	X	X	X	X	X	X	X	X	X	X	X	X	X	X	X	X	X	X			X
International	X	X	X	X	X	X	X	X	X	X	X	X	X	X	X	X		X	X	X	X	X	X	X					
German	X	X	X	X	X	X	X	X	X	X	X	X	X	X	X	X		X	X	X	X		X						
Japanese	X	X	X	X	X	X	X	X	X	X	X	X	X	X	X			X		X	X	X							
French	X	X	X	X	X	X	X	X	X	X	X	X	X	X	X	X		X		X									
Italian	X	X	X	X	X	X	X	X	X	X	X	X	X	X	X	X													
Spanish	X	X	X	X	X	X	X	X	X		X	X	X																
Dutch	X	X	X	X	X	X	X	X	X		X	X	X																
Scandinavian	X	X	X	X	X	X	X	X	X	X	X	X	X																
Canadian																			X				X	X					
Iranian	X	X		X																									

Notes for Catalogs chart:
* 1968– A American, K-18 priced at $2.50.
  1968– B K-18 priced at $3.50.
  1968– English, has paper insert with price change.
** 1969– 1 English, shows Police Car instead of
      Police Wagon in K-23 (Very limited printing).

Matchbox Collectors' Clubs

A great deal of additional information about Matchbox toys is discovered every day by collectors who share an interest in Matchbox. Many of these individuals have organized clubs so that news about Matchbox toys can be exchanged, and several now publish periodical newsletters and magazines for their members.

Lesney toys, dolls, and other products not covered in this book are studied and collected with equal enthusiasm. Through the clubs, collectors will be able to find answers to questions far beyond the scope of this book.

Matchbox Collectors Club
founded 1994
P O Box 977
Newfield, New Jersey 08344

American International Matchbox
founded 1970
522 Chestnut Street
Lynn, Massachusetts 01904

Chesapeake Miniature Vehicle
founded 1978
Collectors Club
c/o Win Hurley
709 Murdock Road
Baltimore, Maryland 21212

Bay Area Matchbox Collectors
     founded 1971
   Association (BAMCA)
P O Box 1534
San Jose, CA 95109

Pennsylvania Matchbox Collectors Club
founded 1980
c/o Mike Appnel
1161 Perry Street
Reading, Pennsylvania 19604

Matchbox U S A
founded 1977 (note date)
62 Saw Mill Road
Durham, Connecticut 06422

Matchbox International Collectors
founded 1985
     Association (M.I.C.A.);
P O Box 28072
Waterloo, Ontario N2L 6J8 Canada

Bibliography

Botwright, Ian and Peter Harrington. **All Our Yesteryears,** 1956-1981, Die-cast model car Publications. 32 St. Peters Street, Ipswich, Suffolk, England, 1981.

Bush, Ray, editor. **U.K. Matchbox Club Magazine,** volumes 1 through 6. Plymouth, England, 1977 through 1982.

Gibson, Cecil. **Model Commercial Vehicles,** The Viking Press. New York, 1971.

_____ . **Model Veteran and Vintage Cars.** New York. A Studio Book. The Viking Press, 1971.

Gunner, H.M. and T.J. **Collectors Catalogue of Matchbox® Models of Yesteryear®,** 3rd edition. Wallington, England, 1981.

Leake, Geoffrey. **A Concise Catalogue of 1-75 Series Matchbox® Toys,** 2nd edition. Worcester, England, 1981.

Mace, Scott. **The Toy Car Catalog: Matchbox® 1-75 Series, a major variation catalog.** San Jose, California, The Toy Car, 1981.

_____ . **The Toy Car Catalog: Matchbox® King Size K1 through K20, a major variation catalog.** San Jose, California, The Toy Car, 1981.

_____ . **The Toy Car Catalog: Matchbox® Major Pack, a major variation catalog.** San Jose, California, The Toy Car, 1981.

_____ . **The Toy Car Catalog: Matchbox® Two-Pack, a major variation catalog.** San Jose, California, The Toy Car, 1981.

Mack, Charles. **"Matchbox" USA K-21 Onward Catalog,** 2nd edition. Durham, Connecticut, "Matchbox" USA, 1981.

_____ , editor. **"Matchbox" USA Club Magazine.** Durham, Connecticut, monthly April, 1980 through 1982.

Sasek, Miroslav. **Mike and the Modelmakers.** London, Lesney Products & Company, Ltd., 1970.

Thompson, G.M.K. **British Diecasts, a collector's guide to toy cars, vans and trucks.** Yeovil, England, A Foulis book, Haynes Publishing Group, 1980.

van den Abeale, Alain, editor-in-chief. **Automobile Year Book of Models 1,** Lausanne, Switzerland, Edita SA, 1981.

Ward, Graham. **The Box Catalogue, 1953-1980 The Models and their Boxes,** 1st edition. Longton, Stoke-on-Trent, England, 1981.

_____ . **The Box Catalogue, 1953-1978 Variations,** 2nd edition. Longton, Stoke-on-Trent, England, 1978.

_____ . **The Box Catalogue, Models of Yesteryear.** 1956-1981, Longton, Stoke-on-Trent, England, 1981.

Price Guide

Compiled by Charles Mack

This is the third revision price guide for this book compiled by Nancy Schiffer. This particular version price guide is set up differently than the 1988 version price guide. Each price denoted is for the particular variation that is photographed on each particular page. Variations of the same model may be considerably different in price both at the low and high end of the scale. An example of this is the Y-7-A5 4 Ton Leyland Lorry as depicted on row 5 of page 77. The particular model shown in the photographs is one of the rarest Yesteryear variations due to the center line of the decal not being printed. This model is in this price guide at $850-1000! However, other variations of this model are considerably less. The "easiest" to obtain version is priced at $60-85. It's very important that when using this particular book that you make sure you have the particular model photographed to match the price. Other price guides are available as well through Schiffer Publishing that cover other variations. Model prices are for mint examples. If boxed you can add 2-10% to the price quoted. On newer models, especially Superfast 1-75 models, these were only available in blisterpack form. If left in the package you can add 2% to the price quoted. A chipped model generally has no collectible valuable unless it's of a very rare version. These can be used as "fillers" until a mint example can be obtained. Remember these prices are only a guide and can be different from one end of the USA to the other as well as other worldwide geographic regions such as Europe or Australia. Preproductions are pictured in this book for interests sake. No prices are given for these models. All of these models are very difficult to obtain and can range from as little as $50 into the thousands of dollars for some Yesteryear rarities. Preproductions are a different kind of collecting aspect in the hobby and prices are determined by the dealer or collector that has them and what one is willing to pay for one. Preproductions are one-of-a-kinds and short runs so prices cannot be "fixed" into any price guide.

77 Lower Valley Road, Atglen, PA 19310

Page 14
Soap Box Racer $1800-2500
Caterpillar Tractor .... $ 200-700
Caterpillar Bulldozer .... $ 200-700
Page 15
Quarry Truck .... (preproduction)
Bread Bait Press $50-85
Muffin The Mule $175-250
Jumbo the Elephant $450-600
Large Ruston Bucyrus $450-700
Page 16
Large Coronation Coach (with king & queen) $800-1200
Rag & Bone Cart $1200-1800
Page 17

Row 1
Large Silver Coronation Coach $500-750

Row 2
Large Gold Coronation Coach $250-450

Row 3
Small gold Coronation Coach $150-200
Small silver Coronation Coach $90-125

Row 4
Covered Wagon (with barrels) $90-125
Covered Wagon (without barrels) $90-125
Page 18

Row 1
Large Cement Mixer $150-250
Large Massey Harris Tractor $500-750
Large Cement Mixer $150-250

Row 2
Aveling Barford Diesel Road Roller $300-450
Large Horse Drawn Milk Float $800-1000

Row 3
Prime Mover w/trailer & bulldozer $350-500
Page 19

Row 1
1-A1 Road Roller. $35-50
1-B2 Road Roller. $50-75
1-C3 Road Roller. $40-60

1-D2 Road Roller. $12-18

Row 2
1-E1 Mercedes Truck $5-8
2-A2 Dumper $35-50
2-A1 Dumper $125-150
2-B1 Dumper $35-40

Row 3
2-C1 Muir Hill Dumper $15-18
2-D2 Mercedes Trailer $5-8
3-A2 Cement Mixer $25-35
3-B1 Bedford Tipper $90-110

Row 4
3-C1 Mercedes Ambulance $5-8
4-A1 Massey Harris Tractor. $35-50
4-B3 Massey Harris Tractor. $45-60
4-C2 Triumph Motorcycle & Sidecar $35-50

Row 5
4-D2 Stake Truck. $50-75
5-A2 London Bus $50-65
5-B1 London Bus $85-100
5-C2 London Bus $35-45
5-D1 London Bus $8-12
page 20

Row 1
6-A3 Quarry Truck $25-40
6-B1 Quarry Truck $175-250
6-C3 Quarry Truck $8-12
6-D1 Ford Pick-Up $8-12

Row 2
7-A2 Horse Drawn Milk Float $50-75
7-B1 Ford Anglia. $15-20
7-C3 Ford Refuse Truck $5-8
8-A1 Caterpillar Tractor $75-90
8-A2 Caterpillar Tractor $75-90

Row 3
8-B1 Caterpillar Tractor $45-60
8-C1 Caterpillar Tractor $45-55
8-D3 Caterpillar Tractor $15-18
8-E1 Ford Mustang $12-15
8-E6 Ford Mustang $90-125

3

Row 4

9-A1 Dennis Fire Escape	$45-60
9-A2 Dennis Fire Escape	$45-60
9-B4 Merryweather Fire Engine	$25-40
9-C1 Boat & Trailer	$5-8

Row 5

10-A1 Mechanical Horse & Trailer	$25-35
10-B1 Mechanical Horse & Trailer	$45-60
10-C2 Sugar Container Truck	$25-40
10-D3 Pipe Truck.	$10-15

Page 21

Row 1

11-A5 Road Tanker	$25-40
11-A4 Road Tanker	$45-60
11-A1 Road Tanker	$250-500
11-B1 Road Tanker	$25-40
11-C1 Jumbo Crane	$15-18

Row 2

11-D1 Scaffolding Truck	$5-8
12-A1 Land Rover.	$25-40
12-B3 Land Rover Series 2	$75-90
12-C5 Land Rover Safari	$8-12
12-C1 Land Rover Safari	$8-12

Row 3

13-B1 Wreck Truck	$40-60
13-A1 Wreck Truck	$35-50
13-C1 Thames Wreck Truck	$35-50
13-C3 Thames Wreck Truck	$25-40
13-D7 Dodge Wreck Truck	$850-1000

Row 4

13-D4 Dodge Wreck Truck	$8-12
14-A1 Ambulance	$25-40
14-B6 Daimler Ambulance	$90-125
14-C1 Bedford Ambulance	$45-60

Row 5

14-D1 Iso Grifo	$5-8
15-A2 Prime Mover	$20-30
15-B3 Atlantic Prime Mover.	$25-40
15-C4 Tippax Refuse Truck	$12-15

Page 22

Row 1

15-D1 Volkswagen 1500	$8-12
16-A1 Atlantic Trailer	$25-40
16-B1 Atlantic Trailer	$35-50
16-B4 Atlantic Trailer	$20-30

Row 2

16-C5 Mountaineer Dump Truck	$25-30
16-C1 Mountaineer Dump Truck	$75-90
16-D4 Case Bulldozer	$12-15
16-D3 Case Bulldozer	$8-12

Row 3

17-A5 Removals Van	$50-75
17-A3 Removals Van	$35-50
17-A1 Removals Van	$150-175
17-A2 Removals Van	$150-175
17-B3 Austin Taxi	$50-75

Row 4

17-C3 Hoveringham Tipper	$12-15
17-D2 Horse Box	$5-8
18-A1 Caterpillar Bulldozer	$45-60
18-B1 Caterpillar Bulldozer	$50-60

Row 5

18-C3 Caterpillar Bulldozer	$25-35
18-C4 Caterpillar Bulldozer	$25-30
18-D3 Caterpillar Bulldozer	$75-110
18-D4 Caterpillar Bulldozer	$15-20

Page 23

Row 1

18-E3 Field Car	$200-300
18-E1 Field Car	$8-12
I9-A1 MG Sports Car	$45-60
19-B1 MGA Sports Car	$55-75
19-B2 MGA Sports Car	$75-90

Row 2

19-C3 Aston Martin	$35-50
19-C5 Aston Martin	$25-30
19-D1 Lotus Racing Car	$20-30
19-D2 Lotus Racing Car	$15-20

Row 3

20-A5 Stake Truck	$25-40

20-A1 Stake Truck $75-100
20-A2 Stake Truck $25-40
20-B1 ERF 686 Truck $35-50

Row 4
20-C5 Chevrolet Impala Taxi $12-15
20-C1 Chevrolet Impala Taxi $250-350
21-A1 Long Distance Coach $25-40
21-B3 Long Distance Coach $60-85

Row 5
21-C1 Milk Delivery Truck $50-75
21-C7 Milk Delivery Truck $50-75
21-D1 Foden Concrete Truck. $5-8
22-A2 Vauxhall Sedan $25-40
Page 24

Row 1
22-B9 Vauxhall Cresta $60-75
22-B1 Vauxhall Cresta $45-60
22-C3 Pontiac Grand Prix $12-15
23-A Berkeley Cavalier Trailer(preproduction)

Row 2
23-B2 Bluebird Dauphine Trailer $45-60
23-C1 House Trailer Caravan $12-15
24-A2 Weatherhill Hydraulic Excavator $25-40
24-B6 Weatherhill Hydraulic Excavator $20-30

Row 3
24-C1 Rolls Royce Silver Shadow $5-8
25-A5 Dunlop Truck $25-40
25-B4 Volkswagen. $35-50
25-C1 BP Petrol Tanker $125-150

Row 4
25-C4 Aral Petrol Tanker $75-90
25-D2 Ford Cortina $8-12
26-A2 Concrete Truck $45-60
26-B1 Concrete Truck $300-450

Row 5
26-C1 G.M.C. Tipper Truck $5-8
27-A1 Bedford Lowloader $500-750
27-B2 Bedford Lowloader $50-75
27-C9 Cadillac Sixty Special $25-40
Page 25

Row 1
27-D2 Mercedes 230SL Convertible $5-8
28-A2 Bedford Compressor Truck $25-40
28-B6 Thames Compressor Truck $25-35
28-C2 Jaguar Mk10 .... $15-18

Row 2
28-D2 Mack Dump Truck $8-12
28-D3 Mack Dump truck $8-12
29-A1 Bedford Milk Truck $25-40
29-B5 Austin A55 Cambridge. $20-25

Row 3
29-C2 Fire Pumper $8-12
30-A2 Ford Prefect $90-125
30-B5 6-Wheel Crane Truck ....
$25-40
30-C3 8-Wheel Crane Truck $5-8

Row 4
31-A1 American Ford Station Wagon $30-45
31-B7 American Ford Station Wagon $90-125
31-B1 American Ford station Wagon $90-125
31-C1 Lincoln Continental $7-10

Row 5
32-A1 Jaguar XK140 Coupe $25-40
32-B3 Jaguar XKE. $35-50
32-C1 Leyland Tanker $5-8
32-C2 Leyland Tanker $35-50
Page 26

Row 1
33-A8 Ford Zodiac Sedan $35-50
33-B1 Ford Zodiac Sedan $25-40
33-C3 Lamborghini Miura $5-8
34-A4 Volkswagen Panel Truck $25-40

Row 2
34-B4 Volkswagen Camper $35-50
34-C1 Volkswagen Camper $8-12
34-D1 Volkswagen Camper $7-10
35-A2 Marshall Horse Box $35-50

Row 3
35-B4 Snow-trac Tractor $18-25
35-B3 Snow-trac Tractor $18-25

5

35-B2 Snow-trac Tractor $18-25
35-B1 Snow-trac Tractor $18-25

Row 4
36-A5 Austin A50. .... $25-40
36-B2 Lambretta Motorscooter & Sidecar $50-75
36-C1 Opel Diplomat $5-8
37-A1 Coca Cola Lorry $85-100
37-C4 Coca Cola Lorry $45-60

Row 5
37-D2 Cattle Truck $5-8
38-A6 Karrier Refuse Collector $25-40
38-B5 Vauxhall Victor Estate Car $20-30
Page 27

Row 1
38-C1 Honda Motorcycle & Trailer $18-25
38-C2 Honda Motorcycle & Trailer $8-12
39-A1 Ford Zodiac Convertible $25-40
39-B3 Pontiac Convertible $75-90

Row 2
39-C1 Ford Tractor $8-12
40-A2 Bedford Tipper Truck $25-40
40-B3 Leyland Royal Tiger Coach $18-25
40-C1 Hay Trailer. $5-8

Row 3
41-A1 D-Type Jaguar $25-40
41-B10 D-Type Jaguar $175-200
41-C3 Ford GT $7-10
42-A1 Bedford Evening News Van $35-50

Row 4
42-B2 Studebaker Station Wagon $10-15
42-C1 Iron Fairy Crane $5-8
43-A2 Hillman Minx $35-50
43-B4 Aveling Barford Tractor Shovel $35-50

Row 5
43-C1 Pony Trailer $5-8
44-A8 Rolls Royce Silver Cloud $25-40
44-B3 Rolls Royce Phantom V. $75-100
Page 28

Row 1

44-C1 Refrigerator Truck $5-8
44-A1 Vauxhall Victor Sedan $25-40
45-B1 Ford Corsair with boat. $12-15
46-A3 Morris Minor. $50-75

Row 2
46-B2 Pickford's Removal Van. $75-90
46-B13 Beales Bealson Removal Van $275-325
46-C1 Mercedes 300SE $8-12
47-A1 Brooke Bond Trojan Van. $25-40

Row 3
47-B1 Commer Ice Cream Truck. $90-125
47-B4 Commer Ice Cream Truck. $150-175
47-B13 Commer Ice Cream Truck $35-50
47-C1 DAF Tipper $20-30

Row 4
48-A4 Meteor Boat & Trailer $75-90
48-B1 Boat & Trailer $50-75
48-C1 Dump Truck $5-8
49-A2 Army Personnel Carrier. $25-40

Row 5
49-B4 Unimog $7-10
50-A11 Commer Pick-up Truck $50-75
50-B1 John Deere Tractor $20-30
50-C1 Kennel Truck. $5-8
Page 29

Row 1
51-A6 Albion Chieftan $25-40
51-A10 Albion Chieftan $75-90
51-B1 John Deere Trailer $20-30
51-C9 8-Wheel Tipper $5-8

Row 2
51-C2 8-Wheel Tipper $10-15
52-A2 Maserati 4CLT $45-60
52-A8 Maserati 4CLT $40-50
52-B3 BRM Racer $7-10
Row 3
53-A1 Aston Martin. $25-40
53-B1 Mercedes Benz 220SE $25-40
53-C2 Ford Zodiac MKIV $5-8
54-A1 Saracen Personnel Carrier $12-15

Row 4
54-B1 S&S Cadillac Ambulance. $7-10
55-A1 D.U.K.W $25-40
55-B4 Ford Fairlane Police Car $75-100
55-C2 Ford Galaxie Police Car $15-20

Row 5
55-D3 Mercury Police Car $7-10
56-A1 London Trolley Bus $175-200
56-A7 London Trolley Bus $45-60
56-B2 Fiat 1500 .... $8-12

Page 30

Row 1
57-A5 Wolseley 1500 .... $25-40
57-B4 Chevrolet Impala $25-40
57-C2 Land Rover Fire Engine. $8-12
58-A2 BEA Coach $30-45

Row 2
58-A3 BEA Coach $25-40
58-B3 Drott Excavator $75-100
58-C1 DAF Girder Truck $5-8
59-A7 Ford Thames Van $90-110

Row 3
59-B1 Ford Fairlane Fire Chief's Car $125-150
59-C2 Ford Galaxie Fire Chief's Car $8-12
60-A5 Morris J2 Pick-up $25-40
60-A8 Morris J2 Pick-up $25-40

Row 4
60-B1 Site Hut Truck $5-8
61-A1 Ferret Scout Car $12-18
61-A1 Ferret Scout Car $12-18
61-B1 Alvis Stalwart $7-10

Row 5
61-B5 Alvis Stalwart $25-35
62-A1 Army General Lorry $35-50
62-B2 T.V. Service Van $125-150
62-B8 T.V. Service Van $35-50

Page 31

Row 1
62-C1 Mercury Cougar $5-8
63-A2 Army Service Ambulance. $35-50

63-B1 Firefighting Crash Tender $18-25
63-C1 Dodge Crane Truck $5-8

Row 2
64-A4 Scammel Breakdown Truck $25-40
64-B1 M.G. 1100 .... $7-10
65-A2 3.4 Litre Jaguar $25-40
65-B4 3.4 Litre Jaguar $20-30

Row 3
65-C1 Claas Combine Harvester $5-8
66-A3 Citroen D.S. 19 .... $45-60
66-B1 Harley Davidson Motorcycle & Sidecar $75-90

Row 4
66-C1 Greyhound Coach $50-75
66-C2 Greyhound Coach $7-10
67-A1 Saladin Armoured Car $15-18
67-B2 Volkswagen 1600TL $10-15

Row 5
68-A1 Austin MK2 Radio Truck. $30-45
68-B2 Mercedes Coach $7-10
68-B1 Mercedes Coach $50-75
69-A4 Nestles Delivery Truck $25-40

Page 32

Row 1
69-B7 Hatra Tractor Shovel $10-15
69-B6 Hatra Tractor Shovel $12-15
69-B8 Hatra Tractor Shovel preproduction
69-B1 Hatra Tractor Shovel $20-30

Row 2
69-B3 Hatra Tractor Shovel $12-15
69-B2 Hatra Tractor Shovel $12-15
70-A1 Thames Estate Car $25-40
70-A6 Thames Estate Car $20-30

Row 3
70-B3 Atkinson Grit Spreader. $5-8
71-A2 Austin 200 Gallon Water Truck $25-40
71-B1 Jeep Gladiator Pick-up. $35-50
71-B7 Jeep Gladiator Pick-up. $18-25

Row 4
71-C2 Ford Heavy Wreck Truck. $60-75
72-A5 Fordson Tractor $75-100

72-A1 Fordson Tractor $30-45
72-A8 Fordson Tractor $30-45

Row 5
72-A9 Fordson Tractor $75-100
72-A2 Fordson Tractor $30-45
72-A6 Fordson Tractor $25-40
Page 33

Row 1
72-B1 Standard Jeep $5-8
73-A3 RAF 10 Ton Pressure Refueller Tanker $35-50
73-B2 Ferrari F1 Racer $20-35
73-B1 Ferrari F1 Racer $20-35

Row 2
73-C1 Mercury Commuter $5-8
74-A2 Mobile Refreshment Canteen $300-350
74-A4 Mobile Refreshment Canteen $25-40
74-A1 Mobile Refreshment Canteen $300-350

Row 3
74-B4 Daimler Bus $7-10
74-B2 Daimler Bus $10-15
74-B3 Daimler Bus $8-12

Row 4
75-A1 Ford Thunderbird $45-60
75-A6 Ford Thunderbird $75-90
75-B1 Ferrari Berlinetta $50-75

Row 5
75-B4 Ferrari Berlinetta $450-600
75-B3 Ferrari Berlinetta $10-15
75-B2 Ferrari Berlinetta $7-10
Page 34

Row 1
1-F4 Mercedes Truck $15-18
1-F6 Mercedes Truck $4-6
1-F5 Mercedes Truck $4-5

Row 2
1-F15 Mercedes Truck $15-18
1-G1 Mod Rod $18-25
1-G3 Mod Rod $10-15

Row 3
1-G18 Mod Rod (Silver Streak) $8-12
1-H1 Dodge Challenger $3-4
1-H8 Dodge Challenger $4-6

Row 4
1-I1 RevinRebel $4-6
2-E3 Mercedes Trailer $15-18
2-E6 Mercedes Trailer $4-5

Row 5
2-E8 Mercedes Trailer $35-50
2-E14 Mercedes Trailer $15-18
2-F1 Jeep Hot Rod $12-15
Page 35

Row 1
2-F14 Jeep Hot Rod $12-15
2-F17 Jeep Hot Rod $5-8
2-G1 Hovercraft $4-6

Row 2
2-G3 Hovercraft $4-6
2-G13 Hovercraft. $7-10
2-H2 S-2 Jet $3-5

Row 3
2-H3 S-2 Jet $2-4
3-D1 Mercedes Ambulance $12-15
3-D8 Mercedes Ambulance $5-8

Row 4
3-E1 Monteverdi Hai $5-8
3-F1 Porsche Turbo $6-8
3-F3 Porsche Turbo $2-5

Row 5
3-F11 Porsche Turbo $2-5
3-F15 Porsche Turbo $2-5
4-E1 Dodge Cattle Truck $15-18
Page 36

Row 1
4-F1 Gruesome Twosome $12-15
4-F14 Gruesome Twosome $8-10
4-G5 Pontiac Firebird $4-6

Row 2
4-H3 '57 Chevy $4-6
4-H5 '57 Chevy $2-4
5-E1 Lotus Europa $50-75

Row 3
5-E5 Lotus Europa $8-12
5-E14 Lotus Europa $15-18
5-F3 Seafire Boat $5-8

Row 4
5-F9 Seafire Boat $15-20
5-F10 Seafire Boat $60-85
5-F12 Seafire Boat $5-8

Row 5
5-G2 U.S.Mail Jeep $3-5
5-H1 4X4 Golden Eagle Jeep. $2-4
6-E1 Ford Pickup. $15-18
Page 37

Row 1
6-F1 Mercedes 350SL $5-8
6-F7 Mercedes 350SL $4-7
6-F13 Mercedes 350SL $5-8

Row 2
6-F10 Mercedes 350SL $25-35
6-F20 Mercedes 350 SL $4-7
6-F22 Mercedes 350 Convertible $4-6

Row 3
7-D1 Ford Refuse Truck $15-18
7-E30 Hairy Hustler $12-15
7-E28 Hairy Hustler $35-50

Row 4
7-E28 Hairy Hustler $12-15
7-F1 V.W. Golf $4-6
7-F5 V.W. Golf $3-5

Row 5
7-F12 V.W. Golf $4-6
7-F21 V.W. Golf $3-5
7-G1 Rompin Rabbit $4-6
Page 38

Row 1
8-F1 Ford Mustang $25-35
8-F2 Ford Mustang $35-45
8-G1 Wildcat Dragster $12-15

Row 2
8-H1 DeTomasso Pantera $3-5
8-H7 DeTomasso Pantera $3-5
8-I1 Rover $2-4

Row 3
9-D1 Boat & Trailer $12-15
9-E8 Javelin $3-5
9-E17 Javelin $3-5

Row 4
9-E25 Javelin $4-6
9-E29 Javelin $3-5
9-E36 Javelin $18-25

Row 5
9-F3 Ford Escort RS 2000 .... $2-4
9-F5 Ford Escort RS 2000 .... $3-5
9-F12 Ford Escort RS 2000 .... $2-4
Page 39

Row 1
9-G1 Fiat Abarth. $2-4
10-E2 Pipe Truck. $15-18
10-F1 Piston Popper $2-4

Row 2
10-F11 Piston Popper $200-250
10-G5 Plymouth Gran Fury $2-4
11-E1 Scaffolding Truck $15-18

Row 3
11-F1 Flying Bug. $15-18
11-G2 Car Transporter $2-4
11-G18 Car Transporter $2-4

Row 4
11-H1 Cobra Mustang $4-6
12-D3 Safari Land Rover $18-25
12-E5 Setra Coach $8-12

Row 5

12-E5 Setra Coach $8-10
12-E8 Setra Coach $8-10
12-F3 Big Bull $4-6
Page 40

Row 1
12-G2 Citroen CX. $2-5
12-G9 Citroen CX. $3-5
12-H 1982 Pontiac Firebird.preproduction

Row 2
13-E2 Dodge Wreck Truck $18-25
13-F1 Baja Dune Buggy $7-10
13-G2 Snorkel Fire Engine $2-4

Row 3
13-H1 4X4 Mini Pickup $2-4
14-E1 Iso Grifo $15-18
14-E6 Iso Grifo $8-12

Row 4
14-E5 Iso Grifo $10-15
14-F1 Mini Ha Ha. $12-15
14-G1 Rallye Royale $6-8

Row 5
14-G2 Rallye Royale $6-8
14-H2 Leyland Tanker $2-4
15-E1 Volkswagen 1500 .... $15-18
Page 41
Row 1
15-E5 Volkswagen 1500 .... $8-12
15-F1 Fork Lift Truck $8-12
15-G1 Hi Ho Silver $6-8

Row 2
16-E1 Badger Exploration Truck $2-4
16-F1 Pontiac $4-6
16-F5 Pontiac $3-5

Row 3
16-G1 Pontiac Trans Am $2-4
17-E1 Horse Box $18-25
17-E2 Horse Box $15-18

Row 4
17-E4 Horse Box $15-18

17-F1 Londoner Bus $8-12
17-F3 Londoner Bus $7-10

Row 5
17-F2 Londoner Bus $150-175
17-F17 Londoner Bus $10-15
17-F14 Londoner Bus $25-40
Page 42

Row 1
17-F22 Londoner Bus $25-40
17-F25 Londoner Bus $25-40
17-F32 Londoner Bus $8-12

Row 2
17-G3 Londoner Bus $7-10
17-G1 Londoner Bus $8-12
18-F1 Field Car $12-15

Row 3
18-F8 Field Car $3-5
18-F16 Field Car. $250-400
18-F15 Field Car. $3-5

Row 4
18-F34 Field Car. $3-5
18-F32 Field Car. $3-5
18-G3 Hondarora $75-90

Row 5
18-G4 Hondarora $7-10
18-G12 Hondarora. $4-6
18-G14 Hondarora. $2-4
Page 43

Row 1
19-E1 Lotus Racer $25-35
19-F1 Road Dragster $10-15
19-F12 Road Dragster $12-18

Row 2
19-G1 Cement Mixer $3-5
19-G17 Cement Mixer $3-5
19-H1 Peterbilt Cement Truck $2-3

Row 3
20-D1 Lamborghini Marzal $12-15

20-D3 Lamborghini Marzal $10-15
20-D5 Lamborghini Marzal $25-40

Row 4
20-E7 Police Patrol $4-6
20-E25 Police Patrol $5-8
20-E6 Police Patrol $12-15

Row 5
20-E24 Police Patrol $7-10
20-E45 Police Patrol $7-10
20-F1 4X4 Jeep (Desert Dawg) $2-3
Page 44

Row 1
21-E1 Foden Cement Truck $18-25
21-F2 Road Roller $15-20
21-F4 Road Roller $7-10

Row 2
21-G1 Renault 5TL $3-5
21-G5 Renault 5TL $3-5
21-G8 Renault 5TL $3-5

Row 3
21-G29 Renault 5TL $3-5
22-D1 Pontiac GP Sports Coupe $25-40
22-E6 Freeman Intercity Commuter $12-15

Row 4
22-E3 Freeman Intercity Commuter $12-15
22-F10 Blaze Buster $3-5
22-G1 Ford Mini Pickup/Camper $3-5

Row 5
23-D3 Volkswagen Camper $7-10
23-D5 Volkswagen Camper $7-10
23-D10 Volkswagen Camper (Dormobile). $5-7
Page 45

Row 1
23-E8 Atlas Truck $4-6
23-E7 Atlas Truck $6-8
23-E9 Atlas Truck $5-7

Row 2
23-F1 GT350 .... $8-12

23-G1 Audi Quattro $2-4
24-D1 Rolls Royce Silver Shadow $6-8

Row 3
24-F1 Shunter $7-10
24-F4 Shunter $3-5
24-E1 Team Matchbox $200-275

Row 4
24-E6 Team Matchbox $275-350
24-E10 Team Matchbox $35-45
24-E3 Team Matchbox $5-7

Row 5
24-G1 Datsun 280ZX $2-4
24-H Datsun 280ZXpreproduction
25-E1 Ford Cortina $20-35
Page 46

Row 1
25-E2 Ford Cortina $15-18
25-F4 Mod Tractor $15-18
25-F10 Mod Tractor $6-8

Row 2
25-G2 Flat Car $4-6
25-G5 Flat Car $4-6
25-H6 Celica GT $3-5

Row 3
25-J1 Celica GT $4-6
25-I1 Ambulance $6-8
26-C1 GMC Tipper. $18-25

Row 4
26-E1 Big Banger. $12-15
26-F1 Site Dumper $3-5
26-F9 Site Dumper $3-5

Row 5
26-F12 Site Dumper $6-8
26-G1 Cosmic Blues $8-10
27-D2 Mercedes 230SL $15-18
Page 47

Row 1
27-E4 Mercedes 230SL $8-12

27-F1 Lamborghini Countach. $6-8
27-F14 Lamborghini Countach $6-8

Row 2
27-G1 Swing Wing Jet $2-4
28-E1 Mack Dumper $18-25
28-E5 Mack Dumper $6-8

Row 3
28-F1 Armoured Vehicle (Stoat) $7-10
28-F3 Armoured Vehicle (Stoat) $4-6
28-G2 Lincoln Continental MK V $2-4

Row 4
28-H1 Formula Racing Car $3-5
29-D1 Fire Pumper $18-25
29-D2 Fire Pumper $6-8

Row 5
29-F3 Racing Mini $12-15
29-E12 Racing Mini $7-10
29-F7 Tractor Shovel $6-8
Page 48

Row 1
29-F3 Tractor Shovel $150-200
29-F28 Tractor Shovel $8-10
30-D2 8-Wheel Crane Truck $18-25

Row 2
30-E2 Beach Buggy $10-15
30-F1 Swamp Rat $3-5
30-G1 Articulated Truck $2-4

Row 3
30-H1 Peterbilt Quarry Truck $2-4
31-D2 Lincoln Continental $18-25
31-E17 Volksdragon $10-15

Row 4
31-F11 Caravan $2-4
31-G1 Mazda RX7 .... $3-5
31-G5 Mazda RX7 .... $3-5

Row 5
31-H Mazda RX7 preproduction
32-E1 Maserati Bora $7-10

32-E11 Maserati Bora $12-15
Page 49

Row 1
32-D1 Leyland Tanker $12-15
32-D2 Leyland Tanker $45-60
32-D5 Leyland Tanker $175-225
Row 2
32-F1 Field Gun $3-5
32-G1 Atlas Excavator $6-8
32-G3 Atlas Excavator $2-4

Row 3
33-D2 Lamborghini Miura $45-60
33-D3 Lamborghini Miura $15-18
33-E9 Datsun 126X $8-10

Row 4
33-F7 Police Motorcycle $3-5
33-F5 Police Motorcycle $25-35
33-F6 Police Motorcycle $6-8

Row 5
34-E1 Formula 1 .... $12-15
34-E3 Formula 1 .... $8-12
34-E4 Formula 1 .... $10-15
Page 50

Row 1
34-E7 Formula 1 .... $8-12
34-F1 Vantastic $4-6
34-F6 Vantastic $4-6

Row 2
34-G3 Chevy Prostocker $4-6
35-C2 Merryweather Fire Engine $10-12
35-D1 Fandango $6-8

Row 3
35-D22 Fandango $6-8
35-E1 Zoo Truck $2-5
35-F1 Trans Am T-Roof $2-4

Row 4
36-D1 Opel Diplomat $15-18
36-E1 Hot Rod Draguar $15-18
36-E6 Hot Rod Draguar $12-15

Row 5
36-F1 Formula 5000 .... $6-8
36-F5 Formula 5000 .... $6-8
36-G1 Refuse Truck $2-4
Page 51

Row 1
36-G4 Refuse Truck $3-5
37-E1 Cattle Truck $15-18
37-F3 Soopa Coopa $12-15

Row 2
37-F8 Soopa Coopa $15-18
37-F10 Soopa Coopa $85-100
37-G3 Skip Truck. $3-5

Row 3
37-G8 Skip Truck. $75-90
37-G6 Skip Truck. $75-90
37-G13 Skip Truck $3-5

Row 4
37-H1 Sunburner $2-4
37-I Matra Ranchopreproduction
38-D2 Honda & Trailer $15-18

Row 5
38-D3 Honda & Trailer $15-18
38-D4 Honda & Trailer $4-6
38-E3 Stingeroo $12-15
Page 52
Row 1
38-F1 Jeep $4-6
38-F10 Jeep $4-6
38-F9 Jeep $5-8

Row 2
38-H1 Model A Truck $3-5
39-D3 Clipper $8-12
39-E1 Rolls Royce Silver Shadow II $4-6

Row 3
39-E2 Rolls Royce Silver Shadow II $4-6
39-E Rolls Royce Silver Shadow II $3-5
39-F Toyota Celica Suprapreproduction

Row 4
40-D1 Guildsman $12-15
40-D9 Guildsman $8-12
40-E4 Horse Box $3-5

Row 5
40-E6 Horse Box $4-6
40-F1 Corvette T Roof $3-5
41-D1 Ford GT $10-15
Page 53

Row 1
41-D4 Ford GT $10-15
41-E1 Siva Spyder $15-18
41-E11 Siva Spyder $15-18

Row 2
41-F1 Ambulance $3-5
41-F2 Ambulance $3-5
41-F13 Ambulance. $20-35

Row 3
41-F7 Ambulance $20-25
41-G1 Kenworth Conventional Aerodyne. $2-4
42-D4 Iron Fairy Crane $35-50

Row 4
42-E5 Tyre Fryer. $12-15
42-E7 Tyre Fryer. $85-100
42-F1 Mercedes Container Truck $4-6

Row 5
42-F3 Mercedes Container Truck $20-35
42-F11 Mercedes Container Truck $7-10
42-F14 Mercedes Container Truck $25-40
Page 54

Row 1
42-F12 Mercedes Container Truck $25-40
42-F13 Mercedes Container Truck $6-8
42-G1 '57 Ford T-Bird $3-5

Row 2
43-D1 Pony Trailer $15-18
43-D3 Pony Trailer $3-5
43-D5 Pony Trailer $3-5

Row 3

43-E2 Dragon Wheels	$15-18
43-F1 0-4-0 Steam Loco	$2-4
43-F2 0-4-0 Steam Loco	$5-7

Row 4

43-G1 Peterbilt Conventional	$3-5
44-D1 Refrigerator Truck	$20-35
44-D2 Refrigerator Truck	$18-25

Row 5

44-E3 Boss Mustang	$4-6
44-F1 Passenger Coach	$3-5
44-F12 Passenger Coach	$6-8

Page 55

Row 1

44-G1 Chevy Van	$3-5
45-C1 Ford Group 6	$12-15
45-C9 Ford Group 6	$12-15

Row 2

45-C20 Ford Group 6	$10-12
45-D1 BMW 3.0 CSL	$5-7
45-D3 BMW 3.0 CSL	$25-40

Row 3

45-D6 BMW 3.0 CSL	$35-50
45-D12 BMW 3.0 CSL	$50-75
45-E1 Kenworth Cabover Aerodyne	$3-5

Row 4

46-D1 Mercedes 300SE	$50-75
46-D4 Mercedes 300SE	$18-25
46-D5 Mercedes 300SE	$7-10

Row 5

46-D7 Mercedes 300SE	$75-100
46-E1 Stretcha Fetcha	$12-15
46-E13 Stretcha Fetcha	$15-18

Page 56

Row 1

46-E11 Stretcha Fetcha	$25-40
46-F8 Ford Tractor	$4-6
46-F4 Ford Tractor	$2-4

Row 2

46-G1 Hot Chocolate	$4-6
47-D1 DAF Tipper Truck	$18-25
47-E1 Beach Hopper	$12-15

Row 3

47-F2 Pannier Loco	$3-5
47-G1 Jaguar SS100	$2-4
48-D4 Dump Truck.	$18-25

Row 4

48-E3 Pi-Eyed Piper	$12-15
48-E5 Pi-Eyed Piper	$75-90
48-F8 Sambron Jacklift	$3-5

Row 5

48-G1 Red Rider	$4-6
49-C3 Unimog	$15-20
49-C8 Unimog	$7-10

Page 57

Row 1

49-D2 Chop Suey	$12-15
49-E5 Crane Truck	$60-75
49-E1 Crane Truck	$3-5

Row 2

49-E10 Crane Truck	$3-5
50-D1 Kennel Truck	$12-15
50-D7 Kennel truck	$15-18

Row 3

50-E1 Articulated Truck	$6-8
50-E18 Articulated Truck	$25-40
50-E20 Articulated Truck	$7-10

Row 4

50-G1 Harley Davidson Motorcycle	$3-5
51-D1 8-Wheel Tipper truck.	$15-18
51-E3 Citroen SM.	$7-10

Row 5

51-E11 Citroen SM	$8-12
51-F1 Combine Harvester	$4-6
51-G1 Midnight Magic	$3-5

Page 58

Row 1

52-C5 Dodge Charger $7-10
52-C9 Dodge Charger $8-12
52-D4 Police Launch $4-6

Row 2
52-D6 Police Launch $6-8
52-E1 BMW M1 .... $2-4
53-D3 Ford Zodiac $15-18

Row 3
53-D6 Ford Zodiac $20-25
53-E1 Tanzara $10-15
53-E4 Tanzara $10-15

Row 4
53-F7 CJ6 Jeep $3-5
53-F9 CJ6 Jeep $4-6
53-F10 CJ6 Jeep $4-6

Row 5
53-G1 Flareside Pickup $2-4
54-C1 Cadillac Ambulance $20-25
54-D3 Ford Capri. $8-12
Page 59

Row 1
54-D8 Ford Capri. $7-10
54-E1 Personnel Carrier $4-6
54-F8 Mobile Home $3-5

Row 2
54-G1 NASA Tracking Vehicle $3-5
55-E1 Mercury Police Car $10-15
55-F4 Mercury Police Stationwagon $12-15

Row 3
55-G1 Hellraiser. $12-15
55-G3 Hellraiser. $12-15
55-H4 Ford Cortina $4-6
Row 4
55-H5 Ford Cortina $3-5
55-I1 Ford Cortina $3-5
56-C1 Pininfarina $15-18

Row 5
56-C6 Pininfarina $18-25
56-C2 Pininfarina $12-15

56-D5 Hi-Tailer $6-8
Page 60

Row 1
56-E2 Mercedes 45OSL $5-8
56-F2 Mercedes Taxi $3-5
56-G1 Peterbilt Tanker $3-5

Row 2
57-D1 Land Rover Fire Engine $25-40
57-E1 Eccles Caravan $7-10
57-E8 Eccles Caravan $4-6

Row 3
57-E11 Eccles Caravan $6-8
57-E12 Eccles Caravan $7-10
57-F1 Wildlife Truck $4-6

Row 4
57-F10 Wildlife Truck $4-6
57-G1 Carmichael Commando $4-6
57-H1 4X4 Mini Pickup $3-5

Row 5
58-D1 Girder Truck $18-25
58-D2 Girder Truck $18-25
58-E3 Woosh-n-Push $12-15
Page 61

Row 1
58-E6 Woosh-n-Push $12-15
58-F1 Faun Dump Truck $3-5
58-F4 Faun Dump Truck $20-35

Row 2
59-D3 Ford Galaxie Fire Chief $18-25
59-E13 Mercury Fire Chief Car $7-10
59-E14 Mercury Fire Chief Car $7-10

Row 3
59-E18 Mercury Fire Chief Car $7-10
59-E16 Mercury Fire Chief Car $6-8
59-E17 Mercury Fire Chief Car $6-8

Row 4
59-F1 Planet Scout $12-15
59-F6 Planet Scout $12-15

59-F7 Planet Scout	$20-25

Row 5

59-F13 Planet Scout	$35-50
59-G6 Porsche 928	$4-6
59-G20 Porsche 928	$3-5

page 62

Row 1

59-G28 Porsche 928	$3-5
60-C1 Site Hut Truck	$20-30
60-D1 Lotus Super Seven	$15-18

Row 2

60-D3 Lotus Super Seven	$18-25
60-E2 Holden Pick-up	$10-15
60-E4 Holden Pick-up	$6-8

Row 3

60-E8 Holden Pick-up	$7-10
60-E11 Holden Pick-Up	$5-7
60-E9 Holden Pick-up	$25-40

Row 4

60-F1 Piston Popper	$5-7
61-C4 Blue Shark.	$12-15
61-D4 wreck Truck	$3-5

Row 5

61-D21 Wreck Truck	$4-6
61-D13 Wreck Truck	$3-5
61-D8 Wreck Truck	$4-6

Page 63

Row 1

61-E1 Peterbilt Wrecker	$3-5
62-Gl Chevrolet Corvette	$3-5
62-G8 Chevrolet Corvette	$2-4

Row 2

62-D2 Mercury Cougar	$12-15
62-E2 Mercury Cougar "Rat Rod"	$10-15
62-E5 Mercury Cougar "Rat Rod"	$18-25

Row 3

62-F3 Renault 17TL	$6-8
62-F1 Renault 17TL	$6-8

63-D1 Dodge Crane Truck	$18-25

Row 4

63-E2 Freeway Gas Truck	$75-90
63-E1 Freeway Gas Truck	$5-7
63-E4 Freeway Gas Truck	$5-7

Row 5

63-E15 Freeway Gas Truck	$18-25
63-E9 Freeway Gas Truck	$6-8
63-E21 Freeway Gas Truck	$5-7

Page 64

Row 1

63-E27 Freeway Gas Truck	$12-15
63-E26 Freeway Gas Truck	$6-8
63-E28 Freeway Gas Truck	$7-10

Row 2

63-F1 Freeway Gas Tanker Trailer	$5-7
63-F2 Freeway Gas Tanker Trailer	$5-7
63-F4 Freeway Gas Tanker Trailer	$5-7

Row 3

63-G1 Dodge Challenger	$8-12
63-G3 Dodge Challenger	$8-12
63-H1 Snorkel Fire Engine	$6-8

Row 4

64-C1 MG 1100	$125-175
64-C2 MG 1100	$18-25
64-D1 Slingshot Dragster	$12-15

Row 5

64-D4 Slingshot Dragster	$10-15
64-D2 Slingshot Dragster	$100-125
64-E2 Fire Chief.	$8-12

Page 65

Row 1

64-F2 Caterpillar Bulldozer	$4-6
64-F9 Caterpillar Bulldozer	$4-6
65-D2 Saab Sonnet	$7-10

Row 2

65-D5 Saab Sonnet	$200-250
65-E5 Airport Coach	$4-6

65-E4 Airport Coach $4-6

Row 3
65-E8 Airport Coach $4-6
65-E16 Airport Coach $7-10
65-E17 Airport Coach $8-12

Row 4
65-E18 Airport Coach $25-40
65-F1 Tyrone Malone Bandag Bandit $3-5
66-D1 Greyhound Bus $15-20

Row 5
66-E3 Mazda RX500 .... $7-10
66-E15 Mazda RX500 .... $4-6
66-F1 Ford Transit $4-6
Page 66

Row 1
66-F12 Ford Transit $4-6
66-E9 Mazda RX500 .... $7-10
66-G1 Tyrone Malone Super Boss $2-4

Row 2
67-C1 Volkswagen 1600TL $25-40
67-C2 Volkswagen 1600TL $15-20
67-C5 Volkswagen 1600TL $12-18

Row 3
67-D1 Hot Rocker. $8-12
67-D5 Hot Rocker. $7-10
67-E1 Datsun 260Z 2+2 .... $2-4

Row 4
67-E2 Datsun 260Z 2+2 .... $6-8
67-E10 Datsun 260Z 2+2 .... $2-4
67-E13 Datsun 260Z 2+2 .... $2-4

Row 5
68-C1 Porsche 910 .... $10-12
68-C3 Porsche 910 .... $20-25
68-D5 Cosmobile $12-15
Page 67

Row 1
68-D8 Cosmobile $15-18
68-10 Cosmobile $20-25

68-D17 Cosmobile. $35-50

Row 2
68-E3 Chevy Van $4-6
68-E9 Chevy Van $6-8
68-E15 Chevy Van. $18-25

Row 3
68-E14 Chevy Van. $7-10
68-E16 Chevy Van. $25-40
68-E17 Chevy Van. $7-10

Row 4
68-E20 Chevy Van. $2-4
69-C1 Rolls Royce Silver Shadow Coupe $15-18
69-C4 Rolls Royce Silver Shadow Coupe $15-18
Row 5
69-D2 Turbo Fury. $12-15
69-E1 Armoured Truck $3-5
69-E6 Armoured Truck $25-40
Page 68

Row 1
69-F1 1933 Willys Street Rodpreproduction
70-C2 Grit Spreader $18-25
70-D11 Dodge Dragster $15-18

Row 2
70-D12 Dodge Dragster $15-18
70-E1 Self-Propelled Gun $2-4
70-F1 Ferrari 308GTB $2-4

Row 3
71-D1 Wreck Truck $18-25
71-D4 Wreck Truck $8-12
71-D5 Wreck Truck $90-125

Row 4
71-E1 Jumbo Jet Motorcycle. $15-18
71-F3 Cattle Truck $3-5
71-F6 Cattle Truck $3-5

Row 5
71-F25 Cattle Truck $3-5
71-F19 Cattle Truck $3-5
71-G 1962 Corvettepreproduction
Page 69

Row 1
72-C1 Jeep $18-25
72-D2 Hovercraft. $3-5
72-E1 Bomag Road Roller $4-6

Row 2
72-F1 Maxi Taxi $2-4
72-G Dodge Delivery Truckpreproduction
73-D1 Mercury Stationwagon. $12-15

Row 3
73-E3 Mercury Stationwagon. $15-18
73-F1 Weasel $4-6
73-F2 Weasel $6-8

Row 4
73-G2 Model A Ford $6-8
73-G6 Model A Ford $4-6
73-G9 Model A Ford $3-5

Row 5
74-C2 Daimler Bus $10-15
74-C6 Daimler Bus $100-125
74-D9 Toe Joe $100-125
Page 70

Row 1
74-D3 Toe Joe $3-5
74-D22 Toe Joe $15-18
74-D16 Toe Joe $100-125

Row 2
74-E1 Cougar Villager $2-4
74-E4 Cougar Villager $2-4
74-F1 Orange Peel $3-5

Row 3
75-C1 Ferrari Berlinetta $60-75
75-C4 Ferrari Berlinetta $18-25
75-D3 Alfa Carabo $10-15

Row 4
75-E1 Alfa Carabo $15-18
75-E3 Alfa Carabo $6-8

Row 5

75-F4 Seasprite Helicopter. $3-5
75-G1 Helicopter. $2-4
Page 71

Row 1
76-A Mazda RX7 .... $12-15

Row 2
77-A Toyota Celica $3-5

Row 3
78-A Datsun 280ZX (white) $12-15
78-A Datsun 280ZX (black) $2-4

Row 4
79-A Galant Eterna $2-4
Page 72
Roman Numeral Models .... $8-12 each
Page 73
Limited Edition Models .... $8-10 each
Page 74

Row 1
5 Datsun 280Z $12-15
2 Mazda RX7 .... $12-15

Row 2
J-21 Toyota Celica $12-15
J-22 Galant Eterna (red) $12-15
J-22 Galant Eterna (yellow) $12-15
Page 75
These models are preproductions. Prices vary greatly depending on color and rarity and what one is willing to pay for one.
Page 76

Row 1
Y-1-A1 1925 Allchin 7-NHP Traction Engine $75-90
Y-1-B4 1911 Model T $18-25
Y-1-C2 1936 Jaguar SS100 .... $10-15

Row 2
Y-2-A2 1911 "B" Type London Bus $60-75
Y-2-B3 1911 Renault Two-Seater $30-35
Y-2-C2 1914 Prince Henry Vauxhall $18-25
Y-2-C8 1914 Prince Henry Vauxhall $18-25

Row 3
Y-3-A1 1907 London 'E' Class Tramcar. $60-75
Y-3-B8 1910 Benz Limousine. $130-150
Y-3-B10 1910 Benz Limousine $25-40
Y-3-C2 1934 Riley MPH $18-25
Y-3-D1 1912 Model 'T' Ford Petrol Tanker $12-18

Row 4
Y-4-A8 Sentinel Steam Wagon $175-225
Y-4-B2 Shand Mason Horse Drawn Fire Engine $150-175
Y-4-C12 1909 Opel Coupe $18-25
Y-4-C6 1909 Opel Coupe $18-25

Row 5
Y-4-D2 1930 Duesenberg Model 'J' Town Car $18-25
Y-4-D3 1930 Duesenberg Model 'J' Town Car $18-25
Page 77

Row 1
Y-5-A4 1929 LeMans Bentley. $60-75
Y-5-B1 1929 4-1/2 Litre (S) Bentley $350-400
Y-5-C1 1907 Peugeot $18-25
Y-5-C5 1907 Peugeot $18-25

Row 2
Y-5-D2 Talbot Van $25-40
Y-5-D3 Talbot Van $12-18
Y-5-D11 Talbot Van $18-25
Y-5-D17 Talbot Van $12-15

Row 3
Y-6-A2 1916 A.E.C. 'Y' Type Lorry $75-90
Y-6-B2 1926 Type 35 Bugatti $25-40
Y-6-B10 1926 Type 35 Bugatti $25-40
Row 4
Y-6C1 1913 Cadillac $20-25
Y-6-C10 1913 Cadillac $18-25
Y-6-C1 1920 Rolls Royce Fire Engine $12-15

Row 5
Y-7-A5 4 Ton Leyland Lorry. $850-1000
Y-7-B3 1913 Mercer Raceabout $35-50
Y-7-B11 1913 Mercer Raceabout $20-35
Y-7-C1 1912 Rolls Royce $25-40
Y-7-C8 1912 Rolls Royce $12-15
Page 78

Row 1
Y-8-A3 Morris Cowley 1926 "Bullnose". $50-75
Y-8-B2 1914 Sunbeam Motorcycle with Milford Sidecar $35-50
Y-8-C2 1914 Stutz $18-25
Y-8-D1 1945 MG TC $25-40
Y-8-D6 1945 MG TC $12-15

Row 2
Y-9-A2 1924 Fowler "Big Lion" Showman's Engine. $75-90
Y-9-B1 1912 Simplex $25-35
Y-9-B8 1912 Simplex $15-18

Row 3
Y-10-A8 1908 'Grand Prix' Mercedes $65-80
Y-10-B1 1928 Mercedes Benz 36/220 .... $45-60

Row 4
Y-10-C2 1906 Rolls Royce Silver Ghost $18-25
Y-10-C3 1906 Rolls Royce Silver Ghost $15-18
Y-10-C6 1906 Rolls Royce Silver Ghost $20-30

Row 5
Y-11-A6 1920 Aveling & Porter Steam Roller $65-80
Y-11-B5 1912 Packard Landaulet $20-35
Y-11-C6 1938 Lagonda Drop-head Coupe $15-20
Y-11-C1 1938 Lagonda Drop-head Coupe. $300-500
Page 79

Row 1
Y-12-A1 1899 London Horse-drawn Bus $65-80
Y-12-B6 1909 Thomas Flyabout $18-25
Y-12-B2 1909 Thomas Flyabout $18-25

Row 2
Y-12-C1 1912 Model T Ford $15-18
Y-12-C5 1912 Model T Ford $35-50
Y-12-C12 1912 Model T Ford. $15-18

Row 3
Y-13-A1 1862 American "General" Loco 'Santa Fe' $65-80
Y-13-B1 1911 Daimler $25-40
Y-13-C2 1918 Crossley RAF Tender $50-75
Y-13-C6 1918 Crossley Coal & Coke Tender $15-18

Row 4
Y-14-A1 1903 "Duke of Connaught" Loco $65-80
Y-14-B5 1911 Maxwell Roadster $18-25

Y-14-C6 1931 Stutz Bearcat. $15-18
Y-14-C7 1931 Stutz Bearcat. $12-15

Row 5
Y-15-A2 1907 Rolls Royce Silver Ghost $18-25
Y-15-B3 1930 Packard Victoria $18-25
Y-15-B13 1930 Packard Victoria $12-15
Page 80

Row 1
Y-16-A2 1904 Spyker $25-40
Y-16-A8 1904 Spyker $20-30
Y-16-B6 1928 Mercedes SS $15-20

Row 2
Y-16-B5 1928 Mercedes SS $125-150
Y-16-B1 1928 Mercedes SS $50-75
Y-16-B7 1928 Mercedes SS $18-25

Row 3
Y-17-A6 1938 Hispano Suiza. $15-18
Y-17-A1 1938 Hispano Suiza. $15-18

Row 4
Y-18-A1 1937 Cord 812 .... $15-18
Y-19-A1 1935 Auburn Speedster $15-18

Row 5
Y-20-A1 1937 Mercedes Benz 540K $12-15
Y-21-A1 1930 Woody Wagon $15-18
Page 81

Row 1
Y-1-B 1911 Model T Ford $45-60
Y-2-B 1911 Renault $45-60
Y-2-C 1914 Prince Henry Vauxhall $45-60

Row 2
Y-3-C 1934 Riley MPH $45-60
Y-4-C 1909 Opel Coupe $45-60
Y-14-B 1911 Maxwell Roadster $45-60

Row 3
Y-5-B 1929 Bentley $50-65
Y-7-C 1912 Rolls Royce $50-60
Y-10-B 1928 Mercedes Benz $45-60
Row 4

Y-10-C 1906 Rolls Royce Silver Ghost. $45-60
Y-13-B 1911 Daimler $45-60
Y-13-C 1918 Crossley Coal & Coal Truck $45-60
Page 82
The models on this page are preproduction models and vary greatly in price
on the collector's market. The following two were issued in limited
quantities on the market.
Row 2- Y-1-B 1911 Model T Ford $300-450

Row 3- Y-4-D 1930 Model J Duesenberg. $1500-2500
Page 83

Row 1
Y-5-D Talbot Van "Nestles Milk n $18-25
Y-12-D Model T Van ~Suze" $15-18

Row 2
Y-12-D Model T Van "25th Anniversary of Yesteryear" $15-18
Y-12-D Model T Van "Smiths Crisps" $15-18

Row 3
Y-5-D Talbot Van "Langendorf" $35-50
Y-5-D Talbot Van "Merita" $35-50
Y-5-D Talbot Van "Taystee". $35-50
Page 84
One-of-a-kindspriceless
Page 85

Row 1
AI-A Petrol Pumps & sign- Esso $30-45
AI-B Petrol Pumps & sign- BP $12-15

Row 2
A2-A Bedford Articulated Four Car Transporter $50-65

Row 3
A3-A Metal Lock-up Garage $25-40
A4-A Road Signs (set of 8). $20-35

Row 4
A5-A Home Store $35-50
A-3B Brroomstick (or Zingomatic) $25-45
Page 86

Row 1
MG1-C Matchbox Garage $20-35

Row 2
MG3-A Texaco Garage & Restaurant $35-50
Page 87

Row 1
M1-A Caterpillar Earth Scraper $45-60
M1-B BP Auto Tanker $15-25

Row 2
M2-A2 Bedford Ice Cream Truck $45-60
M2-B1 Bedford Tractor & York Trailer. $50-75

Row 3
M2-B3 Bedford Tractor & York Trailer. $45-60
M3-A4 Thornycroft Antar & Centurion Tank $45-60

Row 4
M4-A2 Ruston Bucyrus Power Shovel $45-60
M5-A1 Massey Ferguson Combine Harvester $35-50
Page 88

Row 1
M6-A Pickfords 200 Ton Transporter $35-50
M6-B Racing Car Transporter $25-40

Row 2
M7-A3 Jennings Cattle Truck $40-55
M8-A1 Mobilgas Petrol Tanker $75-90

Row 3
M8-B2 Guy Warrior Car Transporter $25-40
M10-A1 Dinkum Dumper $30-45

Row 4
M9-A6 Interstate Double Freighter $60-75

Row 5
M9-A4 Interstate Double Freighter $60-75
Page 89

Row 1
K1-A Weatherhill Hydraulic Shovel $50-75
K1-B 8-Wheel Tipper Truck $20-35
K2-A2 Muir Hill Dumper $20-35
K2-A1 Muir Hill Dumper $25-40

Row 2

K2-B.K.W. Dump Truck $20-25
K2-C2 Scammell Heavy Wreck Truck $15-20
K2-C3 Scammell Heavy Wreck Truck $25-40

Row 3
K3-C Massey Ferguson Tractor & Trailer $15-18
K3-A5 Caterpillar Bulldozer $25-40
K3-A6 Caterpillar Tractor $25-40

Row 4
K3-B1 Hatra Tractor Shovel. $20-30
K4-A1 International Tractor $25-40
K4-A4 International Tractor $20-35

Row 5
K4-B1 GMC Tractor with Freuhauf Hopper Train $35-50
Page 90

Row 1
K4-C1 Leyland Tipper $15-20
K4-C4 Leyland Tipper $18-25
K4-C3 Leyland Tipper $50-75

Row 2
K5-A1 Foden Tipper Truck $20-35
K6-A1 Allis-Chalmers Earth Scraper $25-40
K6-B2 Mercedes Benz Ambulance $12-18

Row 3
K7-A Curtiss-Wright Rear Dumper $25-40
K7-B Refuse Truck $12-18

Row 4
K8-A7 Prime Mover & Transporter with Caterpillar Tractor. $50-75

Row 5
K8-B4 Guy Warrior Car Transporter $35-50
Page 91

Row 1
K8-C2 Caterpillar Traxcavator $12-15
K9-A2 Diesel Road Roller $20-35
K9-B5 Claas Combine Harvester $18-25

Row 2
K9-B1 Claas Combine Harvester $18-25
K10-A2 Aveling Barford Tractor Shovel $25-40

Row 3
K10-B1 Pipe Truck $18-25
K11-A4 Fordson Tractor & Farm Trailer $20-30

Row 4
K11-B1 DAF Car Transporter. $35-50

Row 5
K11-B2 DAF Car Transporter. $18-25
Page 92

Row 1
K12-A1 Heavy Breakdown Wreck Truck $25-40
K13-A1 Ready-mix Concrete Truck $25-40

Row 2
K15-A1 Merryweather Fire Engine $18-25
K14-A2 Taylor Jumbo Crane $18-25

Row 3
K16-A1 Dodge Tractor with Twin Tippers $35-50

Row 4
K17-A1 Low Loader and Bulldozer $25-40
Page 93

Row 1
K18-A1 Articulated Horse Box $18-25
K19-A1 Scammell Tipper Truck $15-20

Row 2
K20-A1 Tractor Transporter & Tractors $35-50

Row 3
K21-A1 Mercury Cougar $25-40
K23-A1 Mercury Police Car $12-18
K24-A1 Lamborghini Miura $12-18
Page 94

Row 1
K1-C3 O & K Excavator $12-15
K2-D3 Car Recovery Vehicle. $15-18

Row 2
K3-D1 Mod Tractor & Trailer $15-18
K4-D4 Big Tipper. $12-15

Row 3
K3-E1 Grain Transporter $15-18
Page 95

Row 1
K5-C2 Muir Hill Tractor & Trailer $18-20

Row 2
K6-C2 Cement Mixer $12-15
K6-D2 Motorcycle Transporter $12-15

Row 3
K7-B4 Refuse Truck $12-18
K7-C8 Racing Transporter $20-35

Row 4
K8-D2 Animal Transporter $20-30
Page 96

Row 1
K9-C1 Fire Tender $12-15
K11-D1 Dodge Delivery Van $10-15

Row 2
K10-C2 Car Transporter $15-18

Row 3
K10D1 Bedford Car Transporter $15-18

Row 4
K11-C1 Tow Truck. $10-15
K11-C4 Tow Truck. $35-50
Page 97

Row 1
K12-C1 Hercules Mobile Crane $15-18
K13-B5 Building Transporter $18-25

Row 2
K13-C2 Aircraft Transporter $12-15
K14-B2 Freight Truck $12-15

Row 3
K13-C6 Aircraft Transporter $12-15
K14-C2 Heavy Breakdown Truck $12-15
Page 98

Row 1
K15-B1 The Londoner- Swinging London Carnaby Street $12-15
K15-B6 The Londoner- Hamleys $20-25

Row 2
K15-B5 The Londoner- Harrods $20-25
K15-B7 The Londoner- Tourist London By Bus $20-25

Row 3
K15-B11 The Londoner- Visit the London Dungeon. $15-18
K15-B4 The Londoner- Silver Jubilee $20-25

Row 4
K15-B12 The Londoner- The Royal Wedding $20-25
K15-B13 The Londoner- 1979 Royal Visitpreproduction
Page 99

Row 1
K16-B1 Petrol Tanker- Texaco $15-18

Row 2
K16-B2 Petrol Tanker- Quaker State $75-100

Row 3
K16-B5 Petrol Tanker- Aral. $35-50

Row 4
K16-B9 Petrol Tanker- Chemco $15-18
Page 100
Row 1
K17-B6 Articulated Container Truck- Gentransco. $15-18

Row 2
K17-B Articulated Container Truck- Ginny Vogue Dolls $225-275

Row 3
K17-B17 Articulated Container Truck- Penguin $18-20

Row 4
K17-B18 Articulated Container Truck- 7-Up $15-18
Page 101

Row 1
K18-B4 Articulated Tipper Truck $15-18
K19-B2 Security Truck $10-15

Row 2
K20-B5 Cargo Hauler & Pallet Loader $18-25
K20-C4 Peterbilt Wrecker $10-15

Row 3
K21-B3 Cougar Dragster $10-15
K21-C1 Tractor Transporter. $15-18

Row 4
K21-D3 Ford Transcontinental $18-20
Page 102

Row 1
K22-A Dodge Charger $12-18
K22-B2 Dodge Dragster $10-15
K22-C1 SRN6 Hovercraft $10-12

Row 2
K23-B1 Lowloader & Bulldozer $15-18
K24-Bl Scammell Container Truck $12-15

Row 3
K24-B3 Scammell Container Truck $15-18
K25-A1 Powerboat & Trailer. $10-15

Row 4
K25-B2 Digger & Plough $15-18
K26-A2 Mercedes Ambulance $10-15
K26-B1 Cement Truck $10-12
Page 103

Row 1
K27-A1 Camping Cruiser $10-15
K27-B2 Boat Transporter $15-18

Row 2
K28-A Drag Pack $20-30
K28-B Skip Truck. $10-15

Row 3
K29-A3 Miura Seaburst Set $20-25
K29-B1 Ford Delivery Van- U-Haul $15-18

Row 4
K29-B2 Ford Delivery Van- Avis $15-18
K29-B7 Ford Delivery Van- Jelly Babies $25-40
K30-A4 Mercedes C.111 .... $10-15

Page 104

Row 1
K30-B3 Unimog & Compressor. $15-18
K31-A1 Bertone Runabout $10-15

Row 2
K31-B3 Peterbilt Refrigerator Truck- Coca Cola. $35-50
Row 3
K31-B6 Peterbilt Refrigerator Truck- Burger King $50-75

Row 4
K31-B5 Peterbilt Refrigerator Truck- Pepsi $35-50
Page 105

Row 1
K32-A1 Shovel Nose $10-15
K32-B1 Farm Unimog & Trailer $15-18

Row 2
K33-A1 Citroen SM $10-15
K33-B1 Cargo Hauler $15-18

Row 3
K34-A2 Thunderclap $12-15
K34-B1 Pallet Truck & Forklift $20-25

Row 4
K35-A1 Lightning. $10-15
K35-B1 Massey Ferguson Tractor & Trailer $15-18

Row 5
K36-A6 Bandalero. $10-15
K36-B2 Construction Transporter $15-18
K37-A1 Sand Cat $10-1
Page 106

Row 1
K37-B1 Leyland Tipper $10-15
K38-A1 Gus's Gulper $10-15
K38-B1 Dodge Ambulance $10-15

Row 2
K39-A1 Milligan's Mill $10-15
K39-B1 Simon Snorkel Fire Engine $15-20

Row 3
K40-A4 Blaze Trailer $10-15
K40-B1 Pepsi Delivery Truck $15-20
K41-A5 Fuzz Buggy $10-15

Row 4
K41-B1 Brabham BT $10-15
K41-C1 JCB Excavator $15-20
K42-A1 Nissan 270ZX $10-15
Page 107

Row 1
K42-B1 Traxcavator Road Ripper $12-18
K43-B1 Log Transporter $15-18

Row 2
K43-A3 Cambuster. $10-15
K44-A5 Bazooka $10-15
K44-B1 Surtees Formula 1 .... $10-15

Row 3
K44-C1 Bridge Layer $35-50

Row 4
K45-A5 Marauder $10-15
K46-A1 Racing Car Pack $20-35
Page 108

Row 1
K47-A1 Easy Rider $10-15
K48-A2 Mercedes 350 SLC $10-15
K49-A1 Ambulance. $10-15

Row 2
K50-A4 Street Rod $10-15
K51-A8 Barracuda. $12-15
K52-A1 Datsun Rally Car $10-15

Row 3
K53-A2 Hot Fire Engine $10-15
K54-A5 AMX Javelin $15-18
K55-A1 Corvette Caper Cart. $10-15

Row 4
K56-A6 Maserati Bora $15-18
K57-A2 Javelin Drag Racing Set $20-35

Row 5

K58-A2 Corvette Power Boat Set $20-35
K59-AI Ford Capri MK II $10-15
Page 109

Row 1
K60-A1 Ford Mustang II $10-15
K60-B2 Cobra Mustang $10-15
K61-A1 Mercedes Police Car. $10-15

Row 2
K62-A2 Doctor's Emergency Car $10-15
K63-A1 Mercedes Benz Ambulance $10-15
K64-A5 Range Rover Fire Engine $10-15

Row 3
K65-A1 Plymouth Trail Duster $10-15
K66-A8 Jaguar XJ12 Police Patrol $15-20
K67-A2 Dodge Monaco Fire Chief Car $15-18

Row 4
K68-A1 Dodge Monaco & Trailer $15-18
K70-A1 Porsche Turbo $10-15

Row 5
K69A-2 Jaguar Sedan & Europa Caravan. $20-35
K71-A1 Porsche Polzei Patrol $50-75
Page 110

Row 1
K72-A2 Brabham BT44B $15-18
K73-A2 Surtees Formula 1 .... $15-18
K74-A1 Volvo Estate $10-15

Row 2
K75-A1 Airport Fire Tender. $12-15
K76-A2 Volvo Rally Set $20-35

Row 3
K77-A1 Highway Rescue Vehicle $12-15
K78-A1 Gran Fury Police Car $10-15
K79-A1 Gran Fury U.S. Taxi. $10-15

Row 4
K80-A3 Dodge Custom Van $10-15
K81-A1 Suzuki Motorcycle $10-15
K82-A2 BMW Motorcycle $10-15
Page 111

Row 1
K83-A1 Harley Davidson Police Motorcycle $10-15
K84-A1 Peugeot 305 .... $10-15
K86-A1 V.W. Golf. $8-12

Row 2
K87-A Massey Ferguson Tractor & Rotary Rake $15-18
K88-A Money Box $25-40

Row 3
K90-A Matra Rancho $10-15
K91-A Motorcycle Racing Set $35-50

Row 4
K98-A Forestry Unimog $35-50
K99-A Range Rover Polizei Set $75-100
Page 112

Row 1
K2001 Raider Command (2 pieces) $20-25

Row 2
K2002 Flight Hunter $20-25
K2003 Crusader $20-25

Row 3
K2004 Rocket Striker $20-25

Row 4
K2006 Shuttle Launcher $75-100
Page 113

Row 1
K77-A Highway Rescue- Strassen Service $35-50
K65-A Plymouth Trail Duster- Bergrettungwacht $35-50
K75-A Airport rescue- Flughafen Feuerwehr $35-50

Row 2
K29-B Ford Delivery Truck- Mr. Softy. $25-40
K28-B Skip Truck- Hoch & Tief $20-35
K26-B Cement Truck- Hoch & Tief $20-30

Row 3
K38-B Dodge Ambulance- Notarzt $25-40
K29-B Ford Delivery Truck- Junge Mode $25-40
K64-A Range Rover- Falck Zonen $35-50

Row 4
K21-D Ford Transcontinental- Barenmarke $35-50
Page 114

Row 1
Buy Matchbox Series $50-65
Buy Matchbox Series $45-60
Players Please $85-100
Visco Static $125-150

Row 2
Pegram (private issue) $75-100
The Baron of Beef $175-200
BP Visco Static $25-40

Row 3
Drink Peardrax $125-175
Players Please $100-125
BP Visco Static $35-45
BP Longlife $8-12

Row 4
Drink Peardrax $175-200
Drink Peardrax $45-60
Page 115
G-2D Railway Set. $20-30
Page 116

Row 1

SB1-A Lear Jet $6-8
SB2-A3 Corsair A7D $6-8
SB3-A A300B Airbus $6-8

Row 2
SB3-B NASA Space Shuttle $5-7
SB4-A2 Mirage F1. .... $7-10
SB5-A Starfighter $7-10

Row 3
SB6-A3 MIG 21 .... $7-10
SB7-A1 Junkers A7B $7-10
SB8-A5 Spitfire $7-10

Row 4
SB9-A Cessna 402. .... $6-8

SB10-A5 Boeing 747 .... $7-10
SB10-B Air Force One $12-15

Row 5
SB11-A2 Alpha Jet $7-10
SB12-A2 Douglas Skyhawk A-4E $7-10
SB12-B Pitts Special $6-8
Page 117

Row 1
SB13-A5 DC10 .... $7-10
SB14-A2 Cessna 210 .... $6-8
SB15-A1 Phantom F4E $6-8

Row 2
SB16-A3 Corsair F4U-5N $6-8
SB17-A Ram Rod $7-10

Row 3
SB20-A1 Helicopter $7-10
SB18-A Wild Wind. $7-10
SB19-A Piper Commanche $6-8

Row 4
SB20-A3 Helicopter $6-8
SB20-A2 Helicopter $6-8

Row 5
SB21-A Lightning. $7-10
SB22-A1 Tornado (M.R.C.A.). $6-8
Page 118

Row 1
SB23-A1 Supersonic Transport $6-8
SB24-A F.16 .... $6-8

Row 2
SB25-A2 Rescue Helicopter (Code Red). $8-10
SB25-A1 Rescue Helicopter $6-8

Row 3
SB26-A Cessna 210 Float Plane $6-8
SB27-A Harrier Jet $6-8

Row 4
SB10-A Boeing 747 (plated). $35-50

Row 5
Gold plated supersonic on penstand $35-50
Page 119

Row 1
BK101 Sherman Tank $15-18
BK102 M48 AZ Tank $15-18
BK103 Chieftan Tank $15-18

Row 2
BK104 King Tiger Tank $15-18
BK106 Tank Transporter & M48 AZ Tank $30-45

Row 3
BK105 Hover Raider $15-18
BK107 155mm. Self-propelled Howitzer. $15-18
BK108 M3A1 Half Track A.P.C. $15-18

Row 4
BK109 Sheridan Tank $15-18
BK110 Recovery Vehicle $15-18
BK111 Missile Launcher $15-18
Page 120

Row 1
BK112 DAF Ambulance $12-15
BK113 Army Aircraft Transporter $18-25

Row 2
K114 Military Crane Truck $18-25
K115 Military Petrol Tanker $18-25

Row 3
BK116 Troop Carrier & Howitzer $20-30
BK117 Self-Propelled 'Hawk' Rocket Launcher $18-25

Row 4
BK118 Kaman Seasprite Army Helicopter $18-25
MM2-A Army Tank Transporter (Military Series) $75-100
Page 121

Row 1
TP7-B Jeep & Glider Set $6-8

Row 2
TP16-C Articulated Truck & Trailer $18-25

Row 3
TP19-A Cattle Truck & Trailer $6-8

Row 4
TP20-A Shunter & Side Tipper $12-15

Row 5
TP21-A Motorcycle Transporter Set $6-8
Page 122

Row 1
TP22-A Double Container Truck $8-12

Row 2
TP23-A Covered Container Truck $8-12

Row 3
TP24-A Box Container Truck (Kodak)preproduction

Row 4
TP24-A Box Container Truck $25-40

Row 5
TP24-A Box Container Truck. $12-15
Page 123

Row 1
TP24-A Box Container Truck. $18-25

Row 2
TP25-A Pipe Truck $12-15

Row 3
TP26-A Boat Transporter $8-12

Row 4
TP2-C Articulated Tanker $6-8

Row 5
PS1 Double Container Truck (from PS1 playset) $15-20
Page 124

Row 1
SK301 Frigate $10-15

Row 2
SK302 Corvette $10-15

Row 3
SK303 Battleship. $10-15

Row 4
SK304 Aircraft Carrier $10-15

Row 5
SK305 Submarine Chaser $10-15
Page 125

Row 1
SK306 Convoy Escort $10-15

Row 2
SK307 Helicopter Carrier $10-15

Row 3
SK308 Guided Missile Destroyer $10-15

Row 4
SK309 Submarine $10-15

Row 5
SK310 Anti-Aircraft Cruiser $10-15
Page 124

Row 1
WD1-A Mickey Mouse Fire Engine $25-30
WD2-A Donald Duck Beach Buggy $18-25
WD3-A1 Goofy's Beetle $60-75
WD3-A2 Goofy's Beetle $18-25

Row 2
WD-4A Minnie Mouse Lincoln. $18-25

WD-5A1 Mickey Mouse Jeep $25-40
WD6-A Donald Duck Jeep $18-25
WD7-A Pinnochio's Traveling Theatre $25-40

Row 3
WD8-A Jiminy Cricket's Old Timer $25-40
WD9-A Goofy's Sports Car $25-40
WD10-A Goofy's Train $50-75
WD11-A Donald Duck's Ice Cream Van $25-40

Row 4
WD12-A Mickey Mouse Corvette $25-40
CS13-A Popeye's Spinach Wagon $25-40
CS14-A Bluto's Road Roller. $25-40
CS15-A Olive Oyl's Sports Car $25-40
Page 127

Row 1
GR1 Light Beamer $4-6
GR2 Speed Blazer. $4-6
GR3 Flamin Vette. $4-6

Row 2
GR4 Streak Ray $4-6
GR5 Twilight TR $4-6

Row 3
GR6 Quicksilver $4-6
GR9 Turbo Flash $4-6
GR10 Dark Rider $4-6

Row 4
GR11 Flash Fire $4-6
GR12 Night Bird $4-6